Entrepreneurial Finance for MSMEs

Joshua Yindenaba Abor

Entrepreneurial Finance for MSMEs

A Managerial Approach for Developing Markets

palgrave
macmillan

Joshua Yindenaba Abor
University of Ghana Business School
Accra, Ghana

ISBN 978-3-319-34020-3 ISBN 978-3-319-34021-0 (eBook)
DOI 10.1007/978-3-319-34021-0

Library of Congress Control Number: 2016953820

Printed on acid-free paper

This Palgrave Macmillan imprint is published by Springer Nature
The registered company is Springer International Publishing AG
The registered company address is: Gewerbestrasse 11, 6330 Cham, Switzerland

To my parents, Mr. Abor Ndobire and Madam Amina Tobga. And to my wife, Dr. Patience Aseweh Abor and children, Ivana, Bastien and Venka for their love, support and encouragement.

Foreword

The important role micro-, small- and medium-sized enterprises (MSMEs) play across the world cannot be overstated. MSMEs represent the 'engine' of economic growth, especially in developing and emerging countries. This book deals comprehensively and clearly with entrepreneurial finance and represents a timely and excellent contribution to our understanding and knowledge of this sector from a managerial perspective. MSMEs are the drivers of entrepreneurship and innovation, and finance lies at the heart of the success or failure of these firms!

Professor Abor must be congratulated on providing such a clear and detailed treatment of this subject. The book is written with exceptional clarity and insight. The 15 chapters deal with the complexity of managerial finance relating to MSMEs in a way that makes the material accessible to a wide readership. The book is essential reading for all concerned with the sector—both those from within the sector itself and others, including analysts, academics, consultants and policy-makers. As more and more developing countries emerge from the 'Base of the Pyramid', we will witness the birth of many new enterprises day by day—and inevitably, there will be many failures. But this book offers hope and guidance for the future of small businesses!

Joe Nellis
School of Management
Cranfield University
Cranfield, UK

Preface

Micro-, small- and medium-sized enterprises (MSMEs) have been noted as important contributors to the economic growth of many countries. Issues regarding MSMEs are therefore critical not only for the entrepreneur, but also for regulators, policy-makers, academics and the general public. Most start-up firms fail in their embryonic stage due to a multiplicity of factors, and especially so in sub-Sahara Africa. One of the main pandemics that plague small businesses is their lack of understanding of financial issues regarding their operations. Finance is critical for the survival of any entrepreneurial venture, and a good understanding of the financial issues confronting MSMEs will increase the chances of the entrepreneur surviving.

Entrepreneurial finance deals with both institutional finance and finance as a structured approach to decision-making. Institutional finance is concerned with identifying the various sources of finance available to MSMEs and showing their extent of use. The focus of finance as a structured approach to decision-making is on the allocation of resources and how the enterprise should be structured. This text combines both approaches, with more emphasis on finance as a structural approach to decision-making. The entrepreneur must consider the sources of finance and how to allocate the funds to productive ventures. The aim of this book, therefore, is to show how entrepreneurs and managers of MSMEs can add value to their firms by applying managerial finance tools. Entrepreneurial finance is also relevant for managers of large corporations because it is increasingly being advocated that these organisations should be more entrepreneurial in their approach. This concept is referred to as **intrapreneurship**, where managers in existing organisations are encouraged to be innovative and are expected to operate like entrepreneurs.

This book is essential reading for entrepreneurs, small business managers, managers of venture capital firms, managers of microfinance institutions, policy-makers and experts in small- and medium-sized enterprises (SMEs) development. The text is also useful for students studying finance and entrepreneurship. Specifically, it is appropriate for both undergraduate and graduate students: MBAs, Executive MBAs as well as Masters in Development Finance.

Divided into 15 chapters, this textbook deals extensively with entrepreneurial finance and provides a comprehensive framework for understanding the MSME sector. The first three chapters, which provide the entrepreneurial setting, focus on the introduction to entrepreneurial finance, new venture development and sources of financing, and business planning. Chapters 4, 5, 6 and 7 examine the financial environment within which MSMEs operate and discuss the importance of venture capital, microfinance and the public sector in supporting MSMEs. Chapters 8, 9 and 10 deal with financial performance and planning. They specifically look at understanding and analysing statements, financial planning and forecasting, and working capital management. The relevance of time value of money, evaluating capital investment decisions and valuation of new ventures and small businesses are discussed quite extensively as useful tools in taking business and investment decisions. These are covered in Chaps. 11, 12 and 13. The last two chapters concentrate on financing choice by the entrepreneurial firm and how entrepreneurs and other investors, such as venture capitalists, can harvest their investments. Though the text gives the reader a global view of entrepreneurial finance, it provides more examples within the context of developing countries, which are often ignored in most books on this subject matter.

Acknowledgements

I am very thankful to the Almighty God for the strength and wisdom to complete this book. I am also grateful to Professor Nicholas Biekpe (University of Cape Town) and Professor Ernest Aryeetey (University of Ghana) for introducing me to research in small business finance. The book has benefitted from useful comments from colleague academics, students, entrepreneurs and private equity and venture capital experts. I am particularly grateful to Professor Joe Nellis (School of Management, Cranfield University, UK), Professor Isaac Otchere (Carleton University, Canada), Professor Charles Blankson (University of North Texas, USA), Professor Paul Alagidede (Wits Business School, South Africa), Dr. Elikplimi K. Agbloyor (University of Ghana Business School), Dr. Agyapomaa Gyeke-Dako (University of Ghana Business School), Dr. Kwame Adom (University of Ghana Business School), Mr. Perci Ampomah (Investment Manager, Venture Capital Trust Fund, Ghana), Mr. Matthew Adjei-Boadu (CEO, Oasis Capital, Ghana), Dr. Michele Ruiters (Development Bank of Southern Africa), Mr. Brendon D. Darroll (Small Business Project, South Africa), Ms. Loyiso Ndlovu (Land Bank, South Africa) and Mr. Clive M. Mulumba (United States Agency for International Development [USAID], Zambia) for reviewing the manuscript. I also appreciate the excellent research support provided by my Teaching Assistants, Abel Agoba, Isaac Ofoeda, Gifty Adjei-Mensah, Vincent Asante-Asiedu, Ibrahim Jabir, Daniel Asante-Amponsah and Richard Akyeanfu. I am thankful to the Carnegie Writing Centre (University of Ghana) for editing the manuscript. However, I am responsible for all other errors in this book.

Contents

List of Figures

List of Tables

Part I

The Entrepreneurial Setting

1

Introduction to Entrepreneurial Finance

Learning Objectives
By the end of this chapter, you should be able to:

- explain the concept of entrepreneurial finance
- discuss entrepreneurship and the importance of finance to the entrepreneur
- distinguish between entrepreneurial finance and corporate finance
- define micro, small and medium enterprises
- explain the characteristics and importance of micro, small and medium enterprises
- identify the constraints to the development of micro, small and medium enterprises

1.1 Introduction

Many new businesses are started year after year, but these businesses face a myriad of challenges. Some succeed while others do not. Micro-, small- and medium-sized enterprises (MSMEs) are regarded as the engine of economic growth not only in Africa but also in the world at large. Issues regarding MSMEs are therefore critical not only for the entrepreneur, but also for regulators, policy-makers, academics and the general public. A good understanding of the issues surrounding MSMEs will increase the chances of the

J.Y. Abor, *Entrepreneurial Finance for MSMEs*,
DOI 10.1007/978-3-319-34021-0_1

entrepreneur surviving and one important issue confronting the growth of most MSMEs is finance.

The aim of this book therefore is to introduce entrepreneurial finance as a decision-making approach and show how entrepreneurs and managers of MSMEs can add value to their firms by applying financial management tools.

This introductory chapter discusses entrepreneurship, finance and the entrepreneur, and the differences between entrepreneurial finance and corporate finance. It then looks at what MSMEs are, the characteristics of MSMEs, the importance of MSMEs to economic development and the constraints to the development of MSMEs.

1.2 Entrepreneurship

While entrepreneurial finance deals with financial decision-making by entrepreneurs and managers of MSMEs, corporate finance is concerned with financial decision-making of large corporate organisations. Clearly, managers of large corporate organisations are mostly confronted with issues and decisions distinct from those affecting MSMEs or entrepreneurial firms.

In order to appreciate the differences in the responsibilities and decisions, it is important to understand who an entrepreneur is. The term 'entrepreneurship' comes from the French word *entreprendre*, which means to undertake or do something. A prominent economist, Richard Cantillon, in the early 1700s considered entrepreneurs as bearers of risk or risk takers who buy at certain prices and assume the risk to sell at future uncertain prices. Modern views of entrepreneurs however go beyond those who bear risk. Providers of risk capital bear risk by financing the enterprise but they are not entrepreneurs. Employees also bear risk due to the possibility of the enterprise failing, but they are also not entrepreneurs.

The use of the term entrepreneurship (entreprendre) was popularised by another French economist in the early 1800s, Jean Baptiste Say, who used the term to refer to people involved in military expeditions and explorations and to merchants. He characterised entrepreneurs as those who improve productivity by shifting resources to higher-gain areas. This definition however is problematic since all those involved in the modern capitalist system are basically trying to achieve higher productivity by shifting resources to higher-gain areas. They are not all entrepreneurs.

Frank Knight (1921) considered the entrepreneur as a manager of uncertainty. He defines entrepreneurship as the process of directing resources, taking into consideration a certain level of uncertainty and achieving a reward for successful performance. Entrepreneurs are also regarded as innovators because they may introduce a new technology, or product or bring something new and unique to bear in the enterprise they undertake. This flavour of innovation is attributed to the Austrian-born economist Joseph Schumpeter. In Schumpeter's view, entrepreneurs are innovators: people who come up with ideas and embody those ideas in high-growth companies. Innovative entrepreneurs, as opposed to replicative entrepreneurs, set off to upset and disorganise the status quo by bringing to birth new ways of organising society's resources to produce distinct and new output. 'Creative destruction' is thus the defining characteristic of the innovative entrepreneur.

According to McClelland (1961), the different level of economic development observed across countries is primarily attributable to the number of entrepreneurs that a country has. From McClelland's point of view, entrepreneurs have a high need for achievement and affiliation which increases their sphere of influence, power and control.

Management expert Peter Drucker (1985) described entrepreneurs as people who create something new and different, and transmute values by challenging the status quo. Therefore, entrepreneurs are risk bearers, they usually innovate by creating something new, and they reallocate resources to higher gain areas. A more recent definition of entrepreneurship given by Howard Stevenson is the pursuit of opportunity beyond the resources you currently control. Going by this definition, the following processes can be identified:

- The entrepreneur must perceive an opportunity to create value.
- The entrepreneur must devise a strategy for marshalling control of resources.
- The entrepreneur must implement the strategy to bring about change.
- The entrepreneur must harvest the rewards that accrue from the innovation and investment.

1.3 Finance and the Entrepreneur

Finance is critical for the survival of any entrepreneurial venture. Entrepreneurial finance or small business finance can be viewed from two main perspectives: institutional finance and finance as a structured approach to decision-making. Institutional finance deals with identifying the various sources of finance available to MSMEs and reporting their extent of use. The focus of finance as a structured approach to decision-making deals with the allocation of resources. It also entails how the enterprise should be set up, that is, whether as a sole proprietorship, a partnership, a private company or a public company. In addition to institutional sources of finance, this book looks at finance as a structured approach to decision-making. The text combines both approaches, with more emphasis on finance as a structural approach to decision-making.

The entrepreneur must consider the sources of funds and how to allocate the funds to productive ventures. This can be looked at from a balance sheet or from a statement of financial position perspective. The balance sheet or the statement of financial position is made up of assets, liabilities and equity. Assets are resources that are controlled by the entity as a result of past events that will lead to future economic benefits accruing to the entity. Liabilities are present obligations as a result of past events, which will lead to resources embodying future economic benefits flowing out of the entity. Equity is the residual between assets and liabilities. Liabilities and equity provide resources or funds for the entrepreneur or firm. Equity involves an investment in a firm that makes the investor a part owner of the firm. Liabilities are debt claims that mature over a given period. The financing decision that an entrepreneur therefore faces is the mix of debt or equity that should be employed to finance the enterprise. This decision, more formally, is referred to as the capital structure decision. After funds are acquired the firm must utilise them by investing in assets that will generate future economic benefits for the enterprise. This decision is referred to as the investment decision. Therefore, whereas assets represent a use of funds, liabilities and equity provide funds.

Entrepreneurs undertake projects with the aim of making profits and gains for themselves and their families. The primary goal is not to create employment for others or further other social objectives. However, as economist Adam Smith shows, in pursuing their own selfish interests, they also serve the needs of society through the so-called process of the invisible hand (market forces of supply and demand).

The key goal of entrepreneurial finance is to create value for the entrepreneur. Others will want to capture some of the gains from the entrepreneurial venture. These other stakeholders include providers of finance and employees. The entrepreneur, however, is interested in maximising his value and not the value of providers of capital or other investors. Maximising entrepreneurial value will coincide with maximising shareholder value if the entrepreneur is the sole shareholder.

It is important for other providers of finance to understand this motivation of the entrepreneur. This is because the entrepreneur will undertake projects that match their risk and return preferences. The entrepreneur also needs to understand this so that he/she can choose financing sources that match the risk/return preferences.

1.4 Entrepreneurial Finance and Corporate Finance

Corporate finance deals with financial decisions for large well established firms. The theory in this area is well developed. However, entrepreneurial finance looks at the financing decisions that concern start-ups, young and small enterprises. The main differences between corporate finance and entrepreneurial finance are outlined explicitly below:

- In entrepreneurial finance, start-ups and entrepreneurial firms face a high level of information asymmetry. In corporate finance, large public companies tend to have less problem of information asymmetry. Information asymmetry refers to various parties having different sets and levels of information. In the case of entrepreneurial firms, the problem of information asymmetry is compounded by the newness of the venture, and the difference between the entrepreneur and the providers of capital. On the other hand, large firms are generally more established, and therefore may be better at dealing with the problem information asymmetry than start-ups.
- In corporate finance, the focus of the finance manager is to maximise shareholder value of the large public company. However in the case of entrepreneurial finance, the focus is to maximise value for the entrepreneur.
- It is difficult to separate the investment and financing decisions when it comes to entrepreneurial finance. In corporate finance, it is assumed that the investment and financing decision are independent.
- In entrepreneurial finance, the owners or finance providers are mostly involved in the management of the firm and therefore the separation of ownership and management is less pronounced. In corporate finance, there is clear separation of ownership and management in large public companies.

- In corporate finance, investors or shareholders of public firms do not have a finite investment horizon and can therefore sell their shares to other investors and such a decision is taken independent of the company. However, in entrepreneurial finance, investors or entrepreneurs have finite investment horizons. They can dispose off their investments during a harvesting event such as public offering of their equity or private acquisition of the firm for cash.

Therefore, the tools in corporate finance are useful in entrepreneurial finance, but with modifications and a different perspective.

1.5 Micro-, Small- and Medium-Sized Enterprises

What is an MSME? There seem to be no generally recognised definition of MSMEs and that what is considered an MSME in a developed country will vary significantly from what constitutes an MSME from a developing country context. The different definitions, to some extent, reflect the differences in geographic and economic conditions. Definitions of MSMEs usually take into consideration the total assets, the level of turnover and the number of employees of the firm.

Various international bodies have come out with definitions for MSMEs. The Bolton Committee (1971) makes a distinction between an 'economic' and a 'statistical' definition of a small firm. With respect to the 'economic' definition, the Committee suggests that, a firm is considered small provided it satisfies the following criteria:

- It has a relatively small market;
- It is managed by owners or part owners personally, and not through the medium of a formalised management structure;
- It is independent, in that it does not form part of a large enterprise.

In terms of the 'statistical' definition, the Committee proposes the following criteria to be considered:

- The size of the small firm sector and its contribution to gross domestic product (GDP), employment, exports and so on;
- The extent to which the small firm sector's economic contribution has changed over time;

- Applying the statistical definition in a cross-country comparison of the small firms' economic contribution.

The European Commission and the United Nations Industrial Development Organisation (UNIDO) define MSMEs in terms of the number of employees. Specifically, the European Commission considers micro enterprises as firms with 0–9 employees, small enterprises are firms employing between 10 and 99 workers, and medium enterprises as those with employee size of between 100 and 499. The UNIDO also defines small- and medium-sized enterprises (SMEs) by giving different classifications for industrialised and developing countries. For industrialised countries, small firms are those with 99 or less employees, and medium firms are those employing between 100 and 499 workers. In the case of developing countries, micro firms are those with less than 5 workers, small firms are those which employ between 5 and 19 workers, and medium firms are those with an employee size of 20 and 99.

In India, the definition of MSMEs per the Micro, Small and Medium Enterprises Development (MSMED) Act, 2006 is based on investment in plant, machinery and equipment depending on whether the investment is in manufacturing or service enterprises. Under manufacturing, micro enterprises are those with investment in plant and machinery up to US$62,500, small enterprises have above US$62,500 up to US$1.25 million and medium enterprises have above US$1.25 million up to US$2.5 million. For service enterprises, micro enterprises are those with investment in equipment up to US$25,000, small enterprises have above US$25,000 up to US$0.5 million and medium enterprises have above US$0.5 million up to US$1.5 million.

In Ghana, the Venture Capital Trust Fund Act 2004 (Act 680) defines an SME as an industry, project undertaking or economic activity whose total asset base, excluding land and building, does not exceed the cedi equivalent of US$1 million in value and employs not more than 100 persons. In China and South Africa, the definition of MSME is based on revenue levels, total asset size and the number of employees, and the thresholds vary across industries.

Clearly, there is no general consensus on what constitutes an MSME, considering the various perspectives and definitions given. Definitions vary across industries and also across countries.

1.5.1 Characteristics of MSMEs in Developing Countries

In developing countries, MSMEs are engaged in varied business sectors ranging from retailing, wholesale, trading, manufacturing and construction to services. The majority of these businesses, however, tend to concentrate in services and retailing.

MSMEs can be male or female owned, but female-owned MSMEs tend to constitute a greater share of the market for MSMEs. Studies have shown that female-owned MSMEs on the whole have a difficulty in accessing finance from formal financial institutions because they often lack the necessary collateral in order to qualify for such loans. They are rather looked at more favourably by microfinance institutions (MFIs) and other informal finance providers. This is because MFIs, for instance, regard females as being more faithful in terms of meeting their loan obligations than their male counterpart. However, because female-owned enterprises are usually small and are operated from home, they are not captured in official statistics and may lose out on more formal financing opportunities beyond microfinance.

MSMEs may be established in rural or urban areas. Urban enterprises are set up and operate mainly in urban areas. Rural enterprises on the other hand are set up and operate mainly in rural communities and are involved in activities such as food production from local crops, bakery, production of soap and detergents, fabrics and wood furniture.

These enterprises may be organised or unorganised. The organised ones have registered offices and have paid workers. The unorganised ones usually do not have registered offices and usually do not employ paid workers. They are made up mainly of artisans who work in open spaces, in temporary wooden structures or at home.

In terms of employment, most MSMEs are managed and operated by their owners. The owners also engage their family members in running the business. These family members mostly help in meeting the labour or human resource requirements of the small business enterprise without taking a regular salary. These firms are also relevant in terms of their contribution to employment generation, considering that they are largely very labour intensive in nature.

Most MSMEs are relatively inefficient because they are labour based; their owners lack appropriate managerial skills and usually do not possess state of the art technology. These factors, as well as the unfavourable policy environment in most developing countries, constrain the level of efficiency of MSMEs. Though MSMEs are recognised to be innovative, they usually do not have the resources to implement and extract the full benefits from their innovations. Larger firms with more resources may pluck up these innovations and implement them, gaining advantages and efficiencies over small firms.

1.5.2 Importance of MSMEs to Economic Development

MSMEs are important contributors to the growth of most economies all over the world and they constitute about 90 % of businesses in African and other developing countries. Even in developed countries with huge multinational companies, MSMEs play a dominant role in these economies. Millineux (1997) suggests that it is the SME sector rather than the multinational companies, which is the largest employer of workers in developed countries.

MSMEs contribute to job creation and employment in a country. Entrepreneurs create jobs for themselves, and also for their family members and other people they engage. They are often described as efficient and prolific job creators, the seeds of big businesses and the fuel of national economic engines. Compared to larger firms, MSMEs are said to create many more jobs and also provide opportunities for more training and advancement for their employees. They are very useful given their contribution to employment generation, thus, reducing the unemployment rate. It is estimated that MSMEs contribute between 60 % and 80 % of employment in developing countries.

Importantly also, MSMEs contribute to the process of economic growth through the demand channel. MSMEs' demand for industrial or consumer goods and other services tend to stimulate the business activity of their suppliers. Similarly, the MSMEs' activity is also stimulated by their clients' demand. Demand in the form of investment plays a dual role, both from the demand-side (by acquiring industrial goods from their suppliers) and supply-side (through improved production resulting from upgraded equipment or capital goods). Also, demand is essential to the income-generation potential of MSMEs and their ability to stimulate the demand for both consumer and capital goods (Berry et al. 2002).

MSMEs contribute to the GDP of any country by either producing goods of value and or by providing services to both consumers and/or other enterprises. This involves the provision of goods and services to foreign customers, and as a result contributes to the country's overall export performance. If MSMEs export their products, this could lead to economic growth by generating more foreign exchange for the nation through exporting. In South Africa, it is estimated that MSMEs contribute between 52 % and 57 % of GDP, while in Ghana their contribution to GDP stands at about 70 %.

Entrepreneurs serve as risk takers in an economy and often make it possible for new lines of business to emerge. Entrepreneurs like Bill Gates took huge risks by venturing into the information technology sector, which has led to rapid growth and expansion of the computing and software business. Therefore, entrepreneurs contribute by making it possible for a 'new economy' to evolve through their initiatives and innovations.

1.5.3 Constraints to MSMEs Development

Though MSMEs are important and contribute significantly to the socio-economic development of any country, they are confronted with several challenges which often prevent them from realising their full potential.

Most entrepreneurs identify limited access to finance as one of inhibiting factors to their growth and development, given that formal financial institutions mostly shy away from financing start-up businesses. The entrepreneur is therefore compelled to depend on personal savings, and family and friends at the initial stages to finance their business. As they grow, they may want to access financial markets to tap funds to finance working capital and other financing needs. However, they may find that financial institutions are not willing to lend to them, that funds provided do not meet their full needs, that the maturity or term of the loans provided may also differ from what they require and that interest rates may exclude them from the market for loans. The inability of MSMEs to acquire funds is due to the fact that they do not have an adequate operational and financial track record. Again due to information asymmetry, lenders shy away from the market for loans for small businesses. Information asymmetry occurs because the potential lender and small businesses possess different quantities and quality of information. Information asymmetry may lead to adverse selection and moral hazards. Adverse selection may occur because the limited nature of information available to the lender will lead to his acceptance of a bad credit risk or the rejection of an otherwise good applicant. Moral hazards occur because the applicant, for example, may use a loan for a purpose other than the intended or agreed purpose. The borrower may use the loan for a wedding or a funeral instead of the expansion of the business, as agreed with the creditor. Asymmetric information can lead to failures in the market for loans, where lenders may not even be willing to lend at any interest rate.

Another key challenge that MSMEs encounter is the inability of the owners to effectively manage the business. Usually, entrepreneurship and management do not coincide. Entrepreneurs are thrilled by forming a business. As the business grows and expands, it may be better for these entrepreneurs to hire professional managers or gain managerial training. The lack of managerial know-how tends to hinder the development of these enterprises. MSMEs mostly have difficulty attracting highly motivated managers because of the fierce competition with large companies in the labour market for such skilled and talented personnel. This has to do with the quality of management.

To compete effectively on the world stage, MSMEs require state of the art equipment and technology so that they can stand up to the competition. However, MSMEs often find these to be too expensive to acquire, and the knowledge and proficiency to operate the equipment and technology may be scarce domestically. Therefore, MSMEs may take a relatively much longer time to produce and then also produce less than their competitors can produce. It stands to reason that higher levels of efficiency can be achieved once the resources are available to acquire and operate the equipment and its technology.

The level and quality of regulation in developing countries is weak and usually inadequate. Regulatory and institutional failures are considered to be more widespread and pervasive in developing countries and these may hamper the development of MSMEs. Proactive regulators, for example, can create differential reporting and regulatory systems for MSMEs. This however assumes that the regulator is well resourced financially and in terms of staff to do this. Regulators in Africa are usually constrained both in financial and in human resource terms. Tax laws and regulations pertaining to large firms may not be suitable for small firms. For example, MSMEs may have difficulties in complying with the requirements of being Value Added Tax registered. Again, most MSMEs do not maintain proper accounting records and it may be problematic trying to determine the amount assessable to tax, based on profits. A flat tax rate may better suit such firms though such a rate may be inequitable in terms of probably being too high or too low. Again, the quality of institutions in developing countries leaves much to be desired. It may take ages for commercial disputes to be settled in law courts. These challenges lead to developing countries achieving low ratings in the World Bank's Doing Business Report.

Another challenge is intense competition from both domestic and international firms. The recent trend of liberalisation of markets has made it even more difficult for MSMEs to compete and survive. The liberalisation of markets has led to the influx of cheap foreign imports which may even have been dumped on these countries. These cheap imports reduce the market share of MSMEs that compete in that line of business and may eventually lead to their collapse.

1.5.4 Overcoming the Constraints to MSME Development

For MSMEs to achieve their full potential, they must be able to surmount the various challenges that they face. An important area by which MSMEs can improve on the operations is to keep proper books of accounts and maintain an adequate accounting and management information system (MIS). For instance, they may consider engaging the services of accounting firms to help them in the preparation of management accounts and financial statements. This will clearly reduce the problem of asymmetric information between MSMEs and finance providers. Also, having audited financial statements will assist in improving the MSMEs' chances of accessing external finance. This is because the audit gives assurance to the financier that the information presented is fair and true. The owners of the business must also understand the basic financial statements since these provide valuable information, which will aid their decision-making and their ability to guide and control their enterprises. Understanding the financial statements and management accounts will aid small firms to manage their financial resources. If financial resources are not well managed, the firm may invest excessively in working capital and may overtrade, leading to its failure. Excessive investment in working capital is expensive and comes at a great opportunity cost.

Entrepreneurs should develop a good and marketable business plan. The business plan should include financial forecasts and needs to be convincing. Having a good business can enhance the entrepreneur's chances of the gaining access to finance from banks as and when they need bank loans. The entrepreneur also needs to demonstrate a good appreciation of the business area. What are the key risks involved in the business? How may these be managed? Who are the main suppliers and customers, and how must the enterprise relate to them? What are the funding needs of the business and how may these be obtained? What is the level of competition and what are the key competences of the firm that will enable it to compete and survive?

If entrepreneurs are able to acquire and improve their management skills set, this has the tendency to increase their growth and survival. The world of business is constantly experiencing rapid changes, and these certainly require complex skills to cope with and to survive in the dynamic and changing trends. Instituting a regular management training regime would be useful in acquiring and developing the requisite skills and expertise.

Improving regulatory and institutional quality and strength in developing countries can help create a business environment friendly to MSMEs.

These institutions need to be resourced financially and in terms of operational capacity. They should also be made accountable to stakeholders since they are public interest organisations. Improving the time it takes to register a business and reducing the number of procedures to establish a business is one area that needs attention. Strengthening and making the judiciary strong, efficient, effective and independent will also help ease the stress and reduce time delays in commercial disputes.

Again, MSMEs may fair better if they are able to gain access to state of the art equipment and technology to improve their productivity. In this regard, the expansion of the leasing market will go a long way in easing these constraints. Banks may also finance these expenditures and use the assets as collateral to back the loans given out.

Another approach for MSMEs is to form groups that can then acquire financing from a financial institution. The group provides guarantees for the payment of the loans. Therefore, individuals in the group can access funding, though individually they do not possess collateral that may be acceptable to a lending institution.

MSMEs also have to manage their workforce effectively. Human capital is essential to the success of the MSME. This is because the level and skill of the human capital available to a firm defines its success and potential. Entrepreneurs must therefore identify the needs and aspirations of their human capital and have adequate motivation in place so that the workforce is motivated to achieve their full potential. Motivation does not always have to be monetary in nature. Commending employees for good work done and having a conducive working environment have the tendency of improving the motivation and productivity of workers.

1.6 Organisation of the Book

This book is organised into 15 chapters. In this chapter, we explain the concepts of entrepreneurship, of finance, of the entrepreneur and of entrepreneurial finance. We examine the difference between entrepreneurial finance and corporate finance. We also provide an overview of MSMEs, their importance to economic development and constraints to their growth and development.

Chapter 2, 'New Venture Development and Sources of Financing', looks at the various forms of business ownership, and discusses the consequence of information asymmetry in new venture and small business financing. We identify the stages of the venture life cycle and discuss financing through the venture. We also describe the sources of financing available to MSMEs and then explain the elements of deal structure and how deals are closed.

Chapter 3, 'Business Planning', considers the purpose of business plans, strategic planning and the business plan, and elements of a business plan. The chapter also discusses how the business plan serves to attract external finance, the relevance of due diligence to the entrepreneur and outside investors, the implementation of business plans, the need for revising the business plan and why some business plans fail.

In Chap. 4, 'The Financial Environment and Small Businesses', we examine how the financial environment affects the decisions of small businesses. We discuss the purpose of the financial market in facilitating the flow of funds. We examine how some financial institutions interact with small businesses in providing access to finance. The chapter also examines interest rates and the factors that affect interest rates in the economy.

The aim of Chap. 5, 'Venture Capital Finance', is to explain how venture capital companies support innovative enterprises and MSMEs with the potential for high growth. The chapter looks at the nature of venture capital, the merits and demerits of using venture capital finance, venture capital markets, how venture capital firms are organised, venture capital contracts, what venture capitalists look for and value creation by venture capitalists.

Chapter 6, 'Microfinance Intervention', explains the concept of microfinance as an importance source of financing MSMEs. It discusses the importance of microfinance, criticisms of microfinance, the operations of MFIs, their sustainability, their lending models and how they manage credits. The challenges confronting MFIs and how banks participate in the microfinance market are also discussed.

Chapter 7, 'Public Sector Interventions and Small Businesses', discusses the channels through which government provides support for MSMEs, the rationale for such interventions and the role of the public sector in MSME development. The chapter also discusses key policy choices with respect to entrepreneurship and SMEs and discusses the government and donor support programmes for MSMEs.

In Chap. 8, 'Understanding and Analysing Financial Statements', we examine financial statements by looking at income statements, balance sheets and cash flow statements. We discuss the problems associated with financial statements. We also discuss the methods of analysing financial statements, the uses and limitations of financial ratios.

Chapter 9, 'Financial Planning and Forecasting', discusses the concept of financial planning, financial planning models and the preparation of a cash budget. It also looks at the financial forecasting of an established business and a new venture, projecting financing needs and growth and financing needs and break-even analysis.

The purpose of Chap. 10, 'Working Capital Management', is to ensure proper management of working capital of entrepreneurial firms. This chapter discusses working capital management in general and also focuses specifically on the various components of working capital management, inventory management, accounts receivable management, cash management, marketable securities management and current liabilities management.

In Chap. 11, 'Time Value of Money', we discuss the concepts of simple interest, compound interest, future value of a lump sum, present value of a future lump sum, the effect of compounding, perpetuities, annuities and amortisation. A good appreciation of the time value of money will enable the entrepreneur to use the techniques to evaluate capital budgeting decisions and other business and financial decisions.

Chapter 12, 'Evaluating Capital Investment Decisions: Capital Budgeting', deals with the steps involved in the capital budgeting process. It also discusses the techniques of capital budgeting. These techniques help enterprises in assessing long-term projects and provide a guide in the selection of the good projects into their capital budget.

The essence of Chap. 13, 'Valuation of New Ventures and Small Businesses', is to examine how entrepreneurial firms are valued. It specifically examines valuation of business ventures and the various methods of valuation. It also discusses the criteria for selecting a valuation model.

Chapter 14, 'Financing Choice', builds on the knowledge obtained in previous chapters. In this chapter, we identify the financing options available to MSMEs and then explain how firms ought to determine their financing needs or requirement. The chapter also examines more closely the factors that affect the choice of financing among the various sources.

In Chap. 15, 'Harvesting the Business Venture Investment', we discuss harvesting as the final stage of investment, where the entrepreneurs or initial investors liquidate their investments. The chapter examines the various forms of harvesting and also discusses the factors that influence entrepreneurs' harvesting decisions.

1.7 Summary and Conclusions

This chapter provided an overview of entrepreneurial finance. The concept of entrepreneurial finance deals with financial decision-making by entrepreneurs and managers of MSMEs. Entrepreneurs are defined as risk bearers who usually innovate by creating something new and who reallocate resources to higher gain areas. Entrepreneurs need to pay attention to the investment and financing decisions regarding their ventures. The investment decision involves investing in assets and projects that yield more than they cost. The financing decision involves how the asset or project should be financed—that is, whether through debt or equity. Finance is critical for the survival of any entrepreneurial venture. Entrepreneurial finance can be looked at from two main perspectives: institutional finance and finance as a structured approach to decision-making. Institutional finance deals with identifying the various sources of finance available to MSMEs and reporting on their extent of use. The focus of finance, as a structured approach to decision-making, deals with the allocation of resources.

The differences between entrepreneurial and corporate finance were examined. Entrepreneurial finance looks at the financing decisions that concern start-ups, young and small enterprises, whereas corporate finance deals with financial decisions for large well-established firms.

Several definitions exist with respect to what constitutes an MSME. In developing countries, MSMEs exhibit certain characteristics and contribute significantly to the economic growth of these countries. However, they are confronted with a number of challenges, including lack of access to adequate finance, lack of managerial competence, lack of technology, weak institutional regulation and intense competition from both domestic and international firms.

Discussion Questions and Problems

1. What is entrepreneurial finance? How different is entrepreneurial finance from corporate finance?
2. What should an entrepreneur do to convince a potential investor about the prospects of his/her venture?
3. How are MSMEs defined in developed and developing countries?
4. What are the characteristics of MSMEs in developing countries?
5. Discuss the importance of MSMEs in the economic development process in Africa.

6. What are the challenges to MSME development in Africa?
7. Discuss the barriers to MSMEs' access to finance in an Africa country of your choice?
8. Explain how MSMEs can increase their access to formal finance.

2

New Venture Development and Sources of Financing

Learning Objectives
At the end of this chapter, you should be able to:

- explain the various forms of business ownership
- discuss the consequence of information asymmetry in new venture and small business financing
- identify the stages of a venture life cycle
- discuss financing through the venture life cycle
- describe the sources of financing available to MSMEs
- explain the elements of deal structure and how deals are closed

2.1 Introduction

Entrepreneurs have various beautiful ideas. However, the challenge is to find the appropriate source of funding and actually implement the idea and bring the product to market. The method of financing can affect the chances of success of the venture. It can also affect the firm for a lifetime and determine the net benefits that will accrue to the entrepreneur. It is therefore important for entrepreneurs to know and appreciate the various sources of financing available and when it is appropriate to use them.

Before the entrepreneur sets out to start a venture, he/she must consider how the business should be organised, whether as a sole proprietorship, a partnership or as a company. This is essential because the form of business owner-

J.Y. Abor, *Entrepreneurial Finance for MSMEs*,
DOI 10.1007/978-3-319-34021-0_2

ship taken by the enterprise has implications in terms of attracting financing, the number of investors, the liability that the entrepreneur bears, tax consequences, succession planning and even attracting talented employees.

This chapter begins with a discussion on the various forms of business and also discusses the consequence of information asymmetry in new venture and small business finance. It then examines the stages of the venture life cycle, financing through the venture life cycle, sources of financing available to MSMEs and closing the deal.

2.2 Business Ownership

An important decision the entrepreneur needs to consider in starting a business is the form of ownership it will entail. MSMEs can be organised under three main forms: sole proprietorship, partnership and limited liability company. We will also discuss franchise as another way of executing a business idea, though this is not a form of business ownership.

The choice of the form of ownership may differ from one entrepreneur to another. The entrepreneur needs to understand the characteristics of the various ownership forms and whether these characteristics fit within their business and personal conditions. The form of ownership structure to adopt may depend on a number of factors, including the size of the business, the type of business, the owner's preferences, the nature of liability, tax advantages, capital requirement, control, managerial ability, management transition plans, cost of information and location of the business.

2.2.1 Sole Proprietorship

Most small businesses are organised as sole proprietorship. A **sole proprietorship** is a form of business owned wholly by an individual who operates it for the purpose of making a profit. In a sole proprietorship, the individual entrepreneur directs and controls the destiny of the business.

2.2.1.1 Advantages of Sole Proprietorship

The sole proprietorship has some advantages over other business forms. There are no strict legal requirements in starting a sole proprietorship, unlike in other forms of business ownership. The entrepreneur or sole proprietor is expected to obtain a license for the purposes of tax, and the fees involved are usually small. Sole proprietorship does not require formal structures and it is not difficult to start. The property and other assets used by the business could be in the name of the owner. The entrepreneur simply needs a good business idea and the willingness to carry out the business in a responsible manner. Considering the limited government regulations, sole proprietorships are the simplest and easiest form of business to establish.

The entrepreneur is the owner–manager of the sole proprietorship and therefore has absolute control over how the business ought to be run. He/she is solely responsible for the daily operation of the business. The flexibility of taking decisions allows the sole proprietor to make prompt decisions in the interest of the business. The owner decides the type of business to go into and can also change the nature or the location of the business. He/she can also decide to discontinue by selling the business without requiring the approval of someone or a board.

Another advantage of a sole proprietorship is the fact that the entrepreneur or proprietor enjoys all the profits alone. The sole proprietorship also has a tax advantage in the sense that it does not pay corporate taxes. Therefore, all the profits of the business are taxed as income of the individual entrepreneur.

2.2.1.2 Disadvantages of Sole Proprietorship

The sole proprietorship also has some disadvantages. There is the difficulty in obtaining finance, specifically through established means, such as issuing shares and securing bank loans or lines of credit. The sole proprietorship has limited access to external sources of finance, and the sole proprietor often relies on personal resources to finance the business. Since the funds invested in the business are mainly from the proprietor, the level of equity that can be raised is dependent on the personal wealth of the entrepreneur.

The sole proprietorship has unlimited liability. There is no distinction between the personal assets of the entrepreneur and the assets of the business. The owner or entrepreneur is responsible for all the debts and obligations of the business and as such bears full liability associated with the business. That is, in law the business and the proprietor are viewed as one and the same person. Therefore, the liability of the proprietor is unlimited. For instance, if the business procures goods on credit from a supplier and is unable to pay, the sole proprietor will become legally liable for that debt. If the business cannot pay its liabilities, lenders can, through legal means, seize the personal assets of the owner.

Organising a sole proprietorship may limit the growth of the business, since the life of the sole proprietorship is limited by the life of the sole proprietor. The business may die off with the death of the entrepreneur. Succession issues are therefore critical for the continued success of the sole proprietorship.

2.2.2 Partnership

Some MSMEs are organised as a partnership. A **partnership** is the association of two or more people to start a business as co-owners with the aim of making a profit. The partners pool resources and share the risk of the enterprise. Based on their capital contribution and the level of their involvement in managing the enterprise, they agree on how to share profits. There are two types of partnership: general partnership and limited partnership. Partnerships are often formed with a formal partnership agreement that details the legal arrangements, and the rights and obligations of each partner.

In a **general partnership**, all partners agree to provide a portion of the capital required and to share in the profits and losses. They also agree to participate in the work involved in the partnership. An important advantage of a general partnership over sole proprietorship is the fact that the partners combine their expertise to execute a business venture. The need for forming a partnership may arise as a result of differences in the level of expertise among the partners. It is easy and inexpensive to form a general partnership. Also, the partners are jointly liable for all the debts of the partnership and this reduces the burden on each partner.

The general partnership also has some disadvantages that are similar to those of sole proprietorship. The partners are liable for the liability of the partnership. The amount of capital raised is limited to what the partners are able to raise from their personal resources. The life of the partnership is also limited and may cease with the death of a partner, except the partnership agreement specifically stipulates that the ownership can be transferred. Income generated from the partnership is taxed as the partners' personal income. Partnerships may also be plagued by in-fighting by the partners.

The **limited partnership** requires some of the partners to have limited liability. That is to say, the liability of such partners is limited to the amount of capital they have contributed to the partnership. In a limited partnership, at least one of the partners is expected to be a general partner and the others are limited partners. The general partner is responsible for the daily operations of the business. The limited partners are investors and are usually not involved in the management of the partnership. With the exception of the general partner having unlimited liability, the limited partnership has the same advantages and disadvantages of the general partnership.

2.2.3 Limited Liability Company

MSMEs can also be organised as a limited liability company. A company is a legal entity that enjoys many of the legal powers of an individual. The company is a separate entity different from its owners. Therefore, it can enter into a contract and therefore may sue or be sued. A company is said to have limited liability in the sense that the liability of the owners is limited to the amount of capital they have invested in the company. This means that, if the company is unable to pay its liabilities, lenders do not have the right to seize the assets of the owners of the company. However, under certain circumstances the veil of incorporation can be lifted by a court of law. In that case, the shareholders may lose their claim to limited liability. Companies have a perpetual life. That is, they can exist forever and do not necessarily die off with the death of their founders. A company may be a public limited company or a private limited company.

A **public limited company** is a company whose ownership has been opened to the general public. It can therefore offer its shares to the public and subsequently list these shares on the organised stock exchange. It also has perpetual ownership, and succession issues are less of a problem in companies since professional managers usually manage them. Public limited companies have limited liability; however, the veil of incorporation may be lifted under certain circumstances. Shares in public limited companies are freely and easily transferrable and shareholders who wish to sell their shares do not need the consent of other shareholders. This is an attractive feature of public limited companies as this can enable them to raise funding even if the investment horizon of the investor does not coincide with the investment horizon of the company. Issuing of shares of public limited companies is easier because the initial investors in the shares have the opportunity to offload or sell their shares on the stock exchange.

A **private limited company** does not sell its shares to the public and therefore has a limited number of investors or shareholders. Since shares of private limited companies are not issued to the general public, shareholders can only sell their shares on the over-the-counter market.

2.2.3.1 Advantages of Limited Liability Company

Limited liability companies have some advantages. Unlike sole proprietorships and partnerships, limited liability companies are often in the position to raise huge amounts of capital by borrowing from banks or issuing shares and bonds.

A limited liability company has an unlimited life in so far as it has the financial capacity to sustain itself. The company is seen as a going concern and is expected to exist forever. The company does not die with the death or withdrawal of a shareholder because it is regarded as a separate legal entity.

Shares represent ownership of a limited liability company and therefore the ownership can be transferred to other people. There is also no limit to the number of shares that can be transferred because the company exists independently of the shareholders.

The owners of a limited liability company have a limited liability in the sense that their liability is limited to the amount of capital they have invested in the company. For instance, Mr. Wood buys US$ 2,000 in shares in Xcom Ltd. Assume that Xcom is involved in a lawsuit involving an amount of US$ 150 million and is therefore forced by the court to liquidate. In this case, the loss to Mr. Wood is only the US$ 2,000 he invested in the company and nothing more.

2.2.3.2 Disadvantages of Limited Liability Company

A limited liability company also has disadvantages. The legal requirements and regulations can be very stringent. These include an annual audit by an independent external auditor. Public limited companies are required to file their financial report regularly and frequently with the Securities and Exchange Commission.

Another disadvantage is that the owners or shareholders are separate from the company and therefore have no control over its daily operations. The shareholders appoint the board of directors, who also appoint management to control or manage the affairs of the company.

There is also the issue of double taxation. The company pays corporate taxes on its profits before paying dividends to the shareholders. The shareholders also pay personal tax on their dividend income. This is not the case with sole proprietorships and partnerships.

2.2.4 Franchise

An entrepreneur can consider franchising as a means of executing a business idea. Though a franchise may not strictly be considered a form of business ownership, it would be useful to discuss it within this context. A **franchise** is a business in which a buyer (franchisee) acquires the right to sell the goods and services of the seller (franchiser). The franchisee and franchiser enter into a signed agreement, which requires the franchisee to conduct business in a manner prescribed by the franchiser for the services provided by the franchiser. The franchiser usually receives a certain percentage of the sales by the franchisee. Franchising is common in fast food chains (such as Steers, Nando's, McDonald's, KFC and Subway Restaurants) and retail stores (such as Walmart, Marvin's Menswear and United Carpets).

Franchising has some advantages, including standardised policies for product and service delivery, reputation, better marketing and marketing communications, targeted training of managers and other staff, and less capital requirement.

One disadvantage of franchising is the fact that the franchisee does not have so much control. He/she must follow directives by the franchiser and is also expected to comply with obligations as stipulated in the franchise agreement. Another disadvantage is the possible disputes between the parties about the residual claimant status.

2.3 Information Asymmetry in New Venture and Small Business Financing

New ventures and MSMEs traditionally have difficulty approaching providers of finance to raise capital. This is because finance providers consider new ventures and SMEs risky businesses. There is therefore often a gap between the supply of finance and the demand for finance, and the 'finance gap' arises as a result of the information asymmetry that exists between lenders and borrowers.

Information asymmetry refers to the disparity between the information available to businesses seeking finance and providers of finance who are typically assumed to be at an informational disadvantage with respect to insiders of the business. The existence of information asymmetry may lead to adverse selection and moral hazard.

Adverse selection suggests that because the borrower has private knowledge or information about the success or otherwise of a project that is not available to the finance provider, the finance provider may end up selecting wrongly. The provider of the finance may not be in the position to differentiate between a high-quality business and a low-quality business and adverse selection can result. The problem of information asymmetry may result in either good lending prospects being rejected by the finance providers or poor prospects being accepted by finance providers. Altman (1968) defined the latter as a type-I error and the former as a type-II error. Finance providers can reduce the risk of type-I/II errors by carefully screening firms at the outset and monitoring projects during the life of the loan. However, screening and monitoring are high-cost activities associated with the lending proposition. If the lender is to recoup these costs, borrower interest rates may be increased, or additional risk may be covered by demanding collateral or may be avoided altogether by rejecting the loan application. Of the Altman error categories, it is the type-II error which is of most concern to MSMEs, that is, a good investment project that is incorrectly rejected by the lender. It is incumbent on the entrepreneur to ensure clarity in the business proposition to the prospective finance provider so as to mitigate the possibility of a type-II error.

Moral hazard refers to the borrower applying the funds for a purpose other than the purpose for which the funds were sourced. The inability of the finance provider to fully control how the entrepreneur uses the funds provided may result in moral hazard. Owners can conceivably benefit economically by, for example, redirecting borrowed funds to invest in higher-risk projects than those approved by the lender. In order to avoid this situation, finance providers can implement contract provisions that discourage borrowers from acting against the interests of the investor or lender, and these precautionary actions can lead to credit rationing. The economic costs incurred by the finance provider to verify the performance or financial status of entrepreneurs can also lead to credit rationing. Certain types of moral hazard play a role in the costly monitoring problem, but these moral hazard problems do not affect the outcome of the entrepreneur's projects. Instead, moral hazard affects costly monitoring problems by adding the risk that entrepreneurs will lie about their returns and profit at the expense of the finance provider.

The problem of adverse selection and moral hazard can be reduced if the borrower can provide adequate collateral and exhibit good reputation. The lack of collateral and reputation may lead to a firm being denied credit: to the extent that small firms possess less collateral and reputation than large firms, they may face yet greater difficulty raising capital than do large firms. Worse still, because there is considerable uncertainty surrounding the survival and growth of SMEs, their asset-backed collateral is usually valued at 'carcass value' to ensure that the loan is realistically covered in case of default and immediate realisation (Binks et al. 1992). This implies that the already disadvantaged small firm may even need proportionately more collateral than do large firms.

Also, small businesses are frequently undercapitalised. That is, the term structure of loans granted to SMEs does not suit their needs. Although many SMEs need long-term capital, finance providers such as banks are usually only willing to grant them short-term loans. SMEs have therefore had to rely on short-term sources such as lines of credit and informal sources to finance long-term needs such as new equipment purchases (Riding and Short 1987; Blanton and Dorman 1994).

2.4 Stages of Venture Life Cycle

MSMEs, like humans, have a life cycle that they go through. They are born, grow, reach maturity, may experience decline and may die off. These stages, however, cannot be predicted. For example, we cannot know beforehand the length of time the firm will spend in the growth phase. Again the stages or phases may not always go in this order. The firm could be at the maturity stage but could develop a new product that will bring it back into the growth phase. Another business may start and go straight to the last stage because it does not survive the start-up phase. However, it is important to note that not all firms go through these stages in the same order or go through all the stages. A pharmaceutical company could have a business life cycle comparable to what is depicted as follows: the research and development phase, the start-up phase, the growth phase and the decline phase.

2.4.1 Research and Development Phase

In this phase, the firm invests in researching and developing the product. Research refers to a planned and purposeful enquiry and investigation to gain new knowledge and improve our understanding of the world. Development is the application of this knowledge to develop new products, processes, systems and services before the commencement of production on a commercial basis. It is impossible to ascertain whether, at the research phase, a product will generate future economic benefits. In the development phase, the firm does not make profits and does not generate sales. Also, its cash flows are negative since these are invested in researching and in developing the product with no accompanying sales and profit. At this stage, the firm has not invested in all the necessary equipment to produce and market the product.

2.4.2 Start-Up Phase

The second phase is the start-up. The start-up phase is where the product is ready to go to the market and a prototype exists. The firm therefore begins to invest in all the equipment and machinery needed to start operations and produce the products. It may also need to employ personnel so that it can take off. Cash flows will be constrained further because of the massive investment in equipment.

2.4.3 Growth Phase

The growth phase can be categorised into the early growth and rapid growth phases. Generally, at the growth stage, the firm experiences improved revenues since the product gains market acceptance. Early growth is the stage when the enterprise's revenues are increasing fairly. At this stage, cash flows and income to investors may still be negative. Rapid growth is the stage when revenues are growing rapidly. Therefore, the firm is expanding at an increasing rate. This may be due to the wider acceptance of its product. Also, it may be operating on a larger scale, therefore reducing production costs, and also because it would have mastered the production technique and therefore can gain from the learning curve. Due to rapid growth, the firm would usually have to source for external capital. Growth should not be undertaken for the mere sake of it. The growth should be adding value to the firm in that the returns exceed the cost and the firm at least earns the weighted average cost of capital of the firm. That is, the projects undertaken should have a positive net present value (NPV).

2.4.4 Decline/Exit Phase

The decline/exit phase is when the firm's revenue and profits are slowing down and the growth rate tends to reduce. The firm is profitable and has more cash than it needs. It can therefore afford to make payments to investors in the form of dividends and regular interest payments without difficulty. At this stage, there is the temptation for management to 'squander' the free cash flows. They may also use the cash flows for an acquisition which has not been well thought through. Some investors may want to harvest their investment at this stage and they may do this by selling their interests or stake in the firm to other interested investors.

2.5 Financing Through the Venture Life Cycle

MSMEs need financing for different reasons at different stages of their development. Therefore, the sequence of financing is related to and is a natural progression from the stages of development of the venture. In the initial or development phase, the enterprise requires funding to develop the product or to explore the feasibility of the project concept. This kind of financing is known as seed financing. The financing provided is usually very small and is meant to enhance product development, market research, putting together a management team and developing a business plan. Seed financing can therefore be used to assess the market and explore the feasibility of going on with the project. This phase is regarded as a pre-marketing phase.

If the concept is feasible and the entrepreneur decides to go ahead with the project, funding will be needed to start up the enterprise. In the start-up phase, funds are needed to acquire equipment and facilities to start operations. If the business is highly sophisticated and therefore needs massive investment in research and development, such as a pharmaceutical company, more funds will be devoted to this, as the seed finance provided is likely to be insufficient. At this stage, the details of the product are likely to have been sorted out and the production method and sources of raw materials and supplies are more certain.

First-stage financing is targeted at an enterprise that has started operations and is making sales but is not yet profitable. Therefore, as the product has just been introduced it is now gaining market acceptance and consumers are now experimenting with the product. As the product gains more market acceptance, the sales of the enterprise will grow and the business will start making profits. At this stage, funding is required to augment the working capital of the enterprise.

Second-stage financing is used when the firm requires more or extra financing. At this stage, the firm's sales are still growing and it is approaching profitability. The enterprise's products are more known and have gained broader market acceptance. The enterprise is usually said to be around the break-even point, where its costs are roughly equal to its revenues.

Third-stage financing is aimed at an enterprise that is experiencing rapid growth and needs more external funds to finance this growth. At this point, though, the enterprise is profitable and has cash flows, this is usually not enough to support the level of growth required. Due to the fact that internal or retained earnings are insufficient to support the planned growth, the enterprise usually has to look to external financiers to finance the growth.

Bridge financing is needed to bridge the gap between current financing needs and the need for permanent financing. At this stage, the business is likely to be around the exit phase. Early investors such as business angels and venture capitalists may want to harvest their investment by taking the enterprise public. The public offering is likely to provide the permanent funds that the enterprise needs. However, if funds are needed before the public offering can take place, the enterprise will seek bridge financing. This type of financing therefore bridges the gap between later-stage financing and harvesting.

An enterprise may need many stages of financing depending on the phases that it is going through. However, the more funds that are sourced externally, the more interest the entrepreneur will have to give up in the firm. This means that the interest or stake of the entrepreneur will be reduced if the provider of the finance obtains all the financing in the form of an equity interest.

2.6 Sources of Financing

Raising capital for a new venture or for expanding an existing business is often a challenge. Many MSMEs have difficulty accessing finance, and as such they often adopt what is referred to as *layering* or *layered financing*. This involves piecing together capital from as many sources as they can obtain, that is, putting together finance from various sources. It is important to now discuss possible sources from which MSMEs can raise finance. The discussion separates the sources of financing into equity-based and debt-based financing. The discussion is, however, not based on a natural progression or order in which the enterprise should obtain financing.

2.6.1 Sources of Equity Capital

Equity refers to the amount contributed by shareholders as capital to finance the activities of their firm. It also includes earnings that are retained by the firm. These retained earnings belong to shareholders and add to the amount they have contributed to the firm. The shareholders are the owners of the firm and they bear the greatest risk in the firm since they are the last to be paid supposing the firm goes bankrupt. The capital they contribute to the firm is therefore referred to as risk capital. Shareholders possess a residual interest in the company. In entrepreneurial firms, sources of equity financing include personal savings, financing provided by business angels, financing provided by venture capitalists, and private and public placements of equity.

2.6.1.1 Personal Savings/Financing

The first and easiest way that entrepreneurs can finance a venture is by relying on their personal savings. External financiers will usually want to see how much of the entrepreneur's own 'blood' is invested in the business. At early stages, external financing is difficult to procure because of the high levels of information asymmetry and the fact that the business does not at this stage have any track record in terms of operation and finance. At the initial stages, the enterprise may also not have sufficient collateral that can serve as collateral to qualify for a loan. The business, however, will possess intangible assets such as its idea. Financing generated from the personal savings of the owner is usually inadequate to meet the full financing needs of the venture. The entrepreneurs can also borrow on a personal basis to augment their savings. The amount the entrepreneurs can borrow will usually depend on the size of their salary (if they are employed) and whether they have adequate collateral such as a home. They can therefore take personal loans from banks to add to what they have been able to save up.

2.6.1.2 Family and Friends

This is the next place that the entrepreneur can seek funding. This is because family and friends are more likely to know the entrepreneur and their abilities. Friends and family can provide funds in the form of equity. However, they may also provide debt capital to the firm. This source of funding, however, may pose serious problems if the venture does not succeed, as family relationships and friendships may be marred. Therefore, the funding should be treated in a professional manner. The terms of the agreement should be documented, and both parties should as much as practicable adhere to the terms of the contract. When accessing funds from friends and family, the entrepreneur does not have to provide collateral to access the funds. Also, interest may not be charged on the amounts provided, or if it is charged it is likely to be low and less than what a financial institution would charge. That is, the interest is likely to be far below market interest rates. A drawback from using this source of finance is that the friend or family member may fall into financial difficulties and may want the amount to be paid before the stated maturity. Just like the entrepreneur's personal savings, these sources are also not likely to be enough to meet the needs of the venture.

2.6.1.3 Business Angels

Business angels are wealthy private investors who can provide equity capital to entrepreneurs or start-ups. Therefore, this kind of financing is provided by high-net worth individuals, as opposed to a formal financial institution. They may also provide debt capital, though most funds provided are in the form of equity. They usually invest in promising fast-growth firms and hope to exit the investment by selling their equity stake to other investors or management or by taking the firm public. They are usually entrepreneurs themselves or successful professionals. Though they invest with the primary aim of making financial returns, they can contribute significantly by bringing their knowledge and experience to bear on the new venture. Therefore, one of their goals may also be to grow and mentor upcoming and promising entrepreneurs. They are usually actively involved in the venture but their level of involvement should be negotiated so that it does not cause problems later on, due to the financing relationship. They are usually willing to provide equity capital for an appreciable length of time, say between 5 and 10 years. Due to this, the financing provided is referred to as 'patient' capital. Business angels usually invest in businesses in their geographical location and in businesses where they have had prior experience. The entrepreneur may find it difficult to locate business angels, since they are not very visible. Entrepreneurs can, however, search for a business angel's network to help them locate possible interested business angels who are willing to provide finance.

2.6.1.4 Venture Capital Financing

Venture capital is private equity invested in new and young businesses with high growth potential. The investment is usually premised on a long-term basis. Venture capitalists usually invest in high-growth firms with a view to taking the firm public at a later date. This is to enable the venture capitalists to harvest their investment. The venture capital fund is set up to last for a definite period of time. There are two main parties in terms of the structure within the venture capital itself: general partners and limited partners. The general partner is actively involved in the operations of the fund and also contributes some of the funds utilised by the venture capital, but the amount contributed is very small compared to what is contributed by limited partners. The general partner manages the fund and his/her expertise and skills are crucial to the success of the venture capital fund. The limited partners are passive investors and they contribute most of the funds that the venture capital firm needs. They are less involved in the operations of the fund and, like shareholders of any company, they attend general meetings of the venture capital firm. Venture capital firms also provide management and technical assistance to the firms they invest in to enable them to grow and to add value to their investment. Like business angels, venture capitalists usually invest in businesses in which they have expertise and to which they can add value, in a geographical area close to where they are located.

Venture capitalists are professional investors who dedicate their time and effort wholly to the portfolio of companies they have invested in. Compared to venture capitalists, business angels are an informal network and do not commit much time to the investments they have made. The amount of financing provided by venture capitalists is usually larger than the financing that a business angel can provide. Also, business angels invest on their own behalf, whereas venture capitalists invest mostly on behalf of their limited partners or investors.

2.6.1.5 Corporate Venturers

Some corporations or companies have venture capital divisions, which are used to invest in new ideas and products that may be worth pursuing. The ideas and products invested in by the company's venture capital division may or may not be related to the main product line of the company. Very large companies with excessive funds are likely to have venture capital divisions. These companies are likely to be 'cash cows' that search for new profitable ventures to invest in to ensure their survival in the long-term.

It is known that large corporations are bureaucratic and are not as entrepreneurial as smaller companies. Large companies may therefore set up venture funds to invest in the ideas of employees. They will support the employees so that the ideas can be brought to market. They will want to do this so that they do not lose their innovative employees. The corporate venture capital may not be limited to investing in ideas from within the company, but may be able to invest in ideas and products outside the company. Therefore, entrepreneurs may be able to access funding from corporate venturers.

2.6.1.6 Private Placements

An entrepreneur can use a private placement to raise equity finance. An entrepreneur can also use this avenue to place its debt. This is possible if the business is registered as a **private company.** To raise private equity, the entrepreneur will have to contact an investment bank. The investment bank then contacts their high-net worth clients who may be willing to invest equity in the business. The investment bank will usually contact institutional investors who it believes may be interested in the offer. These institutional investors are well placed and have high incentives to monitor the firm to reduce agency problems and to increase the value of their investments. Institutional investors may request a seat on the company's board so that their voice can be heard. They will usually also be calling management from time to time to discuss the plans of management and how these can be best carried out.

The investment bank will charge a fee for rendering this service to the entrepreneur/company. An advantage of raising private equity is that the issuing cost is relatively lower compared to a full-blown public equity issue. For example, the requirement for financial statements and a prospectus may be waived in the case of a private placement. Also, the funds can be raised faster because it is less complex and there are fewer compliance requirements. The firm also deals with a small group of investors. Since the company is not going to be listed, the regulations that the company will have to comply with will also be fewer. A private placement can therefore be used to give the firm a low profile if that is the wish of the entrepreneur.

2.6.1.7 Public Offerings of Equity

A public offer is when a company offers its shares to the general public. The public offer is the opposite of the private placement we discussed earlier. Therefore, during the initial public offer (IPO), the company is likely to move from a private company to a public company. The first time the company issues it shares to the general public is referred to as the IPO. The company raises funds from the primary market through the IPO. The general public can subscribe to the shares of the company during the IPO. The amount involved is usually very large, and the finance raised is in the form of equity. A company needs a track record before it can list on an organised stock exchange and raise finance from the general public. Therefore, this source of finance will usually not be available to a start-up firm or a young entrepreneur. The money raised from the issue goes directly to the company, and in exchange for the funds the company issues investors with shares or equity stakes in the company.

The company will have to contact an investment bank just like in the case of private placement. The investment bank then undertakes to bring the firm public for a fee. The investment bank can offer two main services to the firm. It may promise to buy all the shares from the company. In this case, the investment bank buys all the shares from the company and undertakes to sell the shares. The investment bank bears the risk that it may not be able to sell the shares. This is known as a *bought deal* or *firm commitment*. The investment bank will usually buy the shares at a discount, that is, at a price below the issue price. In the second case, the investment bank does not give any guarantees. It merely promises to do its best to sell the shares to investors. This is known as a *best efforts deal*. In this case, the company bears the risk that investors' appetite for the company's shares may be low and that the shares will not sell.

If the company requires more funds, it can go back to the market to raise additional equity to support its activities. This is known as a *seasoned new issue*. However, it will have to justify why it needs the funds. If investors are not convinced, the announcement that the firm wants to issue more equity may cause the share price of the company to fall.

Going public improves the image and visibility of a company, especially if it is listed on a stock exchange. This is because it will receive a lot of publicity and will have to engage stakeholders because of its public interest nature. Suppliers, customers, employees and other interest stakeholders will be attracted to do business with the company. Once the company is a public interest company, a lot of people will want to know more about it and therefore the company's privacy becomes limited. This is because it now has to file regular information with the stock exchange. Listed companies are supposed to make their financial statements available to the investing public and they have to send their annual financial statements to investors and hold annual general meetings. They must also make available all price-sensitive information to the investing public. The printing cost of sending these financial statements and complying with other regulations can be very high.

A drawback of going public is that the entrepreneur will have to give up equity or ownership interest in the company to others. This will diminish the power that the entrepreneur wields. However, the entrepreneur will have to weigh giving up control against the increased ability of the company to grow and undertake more positive NPV projects due to the additional capital that it can raise. Also, the reduced equity can be worth far more because the company can expand and grow faster.

Another drawback is that pressure from shareholders and from investment analysts may force managers to be short-sighted in their approach. This is because shareholders and analysts want to see profits. The managers may, however, be aware of very profitable projects but the profits may take time to materialise. That is, in the initial years the projects may not be very profitable but are likely to be very profitable in the future. Managers will also be aware of short-term less profitable projects. These projects are likely to be average projects with average profits from the very beginning. To avoid the discipline of the capital markets, the firm may be biased towards investing in short-term projects. This is because lower profits than expected by investors and analysts will cause the stock price of the company to fall.

Importantly the IPO market provides a good avenue for early-stage equity investors, like business angels and venture capitalists, to harvest their investments. This is because they can now sell their interests to other investors. IPOs are usually undertaken during bull markets, when the prices of most stocks are rising. The evidence also shows that less IPO activity occurs during bear markets, when there is a general decline in stock prices.

2.6.2 Sources of Debt Capital

These are investors who lend the firm a given amount at an agreed interest rate. The debt repayments are usually made up of interest and principal repayments. However, principal payments may be delayed until maturity. In this case, the borrower only makes interest payments and pays the principal amount at maturity. These are known as balloon payments since the payments balloon from the small interest payments to the full maturity value. The interest rates on debt instruments can be either fixed or floating. A fixed rate loan has the rate agreed on before the loan is given and the rate applies throughout the term on the loan. For a floating rate loan, the rate on the loan adjusts periodically to market interest rates. If market interest rates go up, the rate of the loan goes up and the borrower will have to pay more in terms of interest. If general interest rates fall, the rate on the loan also falls, and the borrower benefits in terms of lower interest payments. Debt holders have priority when the firm runs into financial distress and possible bankruptcy. Debt holders have to be paid first from the assets of the company. If the assets of the company are sufficient, the debt holders can recover the full value of the amounts owed them. Sources of debt finance include bank finance, credit from MFIs, trade credit, factoring, asset-based lenders, issue of bonds, issue of commercial paper and leasing.

2.6.2.1 Bank Finance

MSMEs can resort to borrowing from the bank since banks provide various forms of loans including tailor-made facilities available to firms. Some banks have a specialised MSME division, which provides very useful services to small enterprises. The bank may grant the MSME an overdraft, which enables the firm to withdraw money in excess of what is in their account. The bank usually specifies the limit for the overdraft and can recall the overdraft facility at any particular time. Banks also provide short-term and long-term loans. Short-term loans have a maturity of less than one year, whereas long-term loans have a maturity of more than one year. Short-term loans usually have a lower interest rate than long-term loans.

One major concern about bank financing of MSMEs is the issue of collateral requirement. Banks often require collateral before extending credit to MSMEs. Abor and Biekpe (2007) found that bank financing accounts for less than a quarter of the total debt financing of SMEs in Ghana. They also found that SMEs that have a long-standing relationship with their banks and those with adequate collateral are more likely to access bank finance.

2.6.2.2 Credit from Microfinance Institutions

Microfinance is also an important source of financing MSMEs. It broadly entails the provision of financial services to low-income clients and micro-enterprises that have limited or no access to formal financial services. These financial services include the provision of microcredit, micro-savings, micro-insurance and funds transfer services. Microfinance enables low-income clients and micro-enterprises to gain access to a range of financial services in order to finance their income-producing activities, stabilise consumption, build assets and protect against risks. Given that these financial services normally involve small amounts of funds (such as small loans, small savings, etc.), the term 'microfinance' is useful in differentiating these services from those provided by traditional banks or other formal financial institutions. Essentially, microfinance is the provision of financial services to the underprivileged poor, who form a chunk of the population of developing economies.

MSMEs can therefore access credit from MFIs, and these are normally on a short-term basis. MFIs have adopted various lending models for reaching out to their clients and these include group-based lending, village banking and individual banking. These lending models are discussed in detail in Chap. 6.

2.6.2.3 Trade Credit

Trade credit is the provision of credit by suppliers to their customers. Therefore, an entrepreneur can pick the goods and pay back after the designated period. An advantage of accessing a supplier's credit line is that the firm does not require any collateral. Trade credit is short-term finance given that the normal maximum credit period is 3 months or 90 days. Trade credit can be rolled over continuously to provide the firm with medium-term financing. The payment terms may be specified as follows: net 90 or 3/30, net 90. The first (net 90) means that payment has to be made within 90 days. Therefore, the credit period is 90 days. The quotation of 3/30, net 90 means that the credit period is still 90 days but the firm gets a 3 % discount if it pays within 30 days.

Trade credit provides financing because the firm does not have to pay upfront. However, trade credit is not free. It may be cheaper to purchase the goods upfront, as opposed to purchasing on credit. The discounts lost due to taking credit can be very expensive. The firm can gain at the expense of the creditor if it delays payment and still pays the agreed amount. However, suppliers do not take kindly to this and may restrict future credit. When the firm purchases on credit it has to pay the suppliers after the agreed period. Financing with trade credit is time saving and may not require collateral.

2.6.2.4 Factoring

A firm can factor its receivables to generate liquidity. Receivables are sales that have been made on credit and the debtors have not paid up yet. In essence, the firm has provided financing to its debtors and has therefore locked up cash with these debtors. The firm may itself need cash or liquidity and may generate this liquidity by factoring the receivables. This means that it has to sell (out) the debtors to a financial institution which provides funds to the firm in exchange for the debtors or receivables. There are two types of factoring: factoring without recourse and factoring with recourse. If the factoring is without recourse that means that the debt is sold outright. The financial institution or factor does not have any right of recourse to the firm which sold the receivables if the debtors default. With recourse factoring, if the factor cannot collect the debt, it has a right of recourse to the firm that sold the debt. Therefore, the factor can come back to the firm in case it is not able to collect all the debts. With non-recourse factoring, the firm receives a lower amount for the debt because of the higher risk that the factor is assuming. Therefore, the firm receives a lower discounted amount of the value of the debt. With recourse factoring, due to the lower risk involved, the firm receives a higher discounted amount of the face value of the debt.

Factoring saves the cost of administering the debtors' ledger and it also improves the cash flow of the firm. In addition to the collection and provision of finance, the factor may also provide insurance on debts. One problem with factoring is that the factoring company is usually interested in collecting the debt that it has bought and may use harsh tactics to collect the debts. This may tarnish the reputation of the firm that sold the debt. Again, factoring introduces a third party and the client or debtor may not be comfortable dealing with the factoring company. To deal with this, the firm will usually inform the client that the debts have been factored and so they should forward subsequent payments to the factoring company. Factoring may also create the impression that the firm is in cash flow difficulties and this is likely to cause suppliers of the firm to impose more stringent payment terms.

2.6.2.5 Asset-Based Lenders

These lenders lend to a business based on their assets that are used as collateral. These assets may be inventory, accounts receivable or equipment. The underlying asset must be easily saleable, as the lender relies on this as collateral for the loan granted. If the business is not able to pay the loan, the lender will sell the asset to recover its investment (loan and accrued interest payments). When the loan is based on the accounts receivable of the firm, this is referred to as accounts receivable financing. In this case, the firm has taken a loan against the accounts receivable, which serves as collateral for the loan. The firm taking the loan is required to service the loan. When the loan is supported by inventory, this is known as inventory financing.

2.6.2.6 Bonds/Public Offer of Debt

A bond is a long-term security issued to raise long-term debt finance. The company issues a certificate to investors in return for funds and promises payment of interest and principal. The company has to make payments regularly to investors and these payments are called coupon payments. The term arose due to the fact that companies that had issued bonds sent coupons to investors at the agreed intervals. The investors then have to send the coupons to the company to receive payment. The coupon entitles the investor to receive interest payments. At the maturity date, the investor is entitled to receive the principal amount that was invested in the company or bond. Small firms may find it difficult to issue bonds. One reason is that the cost involved in issuing a bond is high. The firm also needs a good track record to be able to issue bonds, which MSMEs may not possess. Again, bond markets in Africa are under-developed and as such may not be an immediate source of financing for MSMEs.

2.6.2.7 Commercial Paper

Commercial paper refers to a short-term debt instrument issued by highly reputable and credit-worthy firms to raise short-term finance. The interest rate on a commercial paper may be lower than the interest rate on a bank loan. So does it make sense for a firm that can access the commercial paper market to have a good relationship with its bankers? The answer is yes. This is because the firm will require other services apart from loans such as letters of credit. Again, the bank can guarantee the commercial paper issued by the firm, meaning if the firm fails to honour the debt obligation, the bank is liable to pay. Therefore, the bank substitutes the credit rating of the firm with its credit rating. The firm can therefore borrow at a lower rate, as the risk of the issue becomes lower. As economic conditions change, the credit ratings of firms also change. During economic boom periods the credit ratings of firms are usually good. This rating may decline in recessionary or bad economic periods. The firm may therefore lose its credit rating, in which case it will have to resort to its bankers if it needs debt finance. A good relationship with its bankers is therefore essential.

It is important to note that only highly reputable and credit-worthy firms can access the commercial paper market. However, considering that MSMEs in Africa are mostly young and small in size, it may be difficult for them to raise finance from the issue of commercial papers. This is because such firms have not built the reputation or the good name required, and as such may not be known on the market. Diamond (1989) considers reputation as the good name a firm has built up over time and which the market has recognised and observed as important in explaining the firm's ability to meet its obligations in a timely manner.

2.6.2.8 Leasing

MSMEs can also finance their operations by acquiring assets on lease. There are two types of lease: operating and finance leases. An operating lease is basically a rental agreement between a firm (lessee) and a leasing company (lessor). The lessee makes regular lease payments (rentals) to the lessor and these payments are shown as an expense in the statement of comprehensive income (income statement). With an operating lease, the lessor retains the substantial risks and benefits associated with the asset. The asset can also be bought outright using a finance lease. In essence, the lessor has provided a loan to the lessee and the lessee has to capitalise the asset on the statement of financial position. The depreciation expense will also have to be shown, since the asset is shown on the statement of financial position. After capitalising the asset, the liability (i.e. the lease amount owed) also has to be shown on the statement of financial position and the finance cost has to reflect in the financial statements. With finance leases, the lessee bears substantially all the risks and rewards of owning the asset.

Whether leases should be capitalised or not is a hot issue in financial reporting. International Accounting Standards (IAS 17) deals with leases. Firms will not want to capitalise the asset as that will enable them to achieve off-balance sheet financing. If the liability is not shown on the statement of financial position, the leverage (gearing) of the firm is reduced. This reduces the firm's risk and therefore it can borrow at a lower rate. The borrowing capacity of the firm is also increased if the liability is not shown.

2.6.3 Hybrid Instruments

Hybrid instruments have features of both debt and equity. Examples are mezzanine finance and preference shares.

2.6.3.1 Mezzanine Finance

Mezzanine finance has features of both debt and equity. It is debt finance that can be converted into an equity interest. It is usually long-term finance with maturities usually above five years. Mezzanine finance can usually be paid in a one-off manner. The firm does not have to make monthly payments when it comes to mezzanine finance and therefore this eases the constraints on its cash flows, as repayment can be made in a one-off manner. Mezzanine finance is utilised by small companies and is placed privately. Firms with good track records, with proven products and markets, which have been making profits over the years and are looking to expand, can access this type of finance. Mezzanine finance is usually used to support the rapid growth and expansion of an enterprise. It can also be used to finance a management buyout (MBO). In this case managers acquire shares from a shareholder because they want to take the firm private. The managers essentially buy out the shareholders.

The finance appears, or is treated, as equity on the firm's statement of financial position or balance sheet. This gives the firm additional borrowing capacity since it does not show up as debt, which will increase the firm's financial leverage and constrain its ability to raise additional debt finance. The rate charged by lenders is usually very high since the financing is given quickly and therefore less due diligence can be carried out. Additionally, the financier will usually not require any collateral from the firm. Also, in terms of priority in payment, when the firm runs into trouble, mezzanine finance has lower priority compared to bank finance and venture capital finance. Therefore, bank loans and venture capitalists are paid first, before the mezzanine financier. However, mezzanine financiers are paid before shareholders. Considering that they have low priority when it comes to repayment, their level of risk is high.

The finance may be in the form of debt, which can be converted into equity if the firm does not pay on the agreed time and in full. The amount of equity is usually specified as the firm grants the investor warrants to acquire equity stakes. For instance, a debt of US$ 1,000 may entitle the investor to convert into 100 shares at a price of US$ 2. Mezzanine finance is usually expensive as it carries a lot of risk, as we saw earlier (no collateral, lower priority in terms of repayment and low due diligence). Its return will therefore have to be high to compensate the mezzanine financier for the risk he/she is taking. Mezzanine finance will usually have a callable feature, which enables the company to return investors' funds to them. The company will want this option, as this kind of financing is quite expensive. If it can raise other finance at a lower rate, the company will be motivated to pay off the mezzanine finance. Mezzanine financiers will require a higher return if their financing is callable at the option of the company, all other things being equal.

2.6.3.2 Preference Shares

Preference shares are shares issued by a company that entitle the shareholders to receive fixed dividend, and they have features of both debt and equity. They receive a fixed dividend and are sometimes classified as fixed income securities (giving them a debt feature). Preferred dividends are usually larger than ordinary share dividends and are paid regularly and are therefore more predictable than ordinary dividends whose payment is at the discretion of the board of directors/management. Unlike debt, the company may have some flexibility when it comes to the payment of dividends on preference shares. The preference shares may have a cumulative or non-cumulative feature. If the preference shares are cumulative and the firm is not able to pay dividends this year, it will have to pay next year's dividend in addition to this year's dividend. If it is non-cumulative, once the company misses this year's dividend, it is not obliged to pay it and only has to pay next year's dividend. The preference share may also be participating. In this case after receiving their fixed dividends, preference shareholders may receive additional dividends if the company has done extraordinarily well and has met predetermined profitability goals. They are, however, not at risk since they are still entitled to their fixed dividends if performance is not good.

Preference shareholders, like ordinary shareholders, are part owners of the company. However, they usually have limited or no voting rights in a company. They may, however, acquire voting rights if their dividends have been outstanding for a considerable period. Preference shareholders have preference over equity holders since the dividends owed them must be paid before anything can be paid to ordinary shareholders. Also, in the event of liquidation, preference shareholders have preference over ordinary shareholders, since they must be paid before ordinary shareholders can be paid. In other words, they have preference over ordinary shareholders when it comes to distributions to investors and also during liquidation. Preference shareholders, however, rank below debt holders such as bonder holders and banks when it comes to payments of interest or other periodic cash flows and liquidations. Though they are also owners of the company as we mentioned earlier, they bear less risk compared to ordinary shareholders, since they rank higher in terms of payments. In some countries, preference shares are rated just like other company debt.

Preference shares may be converted into equity if there is a convertibility clause. In this case, the preference shareholder will have to make do with a lower dividend rate compared to a similar preference share which does not have the convertibility feature. If the preference shares can be converted into equity, this is favourable to the investor, because he/she can make additional returns or gains by converting into equity. This is because the conversion price is agreed. Therefore, if it is converted into equity at a price higher than the conversion price then the preference shareholder gains. This is why he/she has to contend with a lower return.

Most preference shares, like equity, do not have a set maturity date, though they may be callable. The preference shares are usually callable at the option of the company. This means that the company can force preference shares investors to surrender their preference shares. Companies recall debt instruments in low-interest rate environments, since they can refinance (issue new debt/preference shares) at a lower rate and therefore/thereby save on financing costs. Since the recall is an unfavourable feature for the investor, the company will have to offer a higher return compared to other preference shares which do not have a recall feature.

2.7 Appropriate and Successful Sources of Financing

Financing can be in the form of debt or equity. Usually, a single source of finance is not adequate to meet the full funding needs of the entrepreneur. The entrepreneur may therefore want to raise finance from different sources to add up to what he/she requires to meet the firm's financing need.

MSMEs may require financing to purchase non-current or fixed assets. Financing may also be sought to finance working capital. A firm's working capital is its current assets less its current liabilities. If this figure is positive, the firm requires extra funds to support the remaining current assets, since current liabilities are not enough. Firms usually want to match short-term assets to short-term liabilities. This concept is known as *matching*. The financing may also be to support normal short-term operations such as the payment of salaries and other recurrent expenditure.

Entrepreneurs must be innovative when it comes to financing their ventures. Innovative ways of financing a venture are known as *bootstrap financing techniques* and these involve financing a venture with little or no support from outside capital providers. Examples of bootstrap financing techniques include funds from personal savings, credit cards, amounts from family and friends, taking little or no salary at the beginning stages of the venture (sweat equity), factoring, trade credit, leasing rather than purchasing equipment outright, leasing the business premises or the entrepreneur borrowing against the value of their personal home and using their home as collateral, and finally taking advances from clients to perform work for them. Therefore, the entrepreneur must be alert to possible financing opportunities 'lurking in the dark' around him. Bootstrap financing shows that the entrepreneur is resourceful and this makes investment by outside capital providers easier. It also reduces the need for the entrepreneur to seek external finance, which could lead to the entrepreneur having a reduced interest in the venture.

The finance used usually depends on the stage of the venture. When the enterprise is set up, it is usually easier for the entrepreneur to raise funding from their personal resources as well as from family and friends. As the enterprise is growing it becomes easier to attract equity sources of funding from business angels and venture capitalists. At this stage, the firm has a good track record and can attract debt funding from trade credits given by suppliers. If the enterprise is starved of liquidity, it can factor its debts to generate liquidity or cash. At some point, the early stage investors, like business angels and venture capitalists, will want to harvest their investment. That is, they would want to sell their investment and realise gains on their investment. They would therefore want to take the firm public so that they can sell their investments to other interested investors.

The provision of finance is usually premised on meeting certain conditions. These conditions are known as milestones and they include developing a working prototype, bringing the product to market and the acceptance of the product by the market. Therefore, meeting milestones could entice investors to provide more funds to the enterprise. The milestones also provide a way to evaluate the whole venture so that the entrepreneur and the providers of finance can all decide whether they want to continue with the project. Milestones therefore serve as a road map for both the investor and the financiers or possible financiers.

Some factors are important for the success of small business financing from the entrepreneur's perspective. The entrepreneur should be aware of and choose the appropriate sources of finance at any given point in time. For instance, a business that decides to use/acquire too much debt in the initial or start-up phase is more likely to fail. This is because its revenues are now growing and the market is now 'discovering' its product or service. Its cash flows are likely to be low and it is therefore unlikely that the business will be able to handle the burden of the fixed charges that come with debt. In this case, more patient capital in the form of equity is preferable at this stage.

The entrepreneur should make an effort to search for the various sources of finance available both from traditional and non-traditional sources. The entrepreneur should be aware of the requirements for funding to be granted. This is because a good application can be rejected because it does not meet the specifications of the lender. The process of searching takes time and the entrepreneur should be patient in undertaking the search. A lot of information that could lead to financing is available on the Internet.

The entrepreneur should be prepared before meeting possible financiers. Entrepreneurs should be able to present their case for financing confidently. They should demonstrate that they know the ins and outs of the business and that they have good knowledge of the dynamics of the business. They should also have a good rapport and chemistry with potential fund providers. Good chemistry ensures that the financing relationship starts on a good note and that there is goodwill amongst the parties. Entrepreneurs should therefore not underestimate the chemistry between themselves and their possible financiers.

2.8 Elements of Deal Structure and Closing the Deal

Obtaining financing from external sources is not easy. Entrepreneurs have to do a bit of searching and, after locating possible financiers, engage in several meetings and negotiations with such financiers. The deal reached and its structuring is very important. This is because it will determine the value that will go to the entrepreneur. It will also determine how much finance the potential financiers will provide and how much they are likely to get in return for the risk that they are taking. The purpose of the meetings and negotiations is to enable the potential investor to understand the business and gain more information about it. The information provided will inform the potential investor as to whether he/she wants to invest in the venture. This period also offers the entrepreneur the ability to market and sell the business. The initial negotiations and agreement will be entered in what is known as the *term sheet*. The term sheet is also known as a *letter of intent* and is created by the two parties. It specifies the rights and responsibilities of both parties. The investor, for example, may have the right to appoint members of the board of directors. The investor may also be required to provide further financing if certain milestones are met by the enterprise. In the case of the entrepreneur, he/she may have the right to pay back the investment under certain/specific conditions.

After the negotiations, the parties will meet their legal advisers to finalise the investment agreement. This finalised investment agreement is known as the formal investment agreement. The formal investment agreement can also set out covenants and undertakings with the intention of protecting the investor. Covenants that require the entrepreneur to do something are known as *positive covenants* and those that restrict the entrepreneur from doing what is stated are known as *negative covenants*. An example of a positive covenant is that the entrepreneur will be required to furnish the investor with information such as financial statements and management accounts. An example of a negative covenant is that the entrepreneur may be forbidden from issuing or acquiring additional financing without the prior consent of the investor or from paying excessive salaries or bonuses to management.

2.9 Summary and Conclusions

Entrepreneurs have to consider how their business is organised, as this has various implications. These include the ability of the enterprise to attract highly qualified and skilled employees, the nature of the liability borne by the entrepreneur, tax implications and succession issues. The enterprise can be organised as a sole proprietorship, a partnership or a limited liability company. The 'finance gap' in new venture and small business financing may lead to a situation where credit is rationed. Credit rationing is based on information asymmetries between lenders and borrowers, and the existence of information asymmetry may result in adverse selection and moral hazard. The venture life cycle usually progresses from the research and development phase, to the start-up phase, to the early growth phase, to the rapid growth phase and finally to the exit phase. The sequence of new venture financing is important, especially linking it to the firm's stage of development.

Various sources of finance exist for MSMEs. These sources are discussed based on whether they represent equity or debt finance. Financing that exhibits features of both debt and equity—hybrid finance was also looked at. Equity sources of finance include personal savings of the entrepreneur, financing acquired from business angels, funding raised from venture capitalists, private placements of equity and public offers of equity. Debt sources of finance include bank finance, credit from MFIs, trade credit, factoring, asset-based lenders, bonds, commercial paper and leasing. With regard to hybrid financing, examples include mezzanine financing and finance from preference shareholders. Deal structure and the terms reached are very important for determining the benefits that should accrue to entrepreneurs and how much of their stake can be given up.

Discussion Questions and Problems

1. What are the various forms of business ownership? What factors should an entrepreneur consider in evaluating the various forms of ownership?
2. What are the differences between a private limited company and a public limited company?
3. What is franchising and what are the advantages and disadvantages of an MSME entering into a franchise agreement?
4. An entrepreneur is considering starting a food chain business: How can he/she execute this idea?
5. How does the 'finance gap' lead to credit rationing? What are the consequences of information asymmetry in new venture and small business financing?
6. Discuss the various stages involved in new venture development.
7. Explain the concept of *layering* in small business finance.
8. Discuss the sequence of new venture financing.

9. Discuss the various sources of equity and debt finance available to an MSME.
10. What are the benefits of issuing shares to the general public?
11. What are the sources of finance available to MSMEs in Africa? What are the problems associated with these financing sources?
12. Explain how MSMEs can increase their access to formal finance.

3

Business Planning

Learning Objectives
By the end of this chapter, you should be able to:

- appreciate the difference between the business plans of new ventures and established small businesses
- discuss the purpose and importance of business plans
- describe the elements of a sound business plan
- explain the financial aspect of a business plan
- recognise the importance of using business plans to attract external finance
- appreciate the importance of due diligence to the entrepreneur and outside investors
- explain how to implement a business plan and the need to revise business plan
- provide reasons why some business plans fail

3.1 Introduction

Planning is an essential part of management, which is required for the effective operations of every organisation. It is a systematic process of setting goals, developing strategies and outlining tasks and schedules for achieving those set goals. Engaging in planning enables the firm to analyse its potential for success and by identifying what it needs to do in order to achieve its business

J.Y. Abor, *Entrepreneurial Finance for MSMEs*,
DOI 10.1007/978-3-319-34021-0_3

goals. Business planning is thinking and working out the details of a firm with the aim of achieving the objectives of the firm. The lack of proper planning is often cited as one of the reasons for businesses failing. As Winston Churchill, the British Prime Minister during World War II, highlighted, 'if you fail to plan you are planning to fail.' This goes to buttress the point that planning, as the first function of management, is critical to business growth and success.

Businesses usually begin the planning process by developing a business plan for their operations. A **business plan** is a written document that describes all the important aspects of a business. The business plan helps the firm to identify its goals and objectives and to develop strategies and tactics to reach the set goals. The business plan describes the product and service to be sold, its market and how the product will be made or the service performed, its financial details, as well as the organisational design and management. A business plan is a valuable tool for the entrepreneur to convey the mission (i.e. why the business exists), and the prospects of the business to customers, suppliers and other stakeholders. It can be viewed as the document, which sells the business to potential investors and other stakeholders for investment decision-making.

A potential entrepreneur needs a business plan to start a new venture, and to guide the operations of the firm successfully. On the other hand, an established venture needs a growth plan to accentuate its growth. Previous empirical studies have shown that businesses that are involved in business planning perform better than their counter parts, which are not. Small businesses have been found not to take the issue of business planning seriously. In spite of the numerous benefits of a business pan to the entrepreneur, many entrepreneurs are not ready to invest time and resources to develop one. This may be one of the factors responsible for the failure and collapse of MSMEs in developing countries.

In this chapter, we explain the differences between business plans of new ventures and established businesses. The chapter looks at the purpose of business plans and of strategic planning, and at the elements of a business plan. The chapter also discusses how the business plan serves to attract external finance, the relevance of due diligence to the entrepreneur and outside investors, implementing business plans, the need of revising the business plan and why some business plans fail.

3.2 Business Plans and New Ventures

There are fundamental differences between the business plans prepared for a new venture and an established business. A new venture requires a business plan to take off, while an established venture needs a growth plan to support the growth of the venture. One main difference is the level of precision with respect to the projections for which the business plans are based. Projections made for an established business may be easier since these can be made based on previous actual figures. Such projections may be difficult for a start-up or a new venture. Projection for a new venture may require assumptions: guess work or business modelling and simulation analysis.

The extent to which outsiders rely on the business plan may differ between a new venture and an established business. External finance providers may specifically depend on the current performance and track record of an established business. They are less likely to depend solely on the business plan. In that case, the business plan serves as an internal document to guide management. With respect to a new venture, the business plan is prepared with a different focus. Outsides finance providers rely heavily on the business plan to inform their decision to extend financing to the business.

Another distinction has to do with how detailed the business plan is. The business plan of a new venture appears to be more detailed and elaborate. It normally covers a wide range of issues from marketing, production, product design, organisational design, management, ownership and control to financing. On the other hand, the business plan of an established firm may concentrate mainly on marketing issues. This is because the other issues, such as organisational design and management ownership and control as well as financing might have been addressed in the past. Planning on marketing issues will therefore be based on the existing structures within the firm. However, in a situation where the firm intends to embark on a major expansion project, the business plan then will have to cover a broader scope.

3.3 Purpose of a Business Plan

The business plan serves a number of useful purposes. First and foremost, for a new venture, the process of preparing a business plan is to provide a road map for the future of the business by making the entrepreneur and business owner think through their strategies, evaluate their business concepts, assess the risks that the businesses are likely to be confronted with and develop means to mitigate or eliminate those risks. The business plan guides the entrepreneur by charting a clear path or future course of action for the business and by devising the strategy for success. The business plan details the firm's mission statement, goals, objectives, market analysis, products and services, organisational design and management, financial forecasts and strategies to help the entrepreneur lead the business successfully. Internally, the business plan provides a blueprint for the operation of an entire business.

An important purpose of the preparing a business plan is to attract outside financing. This is not to suggest that if the entrepreneur has enough funds, he/she does not need a business plan. Certainly no! Businesses that are sourcing for finance can use a business plan to attract funding from lenders and investors. In many instances, small businesses have been denied financing by finance providers because of their inability to sell their business concepts with a convincing business plan. The best approach to secure outside finance is to prepare a sound business plan, which serves as a means by which the entrepreneur communicates to these finance providers the potential the business opportunity offers. The business plan describes the ownership structure of the firm, the new venture team, how much finance is required by the firm, how the finance will be utilised, the form the proposed financing will take and, most importantly, how the investors will make a return on their investment and also how the lender's loan will be rapid. In simple terms, business plan can be used by the entrepreneur for applying for loans from banks and other lenders and also to convince investors that the firm is worth investing in.

The business plan allows management to think through the business in detail and to set goals and objectives. It allows key performance indicators to be established against which the firm's future performance can be measured. The firm's future performance and progress can be measured against planned goals involving revenue, expenditures, profits, time frame and strategic direction. The business plan sets out the benchmarks for growth against which the entrepreneur can monitor and measure the actual progress to be made. A business plan integrates the various plans the firm has, including its market plan, financial plan and operational plan.

The business plan can also be used to attract key personnel. The plan serves as a key employment prospects for personnel with specialist skills. The plan is a way by which a certain calibre of entrepreneur can ascertain the prospects of the firm based on its future projections and incentive systems.

Business plans are only as effective as the data on which they are based, so prior to writing a business plan there is the need to gather all the necessary information before writing begins. For example, thorough research needs to be done to obtain information about the industry in which the firm operates: market information, competitors, trends and changes that are likely to affect the operation of the business, and financial information. It is important to note that although business plans may be detailed enough to serve the various purposes, there are aspects of each that may not be too useful for the other. For example, a business plan prepared to attract external financing may be interested in the technical details required in a plan to attract a chief engineer and vice versa.

3.4 Strategic Planning and the Business Plan

Strategic planning involves a systematic approach of setting priorities and assessing the current situation to formulate a strategy, implement the strategy, evaluate progress, assess and adjust the organisation's direction in response to a changing environment. It involves the process of defining a firm's strategy, or direction, and making decisions on resource allocation to pursue the strategy. Determining the direction of the firm involves having an understanding of its current position and possible ways by which it can pursue a particular course of action. Strategic planning focuses not only on where the firm is going and the actions required to get there, but also on how to measure the firm's success.

The strategic planning process involves the following: (1) definition of the firm's goals and/or objectives, (2) analysis or assessment of the current internal and external situation of the firm, (3) formulation of strategy, including identification of strategic alternatives, (4) implementation of strategy by translating strategic plans into more operational plans and (5) evaluation and control, including measuring performance and refinement.

The strategic plan is a document that articulates the firm's goals, define the course of actions required to achieve those goals and to indicate how to improve the firm's performance. The strategic plan is used for implementing and managing the strategic direction of the firm. It is important to note that there is a difference between the strategic plan and the business plan. The strategic plan focuses on developing a sustainable competitive advantage and is long-term in nature, whereas a business plan is useful for assessing the viability of a business opportunity, and is more tactical in nature. Whereas a strategic plan is useful for providing direction and action in order to move the firm from its currents position to where it intends to go, a business plan is used to provide a structure for ideas in order to initially define the business. A strategic plan is also necessary for prioritising resources to enhance the level of revenue and increase the return on investment, but a business plan is useful for the firm when it is seeking external finance.

The strategic plan provides alternative courses of action and has a long-term focus that usually covers a five-year period. The business plan is prepared to facilitate the implementation of a particular strategy that has been selected by the firm, and it usually covers a short-term period. The strategic planning process involves a detailed analysis of the strategic alternatives with the aim of maximising value for the entrepreneur. The business plan will typically not include such great details, especially when the purpose of developing the business plan is to attract external finance.

3.5 Elements of a Business Plan

Though the elements of a business plan are quite standard, the entrepreneur may prepare the business plan and tailor it according to its intended purpose. An entrepreneur writing a business plan for the first time may find it useful to seek the assistance of experts to help in preparing a sound business plan. There are also business planning software that can be used to assist the entrepreneur prepare the business plan. Preparing a business plan can be a costly and time consuming exercise, but it is an important step to take at the beginning. For the business plan to serve as a roadmap, then it must be prepared at the onset to guide the entrepreneur in the venture.

We discuss the common elements of a business plan at this stage. The entrepreneur or small business owner must, however, recognise the fact that, like every venture, every business plan is unique. The outline discussed below covers most of the issues that are relevant to be included in a solid business plan. The entrepreneur can consider these elements as a starting point for preparing a business plan, but can modify them as and when necessary to suit the plan's intended purpose.

3.5.1 Title Page and Table of Content

The business plan must contain a title page with the firm's name, logo, address and other contact information. The business plan should also include a table of content to enable readers to easily locate particular sections of the document.

3.5.2 Executive Summary

The business plan should include an executive summary, which provides a synopsis of all the key points of the business venture. It summarises the various elements of the business plan. The executive summary must be concise, convincing and be able to capture the attention of the reader. A well-written executive summary gives a good first impression of the entrepreneur and the business plan to readers such as potential investors or finance providers. Although the executive summary is the first part of the business plan, it is the last element of the plan to be written because it summarises the entire plan. A reader should be able know what the entire business is all about after reading the executive summary alone.

The executive summary provides readers and potential investors a brief description of the key components of the business plan. The executive summary should stimulate the interest of readers to want to read the entire business plan. Note that, the executive summary is not a preface to or an abstract of the business plan, but instead it is the business plan in a concise form.

3.5.3 Business Description

This element of the business plan shows how the business is organised, the legal form of the business, the venture's vision and mission statements, the objectives, history (i.e. if it is an existing business), current status and plan for the future. It also provides an overview of the industry or market segment in which the venture operates.

The description part should give the reader a good idea of where the firm is, how it got there, and where it foresees itself in the future. When describing the firm's profile, the entrepreneur should indicate the legal name of the business, its legal form and ownership structure. It must state whether the business is a new business, a growing business, or the acquisition of an existing business. It should also indicate the actual business the firm, its products and services, service delivery and so on. This section must indicate where the firm's main office will be or is located as well as any other facility that the firm will use and then explain the reasons for the choice of location. The business description should state the vision and mission statements of the venture. The mission statement expresses in words the entrepreneur's vision about the essence of the firm. The mission statement provides a sense of direction for the entire firm and a guide to decision-making. The mission statement also states the goals and objectives of the venture. The objectives must be specific, measurable, attainable and motivational and time bound.

This section must also provide a brief history and current status of the firm. If the business is already in operation, it must indicate how long the firm has been in business. The history should highlight the significant financial and operational events in the life of the firm. It should describe how the firm has evolved over the period, its achievements and what the entrepreneur envisions for the future. It is important to provide an overview of the industry the firm is entering or operating in, as part of the business description. Businesses operate within a specific context that affects their growth potential. The description of the firm's operating environment may include new products and developments in that particular industry, trends and outlook for the industry, and overall economic trends.

3.5.4 Products and Services

This section gives a detailed description of the products and/or services the venture offers or intends to offer to its potential users. It is the section where firms sell their idea by generating some excitement about their products/services. Information on the product description must be as detailed and factual as possible, as this forms part of the branding process. The firm must indicate the stage of growth of the product/service (introductory, growth, saturation, maturity stage of the product life cycle) and when the products/services were initially developed. In other words, this section is to differentiate a firm's products or services from those of its competitors and what the position of the product/service is in the marketplace. It describes specific customer needs that are uniquely met by the firm's products or services. The section should define the unique features of the firm's products and services and the benefits customers stand to get by patronising them. Product life cycles and their effects on sales and marketing should also be described. It can also catalogue a historical summary of product development, introductions and improvements. The firm's plans for a new generation of products or services may also be included in this section.

3.5.5 Market and Competitor Analysis

This section should define the firm's market, industry, current and potential buyers and the current and potential competitors. The plan must explain the key factors for the market in terms of how buying decisions are made, how the market is segmented, how the firm intends positioning itself and the kind of strategy it has devised to compete with its competitors. This section of the business plan includes industry analysis, and market and competitor analysis. The industrial analysis will enable readers of the plan to better appreciate the industrial structure, and factors driving the competition in the industry. The plan should provide details on the various players in the industry, on the regulatory framework of the industry, on factors that pose threats and opportunities in the industry, on the industrial trends and on size. It must also provide information on the various economic, political, sociocultural, technological and legal trends in the industry and how these affect or will affect the operations of the venture.

In terms of the market analysis, the entrepreneur must describe the specific market in which the firm competes or intends to compete. A thorough analysis of the market and its competitors is a very important aspect of the business plan. It helps the entrepreneur to identify the target market and the behaviours of customers in that market in order to have a better understanding of their needs and expectations. It is crucial at this stage to present a convincing position that there is an unsatisfied/unmet need in the marketplace and that the entrepreneur has a product or service that can address the need. The entrepreneur needs to identify and segment the customers (existing and potential) in the marketplace. It is also necessary to identify the future prospect of the market the firm wishes to enter and to ascertain whether the market is in its growth or maturity stage. Another key area to consider under the market analysis is to evaluate the key/direct competition the firm faces or is likely to face. The firm must list its primary/direct competitors and how it intends to compete with them. Comparing the firm's strengths and weaknesses with its competitors' best does this. The success of the business is dependent on its ability to capture a market share away from its competitors or to focus on a segment of the market that is not being attended to. Competitor analysis also requires identifying the competitors (name and addresses), and indicating the intensity and sources of competition in the industry. Conducting market research on competitors' market share, products and strategy is required in order to write this part of the business plan. Such information can be obtained through interviews, surveys, trade publications, newspapers, demographic profiles, magazine and books.

3.5.6 Marketing Strategy

The entrepreneur and prospective finance providers are mainly concerned about whether there is an immediate and eager market for the firm's products and services. The marketing strategy section is where the entrepreneur shows what strategy is put in place to address the market and competitor situations. This involves developing action plans to achieve the market objective of satisfying the needs the entrepreneur has identified in the marketplace. The marketing strategy is detailed in a marketing plan and a thorough market analysis serves as the basis for the firm's marketing plan. The analysis generally covers the firm's competition, customers, products and market acceptance. The competitor analysis details the competitor's strengths and weaknesses, and provides a basis for identifying market opportunities.

The market plan should include important strategies such as the firm's market segmentation strategy, targeting strategy (this is a strategy on how the firm will approach each of the market segment it has chosen). The targeting strategy may involve either differentiating a product for a particular market segment or going after a niche—going after a small segment with a tailored offer. Small businesses are mostly successful when focusing on a specific niche of the market by meeting the special needs of their customer. The marketing plan should include the positioning strategy, which deals with how to position the firm's products and services in the market. Another integral part of the overall marketing strategy is the pricing strategy. Pricing is a critical success factor and must be looked at carefully as it can make or break the business. This should include how much it costs for the product or service to be produced or delivered, what is the margin and what are the prevailing market prices. It should also include when the pricing strategy will be reviewed. Will it be monthly, quarterly or annually? The distribution strategy is also required. Will the business use wholesalers, cataloguers, mass merchant, retailers or distributors as distribution channel(s)? Another important element of the overall market strategy is the advertising and promotion strategy. This deals with how to communicate to the readers of the business plan (on) how the firm is going to educate its target market about the product or service, inform them about the product's availability and tell them about the benefits of the product or service. The advertising and promotion strategy is necessary for gaining acceptance in the market. The overall marketing strategy should enable the entrepreneur to get the product or service to the target market.

3.5.7 Organisation and Management

This section provides a description of the management team members and their backgrounds as well as the additional key personnel that will be hired. The quality of the firm's management team is a very important aspect of a business plan. This is because investors feel comfortable dealing with a competent management team with some proven records. The entrepreneur needs to describe the key personnel of the firm with their name, position, responsibilities and a short description of their experience. This section should present the strengths of the firm's management team by showing relevant experience and achievements. This should demonstrate the ability of the management team to exhibit planning, organisational and leadership skills. A management team with rich experience and a proven track record of success add to the credibility of the firm. The section also describes specific management and control systems.

The entrepreneur needs to highlight the existing or planned organisational structure that will be used to accomplish the goals and objectives outlined in the business plan. An organisation chart usually depicts the organisational structure. It also describes the facilities, equipment and number of personnel: their key role, skills and responsibilities. This section should also discuss the key advisors and consultants of the firm, including board, lawyers, auditors and bankers. The board of directors or advisors and other consultants add to the credibility and enhance the profile and value of the management team. It is also useful to include information about the firm's ownership structure.

3.5.8 Operations

The operations section details how the firm will be run and how it intends to deliver value for its customers. It involves the processes to be used to deliver the firm's products and services in the marketplace and these may include manufacturing, transportation, logistics, delivery, customer and technical service. There is the need for a detailed operational plan, which details how the entrepreneur will operate the business. The operational plans should be in line with the objectives the business aims to achieve in the marketplace. The entrepreneur also needs to provide detailed description of the scope of the venture's operations by providing milestone and timeline for each of the activities to be carried out.

Again, the plan should be aligned with the marketing strategy of the firm in order to achieve the objectives outlined in the marketing strategy. That is, it should provide a description of how the firm will fulfil its marketing strategy through its operations. The entrepreneur should also cover other important aspects of the operations in the plan, including production methods, cost control techniques, administrative and financial controls that will be or has been established, inventory management techniques, credit policies and working capital management techniques and policies. It is also important to briefly describe how key personnel of the firm will be incentivised in order to retain them.

3.5.9 The Financial Component

The financial component of the business plan includes past and current financial standing of the venture, and it also includes the venture's projected (or pro forma) financial statements for an appropriate period. Lenders and equity investors consider the financial component as the most important element of the business plan of new ventures or entrepreneurs who are seeking finance. For existing firms, the lenders and investors rely on the financial statements to ascertain the financial health of the firm to repay the loan and generate adequate returns or pay dividends to the equity holders. Whether the business plan is developed for a new venture or an existing business, the entrepreneur needs to include pro forma financial statements for the firm (for about three years). The pro forma financial statements include projected income statement, projected cash flow statement and projected balance sheet. The projected financial statements must be consistent with the discussion regarding the firm's past performance trends and the information contained in the other sections of the business plan.

The plan establishes the total financing requirement of the firm over a given period. It should also indicate why the financing is required, and how it is to be utilised. The entrepreneur needs to take into consideration the likely investors' payback and their need for an exit strategy. The plan should also contain budgetary and financial control. The financial projections and forecasts must be supported by verifiable facts and figures. There should be critical assumptions underlying such financial projections. The scope of the financial projections should be looked at in terms of a financial model of the venture. Modelling that is well done should enable the entrepreneur to generate forecasts of sales, income, balance sheet accounts and financial requirements. The use of financial projections assists the prospective investor in making a decision with respect to how much to invest and what proportion of venture's ownership to hold. In the absence of a financial model of the firm, it is difficult to evaluate the effects of financing terms with much such accuracy.

3.5.10 Appendices

The appendices include collection of all of the documentations that are used to support the business plan. They may include a start-up budget, financial history and ratios, a break-even analysis, detailed projected financial statements, market research data, results of surveys and studies, resumes of management team members, staffing plan, photos of products, major contracts, pricing information and references.

3.6 Attracting External Finance

We mentioned earlier that one important purpose of the preparing a business plan is to attract external finance. When the business plan is prepared with the intention of raising finance, it must address the peculiar needs of the finance providers. The needs of the finance provider may depend on whether it is an equity investor or a debt finance provider. Lenders are interested in the ability of the venture to generate the necessary cash flows to service the debt and whether the entrepreneur or venture has collateral to secure the debt. Equity investors, on the other hand, are interested in the return of their investment in the form of dividend and capital gains. They are interested in the valuation of the venture, since this has an effect on their share in the venture. The business plan should therefore be able to demonstrate to the external finance providers that the firm is capable of repaying the loans to the potential lenders and also to offer the investors an attractive return on their investment.

Lenders and investors are often impressed by entrepreneurs who are well informed and have a good appreciation of the business issues. This certainly enhances the entrepreneur's chance of securing the finance. The entrepreneur may have been asked in some cases to make a presentation of the business plan, For instance requesting finance from a venture capitalist may require that the entrepreneur submits a written business plan followed by a face-to-face presentation. The entrepreneur may be given a few minutes to present the business plan to the venture capitalist. This is an opportunity for the entrepreneur to convincingly 'sell' the business ideas to the venture capitalist. Considering the few minutes involved in presenting the business plan, the entrepreneur must avoid unnecessary details and explanation. It therefore requires ample preparation and rehearsals by the entrepreneur to make a good presentation of the business plan in order to attract the finance.

The entrepreneur needs to be aware of the criteria used by external finance providers in evaluating the potential of the small business requiring finance. The entrepreneur must generally bear in mind the expectations of the external finance providers when preparing the business plan as well as when making a presentation of the business plan.

3.7 Facilitating Due Diligence

The business plan provides a means for facilitating due diligence, which is useful for both the prospective investors and the entrepreneur who requires the financing. Due diligence involves the process of obtaining and verifying information associated with an investment decision. In other word, it is the process of evaluating details about a business venture before making the investment decision. Investors are expected to ensure that their decision to invest in the venture is based on accurate and comprehensive information, and such details can be obtained from the business plan. Therefore, the entrepreneur can improve the chance of obtaining finance from investors by providing accurate and comprehensive information in the business plan to facilitate due diligence. Due diligence is not conducted by only prospective investors, it is also important for the entrepreneur to carry out due diligence by investigating the investors. The entrepreneur can evaluate the past records of the investors by obtaining information from other entrepreneurs who have had dealings with such investors.

3.8 Implementing the Business Plan

After developing the business plan, it needs to be implemented. It is important that everyone in the firm understands the business plan and takes ownership of it in order to ensure its successful implementation. Those involved in carrying out the activities outlined in the business plan must have a full appreciation of the various targets, their involvement and how they will be met or achieved. The business plan will typically include all sorts of milestones, objectives, goals and action plans. Therefore, it is important that the implementation indicates clear timelines in relation to the objectives. Implementation also requires monitoring and evaluation of the business plan by the entrepreneur. There is the need for some level of accountability and follow-up. When targets have been met, those involved should know. However, if some targets are not achieved by the expected date, the entrepreneur must figure out why and what remedial actions must be taken to address the issue. Some indicators such as sales volume, productivity benchmarks and market share statistics can be used to gauge whether or not the targets are being met in line with guide you worked out in making a decision as to whether or not the targets as detailed in the business plans are being met.

3.9 Revising the Business Plan

Considering the dynamic nature of markets in which growing firms operate today, it is necessary to periodically revise the business plan so as to maximise the relevance of the plan as a tool for management and investors.

The preparation of the business plan requires the need to revise the business plan, taking into consideration actual developments within the firm and also in the market place. In preparing a business plan, initial projections will have been based on certain assumptions. Over time as the venture develops, it may be realised that these assumptions on which the initial projections were based were not realistic. This will mean that the initial projections will have to be modified, considering the actual developments, and therefore the need to update the business plan. The new set of projections will then be incorporated in revising the business plan. Apart from incorporating the new set of projections, the revised business plan will also include new targets. This is useful for the entrepreneur in tracking progress of the venture. Revising the business plan should entail an examination of the venture's strategic direction and making the necessary changes based on actual happenings.

3.10 Why Some Business Plans Fail

There are a number of reasons why business plans fail. If a business plan is rejected after an initial screening, it may probably be failure on the part of the entrepreneur to communicate the strategy to the readers. Another reason could be that the business plan failed to assure the reader that the marketing strategy can deliver the promised outcomes. The business plan may also lack the operational details required for implementing the plan. It is important for the entrepreneur to set realistic goals and objectives in developing their business plan. There is also the need for the necessary resources in order to implement the plan successfully.

3.11 Summary and Conclusions

In this chapter, we mentioned that a business plan is a written document that describes all the important aspects of a business. The business plan helps the firm to identify its goals and objectives and to develop strategies and tactics to reach the set goals. Business plans prepared for new ventures differ from those of established firms in terms of level of precision with respect to the projections for which the business plans are based, the extent to which outsiders rely on the business plan and how detailed the business plan is.

The business plan serves a number of useful purposes. First and foremost, for a new venture, the process of preparing a business plan is to provide a road map for the future of the business by making the entrepreneurs and business owners think through their strategies, evaluate their business concepts, assess the risks that the businesses are likely to be confronted with and develop means to mitigate or eliminate those risks. The business plan allows management to think through the business in detail and to set goals and objectives. The business plan can also be used to attract key personnel into the firm. Business plans are also used to attract outside financing.

Though the purpose of preparing the business plan may be to inform on how the enterprise should be tailored, there are important elements that need to be included in any standard business plan. These are the executive summary, the product description, information on products and services, market and competitor analysis, marketing strategy, organisation and management, operations and financial information. After developing the business plan, it needs to be implemented. It is also important to revise the business plan taking into consideration current developments within the firm and those that are external to the firm.

Discussion Questions and Problems

1. Why should an entrepreneur be interested in preparing a business plan?
2. How different is the business plan prepared for a new venture from the plan of an established business?
3. Describe the major components of a business plan.
4. As an entrepreneur, how will go about preparing your business plan and presenting it to a venture capitalist?
5. How should a business plan developed to seek funding from a bank be different from one prepared to apply to an equity investor?
6. Explain how the business plan of a small business relates to its strategic plan.
7. Describe the financial component of the business plan. What and what go into that section of the plan?
8. What do investors and lenders look out for in a business plan?
9. Why is due diligence such an important issue to the finance provider and the entrepreneur?
10. What should an entrepreneur do to convince a potential investor about the prospects of his/her venture?
11. How will you go about implementing and revising the business plan of a new venture?
12. Why do some business plans fail in practice?

Part II

The Financial Environment and Finance Providers

4

The Financial Environment and Small Businesses

Learning Objectives
By the end of this chapter, you should be able to:

- identify the components of the financial environment
- explain how the financial environment affects business decisions
- describe the purpose of the financial market
- identify the types of financial institutions
- discuss the functions of financial institutions
- explain how interest rates are determined

4.1 Introduction

Businesses in general and for that matter MSMEs do not exist in isolation. They operate within the financial environment and their decisions are affected by developments within the financial environments. The financial environment includes the financial system, tax and regulatory policies and the state of the economy. The financial system is made up of money, financial instruments, financial markets, financial institutions and financial regulators.

Money serves as a medium of exchange and store of wealth. It is also used as a unit of account and a store of value. A **financial instrument** is the legal obligation of one party to transfer something of value, usually money, to another party at some future date, under certain conditions. It can also act as a means of payment, a store of value, and it allows for

J.Y. Abor, *Entrepreneurial Finance for MSMEs*,
DOI 10.1007/978-3-319-34021-0_4

the trading of risk. Financial instruments are issued by deficit units or entities in need of funds and are bought by the surplus units or savers/lenders. Financial instruments are also known as financial assets or financial securities. Examples of financial instruments include Treasury bills, bank loans, bonds, mortgages and shares. **Financial markets** are markets where financial instruments are traded. **Financial institutions** are financial intermediaries that ensure the transfer of funds between the savers and the borrowers. Examples are banks, credit unions, savings and loans companies, insurance companies, pension funds, mutual funds and finance companies. **Financial regulators** are government institutions that regulate the financial market to maintain financial market stability and to promote financial market efficiency. For example, in South Africa, the South African Reserve Bank regulates the banking sector, while the Financial Services Board oversees the non-banking financial services industry. In Ghana, the financial regulators include the Bank of Ghana (BoG), the SEC, the National Insurance Commission (NIC) and the National Pensions Regulatory Authority (NPRA).

Considering the relevance of the financial environment, it is imperative for the small business manager or the entrepreneur to appreciate current developments in the financial system and the direction of the economy, because these have implications for the firm's financial decisions. A good understanding of the financial environment and its impact on businesses is a very important issue.

The chapter discusses financial markets and the purpose of financial markets. It then looks at various financial institutions and the role they play in facilitating the flow of capital. We examine how some financial institutions interact with small businesses in providing access to finance. We also examine interest rates and the factors that affect interest rates in the economy.

4.2 Financial Markets

Financial markets are markets in which financial assets (securities) are bought and sold. Financial markets exist in an economy to ensure the efficient allocation of capital to the ultimate users. Surplus economic units look out for areas to invest their excess funds and therefore the financial market provides that avenue where they meet deficit units that are in need of funds. Financial markets are not necessarily physical places, but they are mechanisms that facilitate the flow of funds to those who require them to finance investments.

Financial markets are made up of the money and capital markets, primary and secondary markets, organised and over-the-counter markets. The classifications of financial markets are discussed as follows.

4.2.1 Money and Capital Markets

Money markets focus on the purchase and sale of short-term financial securities. Money markets facilitate the flow of short-term funds from surplus units to deficit funds. Short-term securities are those with maturity of one year or less, such as government Treasury bills, commercial paper, negotiable certificates of deposit, bankers' acceptances and repurchase agreements. **Capital markets**, on the other hand, are concerned with the buying and selling of long-term securities. Capital markets facilitate the flow of funds from surplus units to deficit units. Long-term securities have a maturity of more than one year such as bonds or shares.

4.2.2 Primary and Secondary Markets

Primary markets are markets for the issue of new securities. Primary markets provide funds to the initial issuer of the securities and the issue can take the form of a private placement or public offering. A **private placement** is where the securities are issued to specific investors (usually large institutional investors). With respect to **public offering**, the securities are issued to the general public. For instance, firms do **initial public offering** by issuing shares to the public for the first time. **Secondary markets** are markets where already issued or existing securities are bought and sold. In the secondary market, holders of the securities have the opportunity to off-load or sell their securities to new investors. In this sense, the secondary market is said to provide liquidity for the initial investor. In the secondary market, the funds flow from the new investor in the securities to the initial investor but the initial issuer in the primary market is not involved.

4.2.3 Organised and Over-the-Counter-Markets

Organised markets are markets with a comprehensive regulatory framework, with traders linked to one platform. They can easily be identified because they have trading floors or electronic platform, where only authorised members can trade in the securities listed. That means, there is a central location or electronic platform, where buyers and sellers of securities meet to trade in securities. These are stock exchanges, and examples include the Ghana Stock Exchange, the Nigeria Stock Exchange, the Nairobi Securities Exchange, the Uganda Securities Exchange, the Johannesburg Stock Exchange, the Lusaka Stock Exchange, the Stock Exchange of Mauritius, the Egyptian Exchange, Bourse Régionale des Valeurs Mobilières, the Shanghai Stock Exchange, the Shenzhen Stock Exchange, the Bombay Stock Exchange, the National Stock Exchange of India, the New York Stock Exchange and the London Stock Exchange. It is however important to mention that in recent developments, stockbrokers or authorised members of the stock exchange do not have to meet at the physical exchange. They simply sit in the comfort of their offices and trade online or through a virtual platform. **Over-the-counter (OTC) market** is a largely unregulated market, whereby geographically dispersed traders, who are linked to one another via telecommunication systems and computers, trade in securities. In other words, the securities dealers operate at many different locations across the country or the world, but telecommunication systems and computers (tend to) link them. Securities traded on the OTC are not traded on an organised stock exchange.

4.3 Financial Institutions

Financial institutions are financial intermediaries or firms that bring savers/lenders and borrowers together in order to efficiently allocate financial resources. They provide access to the financial market, both to savers who wish to purchase financial instruments and to borrowers who want to issue them. Examples include banks, savings and loans institutions, credit unions, insurance companies, pension funds, investment companies, finance companies, mutual funds, unit trusts, venture capital companies and so on.

In recent times, a number of financial institutions have evolved offering various financial services in the financial market. We present the different types of financial institutions. There are depository financial institutions and non-depository institutions such as contractual savings institutions, investment intermediaries and other financial institutions.

4.3.1 Depository Financial Institutions

Depository institutions are financial intermediaries that accept deposits from individuals and institutions and also give out loans. These institutions include commercial banks, and thrift institutions such as savings and loan institutions, mutual savings banks, and credit unions.

4.3.1.1 Commercial Banks

Commercial banks are financial intermediaries that take deposits from the public and give out short-, medium- and long-term loans to individual and businesses. They mobilise funds primarily by offering current account, saving deposits, time deposits and other investment products. They then use the funds to give out loans to their clients. The variety of the loans they give out include short- and long-term loans, informal lines of credit or revolving credit facilities, construction loans, letters of credit, asset-based lending and accounts receivable financing. The main reason for establishing a commercial bank is to fill an existing need for banking services. Commercial banks have in the past mainly focused on lending to large corporates. In recent times, however, competition within the banking industry has compelled commercial banks to shift their attention to the MSME sector. Small businesses are beginning to benefit from the available bank credits and valuable banking services. Most banks have set up specialised MSME units that focus on lending to the MSMEs.

4.3.1.2 Rural and Community Banks

Rural and Community Banks (RCBs) are unit banks owned by members of a rural community through purchase of shares. They are licensed by the central bank to provide financial services and intermediation in the rural areas. This means they mobilise savings and provide credit and other banking facilities to the people within their operational areas, especially in the rural communities, which are not served by mainstream traditional banks. RCBs are usually established in small business and farming communities which are far from major cities where banking institutions are found, thus, making it difficult to access banking services. They offer services similar to those offered by the commercial banks for small businesses, including RCBs, which perform various functions, including mobilising deposits, granting of loans, investment, transferring funds and custodian services, and also serve as a means of channelling funds to defined targets.

4.3.1.3 Savings and Loans Institutions

Savings and loans institutions engage in the mobilisation of retail savings by accepting deposits from the households and small enterprises and providing credit to the non-corporate sector as well as micro and small businesses. These institutions are mainly located in the urban centres of the country where they provide financial services to the urban poor. MSMEs constitute their main target clients. Small businesses benefit from the savings and loans institutions because they adopt very innovative microfinance models to reach out to poor clients with very small transactions. The interest rates of these savings and loans companies are relatively higher than the traditional banks. However, businesses may place greater value on ready access to funds than on interest charges. The modes of frequent small payments (weekly, fortnightly and monthly) also make it easier for clients to bear.

4.3.1.4 Credit Unions

Credit unions (CUs) are financial institutions or intermediaries owned by members with a common bond. They operate as small cooperative lending institutions organised around a particular group: union members, employees of a firm, a religious group, members of a community and so on. They mobilise funds from deposits from their members (known as shares) and also give out loans to these members. CUs are cooperatives or mutually owned organisations and they help member small businesses by mobilising savings from them and providing them with loans. For instance, members who make predetermined periodic deposits into their accounts may borrow up to two times their savings balance. A member of the union with adequate savings can also guarantee loans on behalf of another member. The interests charged on loans to members are usually below commercial rates, and the interest they pay on members' savings is also low.

4.3.2 Contractual Savings Institutions

Contractual savings institutions acquire funds periodically on a contractual basis and promise their clients future compensation. They pool contributions in the form of premiums and pension contributions and invest these to generate adequate funds to meet insurance compensation and pension benefits. Insurance companies and pension funds are also contractual savings institutions.

4.3.2.1 Insurance Companies

Insurance companies receive premiums by selling insurance policies and also invest the funds to earn sufficient funds to meet insurance compensation. Insurance companies include life and non-life insurance companies. **Life**

insurance companies insure people against financial hazards following death or incapacitation. They raise funds from the premiums paid by policyholders and the funds they acquire are then invested in securities. **Non-life insurance companies** are in the general insurance business. They insure their policyholders against general casualty apart from life, such as loss from theft, fire and accidents. Their operations are similar to those of life insurance companies, and they also raise funds through premiums from their policyholders. However, they generally have a greater risk of losing funds in the event of major disasters occurring. Therefore, they tend to invest in more liquid assets than life insurance companies.

4.3.2.2 Pension Funds

Pension funds are non-depository institutions that provide pension benefits to retired employees by receiving regular pension contributions from the employees and their employers. Funds are obtained from employers' and employees' contributions and these may either be deducted automatically from the payroll or done voluntarily. Pension funds invest the pension contributions in order to generate sufficient funds to meet their liabilities, which are the pension benefits. Pension funds, whether private or public, provide retirement income in the form of annuities to employees who are covered by the pension plan.

4.3.3 Investment Intermediaries and Other Financial Institutions

Investment intermediaries are non-depository institutions and they include mutual funds, unit trusts and finance companies. The other financial institutions discussed here are venture capitals, MFIs, development finance institutions (DFIs) and informal finance.

4.3.3.1 Mutual Funds

Mutual funds are investment companies that raise funds by issuing their own shares and invest the funds in diversified portfolios of shares, bonds and other securities. Investors own shares of the mutual fund and experience profits when the fund goes up and losses when it goes down. Mutual funds provide an opportunity for shareholders to pool their resources in order to take advantage of lower transaction costs when investing in large blocks of shares or bonds. In addition, mutual funds allow shareholders to benefit from diversification by holding more diversified portfolios. **Money market mutual funds** are a form of mutual funds that focus on money market instruments. They also raise funds by issuing their own shares and invest these funds in money market instruments such as Treasury bills and commercial papers. Investments in money market instruments are generally safe and very liquid.

4.3.3.2 Unit Trusts

Unit trusts are investment companies, which buy a fixed, often, unmanaged portfolio of securities and thereafter issue units (shares) in the trust to investors. Unit trusts are typically unmanaged, fixed income security portfolio put together by a sponsor and handled by an independent trustee. Like closed-end funds, unit trusts normally issue only a specific, fixed number of shares, which are called 'units'. Unit trusts mostly invest in bonds. Normally, the sponsor will turn over to the trustee the entire holding of bonds; the trustee holds all the bonds until the issuer redeems them. The assets of unit trusts are usually not traded. Unit trusts tend to meet the steady flow of income objective of investors. However, due to the low risk of unit trusts, there is a commensurate low rate of return on the investment.

4.3.3.3 Finance Companies

Finance companies are non-depository financial institutions that acquire funds by issuing financial instruments such as commercial paper, shares and bonds. The funds they raise are then given to consumers and small businesses in the form of loans. They do no face as stringent regulations as commercial banks do. Leasing companies are an important aspect of finance companies. Given the difficulty MSMEs face in accessing finance from banks and other sources, leasing may be useful for them as a source of short- and medium-term financing. Leasing offers MSMEs the opportunity of using the assets without investing heavily to buy them.

4.3.3.4 Venture Capital Companies

Venture capital companies provide funding to early-stage firms with the potential for high growth that will result in payout for the investors. Venture capital is private equity invested in start-up firms and small businesses with potential for long-term growth. They invest equity recognising that there is risk associated with the investee firm's future profits and cash flow. Most venture capital firms are structured as limited partnerships with pooled investment funds aimed at investing in a portfolio of investee firms. Venture capital companies also provide management and technical assistance to the investee firms to enable them grow and to add value to their investment. They usually invest in businesses they have knowledge and expertise in so that they can nurture them and ultimately make good returns on their investment. Venture capitalists may be a small group of investors or a subsidiary of a large financial institution and invests on behalf clients of the parent company or outside investors.

4.3.3.5 Microfinance Institutions

MFIs are dedicated to providing financial services to small businesses and those who have no access to conventional banking services. They generally include non-governmental organisations (NGOs), microfinance banks and non-bank financial intermediaries. They may operate independently or as the subsidiaries of larger banks. In most developing countries, MFIs include rural and community banks, savings and loans companies, financial NGOs, primary societies of credit unions, rotating savings and credit associations (SCAs), development and commercial banks that have microfinance programmes and linkages, micro-insurance and micro-leasing services. MFIs provide micro credit, micro savings, micro-insurance and funds transfer services to these marginalised small businesses.

4.3.3.6 Development Finance Institutions

DFIs are alternative financial institutions that provide long-term finance to the private sector for investments that promote development. They provide a range of financial services including, long-term loans, equity finance and risk guarantee instruments to private investments and also finance infrastructure projects in developing countries. DFIs focus on areas that traditional finance providers have ignored and they target markets where there is limited access to domestic and foreign capital flows. DFIs occupy the intermediary space between public aid and private investment and are mostly supported by development partners or developed economies. They play an important role in financing MSMEs that are often considered risky by other conventional sources of financing. DFIs are able to raise large amounts of finance on the international capital markets to provide loans or equity investment on commercial and sometimes concessional basis. There are multilateral (such as the International Financial Corporation, and the Multilateral Investment Guarantee Agency), regional (such as the Africa Development Bank, the Development Bank Southern Africa, the Asian Development Bank, the Inter-American Development Bank and the European Bank for Reconstruction and Development) and bilateral or country specific DFIs (such as Export Development and Agricultural Investment Fund in Ghana, International Development Corporation and the Small Enterprise Development Agency in South Africa). DFIs also include MFIs, state development banks, community DFIs and revolving loan funds.

4.3.3.7 Informal Finance Providers

Informal finance, as defined by Adams and von Pischke (1992), involves all transactions, loans and deposits occurring outside the regulation of a central monetary or financial market authority. It includes a wide range of financial activities and services that take place outside a country's formal financial system and financial sector regulations. Informal finance is considered to be an important source of financing, constituting about 30 % of MSMEs' financing in Africa. Considering the difficulty start-up firms and MSMEs' encounter in accessing finance from the formal financial institutions, they are often compelled to resort to informal finance providers. There are different types of informal finance units in Africa and these include savings mobilisation units that are involved in little or no lending, lending units that rarely mobilise savings and units that engage in both deposits mobilisation and lending, albeit mainly of members of distinct associations or groups. Informal finance providers in Africa include SCAs, moneylenders, loans from relatives and friends, traders, mobile banks and cooperative societies.

Informal finance arrangements in Africa range from deposit collectors in West and Central Africa usually referred to as *susu* or *esusu* collectors and *tontines*, to the *hawala* in North and East Africa, and *stokvels* in South Africa.

4.3.4 Functions of Financial Institutions

Financial institutions perform important functions in the financial market, including providing maturity intermediation, reducing risk through diversification, reducing the costs of contracting and information processing, providing payment mechanisms and dealing with adverse selection and moral hazard. These functions are discussed in turn.

4.3.4.1 Providing Maturity Intermediation

Financial institutions provide maturity intermediation by satisfying both surplus units and deficit units in terms of how long they want to invest their resources and how long they want to borrow. For instance, a bank may issue its own financial claims, thus transforming a longer-term asset into a shorter-term one by granting loans to borrowers for the length of time they prefer and also provide depositors the opportunity to deposit their funds for the desired investment horizon. Maturity intermediation provides investors with several options regarding maturity for their investments as well as borrowers with more choices for the length of their loan obligations. In the absence of financial institutions, it may be difficult for borrowers who prefer to borrow long-term to find investors who are willing to lend for that length of time since investors are generally reluctant to commit funds for a longer period of time. They may invest or lend long-term by demanding higher interest from the long-term borrowers. Financial institutions come in handy in addressing this. A bank, for instance, provides short-term deposit products for their depositors and long-term loans for the borrowing customers.

4.3.4.2 Reducing Risk Through Diversification

One important economic function of financial institutions involves transforming more risky assets into less risky ones through diversification. Though individual investors can also diversify by investing in different instruments, they may not be in the position to do this as cost-effectively as financial institutions would, considering the amount of funds that may be involved.

It is less risky for a surplus unit to lend through a financial institution than doing that directly. The reduced risk is mainly because of the diversification advantage the financial institution brings. On the other hand, an individual surplus unit for instance may not be able to make many loans and therefore may be adversely affected by any bad loans. Financial institutions have the capacity to make many good loans and these can offset any possible bad loans. They are able to pool large amounts of resources and invest these in diversified portfolios, thus reducing their risk exposure to the benefits of their depositors. By doing this, financial institutions are able to turn risky assets into safer ones for the benefit of investors. Clearly, attaining cost-effective diversification by investing in financial assets of financial institutions in order to reduce risk, provides economic benefit for financial markets.

4.3.4.3 Reducing the Costs of Contracting and Information Processing

Another important function that financial institutions perform is reducing the costs of contracting and information processing. Since financial institutions handle a large volume of transactions, they are able to enjoy economies of scale in contracting and processing information on financial assets. The reduced contracting and processing costs accrue to the benefit of investors who purchase financial claims of the financial institutions and to the issuers of financial assets, who benefit from lower borrowing costs. Financial institutions are capable of reducing transaction costs substantially, which involve the time and money spent in carrying out financial transactions. Considering their large size and expertise, they are able to take advantage of economies of scale. The low cost of transaction allows these institutions to provide liquidity services, since it is easier to issue financial instruments to raise funds.

4.3.4.4 Providing Payment Mechanisms

Financial institutions such as banks provide payment mechanisms such as cheques, credit cards, debit cards and electronic transfers of funds. Therefore, they are able to transform assets that cannot be used in making payment into other assets that can be used to make payment. Making payments without the use of physical cash is crucial for the effective and efficient functioning of financial markets. However, most African countries operate a cash-based system, where most business transactions are carried out with the use of cash.

4.3.4.5 Dealing with Adverse Selection and Moral Hazard

Financial institutions help in addressing the problems related to imperfect information in financial markets and these include adverse selection and moral hazard. Adverse selection refers to the problem that arises when a loan is granted to a bad borrower or a good borrower is rejected due to information asymmetry. Financial institutions can deal with this problem by obtaining information regarding potential borrowers and by screening bad credit risks. Moral hazard is also concerned with the problem that arises after a loan is made because borrowers may apply the funds for the wrong purpose. Financial institutions have the required structures and expertise to evaluate and screen bad credits and also monitor borrowers' activities.

4.4 Allocation of Funds and Interest Rates

The allocation of funds in any economy takes place on the basis of the interest rate. The interest rate is the price paid on the funds borrowed for a given period of time, and the amount borrowed is the principal. The interest rate is usually expressed as a percentage of the principal or the remaining balance of the loan. The interest rate is explained by a number of factors, but we shall focus our attention on five of these and they are economic growth, inflation, central bank's policy, budget deficit or surplus and international flow of funds.

4.4.1 Economic Growth

The level of economic growth has a major effect on the demand for borrowed funds. The demand for borrowed funds is all the money that is demanded in an economy at a given price or interest rate. An increase in the demand for borrowed funds by economic units such as individuals, businesses and government will cause interest rates to rise. For instance, when businesses increase their demand for loanable funds to expand their operations as a result of economic growth, this will put upward pressure on the interest rates to rise. When demand for loanable funds outweighs supply of funds, the resultant effect is an increase in interest rates. On the other hand, when the demand for funds decreases, probably due to economic down-turns, this will put downward pressure on interest rates. In other words, as demand for borrowed funds exceed the supply of funds, the interest rate is likely to rise.

4.4.2 Inflation

Inflation is the persistent increase in prices of goods and services in an economy. Inflation can be measured by the consumer price index (CPI) or the producer price index (PPI). The CPI, which is mostly used, is the market basket of goods and services an average consumer buys monthly. The basket of goods and services is priced every month to ascertain whether there has been an increase (inflation) or a decrease in the price. The PPI measures average changes in prices received by domestic producers for their output. Inflation affects interest rates because of its effect on the supply of savings and the demand for loanable funds. Assume you expect prices to increase rapidly (inflation), you will prefer to make purchases now before prices rise and therefore you will save less. Expectation of inflation will lead to an economic unit demanding more and saving less and therefore the resultant effect is increased interest rates. Also, households and businesses will be willing to borrow more funds now, so that they can make purchases before prices increase. The demand for loanable funds will increase, leading to higher interest rates. Therefore, if we expect higher inflation, interest rates will increase because less loanable funds will be supplied while more loanable funds will be demanded.

4.4.3 Central Bank's Policy

The demand and money supply affect the level of economic activity and the inflation rate. In any economy, the central bank plays a very important role and is responsible for controlling the monetary supply. **Monetary policy** is the action taken by government to control the money supply with the aim of maintaining a certain level of economy activity. Government increases the money supply in order to expand economic activity. An increase in the money supply, holding demand constant, will cause interest rates to decline due to excess money in the economy. On the other hand, government reduces the supply of money so as to constrict economic activity, and a decrease in the supply of funds should lead to a rise in interest rates. A reduction in the supply of money means less loanable funds in the system, and assuming no change in demand, this should cause an increase in interest rates. The aim of every government is to create employment in the country, ensure interest rate stability, reduce inflation and achieve a favourable balance of payment. Governments try to achieve these goals by using the central banks' money policy. There are three main tools of monetary policy used for controlling the money supply and these are: open market operations, reserve requirement and discount rate.

The **open market operations** involve selling and buying of government securities (such as Treasury bills notes and bonds). If government wants to reduce the money supply, it will sell securities to mop up the excess liquidity. However, if it wants to increase money supply, it will buy back securities. The **reserve requirement is** the ratio of reserves to deposits that must be kept by a commercial bank, and this is mandatory for all banks. These reserves are kept on deposit with the central bank. An increase in the reserve requirement reduces funds available to banks' to give out as loans, and this reduces the money supply. A decrease in the reserve requirement increases banks' loanable funds, thus increasing the money supply. The **discount rate (policy rate)** is the interest rate the central bank charges banks for lending to them. The central bank, as the lender of last resort, lends to banks when they have insufficient funds to give out loans. If the central bank wants to reduce the money supply, it increases the discount rate in order to discourage borrowing. But if it wants to increase the money supply, it would have to reduce the discount rate to encourage banks to borrow more from the central bank for on-lending to bank customers.

4.4.4 Budget Deficit or Surplus

Another important determinant of interest rate is whether the government is running a budget deficit or a surplus. A budget deficit occurs when the government is spending more than it receives from taxes and other revenue sources. The government can finance its budget deficit by borrowing from the financial market. If government demands funds to finance its budget deficit without a corresponding increase in the supply of funds, this will lead to an increase in interest rates. There is a risk that if the government is borrowing too much, it will 'crowd-out' the private sector. This means the increased borrowing by the government will lead to less funds flowing to the private sector. This is because lenders will prefer to lend to the government since loans to the government are risk-free and the government may be willing to borrow at any interest rate. A budget surplus, on the other hand, occurs when government spending falls short of its revenue. If the government runs a budget surplus, the implication is that government has excess funds and might become a net supplier of funds, thus leading to a reduction in interest rates.

4.4.5 International Flow of Funds

The interest rate on the local currency is also determined by international flow of funds. If a country imports more than it exports, it is said to be running a *foreign trade deficit* and the country can finance its trade deficit by borrowing. Assuming a country import bill is US$300 billion but the export revenue is US$250 billion, it runs a trade deficit of US$50 billion and therefore needs to borrow US$50 billion to finance the short fall. The larger the trade deficit of a country, the more it needs to borrow, and by increasing the level of borrowing, this pushes the interest rates upward. On the other hand, if a country exports more than it imports, it will experience a *foreign trade surplus* and therefore an increase in the supply of funds in the country. Increasing the supply of funds in the economy will bring about a reduction in interest rates. Generally, if a country experiences a massive inflow of foreign funds, this will increase the supply of loanable funds in the country, thus leading to a decrease in interest rates in the receiving country.

4.5 Summary and Conclusions

MSMEs operate within the financial environment, and their decisions are affected by developments within the financial environments. The financial environment includes the financial system, tax and regulatory policies and the state of the economy. The financial system consists of the money, financial instruments, financial markets, financial institutions and financial regulators.

Financial markets are markets in which financial assets or securities are bought and sold. Financial markets exist in an economy to ensure the efficient allocation of capital to the ultimate users. Financial institutions are firms that bring savers/lenders and borrowers together in order to efficiently allocate financial resources. Examples include banks, savings and loans institutions, credit unions, insurance companies, pension funds, investment companies, finance companies, mutual funds, unit trust, venture capital companies and so on. Financial institutions perform important functions in the financial market and these include: providing maturity intermediation, reducing risk through diversification, reducing the costs of contracting and information processing, providing payment mechanisms and dealing with adverse selection and moral hazard.

The allocation of funds in any economy takes place on the basis of the interest rate. The interest rate is the price paid on the funds borrowed for a given period of time, and the amount borrowed is the principal. The interest rate is usually expressed as a percentage of the principal or remaining balance of the loan. The interest rate is determined by a number of factors, including economic growth, inflation, central bank's policy, budget deficit or surplus and international flow of funds.

Discussion Questions and Problems

1. What are the components of the financial environment within which MSMEs operate?
2. Discuss the components of any financial system within an economy.
3. What are financial markets and how are financial markets classified?

4. Discuss the purpose of the financial market in any economy.
5. Explain the financial intermediation process.
6. What are the various types of financial institutions and how do they support MSMEs operate?
7. Discuss the functions of financial institutions.
8. What are DFIs and how different are they from MFIs?
9. What is the relevance of informal finance providers in supporting MSMEs?
10. What are interest rates and how are interest rates determined?

5

Venture Capital Finance

Learning Objectives
By the end of this chapter, you should be able to:

- explain the nature of venture capital
- discuss the advantages and disadvantages of venture capital
- show how venture capital firms are organised
- explain how venture capitalists enter into contracts
- indicate what venture capitalists consider before investing
- identify what constitute venture creation by venture capitalists

5.1 Introduction

Innovative enterprises and MSMEs with the potential for high growth can use venture capital finance to fund their growth and expand their enterprises. Venture capitalists usually invest in fast growth promising enterprises. Firms that do not have the potential for fast growth are usually not good candidates for venture capital financing. The firms funded usually can lead to the evolution of new products and markets and have the potential to be revolutionary in nature. Financing is therefore provided to firms with innovative technologies or business models. Given the peculiar aim of venture capital firms, it is useful for entrepreneurs and managers of MSMEs to understand their nature, how they are organised and how they operate.

J.Y. Abor, *Entrepreneurial Finance for MSMEs*,
DOI 10.1007/978-3-319-34021-0_5

This chapter looks at the nature of venture capital, the advantages and disadvantages of venture capital, the organisation of venture capital firms, venture capital contracts with their investee firms and investors, what venture capitalists look for and value creation by venture capitalists.

5.2 The Nature of Venture Capital

Venture capital is the provision of private equity to new and young firms with high growth potential. Venture capital firms invest equity capital in innovative businesses with high growth potential, which are at an early stage of their development. Venture capital financing is regarded as patient capital, since the venture capitalist usually is willing to invest in the enterprise for up to ten years. Venture capitalists invest in firms that at their stage of development may find it very difficult to access funds from capital markets or from the banking system. Venture capitalists therefore provide the needed financing to entrepreneurs with very innovative ideas and who can transform their ideas to form innovative products that can turn into great businesses. Venture capitalists usually invest in businesses from the early stage phase after the business concept has been proven. The investee firms are mainly unquoted or privately held firms.

The venture capital fund is usually set up to have a finite life. The life of the venture capital fund for example could be 12 years. This means that after 12 years, the fund is wound up or is closed down and the investments and gains are realised. Due to the finite life of the venture capital fund itself, its investment in a firm is also usually finite. The popular investment horizon for venture capital funds is between seven and ten years. After the given period of investment, the venture capital will want to harvest its investment. It will want to do this by taking the enterprise public through an IPO, or it could sell its stake to management or to another business which is interested in an equity stake in the investee firm.

Venture capital firms play a unique role in the market for funds. They fill the gap between financing provided by the entrepreneur, family and friends and business angels and that required by public companies. Financing provided by angels is usually smaller than the funding that a venture capitalist can provide. Venture capitalists provide intermediate funding from the time of establishment until when the enterprise goes public. The equity financing is provided based on a valuation of the business so that the interest acquired by the venture capitalist and the amount that has to be paid can be agreed upon. Additional equity financing is usually provided by the venture capitalist as time goes by. That is, the investments are staged. This additional financing are usually termed as 'alphabet rounds'. This is because the investment comes in series such as Series A, Series B, Series C and so on. These denote subsequent provision of funds by the venture capitalist. This additional finance will however be based on how well the enterprise is doing and on whether it is achieving agreed upon milestones. To reduce their risk, venture capitalists invest in a portfolio of firms.

Due to the fact that the funding provided is in the form of equity, venture capitalists provide risk capital to the firm. They therefore become shareholders in the companies in which they invest. The amount of equity provided is not fixed, but could be up to about 70 % of the value of the firm. This stake is usually about 25 % of the equity of the firm. Venture capital is very important to the investee firm because at its early stage of development it may be difficult to access capital markets for the funds that it needs. Also, the firm may find it difficult to raise debt finance in the volumes that may be needed. Another reason is that the firm is risky, though it has potential for huge success. Debt capital will be very risky, and therefore traditional bank finance is not appropriate to finance such firms. That is why equity finance by venture capitalists that are usually willing to invest for up to ten years is essential. Most high technology firms, for instance, do not rely much on debt financing due to the high risk nature of their activities. They tend to rely on venture capital.

The aim of the venture capitalists is usually not just financial in nature. They also seek to add value to their investment by offering advice and making their expertise available to the investee firm. They provide technical, managerial, and networking support and act as a mentor to the entrepreneurs. Venture capitalists' expertise and network of contacts with potential suppliers and customers allow entrepreneurs to focus on what they are best at and that is technical development. Also, due to the fact that venture capitalists become co-owners of the firm, they wield a lot of power over the enterprise. Such powers and privileges include having a seat on the board of directors. Therefore, to attract venture capital funding the entrepreneur usually has to make some concessions. These include giving up an equity stake in the enterprise and also giving up some control to the venture capitalist. To be able to add value to investee firms, venture capitalists usually invest in firms and industries in which they have expertise. Their industry knowledge and expertise are essential for mentoring entrepreneurs and improving their strategies. Venture capitalists' investments are also usually concentrated close to their geographical location.

Venture capital funds are usually divided into various types, and these include seed capital, start-up capital, development capital, and growth capital.

Seed capital is mainly used in financing the preliminary operations such as market research and product development. Seed capital is invested in research and development before the business can start investing.

Start-up capital is used in setting up a business venture. It is used to finance activities such as the hiring of staff, renting of office space, equipping the production system among other things.

Development capital is used to further launch the business and grow the market share so as to increase profitability.

Growth capital is also used in financing the expansion of the business in areas such as launching into foreign markets, creating new product/technology lines, accelerating production and/or acquiring competitors.

Development and growth capital are together known as early stage capital since they are used to fund firms that are already established and ready to pursue further development and expansion.

5.3 Advantages and Disadvantages of Venture Capital

Venture capital financing comes with its own advantages and disadvantages. We shall now discuss the advantages and disadvantages of using venture capital finance.

5.3.1 Advantages of Venture Capital

Financing with venture capital has numerous advantages. First of all, there is no pressure on the company to pay periodic fixed charges like will be the case with debt financing. The pressure on the firm's cash flow is therefore minimal. The cash flows can therefore be used to finance aggressive growth and expansion.

Venture capitalists do not require any form of security in the investee firm or the firm they are investing in. The investee firm does not need to provide collateral to the venture capitalist as would usually be requested for in the case of bank financing.

Since the investment provided is equity in nature, the venture capitalist also bears part of the risk associated with the enterprise. If the investment does very well, the venture capitalist enjoys part of the gains in the form of dividend income and appreciation of the value of their capital. However, if the investment in the investee firm fails, the venture capitalist bears part of the loss and the investee enterprise does not have any obligation to pay back the investment.

Venture capitalists provide non-financial services that can usually add value to the business. They also provide mentorship to management of the investee enterprise. Due to the fact they have a seat on the company's board, they can contribute meaningfully to the formulation, implementation and control of the strategy of the investee firm. Venture capitalists usually specialise in a given industry, and they can bring their accumulated knowledge in the industry to bear on the performance of the investee firm. They can also provide good networking opportunities for the enterprise by linking the investee firm to other providers of capital, value adding services providers, stock exchanges and potential acquirers. This network can be both on a domestic and on an international scale.

The involvement of a venture capitalist in an enterprise can lead to improved corporate governance of the enterprise concerned. This is because both parties would want to adhere to the highest standards of corporate governance. The enterprise will have to be more transparent in making available information about the firm. Improved corporate governance can also lead to better internal control and risk management systems which contribute to safe-guarding the assets of the enterprise.

Using venture capital also provides credibility to a business. This is because other stakeholders such as customers will be happy to see a credible partner (venture capitalist) working with the firm. The credibility of the venture capitalist adds to the credibility of the business. Also, if the enterprise needs resources, it can fall on the venture capitalist. A software company may be able to sell expensive software to corporations partly because of its association with a venture capitalist. This increased credibility can also lead to the firm attracting new customers.

Venture capitalists contribute to the process of economic growth and job creation by providing finance to firms with high growth potential. The funds provided can aid the business to grow astronomically and far beyond any rate that could be supported by using internal finance. Venture capitalists also make good money because investments in private equity tend to outperform investments in public equity markets in the long-term. The higher return is due to the higher risk that private equity and venture capitalists take. Venture capital activity also facilities foreign direct investment by making it easier for foreigners to invest in unlisted enterprises in a country.

5.3.2 Disadvantages of Venture Capital

The entrepreneur will have to give up an equity interest in the firm to the venture capitalist and this will be a dilution of the entrepreneur's interest in the firm. From the pecking order theory (POT), equity is more expensive than debt. Therefore, the cost of venture capital funding is likely to be more expensive compared to bank debt. Also, due to the fact that the venture capital fund manager is more likely to have more knowledge in business valuations the venture capitalists may be able to drive a harder bargain as to the price at which they purchase the equity of the enterprise. Related to this point is the fact that because the business is not trading on an active market, finding the market value of the business is difficult and can be quite subjective. The price paid by the venture capitalist may be at a discount to its true intrinsic value.

Another point is that the enterprise will have to cede some control in terms of decision-making. This is because the venture capitalist will seek to influence major decisions such as finance and investment decisions. Since entrepreneurs want to be independent and control their own destiny, this influence may be viewed as interference.

Accessing venture capital is difficult. The enterprise has to submit a business plan to the venture capitalist. The venture capitalist then thoroughly screens the business and the aim of the screening is to identify potential future 'stars' and to seed out possible 'losers'. For firms seeking venture capital finance, the success rate of accessing funds is very low. Typically, the success rate is about 1 %. This means that only the highly promising firms with potential for high growth are likely to access venture capital funds.

Venture capital firms usually would not sign a non-disclosure agreement with the entrepreneur. There is therefore some risk that the entrepreneur's idea will fall into the wrong hands. That is, another person or business may pick up the idea and implement it ahead of the entrepreneur, which could lead to significantly less revenues due to the fact that first mover advantages may be lost to another enterprise.

Raising finance from a venture capitalist requires the entrepreneur or initial owners to be more accountable to this new partner (i.e. the venture capital firm). The entrepreneur has to provide business forecasts and other management information as well as actual financial information to the venture capitalist. Also, the entrepreneur will have to try hard to meet targets and milestones to keep the venture capitalist interested in the business.

5.4 Organisation of Venture Capital Firms

The venture capital could be organised as an open-end, closed-end investment or a limited liability partnership. Open-end investments continually raise funds and return funds to investors if they require them. With open-end funds, the fund may be exposed to erratic inflows and outflows of investment. Closed-end funds raise capital once and the fund is listed on a stock exchange. Investors who want to invest later in the firm after the IPO have to find people who are willing to buy on the secondary market. Similarly, investors who wish to sell have to find buyers on the secondary market. With the closed-end fund there may be problems of valuing the investments in the fund because of the nature of enterprises in which the fund has invested.

The major form of organisational structure for venture capital firms is the limited partnership. In a general partnership, there must be at least one general partner who manages the fund, and the limited partner contributes the investment capital. The fund then invests the capital in a portfolio of businesses. Most hedge funds, private equity firms and real estate syndicates are also structured as limited partnerships. A limited partnership is made up of general and limited partners.

The general partner is responsible for managing the venture capital firm and raising the needed capital for investment. General partners contribute about 1 % of the capital requirement and share in the profits made. Their share of profits is usually between 20 % and 30 % of the profits made because of their management efforts (i.e. the carried interest). The carried interest represents the portion of the gains made from the sale that goes to the general partner. This is usually about 20 % of the proceeds received. This carried interest is usually received after the investee firm has been sold or harvested. The general partner also receives a management fee, which is usually about 2–3 % of the committed capital of the business annually. General partners usually have experience in corporate finance and other finance related areas, may be as scientists, or may be as successful entrepreneurs in the field in which the venture capital intends to invest. The liability of the general partner is not limited and therefore can extend to the personal worth of the general partner. In addition to raising funds, the general partner is also in charge of generating deal flows (screening possible investment), negotiating an equity interest at a good valuation, monitoring of investments made and finally: harvesting the investments. In essence, the funds raised by the general partner is invested in a portfolio of firms (those with high growth potential) with the objective of adding value to the investee firm so that the venture capital can also benefit.

The limited partners are usually not involved in the management of the business. They contribute capital to the business and share in the profits of the business. They usually contribute about 99 % of the capital requirements of the business and receive about 70–80 % of profits. If significant losses are made, limited partners tend to suffer most, since they contribute the bulk of the capital. However, their loss is limited to their investment made and cannot extend to and attach to their other wealth. The limited partners are usually very wealthy individuals and institutional investors. These institutional investors include banks, university endowments, pension funds, and insurance companies. The institutional investors usually expect periodic reports regarding the performance of their investment in the venture capital from the general partner.

5.4.1 The Venture Capital Investment Process

The official life of the venture capital firm begins when the first close ends. However, prior to that, the general partner would have sought for capital and capital commitments from potential investors. The general partner may also have started screening potential investments before the first close of the fund. After the fund is closed, limited partners are expected to pay down a percentage of their capital commitment. The general partner then makes a capital call to the limited partners requesting them to pay part of their capital commitment.

Over the next year or so, the venture capital firm concurrently does a number of things. It will screen business applications for funding and conduct due diligence on firms in which they intend to invest. During the due diligence phase, the potential investee firm and the venture capitalist will meet several times over a number of weeks which can go into months. The main purpose of the meetings is for the venture capitalist to get to know more about the business, and assess the strength of its management and products. The venture capitalist may also want to interview customers of the enterprise. If the venture capital is satisfied with what it sees, it will go ahead to negotiate a deal and investment terms with the enterprise. The venture capital firm then invests in firms that have been found successful.

The investments made by the venture capitalist are usually like equity in nature, such as through ordinary shares and convertible preference shares. Before an investment is made, the value placed on the firm is known as the pre-money value. The value of the firm after the investment by the venture capitalist is known as the post-money value. If there are lots of deals that require funding, the general partners will make further capital calls on the limited partners.

After an investment has been made, the venture capital will seek to add value by offering its expertise to management. The vast network and contacts of the venture capitalist in the investee firm's industry and beyond can prove very useful to the management of the enterprise. It will also act as a sounding board, because they usually will request for a seat on the investee firm's board. Investments will also be monitored to assess whether the investments are performing as expected.

After seven to ten years of investment, the venture capitalist may want to harvest their investments by selling their stake and realise a gain. The harvest returns may be in the form of cash or shares that can be easily liquidated, for example by being sold on a stock exchange. The most popular form of harvesting a venture capital investment is by Mergers and Acquisitions (M&A's) and taking the enterprise public through an Initial Public Offering. The public can then invest in the investee's firm through the traditional capital markets such as stock exchanges. The venture capital can also sell its stake in the investee's firm to management through an MBO or a leveraged buyout (LBO).

5.4.2 Raising Funds and the Role of Reputation in the Venture Capital Market

It is important to appreciate how venture capitalists raise funds and the role of reputation in the venture capital market. The general partner is responsible for raising capital to invest in firms. The general partner usually looks for institutional investors who are willing to invest in the fund. Finding investors who are willing to invest in the fund can be very hectic for the general partner. The general partner will seek capital commitments from the limited partners who promise or commit to provide funds for the venture capital firm. The general partner will 'close' the fund when sufficient levels of capital commitments have been received from investors to enable the venture capital firm start operations.

There may be more than one 'close' in which case the 'close' is staggered. The first closing officially marks the beginning of the life of the fund and it is sometimes referred to as the 'vintage year'. The general partner makes a capital call to investors to provide funds when sufficient investible opportunities have been identified after the closing. Apart from the periodic capital calls, the limited partners (investors) usually have to pay a stated percentage of their capital commitment upfront. There may be penalties for limited partners who are not able to honour a capital call. Therefore, the reputation of the institutional investor is important in the venture capital market. This is especially the case because the capital calls are made at short notice and are not predictable because they are made based on the investment opportunities that are available. Capital calls are higher during the early years of the venture capital, when deal flows are high and when the fund is actively seeking and investing in potential high growth and profitable firms.

Reputation is important in the entire venture capital industry. It is not limited to only institutional investors or limited partners; it affects all the stakeholders. The venture capitalist must also have a good reputation, a track record and impeccable integrity to survive and continue to attract funds from limited partners. Also, the investee firms must have a good reputation and their management should be of good integrity to earn the trust of the venture capitalist and make the venture capitalist comfortable to want to invest in the firm. Since all possible future scenarios cannot be provided for in a contract, reputation and trust are very important in the dealings among the parties in a venture capital arrangement.

It is important to note that reputation and trust may count more than very detailed and explicit contracts. If the entrepreneur has good integrity and can be trusted by the venture capitalist, a tall list of restrictive covenants may not be necessary. Attempting to put all anticipated scenarios in a contract can be time consuming and very costly indeed (not just in terms of legal costs but the managerial time spent as well as the time of the venture capitalist). The importance of reputation in the venture industry is well demonstrated by the fact that better known entrepreneurs who have previously accessed venture capital funding find it easier to subsequently raise further venture funds. More established and reputable venture capitalists are able to charge higher management fee and may earn higher returns because of the reputation they have established for themselves.

5.5 Venture Capital Contracting

Venture capitalists enter into various contracts. These contracts are usually with suppliers of funds (limited partners) and the portfolio of firms that the venture capitalist has invested in. The essence of entering into these contracts is to protect the interests of all parties. The terms of the contracts have to be thought through carefully and negotiated. As emphasised earlier, not everything can be included in the contract, because some circumstances may not be anticipated at the time of drawing the contract.

5.5.1 Venture Capital Contracts with Investee Enterprises

In terms of the contract between the venture capitalist and the investee enterprise, the venture capitalist may write in a put option into the contract with the enterprise. This means that the venture capitalist has the right, but not an obligation, to sell the interest acquired back to the enterprise. If the venture capitalist decides to exercise the put option, then the enterprise is obliged to buy back the interest. This option gives protection to the venture capitalist because if the enterprise is not performing as expected, the venture capitalist can sell the shares back to the firm.

The venture capitalist can also purchase preference shares which are convertible into equity. In this case, if the enterprise does well, the venture capitalist can convert their preference shares into equity. If the venture turns out to be a failure, the entrepreneur bears the majority of the risk as the preference shares will have preference over the entrepreneur's interest in the event of liquidation.

The venture capitalist may also write pre-emptive rights and the rights of first refusal into a contract with an enterprise. Pre-emptive rights give the venture capitalist the first option to purchase shares if the enterprise wants to raise more funds by issuing equity. Therefore, the shares must be offered first to the venture capitalist in proportion of their interest in the firm before they are offered to outsiders. Pre-emptive rights are sometimes guaranteed by company law. The rationale of pre-emptive rights is to prevent the dilution of the interest of the shareholder. The venture capitalist can exercise this right if the enterprise is performing well. Therefore, pre-emptive rights enable the venture capitalist to benefit when the firm is performing well.

The investment in the enterprise can also be syndicated. This means that a group of venture capitalists come together to finance the enterprise. Therefore, they share the risks and returns associated with the project. Syndication reduces the risk of a single venture capitalist since the source of funding is diversified. The rewards of the investment, however, will have to be shared. Usually, there is a lead venture capitalist that co-ordinates the syndication. The lead syndicator usually provides the larger share of funds among the syndicators. Syndication can also be beneficial in the sense that all parties can contribute in the due diligence process thereby reducing the chances of adverse selection. The expertise of the various syndicators can also be of immense benefit to the enterprise.

The venture capitalist can also use *staging*. In this case, funding is delayed until the venture capitalist gets to know more about the enterprise and the enterprise has met certain benchmarks and milestones. Investments are therefore made in stages or on a piece meal basis and not in a single financing round. Staging therefore improves the chances of the venture capitalist making a good investment decision. It therefore reduces the probability of adverse selection due to information asymmetries. Staging can be used to monitor an enterprise and to reduce agency problems and its associated costs.

The level of involvement of the venture capitalist can also be negotiated and put in a contract. Venture capitalists usually want a seat on the enterprise's board so that they can influence strategic decisions. The venture capitalist may have the right to appoint its representative to the board of the enterprise.

These features and provisions are sometimes in the best interest of the enterprise. This is because they enable the venture capitalist to get as much information and protection as possible. The valuation of the enterprise is therefore likely to be higher, and the entrepreneur is likely to get a larger stake in the enterprise. Some features in a negotiated contract can also be to the benefit of the enterprise. For example, the enterprise may write into the contract a call option that gives the enterprise the right to force the venture capitalist to sell the shares in the enterprise back to the enterprise. The enterprise may want to exercise this option if it thinks its shares are under-valued or that it can get a better deal elsewhere. The buy-back may also be necessitated if the enterprise is not satisfied with the other value adding services that the venture capitalist is supposed to be providing (to it).

5.5.2 Venture Capital Contracts with Investors

The venture capitalist is likely to have a contract with its limited partners (providers of fund). The contract will spell out the rights and obligations of both parties. Contracts that offer protection to the limited partners are likely to lead to the venture capitalist (general partner) being able to raise more funds from institutional and wealthy investors.

Some of the terms that can be incorporated into a contract with institutional investors include the maximum level of investment that the venture capitalist can invest in a single enterprise. This provision seeks to reduce risk for investors by restricting their maximum exposure to a single enterprise. The chances of suffering a huge loss from a single investment are therefore significantly reduced. This provision can be necessary because the general partner may be over-confident of his/her assessment of a firm and therefore overinvest in a single firm. However, if things do not go well, the value of the investments of the limited partners can drop significantly. Investors do not like surprises, especially not negative ones. They will therefore want to limit the chances that the general partner takes with a single firm.

Also, to reduce the risk, investors may write in provisions that prevent the general partner from excessively leveraging the fund. The general partner can leverage the fund by borrowing or taking on a lot of debt. This situation increases the risk of the fund. Returns are likely to be better for a comparatively higher leveraged fund if things go well. However, if expectations are not met, greater losses will be suffered. As we have said earlier, investors do not like 'nasty' surprises and therefore will want to limit the leveraging ability of the general partner.

Investors may also want to limit the investment activity between the general partner and investee firms. They do this by restricting investments separate from the fund by the general partner on their own behalf in the investee enterprise. This is to prevent front-running by the general partner. This provision is therefore to prevent the general partner from putting his/her interests above that of the fund in which the investors have invested. If such prohibitions are not put in place, the general partner may make and exit investments at terms that are advantageous to the general partner but are not in the best interest of the fund that investors have invested in.

Investors may also want to restrict the asset classes in which the general partner invests in. This is to prevent investments in asset classes that are likely to generate a low return. It is also to prevent investment into enterprises in which the general partner will not have to put in a lot of effort. Investments can also be limited into asset classes in which the general partner has little and insufficient experience, because much value cannot be added in such circumstances.

Venture capitalists usually operate more than one fund. Investors may want to limit cross investments. That is using money from one fund to invest in a portfolio firm of another fund. This is to avoid wealth transfer across funds whereby investors in one fund gain at the expense of investors of another fund. If such investment is to be made, then prior approval of the investors from the fund in which the money is being taken may be required.

Some provisions may make it compulsory for the general partner to return some profits to the limited partners under certain circumstances. This is to prevent the situation where the general partner unnecessarily retains profits so as to grow the fund and increase their management fees.

5.6 Venture Capitalists Considerations

We will now discuss what venture capitalists look for before investing in a small business. Entrepreneurs and small business owners must realise that accessing venture capital finance can be difficult, especially when the small business involved is a start-up or is a struggling one. Accessing venture capital finance will require that the small business provides a sound and comprehensive business plan that will convince the venture capital to invest in the firm. Before investing in a firm, a venture capitalist will consider an array of factors, including the following.

5.6.1 Quality of Management

One of the most important factors the venture capitalist will look out for is the quality of the firm's management, their integrity, their performance and experience in the recent past, and their qualifications. As part of the due diligence process, the venture capitalist may interview management about how they see the business and how they have performed in the past and where they see the business going.

5.6.2 Competitive Edge

Also, the venture capitalist will assess the enterprise's products and markets. How strong is the product or brand? How well is the enterprise positioned to compete in its chosen market place? Does it have the potential to substantially change the dynamics in the market? Does the enterprise have a unique competitive advantage and can this advantage be easily replicated? If the advantage can easily be replicated and there are low barriers of entry into the industry, then the competition is likely to erode the advantage very quickly and no substantial gains will accrue to the firm. Is it likely to be a winner in the market place and capture a substantial amount of the industry's market share? Depending on the stage of investment, is the product technically feasible? Are customers happy with the product and would they recommend it to their friends? These questions aim to assess the strength of the enterprise's product or brand and how it is likely to perform in the market place in the future.

5.6.3 Financial Projections

The venture capitalist will also be very interested in the financial projections that the management of the enterprise makes. What are the revenues, profits and cash flows going to be like? Are the assumptions underlying this prospective financial information reasonable? Has the business considered all major items (be they revenue or expenses) and has uncertainty been incorporated into the analysis? Fidelity Capital Partners in Ghana, for instance, requires a minimum internal rate of return (IRR) of 25 % on all projects they consider investing in. Also, the venture capitalists may be interested in the potential growth rates. This is because the venture capitalist has an investment horizon and may want to assess whether the investment can grow fast enough to be 'ripe' for harvesting within the venture capitalist's time-frame.

5.6.4 Level of Financing Required

Venture capitalists also assess the capital needs of the firms. Is the request for funds adequate? Whether the request is not materially above or below what the business will require. Can management effectively utilise the funds provided? The venture capitalist will usually not provide the funds in one go, but in a series of financing arrangements to prevent the firm from 'wasting' the funds provided. The level of financing required is an important consideration for the venture capital firm to guide its investments in the investee firms.

5.6.5 Industry Expertise

The venture capitalists will want to invest in an industry where it has expertise and can add value to the enterprise invested in. Before approaching a venture capitalist, the entrepreneur or enterprise must also do its own due diligence. This will improve the chances of accessing venture financing. The entrepreneur should research among other things the industry in which the venture capitalist has expertise, their geographical focus (if any), the stage of the business in which the venture capitalist prefers to invest, the level of involvement which the venture capitalist is likely to assume, the level of returns expected and the investment horizon of the venture capitalist.

5.6.6 Viable Exit Strategy

Another important consideration of the venture capitalists is the consideration of a viable exit strategy. Venture capitalists will usually invest for some number of years, say ten years before harvesting their investments. In this case, they will be interested in investing in firms for which it may be easier to off load their investment or stake. For instance, will the venture capital firm be able to sell its shares through an IPO? Other harvesting options the venture capitalist may consider include M&A's, MBOs and employee stock ownership plans (ESOPs). The choice of harvesting may also depend on current market conditions and valuation, cost and size of the enterprise, stage of the enterprise's development, synergies, control of firm and taxes. These are discussed in detailed in Chap. 15.

5.7 Value Creation by Venture Capitalists

To be able to add value to the fund, the venture capitalist must be good and efficient in the various processes. These include negotiating and selecting good deals, timing the investment in the enterprise at when it is needed, spending appropriate and effective time with investee enterprises, monitoring and offering expertise to investee firms and exiting the investment at the appropriate time.

The venture capitalist negotiates and selects good deals. The venture capitalist needs good communication and negotiating skills to be able to get an appropriate interest in the enterprise invested in without extracting significant value from the entrepreneur. This is because if value is extracted from the entrepreneur and the entrepreneur therefore feels that his/her enterprise has been under-valued, he/she is unlikely to go ahead with the deal. Therefore, the venture capitalist must balance between the need to get as much value for the fund and expropriating value from the entrepreneur. Also, the venture capitalist must develop expertise in evaluating proposed investments to succeed at this phase. This is likely to be a key skill and can be developed overtime and by training (professional, academic or through specialised training programmes and seminars). Developing such expertise provides some assurance that the venture capitalist will be able to select the best deals that are offered to it. Deal selection is also likely to distinguish between those venture capitalists who turn out to be very successful and those who fall by the wayside.

The venture capitalist will also want to time correctly the investment in the proposed enterprise. Again, tactfulness and a balancing act are required to succeed. If the investment in the enterprise is too early and significant funds are provided to the enterprise, the enterprise may 'waste' away the funds. However, if the investment is delayed and the venture capitalist gets in at the wrong time, the venture capitalist is likely to miss in on the 'action' and therefore earn fewer returns than if investments had been made earlier. Therefore, a key skill required by the venture capitalist is to know and discern when it is appropriate to invest in an enterprise.

One key way by which the venture capitalist can add value to an investee enterprise is by spending sufficient time with the firm, monitoring the activities of the enterprise and offering his/her expertise to the enterprise in ways that are value creating. Monitoring and assisting investee enterprises are likely to take the bulk of the time of the venture capitalist compared to the other activities. An enterprise that requires the venture capitalist to spend an enormous amount of time with it will limit the time that the venture capitalist has to spend with other portfolio enterprises. Again, spending too much time and being too involved in the activities of the enterprise can cause interferences and unintended negative consequences. It may also lead to disagreements on the best way forward and mar the chemistry between the enterprise and the venture capitalist which is so essential for the investment to succeed.

Another key success factor for the venture capitalist is the ability to time exits from investee enterprises. This is essential if the venture capitalist is to create significant value for the venture capital fund. Exiting too early would mean that the venture capital does not earn as much rent as it can. Exiting late too implies that the venture capitalist would have spent too much time with the investee enterprise and the opportunities to add value may have dissipated. Exits are also conditional on market conditions. During a bull market, exiting an investment through a public offering is likely to generate a higher valuation for the enterprise. Exiting during a bear market when markets are down and cautious may mean that the value obtained for the company is likely to be lower than the value that could have been obtained during a bull market. Therefore, the venture capitalist must consider the alternatives and options available to exit an investment and when each of the best options should be exercised.

Regarding the performance of venture backed firms compared to non-venture backed firms, it is obvious that venture capitalists seem to add value to venture backed companies. One line of argument is the level of under-pricing between venture capital backed firms and non-venture capital backed firms. It is generally acknowledged that IPOs tend to be under-priced. However, research indicates that the level of under-pricing seems to be lower for venture capital backed firms. This indicates that the firm and its shareholders and investors (including the venture capitalist) are able to get more value during the public offering compared to the value that non-venture backed companies are able to obtain. Therefore, venture capitalists seem to play an important certification role during the IPO.

5.8 Summary and Conclusions

Venture capital is the provision of private equity to new and young firms with high growth potential. Venture capital firms invest equity capital in innovative businesses with high growth potential, which are at an early stage of their development. The dominant form of organisational structure for venture capital firms has become the limited partnership, which is made up of general and limited partners. The general partner manages the business and shares in the profits of the venture capital firm. The limited partners are usually not involved in the management of the business. They contribute capital to the business and share in the profits of the business.

The venture capital life cycle is made up of raising funds, screening investment proposals, investing in companies, monitoring investments and partaking in the management of the enterprise and finally harvesting the investment. Reputation is very important in the venture capital market. A good reputation is important for all stakeholders, ranging from the general partner, to the limited partner, and the investee enterprise. Venture capitalists enter into various contracts with stakeholders. They usually enter into contracts with fund providers (limited partners) as well as investee enterprises. The contracts serve to protect the interests of the various stakeholders and make funding possible.

Venture capitalists consider an array of factors before 'jumping head long' into an investment. These factors include the quality of the enterprise's management, the enterprise's competitive edge, the financial projections of the enterprise, and what level of financing is required, the industry expertise of the venture capitalist, and the existence of a viable exit strategy. To be able to add value to the fund, the venture capitalist must be good and efficient in the various processes. These include negotiating and selecting good deals, timing the investment in the enterprise at when it is needed, spending appropriate and effective time with investee enterprises, monitoring and offering expertise to investee firms and exiting the investment at the appropriate time.

Discussion Questions and Problems

1. Discuss the relevance of venture capital in small business financing.
2. Discuss the nature of venture capital and explain the various types of venture capital.
3. What are the main differences between venture capital finance and other sources of finance?

4. What are the pros and cons of using venture capital financing?
5. Provide an overview of the venture capital market in a developing country context.
6. Venture capital firms were previously organised as closed-end funds but they are now being organised as limited partnership. What are the main differences between the two forms of organisation?
7. What are the processes involved in venture capital investment?
8. Identify some of the elements in the contracts between venture capital and the investors and also between the venture capital and investee firms.
9. What do venture capitalists consider before investing in a firm and how do they add value to the fund?
10. How do venture capitalists harvest their investments?

6

Microfinance Intervention

Learning Objectives
By the end of this chapter, you should be able to:

- define and provide an overview of microfinance
- discuss the importance of microfinance
- explain the operations of microfinance institutions
- show the sustainability of microfinance institutions
- discuss the lending models and the credit risk management of microfinance institutions
- identify the challenges confronting microfinance institutions
- illustrate how banks participate in the microfinance market

6.1 Introduction

Microfinance can serve as an important source of financing for MSMEs and it covers broadly the provision of financial services to low-income clients and micro-enterprises that do not have access to formal financial services. These financial services include the provision of micro-credit, micro-savings, micro-insurance and fund transfer services. Microfinance enables low-income clients and MSMEs to access different types of financial services to finance their productive activities, stabilise consumption, manage risks and build assets. Given that the provision of such financial services typically involve small amounts of money (small loans, small savings, etc.), the term 'microfinance' helps to

J.Y. Abor, *Entrepreneurial Finance for MSMEs*,
DOI 10.1007/978-3-319-34021-0_6

distinguish between these services and those provided by traditional banks or other formal financial institutions.

This chapter discusses microfinance intervention. We provide an explanation to the concept of microfinance and discuss the importance of microfinance and criticisms of microfinance in general terms. In this chapter, we also try to understand the operations of MFIs, their sustainability, their lending models and how they manage credits. Lastly, we discuss the challenges of MFIs and how banks participate in the microfinance market.

6.2 Overview of Microfinance

Microfinance is said to entail the provision of financial services to low-income clients and micro-enterprises that usually have difficulty accessing formal financial services. Some authors have also defined microfinance in different ways. For instance, Robinson (2001) defines microfinance as small scale financial services for both credit and deposits that is provided to people who farm or fish; provide services; work for wages or commission; gain income from renting out small amounts of land, vehicles, animals or machinery and tools; and to other individuals and local groups in developing countries, in both rural and urban areas. Rogarly et al. (1999) also define microfinance to include the provision of small loans, savings facilities with no (or very low) minimum deposit and other financial services like insurance and money transfer or bill payment designed for people who live on low income or are otherwise excluded from the products of commercial banks. From the above definitions, microfinance in essence involves the provision of financial services to the underprivileged poor, who form a chunk of the population of developing economies.

All the definitions provided above clearly show that microfinance goes beyond the provision of credits and savings facilities. Thus, it is important to show how micro-credit and micro-savings are different from microfinance. **Microfinance** covers a wide range of financial services, which include micro-credit, micro-savings products, micro-insurance, funds transfer services and other financial products designed for poor and low-income earners. In addition to these financial services or intermediation, microfinance provides social intermediation services, including training in business development, management, financial literacy, vocational skills as well as relevant information to their clients. Clearly, microfinance includes both financial intermediation and social intermediation.

Micro-credit, however, refers to the provision of small loans to low-income or poor individuals, households and other economic entities with little or no collateral. Micro-credit is the lending side of microfinance and this lending is targeted at those who have difficulty accessing credit or loans from the traditional or formal financial institutions. The focus of micro-credit is for the borrowers to channel the funds into some economic venture in order to earn returns capable to repay the loans with interest. This will ensure that the micro-credit providers or institutions become sustainable and continue to extend their services at all times.

Micro-saving is also an aspect of microfinance service that provides the poor and low-income earners an opportunity to safeguard their funds and other valuable items and also earn an interest. It involves microfinance clients setting aside money on a regularly basis (series of savings) to be accessed as lump sum at a future date.

It is obvious from the above discussion that microfinance is a broader concept than micro-credit and micro-saving. The main characteristic of microfinance involves small amounts of loans, which are provided to low-income earners to enable them finance their economic activities. The small savings is also an essential element of microfinance, which serve as a form of security for the microfinance clients as well as assist them to accumulate significant amount of capital. The loans given out are usually short-term in nature, with maturity up to one year. Payments for the loans are usually made on a weekly basis and instalments comprise elements of principal and interest, which are usually amortised over a given period of time.

The easy access to the microfinance intermediary's services is time saving for the clients and it also permits the MFI to be able to ascertain the clients' financial and social status. Loan application procedures in microfinance are quite simple unlike the cumbersome processes associated with traditional banks. The processing period between submitting a loan application to an MFI and the loan disbursement is usually shorter and a collateral is often not a requirement in microfinance, as opposed to what pertains in conventional or traditional banks. MFIs usually use collateral substitutes such as group-based lending and joint liability, graduated loans based on prompt payments, frequent collections, compulsory savings, loan guarantors and referees, regular meetings with clients. We will discuss each of these methods later in this chapter.

As discussed earlier, microfinance clients are mostly poor and low-income earners with limited or no access to formal financial services. These clients are usually self-employed and entrepreneurs of micro-enterprises involved in activities such as small retail shops, food processing, farming, street vending, artisanal manufacture and service provision. These micro-entrepreneurs normally access microfinance to finance their micro-enterprises. However, some of the loans are sometimes used to support certain household needs such as stabilising consumption, paying education fees, paying medical bills, financing weddings, funerals and so on.

Though some empirical studies have suggested that microfinance is important in alleviating poverty, it is also important to note that it is not always the most appropriate method, and thus it should never be considered as the only tool for ending poverty. Microfinance, particularly micro-credit, is appropriate if the credit is meant for an economic venture. Micro-credit is said to best serve those who have identified an economic opportunity and can take advantage of it. Microfinance is therefore inappropriate for the poor, who may need grants or other public resources to improve their economic situation, since they may not be in a position to repay such loans.

6.2.1 The Beginning of Microfinance and the Grameen Bank

Globally, microfinance is believed to have gone through four main stages and these include:

- The provision of subsidised credit by Governments from the 1950s as a means to eliminating of poverty.
- The provision of micro-credit mainly through NGOs to the poor between the 1960s and 1970s when the issues sustainability and financial self-sufficiency were not considered relevant.
- The formalisation of MFIs in the 1990s.
- The commercialisation of MFIs and mainstreaming them into the financial sector since the mid 1990s.

It is important to note that credit associations and lending cooperatives have existed for hundreds of years. However, the beginning of modern microfinance is often credited to Mohammad Yunus, an economist who taught at Chittagong University in southeastern Bangladesh. Yunus began a series of experiments by giving small loans to poor households in the close by village of Jobra, Bangladesh in 1976. He used his personal money to give loans to a group of women some of whom dealt in bamboo furniture. He lent an initial sum of US$27 to a group of 42. The group made profits from the loan taken and they were able to pay back the loan with interest and on time. He was convinced that small loans to the poor were not only viable and profitable, but they also had a low default rate, even though they did not have collateral. Realising that he could not do much with his own resources, in 1976, Yunus persuaded the Bangladesh Bank (the central bank of Bangladesh) to assist him to establish a special branch to serve the poor of Jobra, leading to the creation of another trial project. Yunus embarked on this project to form an institution to lend to the poor at the base of the economic pyramid. Yunus therefore sought to raise loans to support this project. He was successful in raising some funds from a government-sponsored bank and other lenders and these were on-lent to the rural poor.

In 1983, Yunus converted the institution, which he had formed to lend to the poor, into what is now known as the Grameen Bank. Grameen introduced innovative methods such as lending to a group of people who were together responsible for paying the loan that they had taken. The group-based lending is a mechanism that enables the poor borrowers to serve as guarantors for each other. This innovation in lending allowed Grameen to grow very fast. Innovation in microfinance has been sustained since then, with the evolution of providers of financial services to the poor. Today, microfinance plays an important role in the provision of financial services to many people, especially in developing countries. Group lending programmes also operate in many other countries including the USA.

In lending to small businesses, Grameen's group lending is quite different from that of mainstream bank lending. In mainstream banking, the borrower provides collateral to the bank as part of the requirements for taking the loan facility. The borrower then invests the loan in a productive venture for a return, which is finally used to repay the loan with interest. If borrowers are not able to repay, the bank seizes the collateral. However, these poor customers of Grameen are not in the position to provide collateral; rather, what Grameen does is to rely on the client's close ties within their community. Relying on those relationships makes it possible for the customers to form groups in order for members to qualify for the loans. This is because the loan contracts in this case are structured based on groups of customers. The groups are formed on voluntary basis, and, while loans are given to individual members within a group, all members of the group are supposed to support each other at difficult moments. Each group usually consists of five members and the mechanism works in the following manner; loans are initially given to two of the members, then to the next two and then finally to the fifth group member, who is usually the group leader. In so far as the group fulfils its debt obligations by repaying the loans, the lending cycle continues. Based on the rules, however, if one member of the group defaults and the other members of the group are unable to repay the loan, all members in the group are refused subsequent loans. This element puts pressure on the customers to pay back their loan on time, to monitor their colleagues and to choose responsible members when forming a group. The five-member group is also part of a 'centre' made up of eight groups. Repayments are made in weekly instalments in public, that is, before the 40 members of the centre. The condition of 'joint liability' is the most notable aspect of the Grameen group lending model, and that explains why microfinance is mostly associated with the concept of group lending.

Yunus and the Grameen Bank for their contribution in leading the microfinance revolution were awarded the Nobel Peace Prize in 2006. The Grameen Bank, since its formation has focused on providing credit and infrastructural assistance to the rural poor who generally lack access to credit from traditional financial institutions because they have no collateral to support their loan applications.

6.3 Benefits and Criticisms of Microfinance

There are benefits and criticisms associated with microfinance by/to the poor, to women and to MSMEs. In the past 20 years, the provision of financial services to poor clients as well as to small and micro-enterprises, including smallholder farmers, has been identified as an important *anti-poverty reduction tool*. Although microfinance is not the solution for poverty and related development challenges, it is considered to play a significant role in a number of respects.

6.3.1 Benefits of Microfinance

One benefit of microfinance is improved economic activity and job creation. The provision of micro-credit to low-income earners enables them to undertake economic activities such as trading, farming and so on in order to increase their income level. MSMEs can also take advantage of business opportunities by increasing the micro-loans acquired to earn returns. Through this means, microfinance is able to improve the income level of the micro-entrepreneur. Improved access to micro-credit to the MSMEs will enable them to increase their economic activities and subsequently lead to job creation.

Another benefit is asset building. Microfinance clients are able to build their asset base through the micro-loans they acquire. Through micro-loans, poor individuals and households are able to acquire and build physical and productive assets such as housing, personal equipment, vehicle, financial assets, livestock and so on. MSMEs are also able to acquire assets such as office equipment, vehicle, office property and so on. Microfinance service like micro-savings also enables poor clients to make savings for investments either in physical assets or financial assets. Building a good asset base is likely to reduce the level of poverty.

The provision of micro-insurance services by microfinance enables MSMEs to buy insurance products to insure their assets and operations against misfortunes. Micro-insurance services also help poor individuals and households to manage their risk. These microfinance clients are able to buy micro-insurance products to protect their assets against fire, theft, and are also protected against accidents and ill health. Microfinance also gives underprivileged people enough capital stability, which, in turn, gives them financial security from sudden financial challenges. Microfinance, in the form of micro-insurance, is therefore important in reducing poverty by protecting the assets of the microfinance clients.

Another benefit is consumption smoothing. Microfinance assists very poor households to take care of their basic needs. Microfinance can increase consumption levels and significantly curtail the need to dispose of assets to meet basic needs. The provision of micro-insurance services can assist the poor to be able to cope with unexpected increases in expenses that may be related to death, serious illness and loss of property.

Microfinance brings about improvement in education levels among the poor. Access to microfinance by poor families enables them to send their children to school. Therefore, drop-out rates are lower among children whose parents participate in microfinance programmes. With the existence of MFIs, parents are now able to save towards their wards' education as well access loans in times when their savings are not enough to cater for their wards' educational expenses.

Microfinance is also important in promoting gender equality and women's empowerment. The support from microfinance enables women to increase their contribution to household income and to the value of their assets, and also to have control over decisions that affect their lives. Microfinance programmes generally target women by empowering them, promoting gender-equity and improving household well-being. Access to microfinance by women improves their status within the family and the community. They become more assertive and confident to the extent that in regions where their mobility is strictly regulated, they have become more visible and are in the position to have a voice in the society.

Access to microfinance leads to reduced child mortality, improved maternal health and nutrition, and general good health, especially among the poor women. Women, who are able to access microfinance, are in a better position to cover the cost of healthcare and provide good nutritional meals for their children. This generally leads to improvement in the health and nutritional status of their children.

6.3.2 Criticisms of Microfinance

In spite of the benefits of microfinance, there are criticisms associated with microfinance. One criticism is the lack of knowledge about microfinance services. Many poor people live in rural communities and tend to have little or no formal education. They therefore lack knowledge about the availability of financial services for the poor. They, as a result, have little access to microfinance services provided by MFIs.

Another criticism is the inability of the poor to offer marketable collateral for loans. Clients of microfinance services are mostly small businesses and poor individuals who lack the necessary collateral, credit history and stable income to qualify for loans. MFIs may be prepared to extend credit to such borrowers by charging high interest rates, otherwise they reject their loan application.

There is also the perceived high risk associated with lending to the poor. The poor and small businesses that access micro-credit from MFIs are often perceived to be risky. This is because they may easily misuse or misapply the loan. This is known as moral hazard. Example, a trader borrows from an MFI to buy goods for resale but uses the money to buy a motorbike. This situation makes it difficult for the trader to repay the loan.

There is the problem of high transaction costs involved in small loans. Microfinance providers are often criticised for the high transaction costs associated with their lending. Considering the small loans they provide, they are not in the position to record low transaction costs like banks that tend to provide big loans. Banks mostly process loans on a large scale and therefore, per unit cost of transaction may be less. MFIs, on the other hand, provide micro-credit, which is associated with high costs and these may be passed on to the borrower.

Microfinance is also associated with high interest rates on loans made to the poor. We mentioned that borrowers of loans from MFIs lack the necessary collateral and are perceived to be risky. We also indicated that microfinance is associated with high transaction costs, because of the small amounts involved in the loans provided. Microfinance providers may therefore charge high interest to cover the lack of collateral, high risk and high transaction costs. This makes microfinance services more expensive, thus driving away potential customers.

6.4 Operations of Microfinance Institutions

MFIs are generally considered a subset of alternative financial institutions. They include NGOs, microfinance banks and non-bank financial intermediaries. They may operate independently or as the subsidiaries of larger banks. In most African countries, MFIs include rural and community banks, savings and loans companies, financial NGOs, credit unions, rotating savings and credit associations, development and commercial banks with microfinance programmes and linkages, micro-insurance and micro-leasing services.

They operate under prudential, regulatory, legal and institutional frameworks tailored for clients, which are traditionally perceived as too risky or unprofitable by mainstream traditional banks. While the operations of MFIs include a social dimension, they consider the business of microfinance as a profitable core venture. Unlike traditional commercial banking, MFIs adapt their financial services targeting low-income earners and MSMEs. Their shareholders tend to value the social dimension of the MFIs' operations and therefore they may expect to earn lower returns on their investments compared to other private investors.

6.4.1 Products and Services of MFIs

MFIs offer a wide range of financial services to low-income households in both rural and urban areas. The services provided to microfinance clients include:

Financial Intermediation Services These include the provision of financial products and services such as savings, credit, insurance, payment systems and so on.

Social Intermediation Services Social intermediation involves the process of building the human and social capital needed by sustainable financial intermediation for the poor. Under this, MFIs try to upgrade or improve on the expertise of the workers engaged in the provision of such services to ensure effective and efficient service delivery. These services may be subsidised by donor agencies, especially in the long-term. Examples of social intermediation services are group formation, leadership training and cooperative learning.

Enterprise Development Services These include non-financial services that assist micro-entrepreneurs in the areas of skills development, training in business plans, marketing, technology and so on. The provision of these services may depend on the clients' ability and willingness to pay for the services. Some clients may also require subsidies in order to access such services.

Social Services These are also non-financial services involving the promotion of the welfare of the poor and micro-entrepreneurs. These services include education, health, family planning, nutrition and literacy training. Such social services require ongoing subsidies provided by the government and/or donor-supporting NGOs.

6.4.2 Functions of Microfinance Institutions

MFIs provide important functions to the people, who are not able to meet the eligibility criteria for bank loans. An important function MFIs perform is to provide access to capital. MFIs provide access to capital for the poor or entrepreneurs to start a business or expand an existing business. This helps the entrepreneur to enjoy a reasonable level of profits. Remember, that capital is necessary for starting or expanding a business.

MFIs also offer basic education to people on how to manage their financial resources and how to run their business effectively and efficiently. In some cases, they may require borrowers to complete education or some form of training before they qualify for loans.

Another function is group lending. Granting of loans without any collateral may result in higher default; however, most of MFIs require what is known as 'collateral substitute'. One form of collateral substitute is group-based lending. MFIs require their borrowers to form a group, so as to ensure timely repayments. Formation of groups act as a support for each other, and every member can guarantee the repayment of other members of the group. Through this way, the MFIs can collect weekly payments more efficiently, because the group supports members if they have problems repaying their loan.

MFIs are interested in women's empowerment. It is well established that, lending to women is better for the broader community because they invest the profits made from loans they receive back into the development of their family. Women tend to use their profits to invest in their children's education and also provide food and clothing to their family. Lending to women generally empowers them and helps close the gender inequality.

One main focus of microfinance is to reduce poverty and develop local communities. In order to raise adequate funds to extend micro-credit to the poor, most MFIs tend to link up with the donor community in developed countries. This is how MFIs connect with the world.

6.5 Sustainability of Microfinance Institutions

In this section, we will look at how to measure the sustainability of MFIs. We will then discuss the determinants of the success and sustainability of MFIs.

6.5.1 Measures of MFIs' Sustainability

Considering the crucial role that MFIs play, it is essential that they are operationally and financially sound. Certain indicators are used to measure the sustainability of MFIs and these include the subsidy dependence index (SDI), operational self-sufficiency (OSS) ratio and portfolio at risk (PAR) measure. These dimensions measure subsidy dependence, operational sustainability and, finally, financial sustainability.

6.5.1.1 Subsidy Dependence Index

The SDI measures by how much average yields have to increase in order for the MFI to exit subsidy dependence given its portfolio size. The SDI can be computed as follows:

$$\text{SDI} = \frac{\text{Net subsidy}}{\text{Loan portfolio} \times \text{Interest rate on loan}}$$

An SDI of 0.5 % or 50 % therefore means that average yields on loans must increase by 50 % for the MFI to exit subsidy dependence. SDI of zero implies full self-sustainability and the MFI does not need subsidy.

6.5.1.2 Operational Sustainability

The OSS ratio measures the ability of the MFI to cover its operating expenses given its operational income. MFIs that are able to cover their operating costs are regarded as more sustainable as compared to those that are not able to cover their operational costs. The OSS is defined as follows:

$$\text{OSS} = \frac{\text{Total operational income}}{\text{Interest expense} + \text{Loan loss provision} + \text{Administrative expenses}}$$

An OSS of 0.5 % or 50 % suggests that the operating income of the MFI is 50 % of its operational expenses. Therefore, its operational income is not sufficient to meet its operational expenses. In this case the operational income of the MFI is less than its operational expenses and therefore the MFI may not be sustainable in the long-term. An MFI with an OSS greater than 100 % is likely to be more sustainable in the long-term since its profits are more than sufficient to cover it basic operating costs.

6.5.1.3 Financial Sustainability

The PAR measure examines the percentage of the loan portfolio of the MFI that is overdue or is likely to be exposed to significant risks in the future. The PAR measure relates the total loan principal outstanding on overdue or delinquent loans to the total amount of loan principal outstanding. The PAR measure is given as follows:

$$\text{PAR} = \frac{\text{Total loan principal on overdue or delinquent loans outstanding}}{\text{Total loan principal outstanding}}$$

As can be seen, the PAR is given as total loan principal on all loans that are overdue or have been delinquent divided by the total loan principal outstanding. The PAR measure can be broken down into amounts overdue over a given period. The MFI can therefore calculate amounts that are overdue for more than a month, three months, six months or any other suitable period. We can adjust the generic PAR to compute the PAR over a given period. This is given as follows:

$$\text{PAR} = \frac{\text{Total loan principal outstanding on loans overdue for more than } x \text{ days}}{\text{Total loan principal outstanding}}$$

The new measure tells us the total principal outstanding on loans that have been delinquent say over the past 30 days or any number of days. So, total principal amounts on loans that have been delinquent for more than 90 days will be riskier compared to the total principal amounts outstanding on loans that have been delinquent for more than 30 days. This is because amounts that have been overdue for longer periods are more likely to turn into bad debts.

The PAR measures the total principal on loans that are overdue or at risk given the total loans outstanding at a point in time. Therefore, if the balance or total principal outstanding on loans that have been delinquent are higher than the PAR measure, it is also going to be high. Higher PAR ratios indicate that the MFI is experiencing problems recovering loans given out. Therefore, a higher PAR ratio indicates credit management problems, whilst a lower ratio indicates good credit administration. The PAR measure can therefore be used to proxy financial sustainability since high PAR ratios may indicate that the MFI is not sustainable in the long-term.

The PAR ratio is a very useful way to measure the quality of the loan book or portfolio of an MFI. It is futuristic in nature because it tells us the amounts that are at risk and not just the principal that is overdue or remains unpaid. It does this by extrapolating past behaviour into the future, and by assuming that those who have defaulted in the past will also default in the future. It is a conservative measure by assuming that customers who have defaulted in the past will also default in the future. Though conservative in nature, it may be appropriate to assume that for loans that have been delinquent in the past, future cash flows are riskier than on loans that have not experienced any default.

Example 6.1

Consider the financial records of Capro Finance, an MFI, based in the rural community, for the year 2015 (Table 6.1).

Compute the following:

(a) Subsidy dependence index
(b) Operational self-sufficiency
(c) Portfolio at risk

Answer 6.1

(a) Subsidy Dependence Index (SDI)

$$SDI = \frac{\text{Net subsidy}}{\text{Loan portfolio} \times \text{Interest rate on loan}}$$

Table 6.1 Financial records of Capro Finance (2015)

Details	US$
Operating income	414,000
Financial expense	94,000
Net impairment loss, gross loan portfolio	68,000
Operating expense	171,000
Gross loan portfolio	283,000
Delinquency + 1 month or more	31,000
Net subsidy	30,000
Interest rate charged on loans = 22 %	

$$\text{SDI} = \frac{\text{US\$ } 30{,}000}{\text{US\$ } 283{,}000 \times 0.22}$$

$$\text{SDI} = \frac{\text{US\$ } 30{,}000}{\text{US\$ } 62{,}260} = 0.4819 = 48.2\%$$

This implies that Capro Finance Ltd. needs to increase its interest income by 48 % in order to exit its dependence on subsidy.

(b) Operational Self-Sufficiency (OSS)

$$\text{OSS} = \frac{\text{Total operational income}}{\text{Interest expense} + \text{Loan loss provision} + \text{Administrative expenses}}$$

$$\text{OSS} = \frac{\text{US\$ } 414{,}000}{\text{US\$ } 94{,}000 + \text{US\$ } 68{,}000 + \text{US\$ } 171{,}000}$$

$$\text{OSS} = 1.243 \text{ or } 124.3\%$$

This implies the Capro Finance Ltd. is sustainable in the long-term since its income is more than sufficient to cover its expenses.

(c) Portfolio at Risk (PAR)

$$\text{PAR} = \frac{\text{Total loan principal on overdue or delinquent loans outstanding}}{\text{Total loan principal outstanding}}$$

$$\text{PAR} = \frac{\text{US\$ } 31{,}000}{\text{US\$ } 283{,}000}$$

$$\text{PAR} = 0.11 \text{ or } 11\%$$

This implies that 11 % of loans given out by Capro Finance Ltd. have become delinquent.

Example 6.2
Clemmie Microfinance Institution has an equity base of US$250,000 and concessionary borrowed funds of US$600,000. Currently, Clemmie Microfinance Institution's does not have any other subsidies apart from the concessionary borrowed funds. Clemmie Microfinance Institution's has a loan portfolio of US$1,000,000. Market interest rates on deposits are given as 15 %. The interest rate on the concessionary borrowed funds is 10 %. The average on-lending interest rate on Clemmie Microfinance Institution's loan portfolio is 23 %. The profit after tax for Clemmie Microfinance Institution for its current financial year is given as US$9000. Tax rate is 20 % on profit of Clemmie Microfinance Institution. Compute the SDI. At what interest rate can it wean off subsidies?

Answer 6.2
Step 1: Subsidy on borrowed funds

$$= \text{US\$}\,600{,}000(0.15-0.10) = \text{US\$}\,30{,}000$$

Step 2: Imputed cost of equity

$$= \text{US\$}\,250{,}000 \times (0.15) = \text{US\$}\,37{,}500$$

Step 3: Subsidy on equity = Imputed cost of equity − profit

$$= \text{US\$}\,37{,}500 - (\text{US\$}\,9000/(1-0.2) = \text{US\$}\,26{,}250$$

(*Note: convert profit after tax to profit before tax*)

Step 4: Total subsidy = US$ 30,000 + US$ 26,250 = US$ 56,250

$$\text{SDI} = \frac{\text{Subsidy}}{\text{Loan portfolio} \times \text{Interest rate on loan}}$$
$$= \frac{\text{US\$}\,56{,}250}{\text{US\$}\,1{,}000{,}000 \times 0.23} = 0.2446 = 24.46\%$$

Step 5: For Clemmie Microfinance Institution to wean off subsidies, the interest rate should increase by 24.46 %. Thus, the interest rate should be:

$$= 0.23(1.2446) = 0.286 = 28.6\%$$

6.5.2 Determinants of the Success and Sustainability of MFIs

There are several factors that determine whether an MFI is likely to succeed or fail in its endeavour to provide financial services to the underprivileged in society. MFIs try to achieve both social and financial objectives. Attempting to achieve these two objectives can raise several conflicts. Therefore, there may be natural trade-offs in attempting to achieve these two targets. For instance, an MFI that attempts to maximise social objectives may find that it will have to compromise some financial goals. For example, conflicts of interest can arise when loan officers are rewarded based on the quality of the loan portfolio through higher repayment rates. In this case, loan officers may prefer more rich clients who can repay, but the goal of poverty reduction may be compromised. Incentive schemes that highlight a larger number of borrowers and good repayments have proven successful for many MFIs. Increasing loan size can increase the profitability of an MFI, but the impact on poverty reduction will be reduced, given the larger loan sizes. Also, achieving a social objective of a larger social outreach and impact may lead to more loan defaults as more and larger loans are given out. Managers of MFIs must therefore be skilful and tactful in order to balance these sometimes conflicting goals.

Why are some MFIs successful whilst others are struggling to survive? We will explain why this occurs in the real world. A number of factors may account for an MFI being successful and these include leadership quality, talented staff, innovative products and services, reliance on subsidies, sound financial management, diversified clientele base and prudential regulation.

Leadership Quality Leadership quality has been identified as one of the attributes that distinguish successful from not so successful MFIs. MFIs with strong, dynamic, as well as visionary leaders are more likely to be successful, compared with the management of similar MFIs without these qualities. The quality of an MFI's management is very important for its success. This is because such leaders are well placed to lead their organisations, motivate staff and ensure that risks are identified and managed and that good internal controls are put in place. The leadership of the MFI, as identified earlier, must be very tactful in achieving financial goals as well as maintaining good social impacts. Therefore, just like formal financial institutions, quality management can better advance the success and sustainability of an MFI.

Talented Staff An MFI must also aim at attracting, and retaining talented staff. The staff should be knowledgeable and possess sufficient skills to perform the tasks assigned them. Since management cannot perform all the work alone, they have to delegate responsibilities to employees. Employees such as loan officers are very important because they deal directly with clients and therefore can tarnish the reputation of the MFI if they are very hard on clients when it comes to the collection of outstanding loans. If they are too soft too, and do not put up much of a 'struggle' when it comes to the collection of outstanding loans, clients are likely to default. If loan officers do not perform their work well in terms of screening, monitoring and collection, the MFI is likely to experience high default rates and may be adversely affected.

Innovative Products and Services Successful MFIs have innovative products that are tailored to their market niche. Most MFIs have adopted the group-based lending mechanism. Such lending mechanisms have proven successful in other places after the Grameen Bank pioneered it. It is argued that MFIs whose loan portfolio is more tilted towards group-based lending tend to be more successful than MFIs whose portfolio is more tilted towards individual lending. Most MFIs tend to focus on the poor and women. The products must be such that the illiterate poor who are likely to form the bulk of the clientele base of an MFI can understand them. It is argued that compared to men, women may find it more difficult to access formal financial services such as accessing loans from the banks. This is because their businesses may be more informal compared to male-owned businesses. Therefore, women groups are more likely to value micro-credit provided by an MFI. One important factor that determines the success or failure of an MFI is its ability to design innovative products that are valued by its clientele and market niche.

Reliance on Subsidies Most MFIs, including the most successful, rely on subsidies to support their operations. These subsidies could be coming from donors, governments or individuals who believe in the ideals of reducing poverty. However, high reliance on subsidies can lead to the MFI being financially unsustainable. To overcome the challenge of relying heavily on subsidies, the MFI can charge market interest rates on its loans. Charging market interest rates can lead to profitability, provided that costs are efficiently controlled. Retained earnings can therefore be accumulated and can help reduce the

MFI's reliance on subsidies. MFIs that charge market interest rates are more likely to be financially sustainable and rely less on subsidies.

Sound Financial Management Sound financial management and risk management are also essential for the success of an MFI. MFIs must be able to effectively and efficiently manage their financial resources and a good MIS can ensure effective financial management. The MIS should make it easier to record transactions such as deposits as well as keep track of loans given out. Another good practice is if MFIs have their accounts audited by professional accountants. This increases the credibility associated with the accounts and also increases the confidence of stakeholders in the MFI's financial statements. Having accounts audited can also reduce the risk of fraud. MFIs must also have and implement effective risk management techniques. Risk management must be part in the culture and systems of the MFI and should not be seen as a one off activity. Therefore, for an MFI to be successful, it must practise good and sound financial management, have strong internal controls as well as implement effective risk management systems.

Diversified Clientele Base Having a large and diversified client base as well as giving out smaller loans has been found to be a useful predictor of MFI success. A large client base helps the MFI to diversify its loan portfolio. This ensures that the risk of failure of the MFI is reduced. Giving smaller loan amounts also means that the MFI can give out more loans and increase its outreach. Outreach is about the spread of the activities of the MFI in terms of the number of clients it is able to reach and serve. The social impact from smaller loans is likely to be higher than larger loans in terms of reducing poverty. Also, operating on a larger scale through a broader outreach will lead to benefits of economies of scale for the MFI.

Prudential Regulation MFIs, which operate in well-regulated markets, tend to perform better than those who operate in unregulated markets. Regulation brings formalisation and recognition of the activities of the MFI. Regulated markets set the rules of the game and also make sure that regulations address the needs and challenges of the industry players. Regulators also ensure that, operators in the MFI industry are doing things the right way, and they reserve the right to shut down non-performing MFIs. This threat of withdrawing the licence of an MFI can in itself motivate MFIs to keep their houses in order.

6.6 Lending Models and Credit Risk Management

It is important at this point to appreciate the lending models and credit risk management mechanisms used by MFIs.

6.6.1 Lending Models of MFIs

The lending models used by MFIs differ from lending models used by banking institutions. Microfinance is developed out of the need to provide financial services to the poor. Traditional banks use western models, which seem not to be effective in reaching the poorest of the poor in developing countries. The traditional lending models employed by banks have not been effective due to the differing circumstances of developing countries. Developing countries have developed new means of reaching out to the poor without having to adopt banking models from the West. Some of the lending models adopted by MFIs are group-based lending, village banking and individual banking.

6.6.1.1 Group-Based Lending

Group-based lending is one of the cornerstone lending models used by MFIs. The MFI transacts business with the group and therefore members of the group have to meet periodically. With this approach, the MFI lends to members in a group but the entire group is liable if a single member of the group defaults or does not pay a loan that has been taken. The group-based lending approach therefore utilises joint liability as all members are jointly and severally liable for the debt of their peers. Due to this joint liability, if a single member of the group defaults, the bank has the right to restrict future credit to the entire group until they pay up. The bank may lend to a smaller group, which is known as a solidarity group. Due to the smaller nature of the solidarity group, it provides more flexibility to members. The group members could be as few as three members. In the classic method employed by the Grameen Bank, the bank lends to a group of five. This is how it works out: initially Grameen lends to two members in the group. If these members pay up, then another two members in the group become entitled to receive loans from the bank. After these two members in the group have paid up, the last member in the group who is usually the group leader becomes entitled to receive his loan.

This system therefore provides incentives for the members who are in line to receive loans to encourage their peers to pay up.

The bank may also lend to a larger group of 40 people made up of eight groups each with five members. What happens is that the bank's loan officer periodically meets this group during meetings, which typically last for about 2.5 hours. This meeting is held in public thus providing transparency to the process. During such meetings, the bank's loan officer sits in the middle of the group. Each five-member group has a leader, and there is a leader for the entire group. The leaders help the loan officer to transact the business of the day. This includes loan collections and savings deposits. In this larger group, the entire group is liable for the loans taken and liability is not restricted to the smaller groups of five. There have been cited instances where loan officers have refused to leave the village unless the entire group of 40 has settled their obligations for the week. Using the group approach, the bank moves to the people since it is the loan officer or bank official that attends the meetings of the group and transacts business with them. Therefore, the group approach provides convenience and enables a single officer of the bank to serve a large number of clients (40) at a sitting.

Group-based lending is suitable to lending to the rural poor and communities that are closely knit. This approach has been employed widely and quite successfully in rural Bangladesh as well as in other places in Asia and Africa. The group-based lending methodology approach may not be suitable to lending to urban poor, due to the higher mobility of such a group.

Group-based lending is very useful for a bank for several reasons. It reduces the cost of the bank because the group essentially performs the task that the bank would have had to perform. This ranges from initial screening and selection, monitoring of group members, and finally aiding in collection, repayment and enforcement of the terms of the loan. The group-based lending methodology is also very useful in that it helps resolve information asymmetries that for so long prevented lending to people at the bottom of the economic ladder, due to market failures. The group-based lending approach helps the bank to avoid adverse selections by inadvertently picking bad credit risks and rejecting good credit applicants. This is because members of the group choose each other. Group members will therefore want to be in a group with people of good repute. This mechanism leads to safe borrowers banding together, whilst riskier borrowers also band together. The bank can therefore afford to price discriminate. Again, the group-based lending mechanism avoids cross subsidisation of risky borrowers by safe borrowers and therefore safe borrowers are encouraged to enter into the market to borrow. The bank can also afford to lend to all borrowers at lower rates since it does not have to charge very high interest rates because it cannot distinguish between good and bad borrowers.

Apart from reducing adverse selection, the group-based lending methodology also serves to reduce moral hazards. Ex ante moral hazards are reduced because the group-based lending methodology means group members can monitor each other in terms of the choice of projects that are undertaken so that excessively risky projects are not undertaken. Moral hazard can also occur ex post when after the borrower has undertaken a project and has realised gains, decides not to pay back the loan owed to the bank. Due to moral hazards, the bank will find it difficult to distinguish between borrowers who cannot actually repay, because the project went sore or because there are those who just want to defraud the bank. The group-based lending methodology helps overcome this problem, which, at worst, results in a market failure because the bank decides not to lend at all because it expects that borrowers will not repay. This is because members are closely knit such as those in a village or rural community. Groups reduce moral hazards because they can impose social and economic sanctions on each other better than the bank can ever hope to. Also because of the group liability feature members who are incentivised to monitor each other, so far as monitoring costs are not excessive and do not outweigh their profits.

We have talked so much about the benefits of group-based lending and the promise they provided when they became popular in the 1970s. Group-based lending is not all that rosy and is associated with some challenges. One of this is high costs, which exist in the process of group members monitoring each other. In this case monitoring will not be effectively undertaken. Also, attending regular meetings can be costly in terms of the time spent to get to the meeting as well as the time that is spent at the meeting. Frequent and long meetings as well as covering long distances to get to meetings have reportedly led to some people quitting the group-based lending mechanism and those who remain probably remain because they have no other option. This may also partly explain why clients prefer to switch to an individual lending scheme once they become more successful. Also, free rider problems can occur because some members of the group work hard and are diligent in monitoring whilst others do the opposite. Due to joint liability some members may be opportunistic and therefore choose risky projects because of the insurance cover provided by the other members of the group. Also clients who genuinely cannot repay loans taken are likely to face excessive peer pressure and social threats (such as exclusion from the group and other social events) in addition to loosing access to future loans. In practice, it can be difficult for sanctions (both social and economic) to be applied because of friendships, family ties and other social ties. Finally, the group-based lending mechanism can become hopelessly ineffective if group members decide to collude to defraud the bank. The MFI can reduce this likelihood by lending to a more diverse group of borrowers in a group. This is because more similar borrowers have a higher likelihood and probability to collude to defraud the MFI.

6.6.1.2 Village Banking

The village banking lending model was pioneered by John Hatch an economist and development expert who formed FINCA in 1984. Other MFIs that use the village lending approach include Freedom from Hunger and Pro Mujer. Using this approach, neighbours come together in financial support groups called 'village banks'. The village bank would invite people who want loans to come and write their names. Once a certain number has been reached, the people on the list are used to form a group. The members of the group therefore do not choose each other and therefore may not even know beforehand who their group members are likely to be. Village banking groups are made up of between 10 and 50 members who meet regularly to provide mutual support. Therefore, neighbours as a group guarantee loans taken by individuals in the group because as individuals they cannot raise the necessary collateral that a bank is likely to require. FINCA using the village banking approach provides working capital to poor people, most of whom are women. The village banking approach fosters communalism and can invigorate entire communities. Though similar to the group-based lending approach, in village banking members are placed in the group by the village bank and they meet at the head office of the village bank. Armendariz and Morduch (2010) suggest that, it is still possible for the costs associated with lending to large groups of people who have no information about each other to be lower compared to utilising an individual lending approach. This is especially the case with village lending where the members are selected by the bank and not by each other and therefore may not know each other.

6.6.1.3 Individual Banking

Individual banking is when the MFI lends to individuals and the individual is responsible for repaying the loan. In this case, the liability rests on the applicant and cannot be passed on to other people. Individual lending is the traditional model employed by banks. Some banks that enter into the microfinance industry still continue to lend on an individual basis. Most MFIs, however, use the group-based lending approach or variants of it. Those who use the group-based lending approach tend to stick to it whilst those who use individual lending approaches also tend to stick to it. Therefore, most MFIs do not mix the various approaches. However, some MFIs such as Grameen are beginning to use individual lending approaches. This is especially used for very successful clients who no longer want to be part of the group they used to be. Research findings indicate that, as MFIs clients become more successful, they would rather opt for the individual loans rather than the traditional group loans.

6.6.2 Credit Risk Management Mechanisms of MFIs

Information asymmetry occurs when the lender does not have adequate information about the borrower. The MFI may not have sufficient information about the loan applicant and this can lead to wrong assessment of the borrower's credit worthiness. Information asymmetry may result in what are known as **adverse selection and moral hazard**.

Adverse selection is when the MFI makes a mistake by selecting a bad borrower or rejecting a good borrower because it does not have sufficient information about the borrower. Moral hazard is that clients use the loans granted to them for a different purpose. For instance, an entrepreneur applies for a loan to acquire equipment for his business and ends up using the loan to buy a car.

Adverse selection and moral hazard have the tendency of increasing the MFI's credit risk. That means loan given to a bad borrower who is likely to default. A borrower who uses a loan obtained for a different purpose is also likely to default. It is therefore necessary to put measures in place that prevents the likelihood of having *lemons* (bad credit risks) whilst actively seeking and rewarding *diamonds* (good borrowers). One approach to reducing likelihood of loan default is to demand collateral before lending. However, clients of MFIs are mostly not in the position to provide such collateral. Therefore, MFIs have been innovative in using what is known as *collateral substitutes*. Collateral substitutes include, group-based lending and joint liability, graduated loans based on prompt payments, frequent collections, compulsory savings, loan guarantors and referees, regular meetings with clients.

MFIs are exposed to several risks in the effort to bring financial services to the doorsteps of the underprivileged in society. One of the most potent risks that confront MFIs is credit risk. This is the risk that loans and advances given out will not be paid back by the recipients. That is, the loan and interest components are not paid back. Also, credit risk occurs even if the loans are repaid but are not paid on schedule. Due to the fact that most MFIs do not demand collateral, credit risk may be heightened if payments are not made or are not made on time. The methods discussed help to reduce information asymmetries and make it more likely that advances given out will be recovered. The mechanisms adopted include group-based lending, graduated loan schemes, frequent collection of loan instalments, compulsory savings, guarantors and referees, and collection of information on clients.

6.6.2.1 Group-Based Lending

MFIs, unlike banks, lend usually through group schemes. In this case, members voluntarily choose the people they want to be in their group. The group-based lending mechanism was pioneered by Muhammed Yunus's Grameen Bank. Grameen gave loans to small groups with a maximum membership of five people. The group-based lending scheme has now become popular among MFIs the world over. There are several advantages of using a group-based lending scheme. The members of the group screen and monitor themselves therefore internalising the screening and monitoring costs. The screen and monitoring costs are therefore transferred from the MFI to the groups. Members will only select other members or want to be in a group with these other members because they are of good integrity and they believe they will honour their obligations. Therefore, members of the group screen each other before they join a group.

The MFI can give loans to some members but not all the members of the group at a particular time. Therefore, until members who have received loans pay up, other members of the group will not have access to credit. Therefore, the other members who are in line to receive loans have incentives to monitor their colleagues and impress on them to pay their loans when they are due. The members of the group are jointly and severally liable for the loans that they take out. This reduces the risk for the MFI because if one member of the group is going to default, the group as a whole is likely to pay up so that they are not cut off from future credit opportunities. Therefore the group-based lending mechanism can serve to reduce the credit risk that an MFI is exposed to. Group-based lending mechanisms are likely to be successful in countries that are more social in nature and are based on an extended family system. It is instructive to note that such group-based lending practices may not be suitable in a typical European or American city. This is because these countries tend to value and promote individualism. Therefore, though the group-based lending mechanism has proven successful in Asia and Africa it may not be that effective everywhere else on the globe.

6.6.2.2 Graduated Loan Schemes

MFIs also use graduated loans also known as progressive lending mechanisms to reduce their exposure to credit or default risk. With a graduated loan payment scheme the amount initially granted by the MFI is very low. Based on the repayment record of the client the MFI may increase the amount of loans that are granted. Clients that are faithful and religious in payments are advanced larger cedi amounts when they next apply for a loan. The client is therefore motivated to repay as that will entitle them to receive larger amounts the next time around. Graduated lending schemes are therefore based on repeated lending. It ensures that the MFI gets to know trustworthy clients therefore reducing information asymmetry and its associated hazards. Therefore, graduated lending schemes reduce the risk of lending larger sums to clients who are not trustworthy and who are more likely to default (bad credit risks). Graduated lending programmes are one of the reasons explaining why the majority of the loan portfolio of MFIs is advanced to women. MFIs realised that women borrowers are more likely to pay loans advanced compared to their male counterparts.

6.6.2.3 Frequent Collection of Loan Instalments

MFIs also use a unique mechanism in terms of collection and repayments. Loan repayments are scheduled to be made frequently, usually weekly. The loans granted therefore become repayable usually after a week when the loan has been granted. Also, apart from the frequent collection periods, MFIs usually grant loans for shorter durations compared to the durations used by banks. Frequent collection periods and short durations therefore may mean the loan recipient may have to rely on general income sources to settle the loan received. Regular repayments ensure that the amounts outstanding are reduced significantly and that the client is not tempted to waste free cash flows. Such a mechanism instils discipline into clients and can help them develop a savings culture. However, such regular payments may not be suitable for all businesses. Such regular payments are likely to affect start-up businesses. This is because the business is unlikely to generate significant cash flows in such short periods to meet loan repayments. Therefore, microfinance programmes based on such schemes are unlikely to promote entrepreneurship in the underprivileged and socially and economically excluded areas.

Also microfinance programmes based on such repayment schemes are unlikely to be suitable for seasonal businesses. Farmers are a good example of such seasonal businesses. The farmer has to plant and then wait for some time before harvesting. The major cash flows of a farmer are therefore generated after the harvesting season. Loan repayments therefore may be difficult prior to the harvesting season. Some MFIs have responded by making payments more flexible, though still requiring regular payments. Therefore a farmer, for example, will pay lower amounts during pre-harvest seasons and pay larger amounts post-harvest.

6.6.2.4 Compulsory Savings

MFIs may require customers to keep compulsory savings with them. Savings schemes may however be voluntary for some other MFIs. MFIs will usually require that clients save with them because it reduces their risk and credit exposure. This is because the savings can be used as collateral for loans that have been given out. It must be noted, however, that savings and taking deposits from clients are not legal in all jurisdictions. For example until May 2008 deposit-taking by MFIs in Kenya was illegal. Deposit-taking is legal in countries that pioneered the microfinance revolution, such as Bangladesh.

6.6.2.5 Guarantors and Referees

Also, MFIs may require guarantors and referees for loans that are given out. In the case of guarantors they guarantee that if the client fails to pay up, then they will make good the debt owed by the client. Referees testify to the good behaviour and reputation of the client. Using guarantors and referees can help reduce the credit risk of an MFI. This is so because guarantors provide a useful safety net, whilst the information provided by referees reduces information asymmetry problems. Also because the guarantor becomes liable if the client fails to pay, he/she is likely to encourage and put pressure on the clients to make good their debts to the MFI.

6.6.2.6 Collecting Information on Clients

MFIs also tend to reduce credit risk by seeking to build solid relationships with their clients. This enables them to collect and gather valuable information that may prove useful in subsequent lending decisions. MFIs also use Know Your Client (KYC) procedures to get to know their clients better. Therefore, they visit the homes and businesses of clients to ensure that the information with which they have been provided is accurate. During such visits they can find out, for example, the integrity as well as reputation of clients from people who are likely to have such information, such as neighbours. Relationships can also be built by having loan officers and other staff periodically join the meetings of lending groups. At such meetings, the loan officer can learn of the difficulties that clients are facing.

They can also offer advice as to how challenges being encountered by the groups can be overcome. Being involved in the activities of clients therefore improves the MFIs' understanding of the business of their clients and this assists them in the critical function of monitoring. MFIs may also organise training seminars for their clients and groups to acquaint them with vital business skills. Such training can be provided on business management and basic entrepreneur skills. These training programmes improve the business skill sets of the clients involved and therefore make it more likely that clients will repay loans granted them.

6.7 Challenges Affecting Microfinance Institutions

Despite the contributions of MFIs to the economies of countries, especially the developing ones, there are challenges that seem to hamper the necessary impact that they are expected to make. The sector's growth has been slower than anticipated due to some constraints and challenges that have tended to hinder their operations of the MFIs. These challenges can be identified as follows.

Lack of Human Capacity Microfinance is a specialised area that tends to combine banking with social objectives, and capacity requirements to be built at all levels, from financial institutions through the supervisory and regulatory bodies and information systems, to government development entities and donor agencies. However, in most African countries, MFIs often lack the necessary technical expertise to operate effectively and efficiently. There is the lack of expertise on the part of the human capital base of most of these institutions, and these shortcomings cause them to perform under capacity.

Inadequate Infrastructural Support MFIs also lack the necessary infrastructure such as electricity, information technology, telecommunication and good roads to support their operations. In most cases, the MFIs are located in rural areas without the necessary infrastructural base to support such institutions. The MFIs often experience high cost of operation due to the inadequate infrastructure base. This is challenging and tends to limit the operations of the MFIs whose existence is to support the rural folks who do not have access to financial services from the traditional or conventional financial institutions.

High Risk The level of risk associated with the operations of MFIs is very high. We mentioned earlier that MFIs experience information asymmetry because they may not have adequate information about the borrower. The MFI may not have access to documented financial information from the potential borrowers, who most often do not keep proper records. Therefore, MFI supervisors are unable to do a good assessment of the credit worthiness of their clients in order to extend credit. In addition, considering the intense competition among MFIs, they have started expanding and diversifying their financial products. Some MFIs are providing individual loans in addition to group loans and/or fixed asset as well as working capital loans. They are also growing fast to gain a greater market share and enter new markets. These developments result in the MFIs taking on excessive risk, thereby increasing their chances of failure.

Lack of Coordination In most developing countries, there appears to be no formal body or institution with the responsibility of coordinating all activities in connection with microfinance, neither is there a common platform or forum for engaging stakeholders of the microfinance sector on policy and programme issues. This has resulted in fragmentation, duplication and inadequate collaboration among donor agencies, development partners, service providers, practitioners and microfinance clients. In addition, the lack of coordination in the microfinance subsector makes the flow of credit information on clients difficult. Clients take advantage of this lapse and tend to take loans from several MFIs without repaying. This is because there is no way they can track the credit history of clients.

Lack of Adequate Information and Dissemination Generally, there is lack of adequate information on MFIs, their operations and clients in most developing countries. There seems to be no uniformity in the approaches and methodology used in obtaining information at the national and institutional levels, thus making it difficult to centrally monitor progress and developments in the sector. There is a lack of a well-defined reporting system by both the government and development partners with respect to their interventions, and an appropriate database used for decision-making and planning is also lacking or is at best inadequate. In addition, the lack of common benchmarks, of universal methods required for measuring and disseminating information further limit the performance of the sector. Therefore, the lack of adequate and reliable information regarding outreach with respect to its depth and breadth remains one of the problems in the microfinance sector.

Lack of Adequate Funding There are essentially three main sources of funding for MFIs, including the institutions themselves, government and development partners. MFIs mostly experience lack of adequate funding and the different sources also come with some conditions, thus distorting the market in some instances. Donor or governmental funding of the activities of MFIs is mostly characterised with conditionalities, which hinder the smooth operations of the MFIs. There is a general call for the need to establish a central microfinance fund, which MFIs can access for on-lending.

Weak Regulation and Supervision In most developing countries, especially in Africa, the legal and regulatory framework of MFIs are weak or not in existence at all. Due to the absence of the necessary regulatory framework, the clients or customers of these MFIs feel unprotected in terms of their dealings with these institutions. This prevents people from patronising the products and services offered by MFIs. MFIs tend to exhibit different characteristics, making it difficult to bring all of them under a single regulatory regime. Some MFIs are deposit-taking, while others such as the financial NGOs are not deposit-taking. Deposit-taking institutions, for instance, require more stringent prudential regulatory requirements than non-deposit-taking ones do. However, in most African countries deposit-taking MFIs appear to come under the same regulation, like mainstream depository institutions such as banks and are regulated by the central bank. Such a regulatory arrangement does not address the unique circumstances of MFIs.

Inadequate Monitoring and Evaluation MFIs do not currently have adequate capacity to effectively monitor and evaluate programmes and activities. A framework for monitoring and evaluation is also non-existent at the national level to direct practitioners on their activities. The use of different monitoring and evaluation frameworks in different programmes makes it difficult to carry out a comparative evaluation of projects and programmes in order to ascertain their impact on the performance of MFIs and their clients.

6.8 Banks and the Microfinance Market

Banks in the past avoided operating in the microfinance market. However, banks in developing countries are currently beginning to consider microfinance as both a valuable public relations tool and as a profitable venture and have started focusing their attention on the microfinance market. Since the early 1990s, there has been a trend whereby mainstream banks have found it necessary and desirable to enter the market for microfinance. Banks are finding that the level of competition in mainstream banking is increasing and therefore regard microfinance as a new area of growth and profitability. Competition leads to dwindling margins and therefore banks in highly competitive markets may want to enter the microfinance market. Also, the deregulation of markets across the globe has meant that banks can charge market interest rates and that the high reserve requirements have been relaxed. Also, some NGOs have also entered the microfinance market. Over time, these successful NGOs and other MFIs have gradually evolved into regular banks.

The entry of banks into the microfinance industry will serve the interest of the poor. Banks have a lot to offer and are likely to have competitive advantages over traditional MFIs. Banks are well placed to compete in the microfinance market. Banks, for example, have a huge financial base and muscle and therefore do not need to rely on funding from donors. They also have large infrastructure in terms of IT systems and a broad branch network, which is likely to be national in nature. Generally, banks that are more oriented towards retail banking are more likely to be successful in the microfinance market compared to banks that focus largely on corporate banking. Banks are also likely to have good reputation, which is essential in providing financial services of any kind.

Also, banks have quality human resources, though these may also turn out to be a challenge, because the bank culture that such employees will be used to is likely not to be suitable for microfinance operations.

In recognition of the roles that banks can play in the fight against poverty, international agencies and donors are providing banks with technical support, training on best practices in microfinance as well as in some cases providing 'cheap money' to encourage banks to enter into the microfinance market.

6.8.1 Differences Between Banks and Microfinance Institutions

Banks generally operate in a completely different environment than do MFIs. Banks have objectives, need policies and capabilities different from those of MFIs. For instance, in terms of objectives, banks are mostly profit oriented whereas some MFIs, especially financial NGOs, do not have profit as their motive.

Banks usually offer large products and services aimed mainly at corporate organisations and individuals in order to earn high returns on their capital. MFIs, on the other hand, provide microfinancial services to micro-enterprises and poor borrowers.

MFIs tend to provide tailor made services to their clients. They provide a doorstep service to their clients because time is of essence to the rural poor clients, as most of them depend on small businesses or daily wages for their existence. On the contrary, banks would not consider doorstep services as very efficient in their operations.

Clients of banks are usually expected to present collateral in the form of landed property or a guaranteed income stream in order to qualify for bank loans. Clients of MFIs are mainly low-income borrowers who are not in the position to present collateral and therefore do not qualify to access formal banking services. The MFI therefore relies on collateral substitutes such as group-based lending and joint liability, graduated loans based on prompt payments, frequent collections, compulsory savings, loan guarantors and referees, and regular meetings with clients.

MFIs usually employ staff from the local community. They also tend to have good knowledge about the local community since they establish a deeper relationship with the clients in the community. Banks recruit professionals who do not necessarily live in the local community. They do not have the same level of closeness with their clients as the MFIs do.

6.8.2 Complimentary Roles of Banks and Microfinance Institutions

Both banks and MFIs can work together to achieve the goals of financial inclusion. Microfinance is distributed primarily through MFIs (including micro-credit banks, NGOs, cooperatives, etc.), to help the rural groups directly. Banks have access to huge funds but tend to focus on large borrowers. It is more practical, effective and efficient for banks to lend to MFIs, which will in turn on-lend to micro-borrowers. The MFIs can thus become the extended arms of the banks to achieve the larger objective of financial inclusion, which banks find difficult to achieve on their own.

Rural clients (would) like to have micro-savings, micro-credit, micro-insurance and pension products from one source. So, MFI can play an agent role or a point of contact for a bank with the rural masses. It would be more commercially viable for banks to deal with the rural poor through MFIs rather than opening their own branches.

Banks can also appoint MFIs as Business Correspondent for distributing their products and services to the rural clients. This could be an efficient means of providing banking services, since the MFIs have a good network outreach.

A strong collaboration between a bank and an MFI can be very beneficial for both parties instead of them competing with each other. Such collaboration can result in a win-win situation for both banks and MFIs, as banks are looking for a footprint, while MFIs are looking for sources of funding. Both parties depend on each other's strength for their mutual benefits. Such benefits can/will ultimately translate into the economic development of the country. Banks and MFIs can have a complimentary role in taking advantage of this opportunity by reaching out to the rural clients.

6.8.3 Approaches to Banks' Entry into the Microfinance Market

In spite of the constraints to banks' entry into the microfinance market, they can still enter and operate successfully in the microfinance market. To be successful, banks seeking to operate in the microfinance market must consider the following:

- Design appropriate legal and organisational structures. The legal structure must address the framework for taking non-traditional collateral or collateral substitutes.

- Adopt appropriate organisational cultures that will increase their chances of success in this tough market.
- Be innovative in developing new products as well as customising existing products to fit the microfinance market.
- Attract and retain appropriate staff. Significant costs will have to be incurred in training new staff. Attracting staff from MFIs operating successfully can also beef up the human resource capabilities of banks' microfinance outfit.
- Determine by what means and to what extent the bank's role in the microfinance industry will be. This is a strategic decision as the methodology employed will affect the success rate of the MFI for a very long time. It is also a strategic decision because it affects the products and markets that the bank will deal in and operate in.

The approaches that banks can employ in order to enter the microfinance market are classified as direct approaches and indirect approaches.

6.8.3.1 Direct Approaches

The direct approaches of entering the microfinance market involve the direct provision of microfinance services by banks and these include establishing an internal microfinance unit, setting up a specialised financial institution and setting up a microfinance service company.

Establishing an Internal Microfinance Unit As identified earlier, one approach a bank can adopt is to set up an internal unit within the bank. The microfinance unit is therefore housed within the bank's existing internal structures and can be linked with other departments of the banks such as retail banking. Under this approach, the microfinance unit is not regarded as a separate legal entity, and it is also not regulated differently from the bank. Such an approach has, however, mostly been found not to be successful. This is because the unit is likely not to have enough autonomy to succeed. Also, the unit will be highly influenced by the existing culture of the bank and is unlikely to adopt the best practices that have been found to work in the microfinance industry, such as group-based lending. Banks that already operate in outreach areas are at an advantage. This approach is the most labour intensive for bank employees, and it is also known as **downscaling**. Currently, a number of banks have set up internal units that focus on providing financial services to MSMEs.

Setting up a Specialised Financial Institution Setting up a specialised financial institution is also a direct approach by which a bank can directly enter the microfinance market. This requires setting up a separate subsidiary as a separate legal entity with its own governance and management structures, to carry out microfinance business. The subsidiary provides a full array of microfinance services and is therefore licensed and regulated differently from the bank. It may be fully owned or partly owned by the parent bank. This is likely to be more successful as it overcomes the weaknesses identified when the microfinance operation is integrated in the bank's existing infrastructure. Though this approach will be more costly because of the separate infrastructure and the additional bureaucratic structures that will have to be put in place, it is likely to be more successful. This is because the subsidiary is likely to have the autonomy to develop the culture necessary to operate successfully in the microfinance market. Again, such an approach makes it easier to develop separate incentive schemes for the loan officers and other staff of the subsidiary. This approach is also referred to as the Greenfield option. Unicredit Savings and Loans Company Ltd., a subsidiary of Unibank Ltd., and EB-ACCION Savings and Loans Company Ltd., a subsidiary of Ecobank Ghana Ltd., are typical examples in Ghana. Rafiki Microfinance Bank, a subsidiary of Chase Bank Kenya Ltd. is an example in Kenya. These subsidiaries specialise in providing microfinance services to micro-enterprises.

Setting Up a Microfinance Service Company Another approach by which a bank can directly enter the microfinance market is by setting up a service company. Under the service company model, the bank establishes a non-banking institution with a separate corporate identity with its own governance and management structures. The service company provides the bank with support services, including credit administration services, whilst the bank provides the funding that is required. The loans that are given therefore represent direct assets of the bank. The service company may be fully or partly owned by the parent bank. One advantage with this model is that the parent bank can involve other equity investors with expertise in the provision of microfinance services. An example in Ghana is the HFC Boafo Microfinance Services Ltd., a service company of the HFC Bank (Ghana) Ltd.

6.8.3.2 Indirect Approaches

The indirect approaches of entering the microfinance market involve working through existing microfinance providers and these include outsourcing microfinance operations, giving loans to existing MFIs, and providing infrastructure and services to MFIs. Each approach has its own advantages and disadvantages. We shall discuss the indirect approaches one after the other.

Outsourcing Microfinance Operations One of the indirect approaches that a bank can use to facilitate its involvement in the microfinance industry is to outsource its microfinance operations. In this case, the bank enters into a contractual relationship with an existing MFI to perform micro-lending, micro-insurance, micro-deposit and money transfer services on its behalf. The MFI performs these services in return for a share in interest income and fees on the products and services provided on behalf of the bank. The contractual relationship between the bank and the MFI may be structured in a way that limits the MFIs from providing services on behalf of other banks.

Giving Loans to Existing Microfinance Institutions Another approach that a bank can use is to lend funds to existing MFIs to on-lend. That is, the bank provides loans to existing MFIs to also lend to low-income clients. Funds can be used by the MFI as working and/or lending capital. The advantage with such an approach is that the bank can enter the microfinance market by relying on an existing microfinance institution that knows the terrain better. Another advantage is that the bank does not have to commit administrative and human resources to get involved in the microfinance market. The disadvantage with using this approach is that the problem of information asymmetry is likely to exist between the bank and the MFI that the loan has been extended to. This is because it may be difficult for the bank to determine the actual state or condition of the MFIs such as an NGO engaged in the microfinance business.

Providing Infrastructure and Services to Microfinance Institutions This is an indirect approach where a bank makes its infrastructure and systems available to MFIs for a fee or commission. The bank, for example, can make available its branch network and ATM facilities to the MFI. The bank can also provide front office facilities such as teller services and back office facilities such as cheque clearing and information technology services to the MFI. Sometimes the MFI places its own staff in the branches to serve its clients. The clients may hold accounts with the bank or use the MFI's account at the bank.

6.8.4 Factors that Facilitate the Entry of Banks into Microfinance

Banks may be encouraged to enter into the business of providing microfinance services. The factors that facilitate the entry of banks into the microfinance market are the policy environment, management commitment, administrative mechanism, start-up and funding sources, cost-effectiveness, human resource management, financial products and services, and the role of donors.

Policy Environment A favourable policy environment with respect to the financial sector plays an important role in facilitating banks' entry into microfinance. In a situation where the country is experiencing substantial financial liberalisation, banks are more likely to enter into microfinance than in countries where there are still restrictions on interest rates, reserve requirements and areas banks can operate in. Financial liberalisation makes it possible for banks to charge relatively high interest rates on their microloans and also cover the transaction costs, credit risk and the opportunity costs of funds; thus a more liberal policy serves as an incentive for them to enter the microfinance market. Also, a low reserve requirement can encourage banks to enter into the microfinance market. The lower the reserve requirement, the higher the loanable funds available to banks to lend to microfinance clients.

Management Commitment The extent of commitment to microfinance at the top management and corporate board levels of a bank is necessary for ensuring the successful microfinance operations. The lack of any solid commitment by the board and management will not help in sustaining the bank's microfinance operations after a few years. There are clearly differences in the methodologies adopted by MFIs and mainstream banking and therefore microfinance methodologies may not be appropriate for banking operations. Also, in cases where the microfinance operation is in competition with other divisions or units of the bank for resources, priority is often given to the other units. Therefore, a strong management commitment is necessary for microfinance business of the bank to succeed.

Administrative Mechanism The type of administrative mechanism employed is also very important. There are a number of administrative structures banks often use to carry out microfinance operations and these are:

(a) Fully-independent retail centres which are affiliated to the bank but have their own lending policies, staff and information systems that report to the larger bank.
(b) A system where the bank provides loans through NGOs that serve as intermediary by also on-lending to micro-enterprise clients.
(c) Semi-independent microfinance units providing loans directly and/or having specialised desks in each bank branch, with an assigned microfinance credit officer. Under this structure, administrative and financial functions are integrated into the main bank.
(d) Fully integrated operations, wherein credit officers of the banks also handle micro-enterprise clients. The financial and administrative systems tend to be fully integrated into the bank.

Banks are mostly interested in an administrative structure that allows them to provide microfinance services through a separate window or bank branch office focusing on only microfinance clients. This separation is useful as it enables both personnel of the bank and the clients to clearly distinguish between the services involved in mainstream banking and microfinance. In addition, banks with specialised independent microfinance units or subsidiaries are better at instituting separate lending policies for their microfinance business. The microfinance unit is therefore able to operate independently without being influenced by the parent bank.

Start-Up and Funding Sources Start-up and funding sources are also an important factor to consider. The ability of the bank to raise the required funding for its microfinance operations will facilitate its entry into the microfinance market. The willingness of the bank for instance to use its resources to subsidise microfinance operations by covering operating cost, and its ability to access donor funds, make it easier for the bank to enter the microfinance business. Generally, where the start-up and operating cost can easily be covered with available resources, this may make microfinance attractive for banks.

Cost-Effectiveness Cost-effectiveness also influences a bank's entry into the microfinance market. Banks consider the costs of providing microfinance in relation to the profitability. It is easier to clearly see the costs of the microfinance operation when the microfinance operation is separated from the mainstream banking activities. The income and expenses of the microfinance operation should be considered differently in order to ascertain the cost-effectiveness of microfinance activity. When the cost is lower in comparison with profits, microfinance will be attractive for banks to consider as an area of business.

Human Resource Management Microfinance services are labour intensive in nature and this poses a key challenge to banks in terms of the recruitment, training and motivation of staff. Most banks often prefer to recruit personnel outside the main bank for their microfinance operations and will typically hire fresh university graduates with little experience. These young graduates are better able to learn the special mission and practices of the microfinance business. A performance-based incentive system used in microfinance for loan officers can create tension between microfinance staff and bank staff, since loan officers of the bank do not enjoy such bonus remuneration. Some banks have tried to manage this tension by largely keeping salaries at similar levels for both groups of staff. They ensure that salaries and other incentives of/for microfinance staff do not exceed salaries of other bank staff. Some banks also give the same incentives meant for microfinance staff to all bank staff, thus eliminating any avenue for tension.

Financial Products and Services Largely, financial products and services provided by banks are different from those provided by microfinance, though there might be some similarities. Banks that are able to adjust and modify their products and services to suit the microfinance market are more likely to excel in their microfinance operations. This calls for banks to be able to institute some microfinance techniques and innovations. It is important for banks to modify their procedures and tailor their products and services in order to make them more attractive and suitable for clients of microfinance. The easier it is to tailor these banking products and services, the easier it is to find/make microfinance attractive.

Role of Donors Donors play an important role in influencing banks to venture into the business of microfinance. Donors, for instance, can impress on governments to remove restrictive financial regulations, such as interest rate ceilings, tight reserve requirements and targeted credit schemes. These changes are helpful for microfinance providers to operate in a more open and competitive market so they can cover operating costs, risks and opportunity costs of capital. Donors can also support banks to enter into the business by providing funding and free technical assistance. Such assistance from donors can be very useful in facilitating banks' attempt to enter into microfinance.

6.8.5 Benefits of Banks' Entry into Microfinance

A number of benefits can accrue to banks for entering into the microfinance market. One of the benefits is the fact that it opens a huge unexplored market. Banks' entry into the microfinance business opens up a huge unexplored market. Such banks are able to provide other banking services that they did not previously provide. For instance, a bank that focused on corporate banking can now provide retail banking by entering into microfinance.

Another benefit is that it creates a pool of bankable customers. Banks that enter into microfinance can build a good pool of microfinance customers who can later become customers of their mainstream banking services. Through the provision of microfinance services to the poor and micro-enterprises, the bank is able to grow these poor borrowers who can become good customers to the bank's mainstream banking services.

Also, banks' entry into microfinance brings about growth and diversification of banks' portfolio. We know from investment fundamentals, that by diversifying your investment portfolio, you are able to reduce your risk and increase your returns. By entering into the business of microfinance, banks are able to diversify their investment and as a result minimise their risk and maximise their returns.

Bank can leverage their human and infrastructure resources to enter into microfinance. Banks tend to have a strong human resource and infrastructure base. They already have experienced bank staff, office building, IT systems, broad branch network and so on. They therefore leverage on these to provide microfinance services to low-income customers. Considering that banks already have such infrastructure, they may be in a better position to provide more efficient microfinance services.

Another benefit is that it enhances banks' corporate image. Through the provision of microfinance services, banks are perceived as good corporate citizens that are also interested in serving the poor and micro-enterprises. We have learnt that low-income earners and micro-enterprises generally have difficulties in accessing mainstream banking services because of their inability to satisfy lending requirement. Therefore, banks that seek to serve the interests of such low-income borrowers tend thereby to enhance their corporate image.

6.8.6 Constraints to Banks' Entry into the Microfinance Market

Though banks may have special advantages that may make them successful as providers of microfinance services, there are several constraints that have prevented banks from entering the microfinance market. We discuss these constraints in the following paragraphs.

High Credit Risk A microfinance operation is associated with high credit risk. Poor borrowers do not present adequate information about themselves, and they also lack the necessary collateral to qualify for loans, therefore increasing the credit risk. Credit risk is generally high when lending to borrowers who do not have regular cash flows, cannot provide collateral and cannot provide financial statements and forecasts of future performance. A bank is likely to expose itself to significant credit risks by entering into the market for microfinance services. Banks recognise that the microfinance market is risky compared to what they are used to. In mainstream banking, the credit risk is lower because banks require adequate information and collateral from their borrowers before they extend credit. Therefore, bankers would want to avoid the microfinance market due to the high credit risk associated with micro-lending.

Lending Methodology One of the main constraints that banks are likely to encounter is that the lending methodologies used in traditional banking are not necessarily suited to providing financial services to micro-enterprises and the poor. In fact banks are likely to avoid this group of clients. This is because banks are unlikely to have the appropriate screening and monitoring mechanisms to provide small loans to such poor borrowers. Most banks that have entered the microfinance market tend to continue to rely on individual lending. The popular mode of lending by traditional MFIs is through the group-based lending approach and this has received wide recommendation among various stakeholders. It is also important to note that whilst traditional bank lending appreciates the role of collateral, MFIs usually do not rely on collateral but rather on collateral substitutes and the good reputation of the client or borrower. Microfinance is a specialised area and may require banks to be innovative in adopting the appropriate lending methodology. Most banks, however, lack the skill and lending methodology to reach and retain low-income clients who need micro-credit or small loans.

Cost-Effectiveness Provision of microfinance services, by nature, is more expensive compared to conventional banking services. It can be very expensive to process several small loans and mobilise deposits on a small scale. The transaction costs associated with granting small loans is usually the same as giving large loans and therefore the per unit transaction cost is higher in the case of the small loans. For example why should a bank grant very small loans of about US$600, which costs the same as giving a loan of US$400,000? Thus, banks cannot provide microfinance services by using their traditional bank mechanisms with the related overhead structures, which makes it difficult for them to operate at lower costs, increase the productivity of staff and expand their micro-loan portfolio.

Pricing Banks may initially encounter some difficulty, from a public relations point of view, in increasing the price of their loans for poor borrowers. Without appropriate pricing, the bank will not be able to make any profit from microfinance and therefore that aspect of its business will not grow within the bank. Usually, the conventional bank pricing models may not be appropriate for microfinance operations that typically involve small transactions. Therefore, the conventional pricing model may not give a true reflection of the profitability of microfinance. In order to price a microfinance product more correctly, it is useful to have a sense of the market prices quoted by other microfinance providers, as well as their product's cost structure. Where the bank does not have a good understanding of the pricing models in microfinance operation, it will constitute a constraint to their entry into the area.

Institutional Commitment Banks that may show interest in the microfinance market may be doing so, not based on their institutional objective, but based on the recommendations of some visionary board members. The main goal of banks is to make profits and deliver value to shareholders. The goal of a bank is more profit oriented compared to MFIs, which have a twin objective of profits and making a social impact. Therefore, the level of social commitment that is required to operate in the microfinance market is unlikely to be seen in the case of banks. The board of the banks must therefore be very interested in microfinance and champion this course in a bank. If such a commitment is not there, banks may not enter the microfinance market. Also, there are opportunity costs with operating a microfinance business. The microfinance unit of the bank may have to compete with other divisions of the bank for scarce resources and therefore without that institutional commitment, the microfinance unit will not survive.

Organisational Structure A bank's organisational structure may also limit its ability and its success rate in its microfinance programme. Formal or traditional banks tend to operate a centralised system. However, operating a microfinance programme within this centralised system is likely to prove problematic. Operating a microfinance unit may require that the bank's organisational structure be designed in such a way that the microfinance outfit operates as a separate subsidiary. The main constraint is that banks find it difficult to integrate microfinance within the structure of a bank that does not focus on providing financial services to low-income clients. We will return to this discussion when we look at approaches banks can adopt to enter the microfinance market in the next section.

Human Resources Bank must be able to attract, train and retain quality and specialised staff in its attempt to penetrate the microfinance market. Attracting such specialised staff from existing MFIs that are operating successfully can serve to complement the bank's microfinance human resources. Some banks find that employing and training fresh graduates from universities may be useful since this staff group will not have been exposed to the traditional banking culture, which can be a hinder to the microfinance operation. Banks will have to incur high costs to train staff so that they can operate effectively and efficiently in this market niche. Apart from the problem of attracting the right personnel and training them, designing performance-based incentives is also critical. Issues regarding recruitment, training and designing performance-related incentives are very essential and therefore need to be properly considered.

Socio-Economic and Cultural Barriers The culture prevailing in a bank can lead to top management and mid-level management not really understanding and appreciating how microfinance works. The culture prevailing in a bank is likely to be very different from the culture that pertains in MFIs. Underestimating the subtle operations of this culture difference is likely to lead to disaster for a bank that does not appreciate these differences. Due to the cultural and economic circumstances of low-income clients, they may feel reluctant to approach a bank. This may partly be due to the fact that, poor and rural folk are likely to be illiterate and therefore are likely to find interactions with banks and the use of modern banking delivery mechanisms (such as ATMs) difficult. Challenges are likely to occur as the bank changes its systems, processes and procedures to serve the microfinance market. It can usually take about three or more years for a bank to actually get its microfinance programme running efficiently and profitably.

Regulatory Compliance Another constraint that banks may encounter in the microfinance market is inadequate and inappropriate regulations. Such inadequate and inappropriate regulations may prove problematic for a bank, especially since the operations of a microfinance unit may need differential regulations or regulatory regimes. It certainly may not be subject to the same regulations as the mainstream banking division. Therefore, complying with the reporting and regulatory requirements in order to reflect the bank's microfinance operations may require new procedures altogether.

6.9 Summary and Conclusions

In this chapter, we discussed microfinance intervention. We mentioned that microfinance is the provision of financial services to low-income clients and micro-enterprises that often do not have access to formal banking services. These financial services include the provision of micro-credit, micro-savings, micro-insurance and funds transfer services.

We also examined the important of microfinance in a number of respects, including improved economic activities and job creation, asset building, assisting microfinance clients to manage their risk, smoothing consumption level, improvement in education levels among the poor, promotion of gender equality and women's empowerment, and reduction in child mortality and improved health and nutrition. In spite of the benefits of microfinance, there are criticisms associated with microfinance and these include lack of knowledge about microfinance services, inability of the poor to offer a marketable collateral for loans, perceived high risk associated with lending to the poor, high transaction costs involved in small loans and high interest rates.

The chapter also examined the operation of MFIs. We defined MFIs as institutions that provide microfinance services and they are generally considered a subset of alternative financial institutions. They provide financial intermediation services, social intermediation services, enterprise development services and social services. Considering the important role MFIs play, it is essential that they are operationally and financially sound. The measures used to measure the sustainability of an MFI include the SDI, the OSS ratio and the PAR measure. These dimensions measure subsidy dependence, operational sustainability and finally, financial sustainability. There are several factors that determine whether an MFI is likely to succeed or fail in its endeavour to provide financial services to low-income earners, and these include leadership quality, talented staff, innovative products and services, a reliance on subsidies, sound financial management, a diversified clientele base and regulation.

We looked at the lending models and credit risk management mechanisms used by MFIs. The lending models adopted by MFIs are group-based lending, village banking and individual banking. The group-based lending model is based on the MFI lending to members in a group but the entire group is liable if a single member of the group defaults or does not pay the loan that has been taken. In this case, members of the group are jointly liable for paying back the loan. If a single member of the group defaults, the MFI has the right to restrict future credit to the entire group until they pay up. The village banking model is based on invitation to people who want loans to come and write their names. Once a certain number has been reached, the people on the list are used to form a group for the loan. Individual banking is when the MFI lends to individuals and the individual is responsible for repaying the loan. In the process of lending to clients, MFIs face credit risk, which needs to be properly managed. The mechanisms adopted by MFIs in managing their risks include group-based lending, graduated loan schemes, frequent collection of loan instalments, compulsory savings, guarantors and referees, and collecting of information on clients. The growth of MFIs has been slower than anticipated, because of some constraints and challenges that have hindered their operations and these include the lack of institutional and human capacity, inadequate infrastructural support, high risk, lack of coordination, lack of adequate information and dissemination, lack of adequate funding, weak regulations and supervision, and inadequate monitoring and evaluation.

In this chapter, we also examined banks' participation in the microfinance market. Banks in the past tended to shy away from providing microfinance services, but in recent times, they are beginning to consider microfinance as a viable area of business. There are direct and indirect approaches banks can adopt in entering the microfinance market. The direct approaches include, establishing an internal microfinance unit, setting up a specialised financial institution, and setting up a microfinance service company. The indirect approaches include, outsourcing microfinance operations, giving loans to existing MFIs and providing infrastructure and services to MFIs. The factors that facilitate banks' entry into the microfinance market include the policy environment, management commitment, administrative mechanisms, start-up and funding sources, cost-effectiveness, human resource management, financial products and services, and the role of donors. The benefits banks can derive by entering into the microfinance business include: opening a huge unexplored market, creating a pool of bankable customers, bringing about growth and diversification of banks' portfolio, leveraging banks' human and infrastructure resources, and enhancing the banks' corporate image. Though banks may have advantages that may make them succeed as providers of microfinance services, they are constrained by a number of issues, including high credit risk, lending methodology, cost-effectiveness, pricing, institutional commitment, organisational structure, human resources, socio-economic and cultural barriers, and regulatory compliance.

Discussion Questions and Problems

1. Discuss the importance of microfinance for micro-enterprises.
2. What are some of the problems associated with microfinance?
3. Describe the products and services MFIs provide.
4. Discuss the functions of MFIs in small business development.
5. Discuss the factors that affect the success and sustainability of MFIs.
6. Explain the lending models used by MFIs in extending credit to micro-enterprises.
7. Discuss the significance of group lending in microfinance.
8. Explain the credit risk management mechanisms used by MFIs.
9. Discuss the challenges confronting the growth of MFIs in Africa.
10. The issue of regulation has been identified as a major challenge confronting MFIs in Africa. Discuss this issue with specific examples.
11. Identify five basic differences between banks and MFIs.
12. How can MFI complement the functions of banks?
13. Discuss the approaches banks can adopt in operating in the microfinance market.
14. Identify the factors that influence banks' entry into the microfinance market. What are the benefits to a bank that decides to provide microfinance services?
15. What are the challenges confronting banks that wish to enter the microfinance market in Africa?
16. Consider the following financial data of Leery Microfinance Limited:

Table A.6.1 Financial data of Leery Microfinance Limited

Details	US$
Operating income	275,000
Financial expense	47,000
Net impairment loss, gross loan portfolio	53,000
Operating expense	122,000
Gross loan portfolio	125,000
Delinquency + 1 month or more	14,000
Net subsidy	26,000
Interest rate charged on loans = 18 %	

Compute the SDI, OSS and PAR of Leery Microfinance Limited. What do the numbers represent?

7

Public Sector Interventions and Small Businesses

Learning Objectives
By the end of this chapter, you should be able to:

- explain the channels through which government supports small businesses
- explain the rationale for public sector interventions
- discuss the role of the public sector in MSME development
- identify government- and donor-supported funding schemes

7.1 Introduction

Considering the important role played by MSMEs in the economic development of countries, governments, through their public sector, provide support and also implement policies and programmes aimed at improving the economic environment and opportunities for MSMEs.

Prior efforts to promote MSMEs in developing countries focused mainly on direct assistance programmes, which were typically started by state or parastatal agencies. In the late 1960s, for instance, Kenya and Tanzania were part of the first African countries to have established industrial estates, while governments in Botswana, Kenya and Ghana, had also introduced entrepreneurial training programmes to support the development of MSMEs in their respective countries.

These efforts, however, were not in tandem with general industrialisation policies laid down in the development plans of these countries. These were

J.Y. Abor, *Entrepreneurial Finance for MSMEs*,
DOI 10.1007/978-3-319-34021-0_7

welfare considerations that rather dominated economic efficiency, resulting from the polarisation of policy-making that separated the MSME sector development from mainstream industrial policies. MSMEs consequently became potential employment generators, means of achieving an evenly distributed growth across regions as well as addressing the issue of the concentration of economic power by larger firms. In the 1980s, MSME development was seen as a strategic initiative tied to the policies aimed at mitigating the negative impact of structural adjustment.

The type of support and the rationale for these support initiatives have, however, changed over time. This chapter discusses public sector interventions in the support of MSMEs. We first discuss the channels through which government provides support for MSMEs. We then discuss the rationale for such interventions and the role of the public sector in MSME development. We also discuss key policy choices with respect to entrepreneurship and SMEs and we discuss the government and donor support programmes for MSMEs.

7.2 Channels of Government Support for MSMEs

Governments provide support to SMEs in three principal ways. These channels include measures aimed at influencing enterprise behaviour and improving the environment for MSMEs and the support provided by intermediary agencies in the promotion of inter-firm linkages and networking, and support also through the government's role in the development of the financial systems aimed at increasing MSMEs' access to financing. These channels are discussed in turn.

7.2.1 Measures Aimed at Influencing Enterprise Behaviour and Improve Environment for MSMEs.

Government can provide support for MSMEs by instituting different incentive schemes such as taxes and subsidies, relaxing regulatory requirements and procurement policies. Taxes and subsidies have been used to facilitate the linkages between large and small enterprises and also to encourage subcontracting between multinational companies and MSMEs. Tax and subsidy schemes are given to large firms who create business opportunities that benefit MSMEs. Subsidies are also used to provide direct support to MSMEs in the areas of R&D and training in marketing and finance. Subsidies can be used to encourage MSMEs to take part in trade fairs. In Brazil for instance, government covers half of trade exhibition costs for small enterprises. Procurement policies can also be used by Government to support MSMEs. Special contracts can be offered to small businesses or MSME associations. The use of procurement policies by government to support MSMEs is commonly used in India and Brazil.

7.2.2 Support Given to Intermediary Agencies to Promote Inter-Firm Linkages and Networking

Another channel of government support for MSMEs is through the provision of support to intermediary agencies. These included state and private agencies that help in the promotion of inter-firm linkages and networking. Government support for the MSME sector has largely focused on improving infrastructure and institutional support. Governments and other international agencies have paid particular attention to the development of the framework required for ensuring fair competition. Governments also support the development of intermediary agencies, including private associations. For example, the Brazilian Micro and Small Business Support Service in Brazil, the Technical Co-Operation Service funds and the Development Partnership Projects in Chile are set up by the governments to encourage participation of the public and private sectors.

7.2.3 Government Policies to Encourage Financial Institutions to Provide Support for MSMEs.

Governments play a very important role in the development of the financial system designed to provide financial services to small businesses. The role of the government in the financial system has an impact on financial institutions in providing these financial services. Governments can therefore participate in various ways in order to motivate financial institutions to increase their involvement in the provision of financial services to MSMEs. Government's role can be seen in terms of formulation and implementation of policies and regulations targeted at improving access to financial services, and in liberalising interest rate to allow financial institutions such as MFIs to charge commercial rates so they can operate more competitively. Government can intervene by allowing state-owned banks, for instance, to focus on financing MSMEs. Government can also support financial institutions with subsidies that can increase the number of MSMEs they can extend credit to at lower cost. Such support from government increases financial institutions' participation in the provision of finance to MSMEs.

7.3 Rationale for Public Sector Interventions

The reasons for public sector interventions in assisting the MSME sector are varied. These interventions are geared towards improving the business environment, assisting MSMEs meet financing requirements, making the financial system more accessible to MSMEs and increasing the supply of finance through the non-financial private sector. We discuss these issues one after the other.

7.3.1 Improving Business Conditions

The public sector intervenes to improve business conditions for MSMEs in their operations by ensuring an enhanced information environment, an effective legal system and an efficient fiscal regime. Proper information is very important for investors and lenders in assessing the economic viability of firms. This can be achieved by adopting clear accounting standards, setting up independent, competent and reputable accounting firms, and creating appropriate credit bureaus to supply data on the solvency of firms. An effective legal system through commercial law reforms can help settle contract disputes, clarify land titles and also ensure effective bankruptcy procedures, which are important for the growth of the business sector. An efficient tax or fiscal regime will either encourage MSMEs to enter the formal sector of the economy or keep them out of it. Governments can also ensure prompt payment to MSMEs for public contracts, since such public contracts are critical to the financial security of MSMEs.

7.3.2 Providing Guarantees for MSMEs

Governments through the public sector, guarantee loans on behalf of MSMEs. This may include guaranteeing the payment of principal and interest in whole or in part, in the event that the borrower defaults. By providing such guarantees, government assures lenders of the viability of the MSMEs and repayment of the loans. Governments have thus set up guarantee funds to ensure repayment of loans extended to MSMEs in case of default. Example is Exim

Guarantee in Ghana, which provides Government guarantee to external financiers who advance funds to Ghanaian firms. The terms of such facilities require the provision of a guarantee from the Government. However, in several countries, especially in Central Africa, the provision of guarantee has not been successful, given that this has resulted in less rigorous choice of investment projects and a lower debt recovery rate. Some MSMEs may default because they know government will come to their aid in terms of repaying the debt.

7.3.3 Making the Financial System Accessible to MSMEs

MSMEs have traditionally had difficulty in accessing finance from the formal financial system. Governments have therefore attempted to address this challenge by opening up the formal financial sector. Some countries, like Kenya, have addressed the issue of lack of finance by supporting the growth of smaller banks. The Philippines and Ghana governments, for instance, have encouraged the setting up of rural and community banks in order to address the problem MSMEs and rural communities face in accessing formal financial services from mainstream financial institutions. In South Africa, two different laws were passed in 2005 to expand the banking system to cover savings and loan institutions (second-tier banks) and co-operative banks (third-tier banks), while relaxing banking regulations for new entrants so that these banks could be free in granting loans. In many countries, banks have also encouraged the setting up of micro-credit services so as to serve the small business sector that hitherto has had limited access to financing.

7.3.4 Expanding the Supply of Finance Through the Non-Financial Private Sector

The interdependence between MSMEs, large firms and sectoral 'clusters' is also a major source of funding, especially in Asia and Latin America. Large firms can assist MSMEs acquire finance more easily by transferring resources and also by guaranteeing MSME solvency with financial institutions. MSMEs' linkages with major firms can also assist them obtain export credits, which is regarded useful in, for example, Zambia's agro-processing industry. Clusters of MSMEs assist member firms to collectively pursue sources of finance, provide collective guarantees or even set up their own financial entity. The threat of exclusion from the cluster ensures that member firms keep their promise, allowing the network to overcome the weaknesses in the legal system.

Frequent interaction with financial authorities and the role of reputation in the cluster can enhance the confidence between member firms and financial institutions, therefore making it easier to obtain loans on favourable terms. Member firms working together can also obtain supplier credits or borrow from other member firms when the need arises, thus, reducing overall costs. Such clusters tend to be common in Nigeria, Kenya, Tanzania, Zimbabwe and South Africa.

7.4 The Role of the Public Sector in MSME Development

The role of the public sector in the development of MSMEs include creating an enabling regulatory environment, improving access to finance and providing business development services (BDS).

7.4.1 Creating an Enabling Regulatory Environment

The business environment in which firms operate plays a significant role in the performance of businesses. It is expected that stable macroeconomic indicators, an open trade and investment regime, and a competitive financial sector will provide the enabling environment for a vibrant private sector. A well-developed physical infrastructure, including transportation, warehousing and port facilities, and modern information and communication technology are necessary for expanding markets and facilitating business transactions throughout the productive sector. Investments in social infrastructure such as education and health are also crucial in building the capabilities of the workforce in the productive sector. However, there are some aspects of the business environment that are particularly importance to MSMEs' competitiveness, and these include those that affect market access, the cost of acquiring information, transactional efficiency and risk, and the fixed costs of doing business. In most countries, these MSME-specific aspects of the business environment include barriers to entry, expensive and time-consuming regulatory requirements, including licensing and registration.

In order to give MSMEs a clearer understanding of relevant laws and regulations, ensure that their legal rights are protected and enhance their competitiveness and ability to adapt to changes in the law, and that governments actively work to create a legal and regulatory environment conducive to MSME innovation and to the growth of the MSME sector as a whole.

To this end, the public sector coordinates the revision of various laws and regulations related to MSME activity, while also providing MSMEs with legal information and consulting services, and undertaking studies and surveys on MSME development policy, with the underlying goal of building a favourable environment for MSMEs to operate in. This also involves ensuring the stability of the legal, political and policy framework and assuring MSMEs that, government will not unfavourably alter the basic conditions underlying their business decisions.

Next is the publicity of the rules and laws to enable MSMEs to have access to applicable laws that govern their operations. There is also the need to ensure clarity and certainty of the legal framework. This allows MSMEs to appreciate which laws are relevant to their situation. Predictability in the application of the law reduces the risks associated with changing interpretation, implementation or law enforcement. Governments also work towards ensuring fairness, the possibility of legal options and due process, thus providing access to independent recourse and mechanisms for settling disputes.

In helping to open access to markets and to accelerate market development for MSMEs, the creation of an enabling regulatory environment includes the formulation of a competition policy, licensing and registration requirements, administrative fees, commercial transaction laws, intellectual and commercial property rights, tax and labour legislation, government procurement laws and flexibility in the implementation of regulations. Creating an enabling regulatory environment also means investing in public goods, as well as building institutional capacity through investing in infrastructure (transport, warehouse and ports, market facilities, information and communications technology), provision of information (on markets, standards, technologies), monitoring of MSME performance and impact of policies and interventions as well as public/private partnerships at the local level to improve the business environment.

7.4.2 Improving Access to Finance

The limited access to financing and the high cost of credit have often been cited as constraints to MSMEs' growth and competitiveness. This is attributed to the transaction cost as well as the high risk associated with providing credit to MSMEs. Lenders find it difficult to assess the credibility of the information provided by MSME borrowers. Again, it is difficult for lenders to ensure that the terms of the contract are adhered to by these MSMEs. The lenders also find it difficult to manage risk since they do not have the appropriate risk management instruments. Usually, the burden of capital adequacy, as well as other supervisory requirements that penalise banks for lending to enterprises that do not have traditional collateral, also tends to compound the situation.

Governments supply credit to MSMEs through the first-tier development banks and second-tier credit facilities channelled through banks and other financial institutions in the traditional approach to MSME development. Also, governments have helped through portfolio requirements to banks and credit guarantee schemes to assist these MSMEs. In the past, MSMEs benefited from subsidised interest rates and guarantees. This still exists in many countries in recent times. To some extent, this presumes that the main constraint to MSMEs financing is the high cost of credit; however, there is evidence that MSMEs are more concerned about access to credit than its cost. The importance of state-owned banks in financial markets of developing and emerging countries may be as a result of the traditional approach of subsidised credit.

The fundamental objective of directed and subsidised credit programmes is to increase the access of small enterprises to financial services, however, very little have been achieved by these programmes. On the contrary, these programmes impede the sustainable development of the financial institutions and rather enhance a 'non-repayment culture' among enterprises. Ex-post subsidies are pushed higher as a result of low rates of loan recovery than what are intended in credit programmes. There is also then a distortion in the financial market due to credit subsidies, since they do not encourage firms to use non-credit forms of financing. The traditional approach has not helped in dealing with the basic problems that increase the cost of credit and make banks unwilling to give credit to MSMEs: that is, the real or perceived transaction cost and the high risks associated with commercial lending to the small-scale segment of the market.

A market-oriented strategy, aimed at increasing the financing accessibility of MSME focuses on lowering the transactions costs and risk of this segment of the market, enhancing the financial institutions' capacity to serve smaller clients and promoting healthy competition in financial markets. This is aimed at increasing the number of financial institutions that perceive the act of lending to MSMEs as profitable, and hence sustainable. The government does this by:

- Reducing entry restrictions, for instance, by reviewing the capital adequacy requirements and prudential regulations that may impede the ability of financial institutions serving smaller clients.

- Reducing lending risk of small businesses, by promoting laws that focus on the enforcement of contract, forfeiture and collection of collateral, as well as the use of movable assets as collateral, to enhance the operations of MSMEs.
- Developing policy frameworks, as well as legal and regulatory frameworks that accommodate financial innovations. This could be an innovation towards the development of financial institutions or instruments such as venture capital, small equity investments and leasing.
- Supporting specialised lending innovative technologies aimed at cutting down administrative cost attributed to credit application, monitoring and payment.
- Enhancing the financial institutions' ability to assess and evaluate the credit worthiness of MSMEs in a cost-effective manner. Credit scoring technique is an example of such a technique used in evaluating MSMEs in a cost-effective manner.
- Establishing more credit bureaus to improve information on the credibility of potential borrowers. Again, the MSMEs can be trained on more efficient ways of preparing business plans and financial projections.

The inability of MSMEs' access to finance can be seen from two angles: firstly, from the MSME side and, secondly, from the point of view of banks or financial institutions. MSMEs face a peculiar type of risk such as their being vulnerable and not having sufficient funds to run their businesses, their dependence on a limited cliental base and issues of credit worthiness, as well as inadequate collateral to secure loan. They are also regarded as costly clients (considering the ratio loan amount to administrative cost). Banks tend to charge higher interest rates on loans to MSMEs due to the high cost associated with managing these MSMEs loans.

MSMEs can have access to the financial market if finances are made accessible to them. This helps in the development of the financial market, especially when healthy competitive policies are formulated and implemented in the financial sector and there is a promulgation of collateral legislation, there are prudential regulations and supervision, there are favourable regulations governing leasing, venture capital and equity markets.

MSMEs' access to finance can be improved by governments if they invest in public goods and build institutional capacity that will enhance the activities of the MSMEs through innovation in loan products, risk assessment models (e.g. credit scoring), credit bureaus, lending methodologies, delivery mechanisms registers and training and technical assistance to financial institutions serving MSMEs.

7.4.3 Providing Business Development Services

Business Development Services (BDS) include a wide variety of non-financial services towards the development of MSMEs. Some of these services include the following: training and managing, providing extension, consultancy, and counselling to MSMEs for them to make informed decision concerning present and future prospects, assisting them in marketing their products and services, as well as providing information services for the MSMEs, assisting them in developing up to date technology and helping them in the ultimate diffusion of the technology, and providing MSMEs with mechanisms that enhance their business linkages through subcontracting, franchising and business clusters. These services help to build MSMEs by forming a paramount component of the 'market support structure' of MSMEs.

Traditionally, public institutions and non-governmental organisations have been the channel through which governments and donors provided BDS to MSMEs, usually on a free or subsidised basis. Publicly provided BDS are usually associated with poor quality, insufficient awareness of cost of control and these services being too general and supply-driven. There is low programme coverage for publicly provided or publicly funded services. This is due to the limited amount of subsidies given to public enterprises. This therefore affects both the quality and quantity of such outfits organising such programmes. There are rare cases of doing a systematic monitoring and evaluation of such programmes to see how they affect MSMEs, but most of the time, MSMEs complain that such programmes are not relevant to their needs.

In recent times, BDS have concentrated on services that look more appropriate to and are demanded by SMEs as well as enhancing the markets for such services. This is in contrast to the traditional way of direct provision of BDS by governments and donors. One effective way of increasing the quality, coverage and sustainability of services and enhancing their impact on the performance of MSMEs is to facilitate the provision of services by private sector providers and stimulate their demand by clients of small enterprise.

Understanding the current or existing market is the first step to developing a BDS market. In doing so, one must be conversant with the current market situations such as the product or services available on the market and the providers of the services and products (including informal and indigenous providers), the nature of market failures that constrain market development, and the characteristics, needs and willingness-to-pay of small enterprises. Due to MSMEs reliance on informal relations, instead of the formal, external relations, as well as the inter-firm relations, it usually makes delivery and price of services not easily visible.

The promotion of BDS market development by the supply-side interventions can help to extend and replicate financially sustainable models, as well as cost-effective services. However, small firms do not have adequate knowledge about the benefits of BDS or perceive them to be risky, therefore, demand-side interventions, such as matching grants and vouchers, may only be justified on a temporary basis, especially if markets are under-developed. Nevertheless, the success of demand-side subsidies is, however, judged based on the impact it has on the market, that is to say, whether they help in the development of the market or cause a distortion of the markets. It is believed that subsidies are less distortionary at the BDS level, but are more distortionary at the pre-delivery stage (such as market assessment, product development) and the post-delivery stage (monitoring and evaluation).

The involvement of the private sector in the delivery of services can help BDS institutions to reduce cost and improve upon the quality of their services. This is made possible through MSMEs linkages with larger firms through demand and supply relationships, and industry associations including other MSMEs. Again, there has been a reduction in cost of information, training, marketing and business linkages due to recent advancement in Internet access and information and communications technology. There are other cost-effective ways of delivering services, such as standardised or group approaches (such as basic business diagnostics), however, these approaches may not be appropriate for more sophisticated services to larger clients (such as technology upgrade).

BDS organisations' performance indicators can serve as solid grounds for appraising and evaluating firms, as well as improving future intervention designs. It is prudent to complement efforts aimed at developing private BDS markets with a reduction and rationalisation of public sector involvement. It will take some time for governments to be able to reduce the traditional roles they play in service provision. This can however be encouraged through a steady rise in recovery cost, aimed at achieving more business-like institutional management, increasing the use of the private sector in service delivery, enhancing financial sustainability and encouraging more rigorous impact evaluation tied to budgetary allocations. Selective privatisation of programmes may help in full cost recovery when public expenditure is rationalised on BDS. In the long run, only firms that assist in the provision of public goods should have access to subsidies. However, in the short run, other firms may be justified on the grounds that their contribution helps in the development of the markets, using a clear strategy that helps to reduce their cost. In addition to the efforts of contribution to the development of the market, there is also the better use of the limited fiscal resources available to firms.

Firms get easy access to market in the presence of BDS. Again BDS helps in the acceleration of market development. This comes about through the use of target subsidies for market development to specific market failure, provision of information on service providers, impact of services and enforcement of competition in service markets. There is an improvement in the investment in public goods and institutional capacity, as a result of using BDS. This is made possible through innovation in products for the MSMEs.

7.5 Key Policy Choices

A number of choices confront those with the responsibility of formulating Entrepreneurship and SME policy. Let us examine two key policy choices and explain how the choices made by policy makers often vary fundamentally among countries. SME policy relates to existing enterprises, whereas Entrepreneurship policy applies to policies seeking to enhance the creation of new enterprises. The distinction is shown in Table 7.1 drawing examples on elements of both policies from Lundstrom and Stevenson (2005).

Irrespective of the disparities between the two policies, there are several common elements in both policies. For instance, both SME policy and Entrepreneurship policy try to reduce the burden of bureaucracy and paper work to its barest minimum. However, it is still important to demonstrate how the two policies differ. The two policies vary sharply between start-ups and established businesses. For instance, for an individual who is considering starting up a new business, his/her relevant measure of 'bureaucratic burdens' may be how long it takes to start up the business, the amount of procedures required, as well as the costs of completing these procedures. On the contrary, what an SME may consider as bureaucratic burdens may include the cost of complying with regulations or legislation requirements, such as health and safety regulations or workforce legislation.

Table 7.1 Features of SME and Entrepreneurship policy

SME policy	Entrepreneurship policy
Reducing red-tape and paperwork burden	Reducing red-tape and paperwork burden
Access to capital/financing	Access to micro loans and seed funds
Provision of information services	Provision of information about start-up
Export and marketing services	Highlighting entrepreneurs as role models
Provision of training and consultancy	Entrepreneurship education
Technology transfer	Facilitating networking services

Source: Lundstrom and Stevenson (2005)

A better way of addressing the question is to distinguish between 'micro' and 'macro' policies. The unit of government responsible for small enterprises normally implements micro policies, which are centred on SMEs and/or entrepreneurship. On the other hand, macro policies are government-wide policies that do not have SMEs and entrepreneurship as their prime targets, but may have some impact on the activities of SMEs and entrepreneurship.

7.6 Government and Donor Support Programmes

There has been collaboration between governments and international development partners in fashioning out programmes that can help sustainable MSMEs. In recent years, there has been emphasis on the development of specific linkage-creation policies by international development agencies. They have helped to lower transaction costs through the introduction of subcontracting exchanges, incentives, venture capital schemes, market reservations and local content requirements. Small-scale sector development is being supported by a collaborative approach aimed at facilitating vertical and horizontal linkages, as opposed to enforced linkages. This consensual trend is emerging as a linkage support that helps the development of the small-scale sector (World Bank 1994; Schmitz 1995a, b). For instance, the Inter-American Development Bank (IADB) has been able to make loans available to SMEs at lower cost, by providing a range of financial support via the Small Projects Programme in Latin America. This is made possible through collaborations between the SMEs and the local co-operatives.

The UNIDO Cluster Development Project in India targets existing clusters of small-scale enterprises. The project specifically helps small-scale enterprises to get access to finance support through the help of NGOs and financial institutions. The project has appealed to financial institutions and NGOs in India to assist in the promotion of cluster activities (Clara et al. 2000).

There have been extensive interventions by bilateral donor agencies to support small-scale enterprises. The German Technical Corporation (GTZ) (now German International Corporation (GIC)) is a classic example of a prominent German aid organisation that helps to develop links and support activities of SMEs. They have helped some SMEs in countries like Ghana, Kenya, Nigeria and Tanzania. For instance, there has been a joint venture between Small Industries Development Organisation (SIDO), Tanzania and GTZ, Germany to support a range of self-help organisations through the Crafts and Small-Scale Enterprise Promotion Project in Tanzania, (Schulz 1995).

German aid again supported the New Business Creation programme, to provide support services, training and advice to small enterprises in Nepal (ODA 1992). Again, the Integrated Experts Programme is a German support programme responsible for providing advisory services to local entrepreneurs. The Company for International Investment and Development is a French-supported initiative that provides investment and also lends to entrepreneurs by assisting in the creation of local investment companies (ODA 1992).

The range of linkages is a variant or type of the inter-firm networking that has developed to increase small enterprises' capacity to enter policy dialogue. The West African Enterprise Network is a classic example of such inter-firm networking. It is based on local and regional cooperation networks. It came into being as a result of political liberalisation becoming popular in Africa in the 1990s, and thereby making private entrepreneurs having the zeal to have greater influence over economic policy. The USAID/OECD sponsored conference initiated this concept and it is aimed at establishing an agenda for private sector action that seeks to improve business conditions for MSMSEs.

Commercial banks and MFIs have made it possible for many donors to concentrate their activities on various credit schemes. This is aimed at strengthening the finances of MSMEs through training and business support services. It is paramount to evaluate the benefits derived by small enterprises to make sure that they are not disadvantaged by the receipt of export rebates and other concessions by large firms (Berry 1997). R&D of SMEs can be supported directly by giving them subsidies. They can also be that support may also be provided in the area of training in marketing and finance (Sandee 1994). Subsidies have also been used to permit SMEs to participate in trade fairs. For instance, Sebrae Expert in Micro Enterprises and Small Businesses motivates SMEs in Brazil by paying half of the costs of exhibition (Humphrey and Schmitz 1995) and also, governments in some countries such as Ghana, Kenya and Botswana have introduced entrepreneurial training programmes in order to support MSMEs development in their respective countries.

7.7 Summary and Conclusions

Considering the important role played by MSMEs in the economic development of countries, Governments through their public sector provide support and also implement policies and programmes aimed at improving the economic environment and opportunities for MSMEs. In this chapter, we examined public sector interventions in the support of MSMEs. We first discussed the channels through which government provides support for MSMEs.

Governments provide support to SMEs in three principal ways. These channels include measures aimed at influencing enterprise behaviour and improve the environment for MSMEs, support provided by intermediary agencies in the promotion of inter-firm linkages and networking, and also through the government's role in the development of the financial system aimed at increasing MSMEs' access to financing. We identified the reasons for public sector interventions in assisting the MSME sector, and these interventions are geared towards improving the business environment, assisting MSMEs meet financing requirements, making the financial system more accessible to MSMEs, and expanding the supply of finance through the non-financial private sector. The chapter also discussed the role of the public sector in the development of MSMEs and these include creating an enabling regulatory environment, improving access to finance and providing BDS.

We examined two key policy issues and explained how the choices made by policy makers often vary fundamentally among countries. SME policy relates to existing enterprises, whereas Entrepreneurship policy applies to policies seeking to enhance the creation of new enterprises. We also noted that governments and international development partners have often collaborated in fashioning out sustainable support programmes for MSMEs.

Discussion Questions and Problems

1. Discuss some of the channels through which the public sector supports MSMEs in developing countries.
2. Why are governments interested in providing support to the small business sector?
3. Examine some of the important roles played by governments in supporting MSMEs.
4. Identify some of the government support schemes targeted at assisting MSMEs. How effective are these support schemes?
5. Distinguish between the key policy choices with respect to entrepreneurship and SMEs.
6. Identify some support programmes provided by the international donor agencies to facilitate MSME development.
7. Discuss the impact of macro policy areas on entrepreneurship development.

Part III

Financial Performance and Planning

8

Understanding and Analysing Financial Statements

Learning Objectives
By the end of this chapter, you should be able to:

- appreciate how businesses prepare and make use of financial statements
- explain the various forms of financial statements
- identify the elements of financial statements
- discuss the problems with financial statements
- perform vertical and horizontal analysis of a firm's financial statements
- evaluate the performance of a firm based on financial ratios
- discuss the uses and limitations of ratio analysis.

8.1 Introduction

MSMEs, just like other businesses, are expected to prepare financial statements. The financial statements of the firm are used for both internal and external purposes. They are prepared to aid the entrepreneur or the manager of the MSME to understand how well the business has performed in the previous year and how to plan for the subsequent year. Apart from the entrepreneur and the managers of the small business, employees of the firm are also interested in the performance of the business to determine whether the firm is in the position to continue paying salaries. External users of the firm's financial statements include investors, lenders, suppliers, customers, govern-

J.Y. Abor, *Entrepreneurial Finance for MSMEs*,
DOI 10.1007/978-3-319-34021-0_8

ment and government agencies and the general public. For instance, investors such as venture capitalists, business angels and other equity investors would want to understand the financial health of the firm to be able to ascertain the prospects of investing in such a firm. Lenders and creditors use these financial statements to determine the financial health of the firm in order to inform the level of credit they should extend to the firm. Customers are interested in the firm's financial performance especially with respect to its ability to continue to trade, since customers' survival largely depends on the operations of the firm. Government agencies such as the tax authority would also want to know how much tax is due government based on the firm's performance.

Financial data based on the firm's transactions in a particular financial year are used to prepare the statements. The financial statements are useful for evaluating the firm's past and present financial performance as well as predicting its future financial direction. Limited liability companies are usually required by law to have their financial statements audited by an independent auditor in accordance with established accounting principles. Although the audits of the financial statements of sole proprietorship businesses and partnerships are not obligatory, it is recommended that accountants are hired to prepare the firm's books of accounts. Generally, most micro and small businesses are organised as either sole proprietorship or as a partnership and they do not keep proper books of accounts, especially not in the developing world.

The preparation and audits of financial statements of MSMEs is very relevant and improves MSMEs' access to finance. Micro and small businesses, at the start, may not really need a qualified or chartered accountant on full-time basis since that comes at high costs. But they still need an accounting officer to capture the financial transactions diligently. There are also good computerised accounting packages on the market that can be acquired and implemented in the firm to perform the accounting function. Implementing a computerised accounting system enables the accounting function to be performed in a faster and more efficient manner.

In this chapter, we examine financial statements by looking at income statement, balance sheet and cash flow statements and then explain the problems association with financial statements. We also discuss the methods of analysing financial statements, and the uses and limitations of financial ratios.

8.2 Financial Statements

Financial statements provide users with information about the financial position of the firm, its financial performance and changes in its financial position. Users of financial statements require the financial information in order to evaluate the ability of the firm to generate the necessary cash, and the timing and certainty of the cash generation. The ability of the firm to generate cash determines whether the entity will be able, for example, to pay its employees' salaries, pay its suppliers, honour its debt obligations with lenders in terms payment of interest and repayment of the loan principal, pay dividends to its shareholders and also pay taxes to government. Financial statements show the result of the stewardship of the assets and resources of the firm.

There are three main forms of financial statements and these are: income statement, balance sheet and statement of cash flow.

8.2.1 Income Statement

The income statement reports the financial results of a firm for a given period of time, such as a year. It shows what has happened during the accounting period with regard to the revenues and expenses of the business. Typically, income statements are generated for a normal accounting period, that is, one year. However, firms may want to generate income statement on a monthly or quarterly basis to determine how the firm is doing and to compare specific month or quarter to the same month or quarter in previous years and to past months or quarters during the current year. Sometimes a business may prepare a **pro forma** financial statement when submitting a business plan or proposal for funding. The pro forma income statement, for instance, provides projected income and expenses based on future forecast of the firm's operations.

The income statement is made up of three main parts. The first part captures the revenue/sales (turnover) minus the cost of sales, which gives us the gross profit. The second part indicates the gross profit minus operating expenses, which equals the net profit before interest and taxes or earnings before interest and taxes (EBIT). The third part includes net profit before interest and taxes minus finance costs such as interest expenses, which equals net profit before taxes minus taxes (if the entity is a company), which equals net profit after tax.

The reporting of items on the face of the income statement should be in accordance with the relevant accounting standards governing the preparation of financial statements in that jurisdiction. Due to the differences in the accounting standards used in the preparation of financial statements across countries, there is bound to be differences in the items reported on the face of the income statement. We however adopt the requirements of the International Accounting Standards (IAS) as well as the International Financial Reporting Standards (IFRS) in our discussion. The International Accounting Standards Board (IASB) reissued its International Accounting

Table 8.1 Income statement (statement of comprehensive income)

Extel Company Limited Income statement for the year ended 31 December 2015		
	2015	2014
	US$'000	US$'000
Sales	10,855	9,260
Cost of sales	(2,500)	(2,200)
Gross profit	**8,355**	**7,060**
Other income	300	200
	8,655	7,260
Operating expenses	(1,700)	(1,400)
Net profit before interest and taxes	**6,955**	**5,860**
Finance costs	(60)	(40)
Net profit before tax	**6,895**	**5,820**
Income taxes	(835)	(590)
Net profit after taxes	**6,060**	**5,230**

Standard (IAS 1) on the presentation of financial statements in September 2007. According to IAS 1 reissued, the Income Statement will now be known as the Statement of Comprehensive Income and the Balance Sheet will also be known as the Statement of Financial Position.

Let us look at a simple income statement of a firm using actual figures as shown in Table 8.1. The income statement for the previous year is normally included in the report for the current year for comparative purposes. For instance, the report containing the income statement for 2015 will include that of 2014 as well. We also discuss each of the items in the income statement.

Sales or turnover are all sales of goods and services for the firm. This however is to be adjusted to take into account the returns of goods that occurred in the course of the year as well as discounts that have been given to customers.

Cost of sales is the amount it costs the firm to obtain the items meant for sale. This includes the cost of materials (purchases), direct labour and overheads allocated to particular products. Cost of sales must be adjusted by deducting goods returned to suppliers. Adjustments must also be made by adding the opening stocks and subtracting the closing stocks of the firm.

Gross Profit of the firm is determined by subtracting the cost of sales from the revenue of the firm.

Other income refers to income the firm receives which does not come from its core business operations. An example is investment income.

Operating expenses are usually made up of distribution expenses, administrative expenses and other expenses, which form part of the operating expenses of the firm. Some of the specific expenses include salaries for management and administrative personnel, utility expenses, rental expenses, insurance, advertising expenses, legal expenses, auditor's fees, depreciation, amortisation and other general expenses.

Finance costs include the interest accrued during the accounting period on funds borrowed by the firm as well as other bank charges in relation to services provided by the bank to the firm.

Net profits before taxes are the earnings or income of the firm before paying income taxes to the government. In the case of limited liability companies, the corporate tax is calculated as a percentage of the net profits before taxes. But in the case of sole proprietorship or partnership, the net profit is added to the other incomes of the individual owners and taxed using the personal income tax rates.

Income taxes are provisions made based on the corporate income of the company. Corporate incomes are subject to a corporate income tax and it is the corporate tax that is owed to the government.

Net Profit after taxes for the period is the profit after provision for income taxes have been taken care of.

8.2.2 Balance Sheet

This is the **statement of financial position,** which shows a firm's accounting value on a particular date. It provides a snapshot of the firm's financial position at a given period, stating its asset holdings, liabilities and owner's equity. It shows all items that are owned (assets) by the firm and all items that are owed (liabilities) by the firm at a specific point in time. The statement of financial position also indicates what resources (assets) the firm controls and how it has financed these assets.

Considering a simple statement of financial position using actual figures as shown in Table 8.2. Again such a statement will normally include reports for the previous year and current year for comparative purpose.

Assets are the resources controlled by the entity as a result of past events, and from which future economic benefits are expected to flow to the entity. It is any item that is used or owned by the firm to produce goods or services to meet the needs of its customers. The assets at the disposal of the firm are further categorised into fixed (non-current) assets and current assets for purposes of presentation on the face of the statement of financial position.

Fixed (non-current) assets are normally not used up during the accounting year. They are the least liquid of assets and it is not easy to dispose of these items and obtain cash. Examples of fixed assets are property, plant and equip-

Table 8.2 Statement of financial position

Extel Company Limited		
Statement of financial position as at 31 December 2015		
	2015	2014
Assets	US$'000	US$'000
Non-current assets		
Property, plant and equipment	16,610	18,580
Goodwill	1,570	1,570
Other intangible assets	880	1,820
Total non-current assets	**19,060**	**21,970**
Current assets		
Inventories	5,780	3,960
Accounts receivable	4,980	2,500
Other current assets	3,200	3,160
Bank and cash	10,180	5,370
Total current assets	**24,140**	**14,990**
Total assets	**43,200**	**36,960**
Equity and liabilities		
Equity		
Share capital	12,000	9,000
Other reserves	2,690	2,690
Retained earnings	6,060	5,230
Total equity	**20,750**	**16,920**
Non-current liabilities		
Long-term borrowings	6,000	6,000
Deferred tax	450	450
Long-term provisions	3,450	3,450
Total bon-current liabilities	**9,900**	**9,900**
Current liabilities		
Accounts payable	8,210	6,900
Short-term borrowings	1,420	1,055
Current Portions of long-term borrowings	1,500	1,000
Tax Payable	1,420	1,185
Total current liabilities	**12,550**	**10,140**
Total liabilities	**22,450**	**20,040**
Total equity and liabilities	**43,200**	**36,960**

ment, investment property, intangible assets and long-term financial assets. Since fixed assets have expected life of more than one year, they are usually depreciated according to the tax regime prevailing in the country.

Depreciation is the wear and tear of the tangible fixed assets during the useful life of the asset. The rationale behind depreciation is simply making provision for replacing the asset in the future. The portion of the asset used is then set aside for future replacement of the asset. The depreciation charge matches that portion of the value of the assets cost with the period's revenues the asset helped to generate. The depreciation method adopted by the firm may be based on either a *straight line* method which involves dividing the cost of the asset by its useful economic life (less salvage value) or a *modified accelerated cost recovery system* (MACRS) method which accelerates the depreciation write-off by apportioning a greater percentage of the total expense to early life of the asset. However, for the purpose of tax, the capital allowance concept is used and the percentages are determined by the tax authority. The capital allowance schedule is provided by the tax authority in order to ascertain the amount of depreciation (capital allowance) which is allowed to be charged to the income statement before arriving at the taxable profits. The depreciation of intangible fixed assets is known as **amortisation.**

Current assets are assets, which can normally be converted into cash during the accounting year. Also, current assets are held by the firm for trading purposes or the entity expects to realise it 12 months after the operating period. The following items could be considered as current assets: inventories, trade and other receivables, marketable securities, cash at bank and cash in hand.

Liabilities are all items that the firm owe. They represent the part of firm's total assets that is owed to other parties. Liabilities are made up of long-term liabilities and current liabilities.

Long-term liabilities are all amounts the firm owes which are usually due in more than one accounting year. It means the debt is not expected to be paid in the current accounting year. Examples are mortgage loans, long-term bank loans for equipment.

Current liabilities are also amounts owed by the firm, which are due in one accounting year. They include accounts payable, short-term debt, notes payable, accrued expenses, taxes payable.

Equity is the residual interest of an entity after all the value of its liabilities has been deducted from the value of all its assets.

Owner's Equity is the difference between assets and liabilities. It is the residual interest in a firm after all the value of liabilities has been deducted from the value of all its assets. In other words, when we subtract the firm's total liabilities from its total assets, we get the owner's equity or the net worth of the firm. Equity may be subclassified in the statement of financial position as share capital, retained earnings and other reserves. The balance sheet of the firm is derived from the *double-entry bookkeeping* concept as expressed in the following accounting equation:

$$\textbf{Assets} = \textbf{Liabilities} + \textbf{Owner's equity}$$

Or

$$\textbf{Owner's equity} = \textbf{Assets} - \textbf{Liabilities}$$

Or

$$\textbf{Liabilities} = \textbf{Assets} - \textbf{Owner's equity}$$

This suggests that the balance sheet of the firm must always balance.

8.2.3 Statement of Cash Flows

Income statements and balance sheets are usually prepared based on the accrual concept of accounting. The accrual concept assumes that revenues are recognised when *earned* and not when cash is received, while expenses are recognised when incurred and not when payment is made. This means the income statements and balance sheets will not be able to tell us the actual inflows and outflows of cash during the accounting year. To be able to show how cash flowed into and flowed out of the firm during the accounting, we need to prepare a statement of cash flows.

IAS 7 enforces the preparation of statement of cash flows for entities. The statement of cash flows shows changes in cash and cash equivalents of an entity and it classifies the cash flows based on operating, investing and financing activities. Cash consists of cash on hand and demand deposits. Cash equivalents are short-term, highly liquid investments that are readily convertible to known amounts of cash and which are subject to an insignificant risk of changes in value. Information regarding the cash flows of the firm is useful in providing users of the financial statements with a basis of assessing the enterprise's ability to generate cash and cash equivalents and the needs of the enterprise to utilise the cash flows.

The statement of cash flows is made up of four main parts and these are cash flows from operating activities, cash flows from investing activities, cash flows from financing activities and net increase (decrease) in cash plus previous year's cash balance to arrive at current year's cash balance.

Cash flows from operating activities represent cash flows from transactions and events aimed at determining profit or loss. Cash flows from operating activities is the difference between total cash received by the firm and total cash paid out by the firm in carrying out its daily operations. The receipts include all cash received from sales, changes in accounts receivable, changes in inventory. The payments also include all payments made by the firm to all accounts (suppliers, employees, rent, utilities, etc.).

Cash flows from investing activities include cash flows from acquisition and disposal of long-term assets and other investments. Investing transactions generate cash outflows, such as capital expenditures for plant, property and equipment, business acquisitions and the purchase of investment securities. Inflows come from the sale of assets, businesses and investment securities. Cash flows from investing activities represent the net difference between property, plant and equipment or fixed assets on the two balance sheets. An increase represents an acquisition (which is an out flow) and a reduction suggests a sale (which involves an inflow).

Cash flows from financing activities include cash flows from activities that result in changes in the size and composition of the equity. Cash flows from financing activities represent the net difference between increase in equity resulting from sale of shares to raise funds and increase in debt as a result of issue of long-term debt instrument to raise debt finance. An increase represents an inflow from the proceeds of the issue of the shares or debt instruments and a decrease represents an out flow because the firm might have repurchased its shares or repaid its long-term debt.

The fourth part involves adding the total cash flow from operating activities, investment activities and financing activities. This will give us the **net increase (decrease) in cash**, which is then added to the previous year's cash balance to arrive at the current year's cash balance.

When preparing the cash flow statement, one must analyse the balance sheet and income statement for the coinciding period. Analysing the cash flow statement entails examining changes in account balances on the balance sheet. The general rules for this process include:

- Transactions that bring about an increase in assets will lead to a decrease in cash flow.
- Transactions that result in a decrease in assets will lead to an increase in cash flow.
- Transactions that result in an increase in liabilities will lead to an increase in cash flow.
- Transactions that result in a decrease in liabilities will lead to a decrease in cash flow

Let us look at the statement of cash flows for Extel Company Ltd. for the year 2015 (Table 8.3).

Table 8.3 Statement of cash flows

Extel Company Limited Statement of cash flows as at 31 December 2015		
Cash flows from operating activities	US$'000	US$'000
Net income		6,060
Adjustments to reconcile net income to net cash		
Provided by operating activities		
Depreciation expense	590	
Increase in accounts receivable	(2,480)	
Increase in other current assets	(40)	
Increase in inventory	(1,820)	
Short-term borrowings	365	
Current portions of long-term borrowing	500	
Tax payable	235	
Increase in accounts payable	1,310	
Net cash provided by operating activities		(1,340)
		4,720
Cash flows from investing activities:		
Acquisition of plant, property and equipment	(1,970)	
Other intangible assets	(940)	
Net cash outflow from investing activities		(2,910)
Cash flows from financing activities:		
Proceeds from issuance of ordinary shares	3,000	
Net cash inflow from financing activities		3,000
Net increase in cash		4,810
Cash balance, 31 December 2014		5,370
Cash balance, 31 December 2015		**10,180**

8.3 Problems with Financial Statements

Financial statements are useful for better financial decision-making. It is however important to appreciate the limitations of these statements in forming those decisions. Some of these problems include differences in laws, differences in accounting policies, use of historical cost, measurability and errors

Preparing financial statements is associated with certain problems. Financial statements are subject to the tax and other laws of the particular country. Differences in these laws across countries and changes in the laws in specific countries may affect the preparation of the financial statements.

Financial statements are also prepared based on the accounting policies and methods adopted by the firm. Some firms use accrual method of accounting, which requires that revenues be recognised when they are earned and expenses also recognised when incurred. Other firms may use cash basis where revenues are recognised when cash is received and expenses are based on actual payment of the expense item. Other firms may also adopt different methods for determining depreciation and also for valuing inventory. Such differences in accounting methods also affect the preparation of the financial statements and bring about differences in how the profit figures are arrived at.

Financial statements use historical cost as the basis of measuring the assets. The problem with the use of historical cost is the fact that it does not account for the change in price levels of assets over a period of time. This tends to reduce the relevance of accounting information by posting assets at values below their realisable value as well as failing to account for the opportunity cost of utilising those assets. The financial statements lack predictive value as they provide limited insight into the future prospects of the firm due to the reliance of previous performance.

Accounting information recognises transactions that can be measured in monetary terms. Thus, financial statements do not capture all relevant information on how the firm is doing today in order to predict its future direction. Important information such as quality and experience of management, brand name and strike action by workers will not be captured in the financial statements but these are also relevant in determining business success.

Another problem is in respect of errors that may occur with the preparation of the accounts. Errors associated with the preparation of accounts may lead to producing wrong financial statements, thus, wrong decisions can be taken as a result. Sometimes the errors may be unintentional human errors arising from miscalculation or from applying an item to the wrong accounting ledger. Even when a computerised accounting system is used, errors may arise. This could come from wrong figures being posted or postings being made to wrong accounts. Like it is usually said in the case of computerised systems 'garbage in, garbage out', meaning once you make mistakes in what you input into the system, the output will also be wrong. In some other cases, the errors come about as a result of accountants attempting to perpetuate a fraud.

8.4 Analysis of Financial Statements

Financial statements in themselves do not tell us much unless we begin to interrogate the figures and establish relationships among the variables and figures in the financial statements. An entrepreneur may be interested in rewarding employees based on their performance but does he know how well they have really performed? How does the entrepreneur determine how well the firm has performed? How does the small business manager ascertain at what point existing capacity will be exceeded and a bigger capacity will be required?

How do lenders and creditors ascertain whether the small business will be able to settle its debt as expected? All of these questions can be addressed by analysing the financial statements.

Analysis of financial statements or financial analysis involves gathering information about a firm, its industry and the economy and providing an evaluation of the firm's performance as well as it future financial condition.

Financial statement analysis may be useful for both internal and external purposes. Internally, it can be used to evaluate employee performance, the efficiency of the firm's operations and the firm's credit policies. Externally, financial analysis can be used by lenders and creditors to evaluate the potential pertaining to the credit worthiness of borrowers. Investors such as venture capitalist also use financial analysis to determine whether the firm presents a viable investment avenue.

There are three main methods of analysing financial statements and these include vertical analysis, horizontal analysis and ratio analysis. The use of vertical analysis and horizontal analysis are also referred of ***common-size analysis***.

8.4.1 Vertical Analysis

This is the process of using a single variable on the financial statement as a constant and determining how all other variables relate as a percentage of the single variable. In the case of vertical analysis of income statement, income statement items are expressed as a percentage of sales. The essence is to determine what percentage of sales is being consumed by the item. The formula for the vertical analysis of income statement is given as follows:

$$\text{Percentage of sales} = \frac{\text{Income statement item in US\$}}{\text{Sales in US\$}} \times 100$$

The vertical analysis of the balance sheet is done using total assets as a constant, and expressing each of the other items in the balance sheet as a percentage statement of the total assets. It signals how much of the firm's total assets are claimed by owners and how much is obligated to creditors. The formula below is used in the vertical analysis of balance sheet (statement of financial position):

$$\text{Percentage of total assets} = \frac{\text{Statement of financial position item in US\$}}{\text{Total assets in US\$}} \times 100$$

8.4.2 Horizontal Analysis

Horizontal analysis covers a trend analysis of items in the financial statements. It determines the percentage increase or decrease in an account from a base time period to subsequent time periods. The percentage in the financial statement items is calculated as:

$$\text{Percentage change} = \frac{\text{Current period amount} - \text{Previous time period amount}}{\text{Previous time period amount}} \times 100$$

8.4.3 Financial Ratio Analysis

Ratio analysis seems to be the most commonly used tool in analysing financial statements. A financial ratio is a mathematical relationship between two variables. In other words, it is the relationship between two variables expressed as a fraction. Ratio analysis involves comparing one figure against another to produce a ratio and assessing whether the ratio indicates a weakness or strength in an entity's affairs.

Financial ratios can be classified according to the way they are constructed and their general characteristics. The different ratios address specific address specific aspects of the firm's operations.

Several ratios calculated from accounting data can be grouped into various classes according to the financial activity or function to be evaluated. Each category addresses a particular area of financial health within a firm. Ratios are mainly classified as liquidity ratios, profitability ratios, activity/efficiency ratios, leverage/coverage ratios and market ratios.

8.4.3.1 Liquidity Ratios

Liquidity is the amount of cash an entity can put its hands on quickly to settle its debts. Liquid funds includes cash, short-term investments, fixed deposits with a bank, trade receivable, bills of exchange and so on. Liquidity ratios indicate the ability of the firm to meet future short-term financial obligations as and when they fall due. They compare near-term financial obligations, such as accounts payable or notes payable, to current assets or cash flows that will be available to meet these obligations. Liquidity ratios are useful for potential investors, banks and creditors. There are specific ratios that come under liquidity ratios and they include current ratio, quick ratio and acid test ratio.

Current Ratio This ratio measures the adequacy of current assets to meet the liabilities as they fall due. A high ratio may be an indication of good liquidity position. As a conventional rule, a current ratio of 2:1 or more is considered satisfactory. However, a high current ratio needs to be analysed with caution since a high ratio could mean that there are high levels of inventory and trade receivables, or high cash levels, which could have been put to a better use such as investing it in non-current assets. The current ratio is calculated by dividing total current assets by total current liabilities.

$$\text{Current ratio} = \frac{\text{Current assets}}{\text{Current liabilities}}$$

For Extel Company Ltd., the current ratio of the firm increased from 1.47 (14,990/10,140) in 2014 to 1.92 (24,140/12,550) in 2015. Even though there was an increase over the years, the ratios indicate that the available current assets are not even able to meet the current liabilities of the as and when they fall due. This indicates a very weak liquidity position of the firm compared to the benchmark value of 2:1. This could be because of the huge trade payables on the financial statements of the firm.

Quick Ratio This ratio establishes a relationship between quick or liquid assets and current liabilities. Quick ratio relates current liabilities to only relatively liquid current assets (cash items and accounts receivable). Generally a quick ratio of 1:1 is considered to represent a satisfactory current financial condition. Although the quick ratio is a more penetrating test of liquidity than the current ratio, yet it should be used cautiously. A quick ratio of 1:1 or more does not necessarily imply a sound liquidity position. It is calculated by dividing the sum of total current assets minus inventory by total liabilities.

$$\text{Quick ratio} = \frac{\text{Current assets} - \text{Inventory}}{\text{Current liabilities}}$$

Also, there is a marginal increase in the quick ratio of Extel Company Ltd. from 1.09 (14,990–3,960)/10,140 in 2014 to 1.46 (24,140–5,780)/12,550 in 2015. This further corroborates a stronger liquidity position of the firm against the benchmark figure of 1:1.

Acid Test Ratio This ratio relates the firm's cash and short-term marketable securities to its current liabilities. It measures the ability of the firm to meet its short-term obligations without liquidating its inventory, which is extremely important in certain industries especially for those firms that have high seasonal sales or are in industries that have rapid changes in product lines. It is calculated as follows:

$$\text{Acid test ratio} = \frac{\text{Cash} + \text{Marketable securities}}{\text{Current liabilities}}$$

Further, the acid test ratio indicates that cash and cash equivalents could pay the current liabilities of the firm as and when they fall due on only 0.53 times (5,370/10,140) in 2014 and 0.81 times in 2015.

8.4.3.2 Profitability Ratios

These ratios measure the ability of the firm to generate profit from its operations to pay a return to equity and debt holders. They also measure the entity's potential to earn income in excess of its operating costs to ensure return on equity and assets. There are two main types of profitability ratios, namely profitability ratios in relation to sales and profitability in relation to investments.

A firm should be able to make adequate profit on each US$ of sales. If sales do not generate sufficient profits, the firm will have difficulty in covering its operating expenses and interest expense as a result, and it will fail to pay returns to the owners. Profitability ratios in relation to sales include:

Gross Profit Margin This ratio reflects the level of efficiency with which management produces each unit of product. It indicates the average spread between sales and cost of sales. A high gross profit margin relative to the industry average implies that the firm is able to produce at relatively lower cost. A high gross profit margin signals good management. This ratio is computed as:

$$\text{Gross profit margin} = \frac{\text{Gross profit}}{\text{Sales revenue}}$$

The gross profit margin of Extel Company Ltd. is 76 % (7,060/9,260) in 2014 and 77 % (8,355/10,855) in 2015. This indicates an improvement in the gross profit margin of the firm. This is as a result of the over 17 % increase in the sales revenue of the firm.

Operating Profit Margin This is gross profit minus sales, general and administrative expenses. It is used to ascertain how much each dollar of sales can generate operating income. It is actually the firm's EBIT. It is calculated using the following formula:

$$\text{Operating profit margin} = \frac{\text{Operating profit(EBIT)}}{\text{Sales revenue}}$$

Again, the operating margin for the firm is 63.28 % (5,860/9,260) in 2014 and 64.07 % (6,955/10,855) in 2015. Although there was an improvement in the operating margin, the difference between the operating margin and the gross profit margin means that the firm is spending too much on selling & distribution and administrative expenses. The firm should therefore undertake strategies geared towards the reduction of these expenses.

Net Profit Margin It indicates the relationship between net profit and sales and signals management's level of efficiency in manufacturing, administering and selling the products. This ratio is the overall measure of the firm's ability to turn each dollar sale into net profit. A firm with a high net margin is capable to surviving in a situation of increasing costs of production and low prices and demand for its products. This ratio is computed as:

$$\text{Net profit margin} = \frac{\text{Net profit}}{\text{Sales revenue}}$$

Also, Extel Company Ltd.'s net profit margin is 56.48 % (5,230/9,260) in 2014 and 55.83 % (6,060/10,855) in 2015. This is an indication that the firm is spending too much on operating expenses which should be carefully looked at to improve the firm's profitability.

The profitability of the firm should also be evaluated in terms of the firm's investment in assets as well as the capital provided by the creditors and owners. A firm's survival is threatened if it is unable to earn satisfactory return on investment. Profitability ratios in relation to investment include:

Return on Assets (ROA) This tells us how much a firm earns on each dollar in assets after paying both interest and taxes. This ratio is useful in deciding if the firm is a good investment compared with other alternatives. The formula for return on assets is:

$$\text{Return on assets} = \frac{\text{Net profit}}{\text{Total assets}}$$

Figures from the financials of Extel Company Ltd. indicate that return on assets is 14.15 % (5,230/36,960) in 2014 and 14.03 % (6,060/43,200) in 2015. This means that the return accruing to all investors for investing in Extel Company Ltd. is 14.15 % and 14.03 % in 2014 and 2015, respectively.

Return on Equity (ROE) This indicates how well the firm has used the resources of owners. It tells the shareholders, or individual owner, what each dollar of his or her investment is generating in net income. The earning of a satisfactory return is the most desirable objective of business and therefore this ratio reflects the extent to which this objective has been accomplished. The formula for ROE is:

$$\text{Return on equity} = \frac{\text{Net profit}}{\text{Owners' equity}}$$

Information from the financial statement indicates that equity holders made a return of 30.91 % 5,230/16,920) and 29.20 % (6,060/20,750) in 2014 and 2015, respectively.

8.4.3.3 Activity/Efficiency Ratios

Activity ratios are used to evaluate the efficiency with which the firm manages and utilises its assets. Activity or efficiency ratios examine how the management uses its assets and capital. Assets are worthless if they cannot be turned into cash in a timely manner to generate the revenue required by the firm to meet its obligations. Activity ratios include creditors' payments period, debtors' collection period, asset turnover, stock turnover.

Inventory Turnover This ratio indicates the efficiency of the firm in selling its product. It basically states how many times per year the firm moves its average inventory. This ratio may be usually higher for retailing entities such as the supermarkets and entities selling fast moving products.

$$\text{Inventory turnover} = \frac{\text{Cost of sales}}{\text{Average inventory}}$$

The average inventory is the average of opening and closing balances of inventory. From the financials of Extel Company Ltd, the inventory turnover is 0.58 times (2,200/3,780) in 2014 and 0.45 times (2,500/5,540) in 2015. This implies that the firm could not turn over its inventory even for once in a year. This is an indication that the products being sold by the firm are slow moving and the firm needs to step up its marketing efforts in order to improve sales. *Assume opening inventory to amount to 3,600 and 5,300 in 2014 and 2015, respectively.*

Inventory Turnover Period This ratio indicates how many days it takes the firm to convert its inventory into cash. An increasing number of days mean that inventory is turning over less quickly and may be an indication of lack of demand for the entity's products, poor inventory control or increasing costs. However, increased inventory days could also mean that an entity is buying inventory in larger quantities to take advantage of trade discounts or of increasing stock levels to avoid stock outs.

$$\text{Inventory turnover period} = \frac{\text{Inventory}}{\text{Cost of sales}} \times 365$$

Again, the inventory period of Extel Company Ltd. is 657 (3,960/2,200) × 365 days in 2014 and 843 (5,780/2,500) × 365 days in 2015. This means that it takes the firm more than one year to sell its stock of inventory, which is an indication of poor marketing of the products of the firm. This is also corroborated by the inventory turnover figures for Extel Company Ltd.

Debtors/Accounts Receivable Turnover When a firm provides credits to its customers, debtors or receivables are created in the firm's accounts. The receivables are expected to be converted into cash over short period, thus, they are included in current assets. The liquidity position, to a large extent, depends on the quality of accounts receivable. This ratio is to determine how fast a firm is turning its credit sales into cash. Generally, the higher the value of debtors' turnover, the more efficient is the management of the credit.

$$\text{Accounts receivable / debtors' turnover} = \frac{\text{Credit sales}}{\text{Accounts receivables}}$$

The accounts receivable turnover for Extel Company Ltd. 1.85 times (4,630/2,500) in 2014 and 1.09 times (5,427.5/4,980) in 2015. This means that the firm could only turn its accounts receivable into cash for 1.85 times and 1.09 times in 2014 and 2015, respectively in a year. This indicates a weak credit policy on the part of the firm. *Assumes 50 % sales were made on credit.*

Debtors'/Accounts Receivable Collection Period It represents the average length of time that the firm must wait after making sale before receiving cash, which is the average collection time. This ratio measures the quality of debtors since it shows the rapidity or slowness of their collectability. This should be compared against the firm's credit terms and policy to judge its credit-and-collection efficiency. Increasing the accounts receivable collection period may be an indication of lack of proper credit control, which may lead to irrecoverable debts. Increased ratios may however be due to an entity's deliberate policy to attract more trade or a major customer being allowed flexible credit terms. This ratio is calculated as follows:

$$\text{Accounts receivable collection period} = \frac{\text{Days per year}}{\text{Accounts receivables turnover}}$$

or

$$\text{Accounts receivable collection period} = \frac{\text{Accounts receivables}}{\text{Credit sales}} \times 365$$

Further, the accounts receivable collection period has increased from 197 (2,500/4,630) × 365 days in 2014 to 335 (4,980/5,427.5) × 365 days in 2015. This suggests that the number of days it takes the firm to collect its debt is increasing, which is an indication of poor credit policy and the inability of the firm to collect on its debt.

Payables Payment Period This ratio indicates the length of time it takes the firm to make payment to its creditors. It represents the credit terms that have been extended to the firm by its suppliers. A long credit period may be good as it represents a source of free finance. However, long credit periods could also indicate that an entity is unable to pay more quickly because of liquidity problems.

$$\text{Accounts payables period} = \frac{\text{Accounts payables}}{\text{Credit pruchases or costs of sales}} \times 365$$

The payables period of the firm is 1,144 (6,900/2,200) × 365 days in 2014 and 1,198 (8,210/2,500) × 365 days in 2015. This means that it is taking the firm a longer time to pay its creditors. The firm is taking over two years to pay the amount owed to creditors. This is an indication that the firm is facing liquidity problems as evidenced by the liquidity ratios.

Fixed Assets Turnover Assets are used to generate sales. Therefore, a firm should manage its assets efficiently to maximise sales. This ratio indicates how efficiently fixed assets are being used to generate revenue for a firm.

$$\text{Fixed assets turnover} = \frac{\text{Sales revenue}}{\text{Fixed assets}}$$

The fixed assets turnover of Extel Company Ltd. is 0.42 times (9,260/21,970) in 2014 and 0.57 times (10,855/19,060) in 2015. This means that the firm's fixed assets could only generate sales 0.42 times in 2014 and 0.57 times in 2015. This is an indication of under-utilisation of the fixed assets of the firm.

Total Assets Turnover Ratio This ratio indicates how efficiently a firm uses its total assets to generate revenue for the firm. Unutilised or under-utilised assets increase the firm's need for costly financing as well as expenses for maintenance.

$$\text{Total assets turnover} = \frac{\text{Sales revenue}}{\text{Total assets}}$$

The total assets turnover of the firm is 0.25 times (9,260/36,960) in 2014 and 0.25 times (10,855/43,200) in 2015.

8.4.4 Leverage Ratios

Leverage ratios indicate what percentage of the business's assets is financed with creditors' dollars. In other words, it indicates what percentage of the business's assets actually belongs to the owners and what percentage is subject to creditors' claim. These ratios are concerned with an entity's long-term stability. Such ratios may consider for examples how much an entity owes in relation to its size, whether it is getting into heavier debt or improving its situation. Leverage ratios are very important to the providers of capital.

Debt-to-Equity Ratio This ratio indicates what proportion of the firm's capital is derived from debt, compared to other sources of capital, such as preference shares, ordinary shares and retained earnings. A higher percentage of debt in relation to equity capital increases the volatility of earnings. This is because of the larger fixed financial charges it increases the probability defaulting on the debt and interest payments.

$$\text{Debt}-\text{to}-\text{equity} = \frac{\text{Total debt}}{\text{Owners' } equity}$$

The debt-to-equity ratio of Extel Company Ltd. is 1.18 (20,040/16,920) in 2014 and 1.08 (22,450/20,750) in 2015. This means that for every dollar of equity, the debt component is 1.18 and 0.94. This is an indication that firm is lowly leveraged.

Debt Ratio This ratio shows the proportion of a firm's assets that is owned by creditors. The total debt includes both current liabilities and long-term debt. Creditors prefer low debt ratios since a lower ratio cushions them against losses in the event of liquidation.

$$\text{Debt ratio} = \frac{\text{Total debt}}{\text{Total assets}}$$

Again, the debt ratio of the firm is 0.54 (20,040/36,960) in 2014 and 0.52 (22,450/43,200) in 2015. This implies that the total assets of the firm were financed by 54 % in 2014 and 45 % in 2015 by debt.

Times Interest Earned Ratio The times-interest-earned ratio shows the relationship between operating income and interest payment to the firm's creditors annually. This ratio shows the number of times the firm can cover its fixed interest charges with the earnings.

$$\text{Times interest earned ratio} = \frac{\text{Earnings before interest and taxes}}{\text{Interest payments}}$$

Extel Company Limited's times interest earned was 146.5 times (5,860/40) in 2014 and 115.92 times (6,955/60) in 2015. This means that the earnings before interest and tax could pay for the interest payments of the firm 146.5 times and 115.92 times in 2014 and 2015, respectively. The fall is due to the over 50 % increase in the financing cost of the firm.

8.4.4.1 Market/Investment Ratios

Shareholders' investment ratios help equity shareholders and other investors to assess the value and quality of an investment in the ordinary shares of an entity. The value of investment in ordinary shares in a listed company is its market value. Hence, investment ratios must consider not only the information in published financial statements, but also the current price of the company as measured by the existing share price. These ratios are used to compare firms within the same industry. They are primarily used by investors to determine if they should invest in a company in exchange for ownership. These ratios include:

Price–Earnings Ratio This ratio is widely used by the security analysts to value the firm's performance as expected by investors. It indicates investors' judgement or expectation about the firm's performance. The *P*/*E* ratio reflects investors' expectations about the growth in the firm's earnings. In other words, this ratio usually reflects the confidence of the market, that is, the market's view of the future prospects of the share. A high *P*/*E* ratio suggests that a high growth is expected.

$$\text{Price} - \text{earnings ratio} = \frac{\text{Market price per share}}{\text{Earnings per share}}$$

Earnings Per Share (EPS) This ratio represents the amount of income earned during the period per share of ordinary shares.

$$EPS = \frac{\text{Profit after tax}}{\text{Ordinary shares outstanding}}$$

8.5 Uses of Financial Ratios

Financial ratios are useful in a number of respects. These include managerial decisions, investment decisions, credit analysis and they also predict the long-run profit potential of the firm. Financial ratios provide useful analysis regarding the profitability, financial health and direction of the firm, which can assist management in taking better managerial decisions.

Also, financial ratios allow for intra-firm and inter-firm comparative analysis. That is, a firm can compare its performance over two different periods (intra-firm) and performance with other firms in the same industry (inter-firm).

Financial ratios serve as a guide for making investment decisions. Potential investors of the firm such as venture capitalist and business angels also rely on financial ratio analysis to inform their decision to either invest in the firm or not.

Credit analysis can easily be carried out with the use of financial ratios. Ratios assist banks and other lenders evaluating the firm for the purpose of granting loans. Creditors also rely on ratio analysis for evaluating the credit worthiness of the firm for the purpose of giving credit.

Financial ratios are useful for predicting the long-run profit potential of the firm. A firm's ratios may also be analysed over a full economic cycle. This is useful in understanding and estimating the firm's performance in changing economic conditions and also allows for projecting its future performance.

8.6 Limitations of Ratio Analysis

There are limitations with respect to the use of financial ratios. It is important to note that the financial ratios of a firm have meaning provided they are compared with existing standards. It is often difficult to find or establish a proper basis of comparison. The general recommendation is to compare such ratios with industry averages. However, industry averages are not easily available.

Differences in the firms also constitute a limitation. Situations of two firms are never the same. Similarly, the factors that influence a firm's performance in one particular year may differ in other years. Therefore, comparing the financial ratios of two different firms is a meaningless and difficult exercise, especially when these firms operate in different situations or under different circumstances.

Financial ratios also rely on financial statements and financial statements are prepared based on book value (largely historical cost), which do not reflect current reality in the business. Such ratios (mostly asset-based ratios) may not give a true picture of the financial situation of the firm. Assets may be worth more or less than the value stated in the balance sheet. For instance, if a firm is in financial distress, the liquidation value of those assets will be the more relevant than the book value.

The effect of inflation can lead to distortion when evaluating or predicting performance, since financial ratios are based on historical cost. Balance sheet values are often significantly different from their true values. Also, since inflation affects both depreciation expenses and cost of inventory, profits are also affected. Therefore, ratio analysis for one firm over time, or a comparative analysis of firms of different ages must be interpreted with judgement

Another problem is that there is no indication of cause of change. Ratios simply tell the business owner what happened but not the cause of it. It is important to go beyond the numbers to actually find out why the ratios are changing over time. Consider Accounts Receivable Turnover, for instance. This ratio indicates how quickly accounts receivable are being collected. If the turnover slows, it suggests accounts receivable is increasing in relation to sales for the period. This increase may be affected by factors such as employee inexperience, loosened credit policies or growing customer dissatisfaction with the product. The entrepreneur or business manager must investigate the causes of the problem in order to address it.

Firms can engage in window dressing techniques in order to make their financial statements look stronger. In that case the financial ratios to be computed will not provide any meaningful guide for good decisions to be made.

Financial ratios based on the financial statement only signal activities which have monetary value. Issues such as management changes, industry changes, labour unrest are not reported since they are not expressed in terms of money. Therefore, ratio analysis does not reveal the firm's complete situation with respect to its activities.

Ratios are constructed from accounting records and such data are subject to different interpretations and even manipulation. Firms may adopt different accounting policies and methods and that can impact the preparation of the financial statements and computation of the ratios. For instance, two firms may use different depreciation methods or inventory valuation methods and the different methods can lead to different profit figures. Therefore, it is difficult to compare the ratios since the valuations are not comparable. Firms also tend to have different fiscal years. This makes it difficult to carry out a comparative analysis if the financial statements are prepared at different times and as such the ratios are constructed using different fiscal years.

8.7 Summary and Conclusions

In this chapter, we looked how to understand and analyse financial statements. We mentioned that MSMEs, just like other businesses are expected to prepare financial statements and these are very relevant for both internal and external users. The income statement measures the financial performance of a firm over a period of time. It shows what has happened during the accounting period with regard to the revenues and expenses of the business. The balance sheet is the statement of financial position and it shows a firm's accounting value on a particular date. It indicates all items that are owned (assets) by the firm and all items that are owed (liabilities) by the firm at a specific point in time. The statement of cash flows captures the firm's actual cash inflows and out flows in the accounting year.

We identified problems associated with the preparation of financial statements to include differences in tax laws and regulations governing the preparation of financial statements in countries, differences in the accounting methods of firms, use of historical costs, issues of measurability and also errors in the preparation of the accounts.

We mentioned that analysis of financial statements involves gathering information about a firm, its industry and the economy and providing an evaluation of the firm's performance as well as it future financial condition. The three methods of analysing financial statements are vertical analysis, horizontal analysis and ratio analysis.

Analysis of financial statements is important to the entrepreneur and small business manager. Financial ratios provide useful analysis regarding the profitability, financial health and direction of the firm, which can assist management in taking better managerial decisions. Financial statement analysis helps the owners to gauge the performance of the firm in relation to previous years and competitors. Potential investors such as venture capitalist or business angels are also interested in the financial statement analysis to inform their decision to either invest in the firm or not. Creditors, banks and other lending institutions are interested to ascertaining the credit worthiness of the small business. Financial ratios are useful for predicting the long-term profit potential of the firm.

Discussion Questions and Problems

1. How relevant are financial statements to the internal and external users of an MSME?
2. What are the problems with financial statements?
3. Construct a statement of financial position for Hamza Enterprise Ltd. using the following financial information: land and building US$870,000; motor vehicle US$590,000; plant and equipment US$400,000 furniture and fittings US$469,000; inventory US$79,000; accounts receivable US$69,000; cash at bank US$72,000; cash in hand US$41,000; loan US$800,000; accounts payable US$50,000.
4. Prepare an income statement for ABL Limited given the information below: sales US$4,290,000; inventory at start US$378,000; Inventory at end US$249,000; depreciation is 30 % on cost (cost of motor vehicle and equipment are US$900,000 and US$700,000 respectfully); interest expense US$97,000; lease payments US$50,000; wages and salaries US$360,000; goods purchased US$705,000; repairs and maintenance US$47,000; discount allowed and received amount to US$50,000 and US$70,000 respected; corporate tax is 25 % on profit.
5. What are the uses and limitations of financial ratios?
6. The following information relates to the financial statements of Rand Limited for the year 31 December 2015 together with comparative figures for the year to 31 December 2014:

Table A.8.1 Rand Limited income statement for the year ended 31st December 2015

	2015	2014
	US$'000	US$'000
Revenue	120,000	95,600
Cost of sales	(69,000)	(53,000)
Gross profit	**51,000**	**42,600**
Other income	12,000	13,000
	63,000	55,600
Operating expenses	(20,000)	(18,900)
Net profit before interest and taxes	**43,000**	**36,700**
Finance costs	(8,000)	(6,000)
Net profit before tax	**35,000**	**30,700**
Income taxes	(10,550)	(9,025)
Net profit after taxes	**24,450**	**21,675**

Table A.8.2 Rand Limited statement of financial position as at 31 December 2015

	2015	2014
Assets	US$'000	US$'000
Non-current assets		
Property, plant and equipment	128,000	126,000
Goodwill	12,500	12,500
Other intangible assets	9,500	13,000
Total non-current assets	**150,000**	**151,500**
Current assets		
Inventories	35,890	29,870
Accounts receivable	31,685	39,500
Other current assets	15,600	13,500
Bank and cash	87,920	79,000
Total current assets	**171,095**	**161,870**
Total assets	**321,095**	**313,370**
Equity and liabilities		
Equity		
Share capital	100,000	100,000
Other reserves	4,020	4,250
Retained earnings	89,700	76,980
Total equity	**193,720**	**181,230**
Non-current liabilities		
Long-term borrowings	80,000	60,000
Deferred tax	8,950	9,870
Long-term provisions	895	985
Total non-current liabilities	**89,845**	**70,855**
Current liabilities		
Accounts payable	21,120	35,185
Short-term borrowings	7,805	13,500
Current portions of long-term borrowings	5,000	10,000
Tax payable	3,605	2,600
Total current liabilities	**37,530**	**61,285**
Total liabilities	**127,375**	**132,140**
Total equity and liabilities	**321,095**	**313,370**

You are required to compute relevant ratios from the financial statement for 2015 and 2014 and comment on the performance of Rand Limited.

9

Financial Planning and Forecasting

Learning Objectives
By the end of this chapter, you should be able to:

- explain the concept of financial planning and the financial planning process
- understand how to prepare a cash budget
- appreciate how to prepare a sales forecast for an existing business
- understand how to prepare a sales forecast for a new business
- show the interrelationship between planning, budgeting and forecasting
- illustrate how to project financing needs and growth of MSMEs
- explain how to project financing needs using break-even analysis
- identify the determinants of MSMEs' financing needs

9.1 Introduction

Entrepreneurs and managers of MSMEs require financing to operate their business. However, we know that financing is not always enough for businesses. Financial planning and forecasting are necessary to enable the entrepreneurs plan their finances in such a way that value will be added to the firm. Financial planning and forecasting are important for the entrepreneur to evaluate and ascertain how much external financing may be required. They are also useful in gauging the actual performance of the firm based on the standard and the effect of the necessary corrections where necessary.

J.Y. Abor, *Entrepreneurial Finance for MSMEs*,
DOI 10.1007/978-3-319-34021-0_9

In this chapter, we discuss the concept of financial planning and forecasting. We first look at the financial planning process, at budgeting and preparation of a cash budget. The chapter also looks at financial forecasting by discussing how to do forecasting of sales in an existing business and that of a new business. The chapter also discusses projecting financing needs and growth, and also how to project financing needs using break-even analysis.

9.2 Financial Planning

Financial planning deals with the orderly acquisition of capital, as well as the utilisation of the capital, through the establishment of well-crafted plans directed towards such goals. It entails identifying the sources of funds and the application of the funds in relation to enhancing the financial future of the firm. It is therefore a paramount success factor that cannot be underrated by firms because it acts as a guide to the financial future of firms. A good financial planning involves the coordination of a firm's financial activities geared towards maximising the entrepreneurial value.

The financial planning process involves the following steps:

- Set enterprise goals: It involves setting long-term goals of the firm.
- Develop long-term financial plans: It serves as the roadmap towards achieving the firm's long-term goals.
- Develop short-term financial plans: Short-term financial plans are centred on short-term financial outcomes of the firm.
- Develop individual budgets: Individual budgets including sales, selling expenses, production and administrative budgets need to be prepared.
- Develop a consolidated budget: The individual budgets must be put together in a consolidated budget.

9.2.1 Budgeting

A budget is a financial plan that sets out expected future results expressed in monetary terms, usually for a limited period. Firms use various types of budgets. An income and expenditure budget shows how much a firm expects to receive and spend in future periods, a production budget illustrates how much the firm must produce in the coming periods of time in order to meet demand, and a profit budget also combines planned sales, costs and profit figures.

The budget is also useful to MSMEs in a number of respects. It enables the entrepreneur to communicate his/her targets clearly and motivate employees towards achieving these targets. It provides an indication of the amount and timing of cash flows. It enables the entrepreneur to control and monitor performance by comparing actual outcomes against planned targets. This affords the MSME the opportunity to take corrective actions when discrepancies exist between budget and actual results.

9.2.1.1 Cash Budget

A cash budget is a financial projection of a firm's cash receipts and disbursements for a specified future time period. It predicts the future cash receipts and expenditures for a particular time period, usually covering a short period of time. The cash budget helps the MSME determine when income will be sufficient to cover expenses and when the enterprise will need to seek outside financing.

The cash budget has three main components: cash receipts, cash disbursements and cash summary. A cash budget may also contain a financing section, which details the expected amount of borrowing and repayment of loan or debt during the budget period.

The steps involved in preparing a cash budget are:

1. ***Select the time horizon.*** The time horizon is the planning period covered by a cash budget. The time horizon depends on the MSME owner's needs. Cash budgets are usually prepared monthly, however, it could be done on a weekly or daily basis for businesses with more volatile cash flows.
2. ***Forecast sales/revenues.*** The cornerstone of the cash budget is the sales forecast. The sales forecast helps in estimating the variables contained in the cash budget. The ability to estimate an accurate cash budget largely depends on estimating an accurate sales forecast.
3. ***Estimate cash receipts.*** The inflows expected during a given period are the cash receipts of the firm over that given period. Cash receipts are usually prepared on a separate schedule. The sources of cash receipts include collections of accounts receivable, cash sales, other items indirectly related to sales such as proceeds from sale of assets (e.g. equipment and vehicles) and interest received by the firm.
4. ***Estimate cash disbursements.*** The outflows expected during a given period are the cash disbursement of the firm over that given period. Cash disbursements are usually prepared on a separate schedule. The sources of cash disbursements are overheads, other operating items such as utilities and leases,

current cash purchases, payment of accounts payable resulting from purchases in prior periods, direct labour, selling expenses and general and administrative expenses, capital expenditures, taxes, interest and dividends.

5. ***Compute the next cash flow***. This is the result after finding the difference between the cash receipt and cash disbursement. It could result in a positive or negative balance depending on which of the two cash flows is higher.
6. ***Develop a cash summary.*** This shows whether the firm is in need of additional cash or has got excess cash to spare or invest over a specific time period. The cash summary is determined by:
   - Finding the ending cash balance of the firm by adding the net cash flows (NCF) to the beginning cash of the firm.
   - Finding the cash surplus (i.e. when the ending cash exceeds the minimum cash balance) or cash shortage (i.e. when the ending cash is less than the minimum cash balance) by subtracting the minimum cash balance from the ending cash. The desired amount of cash an MSME wants to have on hand during any period is referred to as the minimum cash balance. This balance depends largely on the certainty of the firm's environment. Ideally, it is expected that higher minimum cash balances are held by firms in more volatile environments, especially when the cash flows are more uncertain than those in more stable environments.

Example 9.1 To demonstrate the preparation and use of a cash budget by an MSME, let us consider an example of quality mechanics, a small business, which repairs and services vehicles on contract for some corporate bodies at the Suame Magazine. Its owner is in the process of preparing a monthly cash budget for the period September to December 2016. Revenues are highly seasonal, peaking in the months of October and November. The following information is used in preparing the cash budget.

1. About 25 % of quality mechanics' revenue is collected one month after the service delivery and the balance (75 %) is collected two months after the servicing is rendered.
2. Quality mechanics purchases amount to 55 % of revenues and are made one month in advance of anticipated revenues. Payments are made in the month following the purchase. For example, September sales are estimated at US$6,000; therefore, August purchases are US$3,300 (0.55 × US$6,000) and are paid in September.
3. Wages, salaries, rent and other cash expenses are recorded in Table 9.1, which gives quality mechanics' cash budget for the four-month period ended December 2016.

4. In addition, expenditures are recorded in the cash budget in relation to the purchase of equipment to the tune of US$1,000 in September and the repayment of a US$800 loan in November.
5. In September, quality mechanics will pay interest expense of US$400 on its medium-term debt. The interest expense relates to the period September–December.
6. Interest on the US$800 short-term debt for the period September–November is US$20, which is paid in November.
7. A tax payment of US$590 is made in November.
8. Quality mechanics has a cash balance of US$1,500 and maintains a minimum cash balance of US$1,500 to meet any unanticipated shortfall in NCF.
9. Quality mechanics needs to borrow in order to maintain that minimum cash balance and this is estimated in the final section of Table 9.1. Borrowing is done at the beginning of the month in which the funds are needed. Interest rate on funds borrowed is 12 % per annum, or 1 % per month, and this is paid in the month following the month in which funds are borrowed. Thus, interest rate on funds borrowed in October will be paid in November equal to 1 % of the loan amount outstanding in October.
10. The financing needed in quality mechanics' cash budget indicates that the firm's cumulative short-term borrowing will be US$1,136.5 at the end of November. In December, the firm will be in the position to repay all short-term debts in October and November. Note that the cash budget indicates not only the amount of financing needed during the period but also when the funds will be needed.
11. Sales for 2016 are estimated to be July US$6,200; August US 5,000; September US 6,000; October US 8,000; November US 8,500; December US$ 7,000 while sales for January 2017 are expected to be US$6,500.

9.3 Financial Forecasting

Financial forecasting is an important element of planning. It is a planning tool that helps the firm to prepare and cope with uncertainties in the future by relying on the analysis of trends from past to present data. To begin the process of forecasting, certain assumptions need to be made on the basis of experience, knowledge and judgement. These assumptions or estimates are then projected into the future or a specified period using various estimation techniques such as exponential smoothing, moving averages, regression analysis and trend analysis. Financial forecasting projects or estimates future financial events of

Answer 9.1

Table 9.1 Quality Mechanics, cash budget for the four months ending 31 December 2016

WORKSHEET	JUL.	AUG.	SEPT.	OCT.	NOV.	DEC.
	US$	**US$**	**US$**	**US$**	**US$**	**US$**
Sales/Revenue	6,200	5,000	6,000	8,000	8,500	7,000
Collections:						
First month (25%)		1,550	1,250	1,500	2,000	2,125
Second month (75%)			4,650	3,750	4,500	6,000
Total Collections			5,900	5,250	6,500	8,125
Purchases (55% of next month's sales)	2,750	3,300	4,400	4,675	3,850	3,575
Payments (one-month lag)		2,750	3,300	4,400	4,675	3,850
CASH BUDGET						
Cash receipts						
Collections (see above)			**5,900**	**5,250**	**6,500**	**8,125**
Cash Disbursements						
Purchases			3,300	4,400	4,675	3,850
Wages			250	650	750	350
Rent			250	250	250	250
Other expenses			200	600	400	75
Interest expense on existing debt			400		20	
Taxes					590	
Purchases of equipment			1,000			
Loan repayment					800	
Total disbursements			**5,400**	**5,900**	**7,485**	**4,525**
Net monthly change			500	(650)	(985)	3,600
Plus: Beginning cash balance			1,500	2,000	1,500	1,500
Less: Interest on short-term borrowing			0	0	(1.5)	(11.4)
Equals: Ending cash balance before			**2,000**	**1,350**	**513.5**	**5,088.6**
Short-term borrowing						
Financing needed			0	150	986.5	(1,136.5)[b]
Ending cash balance			2,000	1,500	1,500	3,952.1
Cumulative borrowing			**0**	**150**	**1,136.5**	**0**

[a]The firm needs US$1,500 to raise its ending cash balance to its desired financing cash balance

[b]When a firm has excess cash to retire a part of its short-term borrowing from prior months then it has negative financing needed

the firm, and forms the basis for preparing budgets, for making estimates of future financial affairs and for monitoring the financial affairs of the firm.

Preparing a sales forecast is usually the first step in financial forecasting. A sales forecast estimates the firm's sales for a planned period in the future. The estimates developed in a sales forecast are essential elements or inputs that enhance other activities such as production scheduling, stock management, personnel planning, plant design, financial planning and budgeting. If the entrepreneur has not tried to anticipate the MSME's future financing requirement, then a crisis occurs whenever the MSME's cash inflows fall below its cash outflows. Proper planning involves anticipating and preparing for times when the MSME will require additional financing and for times when it will have surplus cash. For instance, the financing needs of growth of MSMEs often outweigh their ability to generate cash. Planning for growth means that the MSME owner can anticipate the firm's financing needs and prepare ahead. Planning ahead suggests the entrepreneur or MSME owner is in the position to explore alternative sources of financing in order to acquire the most favourable terms of finance.

9.3.1 Approaches to Forecasting

Entrepreneurs and MSME managers can concentrate on using three general approaches to financial forecasting in their enterprises. These approaches are experience, probability and correlation.

- ***Experience.*** MSME owners/managers can on the basis of past experiences with happenings in the business environment, forecast how things would be in the future. Thus, they can assume that sales, expenses or earnings will grow at certain rates on the basis of trends from the past.
- ***Probability.*** MSME owners/managers can use the probability of things happening to forecast future figures and activities. Thus, supposing it has been estimated that teenagers have a probability of buying yoghurt at US$0.30 during the dry season, then the SME owner can estimate that its sales in a Junior High School of a population of 1000 will be at least 300 units (0.3 × 1000) in the dry season. This will be multiplied by the price per unit of yoghurt to determine sales from teenagers for the dry season in the Junior High School. MSME owners can forecast the number of customers who will not pay their debt and so on based on probability of default.
- ***Correlation.*** When it is identified that there exists some correlation between the behaviour of one known variable and the behaviour of another unknown variable, then forecasts of the unknown variable can be made from the estimates provided by the known variable. Thus, if the MSME owner knows that most people who buy yoghurt also buy meat pie, then they can forecast how many units of meat pie will be bought.

9.4 Forecasting Sales

Forecasting sales is central to financial forecasting in every business including MSMEs. At a minimum, the sales forecast should reflect any past trends in sales that are expected to carry through into the planned period and the effect of any events that have the tendency of materially affecting such trends.

Preparing a sales forecast is not entirely a financial task. The estimates of future sales depend on the demand for the MSME's products and the strength of any competition in the market place. In larger firms, sales and marketing departments normally provide assessments of demand and the competition. Production staff will also provide estimates of manufacturing capacity and other production constraints. With the MSME, the owner may have to probably do all these things due to the small nature of the business.

Sales forecasts are usually used as a link between product-market performance and the financial needs of the firm. The level of forecasted sales therefore serves as a barometer for making future predictions as to the cash flows from operation that are expected to be available for future use. The expected external financing needs of a firm can be derived from the estimates of the productivity of assets, which is measured in terms of the firm's ability to support its sales.

For established businesses, the sales forecast is usually developed from their past experiences or track records. This could be done by, for instance, studying the trends in sales growth over the last six years, and then estimating average sales rates from such data.

New ventures usually do not have any historical data to rely on to make sales forecast. This makes it very difficult for them to develop such a forecast for the new venture. Even when a sales forecast is developed for such a new firm, it is often difficult to be accurate. How does an entrepreneur then project sales or arrive at a sales forecast when the product has never seen the market, and the entrepreneur does not even know how competitors will respond to such a product? There are, however, ways of making a sales forecast for new ventures, including yardstick and fundamental analysis. ***Yardstick*** is an approach that uses the past information of an existing firm that is comparable to the entrepreneur's venture in some respect, to develop the sales forecast. ***Fundamental analysis*** involves estimating the aggregate size of the relevant market. With this approach, the entrepreneur has to identify the trade area that his/her business intends to serve taking into consideration the fact that the business can grow geographically by adding a new location to the original one, or through the expansion of the customer base. He/she should also estimate the number of potential customers and their buying characteristics. The entrepreneur needs to ascertain how often a customer makes purchases and the volume of such purchases. This should give the entrepreneur a sense of the amount of revenue to be generated over time.

9.4.1 Forecasting Financial Statements

After forecasting sales, it is important to know if the enterprise's finances can support the sales forecast by extending the SME's financial statements into the future time periods. These forecasted financial statements are referred to as pro forma financial statements. The pro forma financial statements give the picture of the SME assuming that management's plans is carried out and the sales forecasts are realised. Analysis of the projected financial statements is essential to the owners of the enterprise since it helps them to know if they can get the needed funds to make purchases, if the firm can meet its loan repayment times as scheduled, whether the firm will need external financing, whether the return on investment to the SME's owner or potentials investor will be rewarding.

In forecasting a financial statement, it is important to include the cash budget and capital budgets in addition to the sales forecasts. The capital budget gives a gist of planned expenditure for major assets acquisitions by the firm, while the cash budget depicts the projected inflow and outflows of the cash of the business for a specified time period. The two can however be joined together as one, as done in some businesses.

9.4.1.1 Using Percentage of Sales Method to Forecast Financial Statements

The relationship between the sales and other financial variables are used to determine the percentage of sales forecasts. In order words, sales serve as the underlying estimator for the forecast variables. This is so because in the long-term, most financial variables will relate to sales. Other financial variables are usually independent on sales in the short run, for example, non-current assets and sunk costs.

One must first estimate the ratio between the forecast variable and sales, usually on the basis of historical data and/or one's personal opinion, when using the sales forecast to estimate a financial variable. Then a forecast of sales is made, from which the forecast variable is determined on the basis of established relationship with sales.

$$\text{Forecast variable} = \text{Ratio} \times \text{Sales forecast}$$

Thus, for an enterprise which wants to forecast its selling expenses knowing that the past relationships between sales and selling expenses have been that higher, sales require higher selling expenses, the ratio of selling expenses to sales is estimated to be 11 %. This means that with a sales forecast of US$25,000, selling expenses are expected to be US$2750.

$$\text{Selling expenses forecast} = 0.11 \times \text{US\$25,000}$$
$$\text{Selling expenses forecast} = \text{US\$2,750}$$

In the short run, the percentage of sales forecasting can be used to forecast if and only if the relationship between the forecast variable and sales is constant, which is a more realistic assumption in the short run.

	Year	Selling expenses	Sales
		US$	US$
Historical	2013	1,350	15,000
	2014	1,620	18,000
	2015	2,025	22,500
Forecast	2016	X	35,000
	2017	Y	38,000

The values of X and Y can be estimated by first establishing the relationship between sales and selling expenses from 2013 to 2015. The relationship is that selling expenses is 9 % (i.e. US$1,350/US$15,000) of sales. From this relationship, we can forecast that selling expenses from 2016 and 2017 will be 9 % of the sales figures for those two years. Thus,

$$X: \text{Selling expenses forecast 2016} = 0.09 \times US\$35,000$$
$$X: \text{Selling expenses forecast 2016} = US\$3,150$$
$$Y: \text{Selling expenses forecast 2017} = 0.09 \times US\$38,000$$
$$Y: \text{Selling expenses forecast 2017} = US\$3,420$$

9.5 Projecting Financing Needs and Growth

Any additional funds needed by the firm can be estimated or forecasted by the percentage of sales method. In order to support a projected increase in the sales level, an enterprise can forecast the amount of external financing it needs using the percentage of sales method. This is done on the assumption that changes in specific balance sheet accounts have a direct relationship with sales and remain a fixed percentage of sales over time.

On the assets side, current assets including cash, accounts receivable and stock increase spontaneously with increases in sales. Usually, non-current assets do not depend on sales unless an enterprise is operating at full capacity, in which case non-current assets must also increase to support a higher sales level.

On the liabilities and equity side, current liabilities such as accounts payable, notes payable and accrued wages and taxes generally increase spontaneously with sales. Retained earnings may also increase, but not in direct proportion to increase in sales. Permanent sources of capital do not increase spontaneously with increases in sales.

$$\begin{aligned}\text{External funds needed} \\ &= \text{Increase in assets} - \text{Increase in libilities} \\ &- \text{Increase in retained earnings}\end{aligned}$$

$$\text{External funds needed} = \frac{A}{S}(\Delta S) - \frac{L}{S}(\Delta S) - (PM)(PS)(1-d) \qquad (9.1)$$

where:

$$\frac{A}{S} = \frac{\text{assets that increase spontaneously with}}{\text{sales as a percentage of current sales}}$$

$$\frac{L}{S} = \frac{\text{liabilities that increase spontaneously with}}{\text{sales as a percentage of current sales}}$$

ΔS = change in sales.
PM = profit margin on sales.
PS = projected sales.
d = dividend payout ratio (the percentage of earnings paid out as dividend).

Example 9.2 Dallima Minerals Ltd. wants to forecast its financial requirement for 2016. The firm's current sales are US$300,000. Dallima Minerals Ltd. expects to increase sales by US$15,000 in 2016, earn a profit margin on sales of 18.7 %, and pay 60 % of its earnings out as dividends to its owners. The firm has sufficient capacity to increase sales to US$315,000 without requiring additional fixed assets. Dallima Minerals Ltd. believes that all current assets and only accounts payable vary directly with sales (Table 9.2).

The balance sheet items, which vary directly with sales, are shown below as a percentage of US$300,000 in current sales (Table 9.3).

Answer 9.2 The following figures are inserted in the equation:

$$\frac{A}{S}(\Delta S)-\frac{L}{S}(\Delta S)-(PM)(PS)(1-d).$$

Table 9.2 Dallima Minerals Ltd. Balance Sheet as at 31 December 2015

Non-current assets	US$	US$	US$
Plant and machinery		75,000	
Less accumulated depreciation		(25,000)	
Net non-current assets			**50,000**
Current assets			
Cash	3,750		
Accounts receivable	11,250		
Stock	5,000		
Total current assets		**20,000**	
Current liabilities			
Accounts payable	6,750		
Other current liabilities	750		
Total current liabilities		**7,500**	
Working capital			12,500
Total net assets			**62,500**
Financed by:			
Long-term debt (10 %)			30,000
Owner's equity			25,000
Retained earnings			7,500
Total equity and liabilities			**62,500**

Table 9.3 Dallima Minerals Ltd. Balance Sheet as at 31 December 2015 (as a percentage of sales)

Current assets	US$	Current liabilities	US$
Cash	0.0125	Accounts payable	0.0225
Accounts receivable	0.0375	Other current liabilities	n.a.
Stock	0.016667		
Total current assets	**0.066667**	Total current liabilities	**0.0225**
		Financed by:	
		Long-term debt (10 %)	n.a.
Non-current assets		Owner's equity	n.a.
Plant and machinery	n.a.	Retained earnings	n.a.
Total assets	**0.066667**	**Total equity and liability**	**0.0225**

$\frac{A}{S} = 0.07$, $\frac{L}{S} = 0.023$, $\Delta S =$ US\$15 , 000, PM = 0.187, PS = US\$315,000 and $d = 0.6$.

External funds needed :

$$= 0.07(15{,}000) - 0.023(15{,}000) - (0.187)(315{,}000)(1-0.6)$$
$$= 1{,}050 - 345 - 23{,}562$$
$$= -\text{US\$}22{,}857$$

The negative balance shows that Dallima Minerals Ltd. does not need any external funds to finance a US\$15,000 increase in sales, but has additional funds available of US\$22,857.

The income statements and balance sheets can be forecasted from the percentage of sales method, using the sales forecast as the starting point. Income statement or balance sheet accounts that vary proportionately with sales are usually estimated based on historical relationships. These percentages are multiplied by estimated sales and then are adjusted to account for expected future events and trends. Items that do not vary directly with sales are also estimated and used to forecast future financial statements. The major advantage of the percentage of sales method of forecasting is that it is simple to use.

Example 9.3 The management of Dallima Minerals Ltd. wants to forecast its income statement for the year ending December 2016, assuming:

1. Sales are forecast to be US\$315,000.
2. Items varying directly with sales are:
   - Cost of goods sold at 55 % of sales.
   - Other operating expenses at 17 % of sales.
3. Items not varying directly with sales are:
   - Total depreciation expenses, estimated to be US\$8205.
   - Interest expense, which remains unchanged from 2015 at US\$3000.
4. An income tax rate of 25 %.
5. A dividend payout ratio (percentage of earnings distributed to its owners in the form of dividend) of 60 %.

Answer 9.3 The forecasted income statement is presented below (Table 9.4):

Table 9.4 Dallima Minerals Ltd. Forecasted Income Statement for the Year Ending 31 December 2016

	US$
Net sales	315,000
Cost of goods sold (0.55 × US$315,000)	(173,250)
Gross profit	141,750
Other operating expenses (0.17 × US$315,000)	(53,550)
Depreciation	(8,205)
Earning before interest and tax	79,995
Interest expense (0.10 × US$30,000)	(3,000)
Earning after interest	76,995
Income tax (0.25)	(19,249)
Net Income after tax	57,746
Dividends (0.6)	(34,648)
Retained earnings	23,098

Example 9.4 The management of Dallima Minerals Ltd. wants to forecast the balance sheet for the year ending 31 December 2016 using the assumptions in Example 9.2 above and the additions to retained earnings of US$22,857. If the assets do not equal the liabilities and the owners' equity, they plan to plug-in additional available or required funds as needed to balance the statement.

The forecasted balance sheet for Dallima Minerals Ltd. would appear as shown below. Firms may opt for external finance by borrowing on short-term basis (notes payable), borrowing on a long-term basis (long-term debt), issuing equity (ordinary shares) or use a combination of these financing sources. The approach is known as the ***plug***.

The plug-in figure of US$31,062 represents the US$22,857 in additional available funds, using Eq. (9.1), in Sect. 9.5, plus US$8,205 in depreciation as a non-cash outlay (Table 9.5).

Answer 9.4 Example 9.5 We are contemplating a new business, Everlasting Products Enterprise. The business will be in the business of making artefacts for sale. Newly developed software will enable the new firm to be more responsive to different design specifications. By examining the market and the economics of the business, the following estimates have been made for the next three years:

Table 9.5 Dallima Ltd. Balance Sheet as at 31 December 2016

Non-current assets	US$	US$	US$
Plant and machinery		75,000	
Less accumulated depreciation		(33,205)	
Net non-current assets			**41,795**
Current assets			
Cash (0.0125 × US$ 315,000)	3,938		
Accounts receivable (0.0375 × US$ 315,000)	11,813		
Stock (0.016667 × US$ 315,000)	5,250		
Total current assets		**21,001**	
Additional available funds			**31,062**
Current liabilities			
Accounts payable (0.0225 × US$ 315,000)	7,088		
Other current liabilities	750		
Total current liabilities		**7838**	
Working capital			13,163
Total net assets			**86,020**
Financed by:			
Long-term debt (10 %)			30,000
Owner's equity			25,000
Retained earnings			31,020
Total equity and liabilities			**86,020**

1. Everlasting Products Enterprise's forecasted sales for the next three years are as follows:

	Projected Unit sales	Projected Dollar sales
Year 1	1000	US$100,000
Year 2	1600	US$160,000
Year 3	2400	US$240,000

The dollar sales projections assume that the average unit sales price for each artefact will be US$100.

2. The fixed production costs are expected to be US$50,000 per year, while the fixed operating expenses (marketing expenses and administrative expenses) should be about US$10,000. Thus, the total fixed operating costs will be US$60,000.
3. The variable costs of producing the artefacts will be around 20 % of dollar revenues (sales), and the variable operating expenses will be approximately 25 % of dollar sales. In other words, given an expected US$100 sales price, the combined variable costs per unit, both for producing the arte-

facts and for marketing the products will be US$45 [(20 % + 25 %) × US$100].

4. The bank has agreed to loan the firm an increasing amount over the next three years at an interest rate of 12 %. The bank will loan US$100,000 in the first year, another US$50,000 in the second year, and an additional US$50,000 in the third year. Thus, the loan balance each year would be as follows:

Year 1	US$100,000
Year 2	US$150,000
Year 3	US$200,000

5. Corporate tax rate is assumed to be 25 %.

Answer 9.5 Considering the foregoing assumptions, we may forecast Everlasting Products Enterprise's profits follows (Table 9.6):

The following steps are taken to project the firm's net income for the next three years:

1. First of all, compute the expected cost of sales (line 4) and the operating expenses (line 8) for the given level of sales. Subtracting these costs and expenses from the firm's sales gives us the firm's operating profits or earnings before interest and taxes (line 9).

Table 9.6 Everlasting Products Enterprise: projected income statements

	Year 1	Year 2	Year 3	
	US$	US$	US$	
Sales	100,000	160,000	240,000	*Line 1*
Cost of sales				
Fixed costs	50,000	50,000	50,000	*Line 2*
Variable costs (20 % of sales)	20,000	32,000	48,000	*Line 3*
Total cost of sales	70,000	82,000	98,000	*Line 4*
Gross profits	30,000	78,000	142,000	*Line 5*
Operating expenses				
Fixed expenses	10,000	10,000	10,000	*Line 6*
Variable expenses (25 % of sales)	25,000	40,000	60,000	*Line 7*
Total operating expenses	35,000	50,000	70,000	*Line 8*
Operating profits	(5000)	28,000	72,000	*Line 9*
Interest expenses (interest rate 12 %)	12,000	18,000	24,000	*Line 10*
Earnings before tax	(17,000)	10,000	48,000	*Line 11*
Taxes (25 % of earnings before tax)		02,500	12,000	*Line 12*
Net income	(17,000)	7,500	36,000	*Line 13*

2. Next is to compute the interest expense for each year line (10), which in this case, was calculated as follows:

Year 1:	12 % × 100,000	=	US$12,000
Year 2:	12 % × 150,000	=	US$18,000
Year 3:	12 % × 200,000	=	US$24,000

3. Finally, calculation includes estimating income taxes, which in this case is 25 % of earnings before tax. However, it is important to recognise the little complication resulting from the US$17,000 loss in the first year. Depending on the jurisdiction, the tax laws may permit a company to carry forward losses to be set off against future profits. For the sake of simplicity, let us assume that taxes are not paid when losses are incurred.

From the computations, it can be seen that the firm will lose money in the first year to the tune of US$17,000, followed by positive net profits of US$7500 and US$36,000 in the second and third years, respectively.

9.6 Financing Needs and Break-Even Analysis

After completing the first task of projecting the future profits of the firm, it is now appropriate to look at how to determine the break-even point of the firm, an important issue to any entrepreneur or investor in an MSME.

9.6.1 Break-Even Analysis

An entrepreneur or investor in a start-up business will be interested to know how long it may take for the firm to start posting profits. It is important for the entrepreneur to ascertain the number of units of the firm's product that must be sold before becoming profitable. Considering the number of break-even units, along with our sales forecast, it may be easy to conclude on the time required for the firm to become profitable.

We can adapt an equation from the income statement to determine the break-even point. Using the income statement as presented in Answer 9.5, we understand that operating profits, or earnings before interest and taxes, is computed as follows:

$$\begin{matrix}\text{Total} \\ \text{dollar sales}\end{matrix} - \begin{matrix}\text{Cost of} \\ \text{goods sold}\end{matrix} - \begin{matrix}\text{Operating} \\ \text{expenses}\end{matrix} = \begin{matrix}\text{Operating} \\ \text{profits}\end{matrix} \tag{9.2}$$

From this equation, we are interested in finding out the number of units sold, and the corresponding dollar sales that result in *operating* profit of zero. This means, we want to compute the sales level where:

$$\frac{\text{Total}}{\text{dollar sales}} - \frac{\text{Cost of}}{\text{goods sold}} - \frac{\text{Operating}}{\text{expenses}} = 0 \qquad (9.3)$$

From the above equation, it is possible to establish the break-even sales level, by using trial and error. Another approach is to restate the equation by looking for the sales level that fully covers the variable and fixed costs. This can be restated as:

$$\frac{\text{Total}}{\text{dollar sales}} - \frac{\text{Total}}{\text{variables cost}} - \frac{\text{Total}}{\text{fixed cost}} = 0 \qquad (9.4)$$

Also, considering that a firm's total dollar sales can be calculated as:

$$(\text{selling price per unit}) \times (\text{the number of units sold,})$$

And, total variable costs can be computed as:

$$(\text{variable costs per unit}) \times (\text{the number of units sold}),$$

The break-even equation can then be restated as:

$$\left[\frac{\text{Sellng price}}{\text{per unit}} \times \frac{\text{Units}}{\text{sold}}\right] - \left[\frac{\text{Unit}}{\text{variable cost}} \times \frac{\text{Units}}{\text{sold}}\right] - \frac{\text{Total}}{\text{fixed cost}} = 0 \qquad (9.5)$$

Finding for the numbers of units sold that give operating profit of zero, we have

$$\frac{\text{Break}-\text{even}}{\text{units sold}} = \frac{\text{Total fixed costs}}{\text{Selling price} - \text{Unit variable cost}} \qquad (9.6\text{a})$$

Therefore, we observe that the break-even point is a function of: (1) the total fixed operating costs of the firm (numerator) and (2) the unit selling price minus the unit variable cost (denominator). If fixed costs go higher, more units must be sold in order for the firm to break even. If the difference between the selling price per unit and the variable cost per unit is larger, then fewer units must be sold for the firm to break even. The difference between the selling price per unit and the variable cost per unit is known as the *contribution margin*, that is, for each unit sold, a contribution is made towards covering the firm's fixed costs.

Finally, we can shorten Eq. (9.6a) by using the following notations:

Let Q_B = the number of units sold to break-even.

F = the total fixed operating costs (includes all operating costs that are constant at various levels of production/sales).

P = the unit selling price.

V = the variable cost per unit (includes all costs that vary directly with the volume produced/sold).

Equation (9.6a) may now be stated more succinctly as follows:

$$Q_B = \frac{F}{p - V} \tag{9.6b}$$

Example 9.6 Recall the Everlasting Products Enterprise example, where we forecast the firm's profits. As seen in Answer 9.5, the firm achieved profitability in the second year. Now the question is how many units must be sold, and the corresponding dollars sales in order for the firm to reach the break-even point in operating profits. The following information is required from the example:

F = the total fixed operating costs = US$60,000.

P = the unit selling price = US$100.

V = the variable cost per unit = US$45

Answer 9.6 Therefore, considering the information, the break-even point in number of units, Q_B, is calculated as follows:

$$Q_B = \frac{F}{P - V} = \frac{US\$60,000}{US\$100 - US\$45} = 1091 \text{ units}$$

Also, we can compute the break-even in dollar sales as follows:

$$\frac{\text{Dollar}}{\text{break} - \text{even}} = \text{Break} - \text{even units} \times \text{Sales per unit}$$

$$\begin{array}{c}\text{Dollar} \\ \text{break}-\text{even}\end{array} = 1{,}091\,\text{units} \times US\$100 = US\$109{,}100$$

It is now clear how to forecast profits and how to compute the break-even point in terms of profits.

9.7 Determinants of Financing Needs

Financial forecasting is an essential tool used in assessing the financial needs of firms. Smith et al. (2011) identified a number of determinants of the financing needs of a business venture, including profitability, cash flow, minimum efficient scale and sales growth. These are discussed in turn:

9.7.1 Profitability

Firms need to be profitable in order to stay in business. This helps firms to reduce their external financing needs since they are able to generate enough funds internally to stay in business. The higher the profitability of a firm, the lower the financial needs of the firm, all other things being equal. Though highly profitable MSMEs may have better access to external sources of finance than less profitable ones, their need for external finance will be lower if retained earnings are sufficient to finance new investments. According to the pecking order theory, firms prefer internal sources of finance to external sources. Profitable firms will utilise retained earnings as opposed to depending on external finance. Retained earnings constitute the cheapest source of finance followed by debt and external equity.

9.7.2 Cash Flow

Though profitability reduces the need for external financing, it may however increase a firm's demand for financing due to its other considerations factors. Firms thrive well on cash but not on profit. It is possible for a firm to be making profit, however it may be suffering from not meeting its financial needs. The fact that a firm is profitable does not mean that it has cash to spend. Payments are made with cash but not profit. It is therefore necessary to consider the cash flow of the firm since it is the cash flows that enable the firm to meet its daily operational expenses and cost. A firm that sells for cash may better meet its internal operations (though may not be profitable) than a profitable firm that sells on credit. This is because the firm that sells on credit does not receive immediate cash for their credit sales and this can affect the operations of such a firm, especially when it is in need of funds. Other factors such as buying inventory on credit and timing of payments to employees may also affect the cash flow of the firm.

It is also useful to recognise the difference between cash flow and profit in the sense that firms do not record capital expenditures in the income statement in the period when they are incurred. Capital expenditures are recorded in the balance sheet as fixed assets. It is only a portion of the assets that would be written off over several years in relation to the assets useful life (this is however dependent on the tax laws of a particular jurisdiction). A firm underestimates its financing needs when it focuses on the profitability rather than on cash flows in the year that a fixed asset is bought. It, however, overestimates the need for financing in the later years when the asset is depreciated.

9.7.3 Minimum Efficient Scale

The production of goods and services of firms is carried out by the use of inputs. The nature of a firm usually determines whether it should use too much of fixed inputs or variable inputs (employees and materials). Broadly, inputs of a firm can be classified as employees, materials and fixed assets. What usually determines a firm's scale of operation is the kind of activity that the firm engages in. Firms that engage in services usually do not have to incur a lot of capital investment in their operations. This reduces their investment in fixed assets. As a result, such firms will therefore invest in employees and other materials that propel the rendering of their services. However, capital intensive businesses usually need a great amount of fixed assets compared to other inputs. The inputs of a start-up firm are decided by whether the business venture is capital intensive or labour intensive.

For firms to enjoy economies of scale, as the volume of output per time increases, the long-run average cost must decline. Firms should endeavour to produce at the minimum point of the long-run average curve, since declining below this point puts the firm at a competitive disadvantage.

9.7.4 Sales Growth

As firms grow, they sometimes find it difficult to generate enough cash to finance their operations. This is because growing may need to inject more capital investment into the firm's operations. Cash allocations to items like inventory, investment in equipment, as well as wages and salaries, increase with the growth of the firm. The growth rate of the firm should be at least proportional to its profitability in order not to put so much pressure on the firm to resort to outside generated funds. When this happens, the internally generated funds (cash flows) are usually not sufficient to cater for the financial needs of the firm.

9.8 Summary and Conclusions

In this chapter, we examined the concept of financial planning and forecasting. Financial planning deals with the orderly acquisition of capital, as well as the utilisation of the capital, through the establishment of well-crafted plans directed towards such goals. It entails identifying the sources of funds and the application of the funds in relation to enhancing the financial future of the firm.

The financial planning process involves setting enterprise goals, developing long-term financial plans, developing short-term financial plans, developing individual budgets and developing a consolidated budget. A budget is a financial plan that sets out expected future results expressed in monetary terms, usually for a limited period.

Forecasting sales is central to financial forecasting in every business, including MSMEs. At the minimum, the sales forecast should reflect any past trends in sales that are expected to carry through into the planned period and the influence of any events that might materially affect those trends. Sales forecasts are usually used as a link between product-market performance and the financial needs of the firm. The level of forecasted sales therefore serves as a barometer for making future predictions as to the cash flows from operations that are expected to be available for future use. The expected external financing needs of a firm can be derived from the estimates of the productivity of assets, which is measured in terms of the firm's ability to support its sales.

Financial forecasting is an essential tool used in assessing the financial needs of firms. The determinants of the financing needs of a business venture include profitability, cash flow, minimum efficient scale and sales growth.

Discussion Questions and Problems

1. What is the significance of preparing and producing forecasts for MSMEs?
2. For the last five years, cost of goods sold for Beauty Ltd. has averaged 60 % of sales. This trend is expected to continue for the foreseeable future. If sales for 2016 are expected to be US$20,000, what would be the forecast 2016 value for cost of goods sold?

3. The Happy Ltd.s pro forma balance sheet for 31 December 2015 indicates that total assets will be US$12,000, but total liabilities and equity will be only US$8000. What should Happy Ltd. do to resolve the discrepancy between assets and liabilities?
4. Bans Bakery Ltd. has just come out with a new bread flavour that they are sure will cause sales to double between 2015 and 2016. Using the following worksheet, complete Bans Bakery's pro forma financial forecast and answer the related questions.
   Assume that cost of sales, current assets, and current liabilities will maintain the same percentage of sales as in 2015. Further, assume that no new fixed assets will be needed in 2016, and the current dividend policy will be continued in 2016.

   Estimate the additional funds that Bans Bakery Ltd. will need in 2016.

5. Mr. Yin owns Sugar Cane Farms', a small-sized farm. He would like to expand his farms and buy a nearby land. Mr. Yin does not have the capital to undertake this project and would like to borrow the money from the local bank. He knows the banker will need projected income statement for his current farms when considering his loan application. Net sales for 2015 were US 80,000. Considering the previous growth rates in his business and the anticipated increase in tourism, projected net sales for 2016 is US 100, 000. Cost of goods sold and selling and marketing expenses will remain the same value as 2015 at US 4,000. Mr. Yin uses the straight-line method of depre-

Table A.9.1 Bans Bakery Ltd.: Financial Status and Forecast

	2015 US$	Estimate for 2016 US$
Sales	12,000	
Cost of sales	6,000	
Gross profit	6,000	
Fixed expenses	3,000	
Before-tax profit	3,000	
Tax @ 25 %	750	
Net profit	2,250	
Dividends	0	
Current assets	25,000	
Net assets	15,000	
Total assets	**40,000**	
Current liabilities	17,000	
Long-term debt	3,000	
Ordinary shares	7,000	
Retained earnings	13,000	
Total liabilities and equity	**40,000**	

ciation, so the previous year's depreciation expense figure of US 1,000 can also be applied to 2016.

Answer the following questions based on the following assumptions.

(a) Cost of goods sold in 2015 was US 47,000. What is the forecasted value of Cost of goods sold for 2016?
(b) What is the forecasted gross profit for 2016?
(c) Selling and marketing expenses for 2015 were US 12,000. What is the forecasted value for 2016?
(d) Calculate the forecasted operating income for 2016.
(e) Assume the interest expense for 2015 is US 700 and the tax rate is 30%. Calculate earnings before interest and tax (EBIT) and net income expected for 2016 to the nearest dollar.
(f) If US 9,000 is distributed in dividends in 2016, what will be 2016's addition to retained earnings?

6. After completing the pro forma income statement in Question 5, Mr. Yin now realises he should also complete a pro forma balance sheet. Net sales in 2015 was US$80,000 and his forecasted sales for 2016 is US$100,000. All of Sugar Cane Farms' current assets will remain the same percent of sales as they were in 2015. Mr. Yin does not plan to buy or sell any equipment, so his gross property and equipment amount will remain the same as in 2015. In the liabilities and equity section, only accounts payable will remain the same percent of sales as 2015. Except for retained earnings, the other accounts are expected to remain the same as in 2015. The following balances were taken from Sugar Cane Farms' end of 2015 balance sheet:

(a) Calculate the forecasted end of 2016 values for each of the current asset accounts.
(b) Depreciation expense for 2016 is estimated to be US$1000. Calculate the estimated total assets for the end of 2016.
(c) Forecast the accounts payable for the end of 2016.
(d) What will total liabilities be at the end of 2016?
(e) Assuming the forecasted net income for 2016 is US$18,351, and cash dividends paid equals US$9,000, what total amount will be forecasted for the end of 2016 total liabilities and equity?
(f) Based on these calculations of the pro forma balance sheet, are additional funds needed?

(g) Net income for 2015 was US$13,859. What was Sugar Cane Farms' net profit margin for 2015? The forecasted net income for 2016 is US$18,367. What is Sugar Cane Farms' forecasted 2016 net profit margin?

7. Africagrowth Ltd. expects rapid sales growth next year. Sales for the current year were US$8 million, and are expected to grow by 15 % next year. Africagrowth Ltd. wants to estimate the external capital that will be required to finance this growth. The company estimates that additional assets equal to 25 % of the increase in sales will be required. Liabilities will increase by 20 % of sales. The net profit margin is 5 % and Africagrowth Ltd. expects to pay US$50,000 in dividends to its ordinary shareholders. Compute the external capital required by Africagrowth Limited.
8. Use the percent of sales method to prepare a pro forma income statement for Calico Enterprise. Projected sales for next year equal US$20,000. Cost of goods sold is expected to be 70 % of sales, administrative expense equals US$5000, and depreciation expense is US$7000. Interest expense equals US$5,000 and income is taxed at a rate of 40 %. The firm plans to spend US$1,000 during the year to renovate its office facility and will retire US$7,000 in notes payable. Finally, selling expense equals 5 % of sales.
9. Grace Enterprise has estimated sales and purchase requirements for the last half of the coming year. Past experience indicates that it will collect 20 % of its sales in the month of sale, 50 % of the remainder one month after the sale, and the balance in the second month following the sale. Grace Enterprise prefers to pay for half its purchases in the month of the purchase and the other half the following month. Labour expense for each month is expected to equal 5 % of that month's sales, with cash payment being made in the month in which the expense is incurred. Depreciation expense is US$200 per month; miscellaneous cash expenses of US$2,500 per month are paid in the month incurred. General and administrative expenses of US$900 are recognised and paid monthly. A US$24,000 truck is to be

Table A.9.2. Sugar cane farms' end of 2015 balance sheet

Cash	9,000
Accounts receivable	1220
Inventory	7,000
Property and equipment (gross)	24,000
Accumulated depreciation	3,000
Property and equipment (net)	20,000
Accounts payable	480
Long-term notes payable	7,000
Retained earnings	4,000
Ordinary shares	25,840

purchased in August and is to be depreciated on a straight-line basis over ten years with no expected salvage value. Grace Enterprise also plans to pay a US$9,000 cash dividend to stockholders in July. The Enterprise feels that a minimum cash balance of US$12,000 should be maintained. Any borrowing will cost 12 % annually, with interest paid in the month following the month in which the funds are borrowed. Borrowing takes place at the beginning of the month in which the need for funds is made. For example, if during the month of July, the firm should need to borrow US$5000 to maintain its US$12,000 desired minimum balance, then US$5000 will be taken out on 1 July with the interest owed for the entire month of July. Interest for the month of July would then be paid on 1 August. Sales and purchase estimates are shown in the following chart.
Prepare a cash budget for the months of July and August (cash on hand 30 June was US$12,000, whereas sales for May and June were US$4000 and purchases were US$1500 for each of these months).

Table A.9.3 Sales and purchase estimates

Month	Sales US$	Purchases US$
July	8,000	5,000
August	9,000	4,000
September	10,000	3,000

10

Working Capital Management

Learning Objectives
By the end of this chapter, you should be able to:

- explain the concept of working capital management
- describe the components of working capital management
- discuss the importance of proper inventory management
- appreciate how accounts receivable are efficiently managed
- explain the relevance of good cash management among firms
- discuss how firms invest excess cash through marketable securities management
- explain how firms' current liabilities are managed

10.1 Introduction

Entrepreneurs and manager of MSMEs are often confronted with the issue of proper management of their working capital. Small businesses on regular basis have to make payments with respect of inventory purchased from suppliers, utility bills, staff salaries, insurance premiums, rent and so on. They also expect some receipts out of the revenues generated. The problem often has to do with the fact that these receipts may not come in at the time payments are supposed to be made. How does the entrepreneur or small business manager deal with this problem? The purpose of this chapter is to help better manage such a situation to ensure that the entrepreneurial value or value of the MSME is enhanced.

J.Y. Abor, *Entrepreneurial Finance for MSMEs*,
DOI 10.1007/978-3-319-34021-0_10

This chapter discusses working capital management in general. It then specifically focuses on the various components of working capital management, inventory management, accounts receivable management, cash management, marketable securities management and current liabilities management.

10.2 Concepts of Working Capital

Working capital is the capital available for conducting the daily operations of a firm and it consists of the current assets and the current liabilities. The current assets are assets, which can normally be converted into cash within one year. Current assets are also known as **gross working capital** and they are made up of inventory, accounts receivable, cash and marketable securities. Current liabilities are amounts owed by the firm, which are normally due within one year, and they include accounts payable, notes payable, accrued expenses and taxes payable. The difference between the firm's current assets and the current liabilities is referred to as **net working capital**. The net working capital is a measure of the firm's liquidity, which is the ability of the firm to convert its assets into cash. Net working capital is mathematically defined as follows:

$$\text{Net working capital} = \text{Current assets}\left(\text{gross working capital}\right) - \text{Current liabilities.}$$

For instance, if a firm has current assets of US$6,500,000 and current liabilities of US$3,000,000, then its net working capital will be US$3,500,000. The US$3,500,000 is an indication of the firm's ability to pay its short-term debt or current liabilities. It also means the current assets can pay for short-term liabilities 2.17 times. We had this ratio by simply dividing the current assets by the current liabilities (i.e. US$6,500,000/US$3,000,000 = 2.17).

10.3 Working Capital Management

Working capital management involves the management of all aspects of the firm's current assets and current liabilities in order to maximise returns on its assets and minimise payments on its liabilities. Working capital management involves maintaining optimum levels of all items that constitute net working capital. There is, however, a trade-off between the risk of having small working capital on one hand and the reduced profitability that results from having excess working capital on the other. The basic goal of working capital management is to maximise returns on assets and to ensure that the firm is able to continue its operations and that it has sufficient funds to satisfy short-term debt obligations as and when they fall due.

10.3.1 Determining Working Capital Requirement

In determining the working capital requirement of a firm, there are two basic concepts to be employed and these are the operating cycle, and the funds required per dollar of sales.

10.3.1.1 The Operating Cycle

The operating cycle refers to the process of turning raw materials into finished goods, and turning the finished goods into credit sales and finally converting the credit sales into cash. It shows the number of days or length of time it takes the firm to convert the raw materials into cash. It is calculated as the average age of inventory plus average age of accounts receivable less average age of accounts payable. The operating cycle is also known as the working capital cycle, trading cycle, cash conversion cycle (CCC) or cash cycle. The faster a firm can 'push' items around the cycle, the lower its investment in working capital and the better its cash flow position is.

The CCC shows the average duration of a firm's cash that is invested in inventory and accounts receivable, both of which do not yield any interest. It is therefore prudent for the firm to keep the CCC as short as possible. Let us try and go through the process of calculating the CCC.

Example 10.1 The following information relates to Bapela Brothers Enterprise, a private company which deals in the production of cement: sales US$2,000,000; purchases US$1,200,000; cost of sales US$1,500,000; debtors US$400,000; creditors US$180,000; raw materials US$280,000; work-in-progress US$120,000 and finished goods US$200,000.

Calculate the Bapela Brothers Enterprise's CCC for a period of one year, assuming 365 calendar days.

Answer 10.1

$$\text{Raw materials turnover period} = \frac{\text{Raw materials}}{\text{Purchases}} \times 365 = \frac{280{,}000}{1{,}200{,}000} \times 365 = 85\ \text{days}$$

$$\text{Work in progress turnover period} = \frac{\text{WIP}}{\text{Cost of sales}} \times 365 = \frac{120{,}000}{1{,}500{,}000} \times 365 = 29\ \text{days}$$

$$\text{Finished goods turnover period} = \frac{\text{Finished goods}}{\text{Cost of sales}} \times 365 = \frac{200{,}000}{1{,}500{,}000} \times 365 = 49\ \text{days}$$

$$\text{Accounts receivable or debtors turnover period} = \frac{\text{Debtors}}{\text{Sales}} \times 365 = \frac{400{,}000}{2{,}000{,}000} \times 365 = 73\ \text{days}$$

$$\text{Accounts payable or creditors turnover period} = \frac{\text{Creditors}}{\text{Purchases}} \times 365 = \frac{180{,}000}{1{,}200{,}000} \times 365 = 55\text{days}$$

CCC = Raw materials turnover period + Work-in-progress turnover period + Finished goods turnover Period + Debtors turnover period – Creditors turnover period

$$\text{CCC} = 85\ \text{days} + 29\ \text{days} + 49\ \text{days} + 73\ \text{days} - 55\ \text{days} = 181\ \text{days}$$

This means that it takes the Bapela Brothers Enterprise 181 days to purchase raw materials, produce goods, sell to customers and recover cash from customers. The lower the CCC, the quicker the firm is able to convert raw materials into cash.

10.3.1.2 Working Capital Required per Dollar of Sales

Under the working capital required per dollar of sales approach, we use the relationship between sales and relevant items of current assets and current liabilities in estimating the level of working capital required. For example, if for every US$1 of sales, the firm requires US$0.40 of working capital, then the working capital requirement of the firm if sales for next year is US$7,000,000, this will be US$2,800,000 (i.e. US$7,000,000 × US$0.40).

10.3.2 Determinants of Working Capital Levels

Holding or maintaining adequate working capital is very crucial to the operations of firms. Indeed, MSMEs are also expected to have adequate working capital to carry out their day-to-day business activities. The level of working capital of the firm is determined by the nature and size of the business, the production cycle of the firm, the level of sales growth, the firm's credit policy, and the availability of suppliers' credit.

The nature and size of the firm can influence its level of working capital. For instance, trading firms may require very small investments in fixed assets, but may need huge amount of cash and inventory by way of working capital. A manufacturing firm also requires huge investments in inventory. Service firms may not require huge investment in inventory but may need to hold sufficient cash. Generally, larger firms or those with a large scale of operation that will need more working capital than smaller ones.

The level of working capital requirement of a firm is affected by its production cycle: the longer the production cycle, the larger the firms' working capital requirement. A shorter production cycle, on the other, may not require that the firm hold too much working capital.

Level of sales growth is also an important determinant of a firm's level of working capital requirement. Higher levels of sales growth will require that the firm maintains or holds a reasonably high level of working capital.

The firm's credit policy is a determinant of the level of credit. The credit policy of a firm affects the level of financing given to customers. A lenient credit policy will require that the firm increases its working capital or maintains a high level of working capital. A firm with a tight credit policy may not require a high level of working capital.

Availability of credit provided by suppliers is also an important factor influencing the level of working capital. Accessing credit from suppliers reduces the level of working capital that the firm will have to hold. However, where firm's suppliers are unwilling to offer credit terms, this will increase the level or working capital the firm has to hold.

10.4 Inventory Management

Inventory management is concerned with ensuring that sufficient levels of inventory or stock are maintained in order to meet the demand of customers while minimising the associated holding, administrative and stock-out costs.

An efficient inventory management requires that adequate inventory must be held to satisfy customers' demand. Too much inventory is actually expensive and wasteful, as the firm incurs costs such as capital tied up, storage costs, deterioration, obsolescence and even pilferage. Not having sufficient inventory can result in lost sales. The firm should therefore aim at minimising the total inventory costs while maximising customers' satisfaction. In order to strike that balance, the firm must determine the reorder quantity (number of items to order) and the reorder level (the level of inventory at which the new order will be placed). There are four main types of inventory and they are raw materials, work-in-progress, finished goods and maintenance, repair and operating inventories.

10.4.1 Economic Order Quantity of Inventory

The economic order quantity (EOQ) is an inventory management system that is mostly used for determining the optimum reorder quantity at any time. The EOQ model tries to balance the ordering costs against holding costs and it provides the firm with the optimal economic quantity to order which will minimise overall inventory costs. The main assumptions underlying the EOQ model are:

(i) Demand or inventory use is constant in a year.
(ii) Lead time is constant or zero.
(iii) Purchase costs per unit are constant (i.e. no bulk discount).

The formula is stated as follows:

$$EOQ = \sqrt{\frac{2DCo}{HC}}$$

Where:
D = total annual demand for the item
Co = ordering cost per order
HC = holding cost per unit for one year
EOQ = economic order quantity

Note that in situations where the firm produces its own stock instead of buying, you may be asked to calculate the size of each production run. In this case, the model is modified as follows:

$$EOQ = \sqrt{\frac{2DCs}{HC\left(1 - \frac{D}{R}\right)}}$$

where:
Cs = set-up cost
R = production run per annum

Example 10.2 Let us assume Easybuy's demand for a commodity is 40,000 units a year, at a steady rate. It costs US$20 to place an order, and US$0.40 to hold a unit for a year. Compute:

(a) the order size to minimise stock costs,
(b) the number of orders placed each year,
(c) the length of the stock cycle,
(d) total annual inventory costs.

Answer 10.2 (a) The order size to minimise stock costs is:

$$EOQ = \sqrt{\frac{2DCo}{HC}} = \sqrt{\frac{(2)(40{,}000)(US\$20)}{US\$0.4}} = \sqrt{4{,}000{,}000} = 2{,}000 \text{ units}$$

(b) The number of orders placed in a year will be:

$$\frac{D}{Q} = \frac{40{,}000}{2{,}000} = 20 \text{ orders}$$

(c) The length of the stock cycle will be the number of days in the year divided by the number of orders and this will give us:

$$\frac{365}{20} = 18.25 \text{ days}$$

This means orders will be placed approximately every 18 days.

We could also divide the number of weeks in the year by the number of orders and we will get:

$$\frac{52}{20} = 2.6 \text{ weeks}$$

This means orders will be placed every 2.6 weeks and this works out to be every 18 days.

(d) The total annual inventory cost is also computed as:

$$TC = \text{Ordering cost} + \text{Holding cost}$$

The number of orders placed in a year is equal to the annual demand (*D*) divided by the order quantity (*Q*) (i.e. *D*/*Q*). We then multiply the number of orders by the ordering cost per order (Co) to get the total ordering cost, or $\frac{D}{Q}(\text{Co})$.

Since inventory is used at a constant rate during the year, the average inventory at any given point in time is half the order quantity (*Q*) (i.e. *Q*/2). We then multiply the average inventory by the holding cost per unit (HC) to get the total holding cost, or $\frac{Q}{2}(\text{HC})$.

Therefore, we can restate our total cost (TC) formula as follows:

$$TC = \frac{D}{Q}(\text{Co}) + \frac{Q}{2}(\text{HC})$$

$$TC = \frac{40{,}000}{2{,}000}(\text{US\$}20) + \frac{2{,}000}{2}(\text{US\$}0.4)$$

$$TC = \text{US\$}400 + \text{US\$}400 = \text{US\$}800$$

Example 10.3 For each unit of a computer manufactured, 4 units of raw materials are required. Denzel Tech manufactures 100,000 computers per annum and the demand for computers is stable throughout the year. It costs US$400 each time raw materials are ordered and carrying cost is US$20 per unit of raw materials per annum.

Required:

(a) Determine the EOQ of raw materials
(b) Determine the inventory cost

Answer 10.3 Note that we are interested in the EOQ of raw materials and since the four units of raw material are required to produce 1 unit of computer, to produce 100,000 computers a year, the annual demand for the raw materials will be 400,000 units (i.e. 100,000 × 4).

$D = 100{,}000 \times 4 = 400{,}000$ units
$\text{Co} = 400$
$\text{HC} = 20$

$$\text{EOQ} = \sqrt{\frac{2\text{DCo}}{\text{HC}}} = \sqrt{\frac{(2)(400{,}000)(\text{US\$}400)}{\text{US\$}20}} = \sqrt{16{,}000{,}000} = 4{,}000 \text{ units}$$

The total inventory cost will be:

$$\text{TC} = \frac{\text{D}}{\text{Q}}(\text{Co}) + \frac{\text{Q}}{2}(\text{HC})$$

$$\text{TC} = \frac{400{,}000}{4{,}000}(400) + \frac{4{,}000}{2}(20) = \text{US\$}40{,}000 + \text{US\$}40{,}000 = \text{US\$}80{,}000$$

Example 10.4 Rainbow Limited has a large warehouse storing building materials. The company uses 8,000,000 bags of cement in a year. The cost of a bag of cement is US$125. The cost of processing an order is US$300 and holding costs are 15 % of average dollar inventory value. Antack Enterprise, the supplier of cement to Rainbow Construction Limited has offered to give a discount of 10 % if lots of 20,000 bags of cement are purchased. Determine:

(a) The optimal order quantity when discounts are not offered.
(b) The total inventory cost when discounts are not offered.
(c) Should Rainbow Construction Limited take the discount offer?

Answer 10.4 (a) **When discounts are not offered:**
The EOQ is determined as:

$$\text{EOQ} = \sqrt{\frac{2\text{DCo}}{\text{HC}}} = \sqrt{\frac{(2)(8{,}000{,}000)(\text{US\$}300)}{(0.15)(\text{US\$}125)}} = \sqrt{256{,}000{,}000} = 16{,}000 \text{ bags}$$

The total inventory cost will be:

$$TC = \frac{D}{Q}(Co) + \frac{Q}{2}(HC)$$

$$TC = \frac{8,000,000}{16,000}(US\$300) + \frac{16,000}{2}(0.15 \times US\$125)$$

$$TC = US\$150,000 + US\$150,000 = US\$300,000$$

(b) **When discounts are offered:**

Note that in cases where discounts are offered, we need to use the discount price. In this case, the discount price is US$112.5 (i.e. US$125 minus the 10 % discount). Therefore, our holding cost per unit will now be US$16.875 (i.e. 0.15 × US$112.5). The quantity to be ordered in this case is 20,000.

The total inventory cost will be:

$$TC = \text{Ordering cost} + \text{Holding cost}$$

$$TC = \frac{8,000,000}{20,000}(US\$300) + \frac{20,000}{2}(0.15 \times US\$112.5)$$

$$TC = US\$120,000 + US\$168,750 = US\$288,750$$

(c) **Decision to accept discount or not:**

In deciding on whether to accept the discount or not, we need to include the total value of purchases in our analysis, since the discounts are usually on the purchase price.

Under the condition of no discount, the value of purchases was US$1,000,000,000 (i.e. 8,000,000 bags × US$125). In that case the total cost under condition of no discount will be:

$$\text{Overall total cost} = US\$300,000 + US\$1,000,000,000 = US\$1,00,300,000$$

Under the condition of discount, the value of purchases was US$900,000,000 (i.e. 8,000,000 bags × US$112.5). In that case the total cost under condition of discount will be

$$\text{Overall total cost} = US\$288,750 + US\$900,000,000 = US\$900,288,750$$

Since the overall total cost is lower when discount is taken, it is advisable for Rainbow Construction Limited to accept the discount offer.

10.4.2 Reorder Point Calculation

The **reorder point (ROP)** is the level that requires putting into action the replenishment of stock. It is the level where management must place an order for new stock to be supplied. It is the level below which stock is not supposed to fall. The reorder point is determined by the lead-time, daily demand, and safety. **Lead time** (L) is the time between when a firm places an order for stock and when the stock is actually received. **Daily demand** (d) is the quantity of the stock that is used per day. **Safety stock (ss)** is the minimum quantity of stock held as a buffer and only used in times of emergency. We can depict these in Fig. 10.1.

The reorder point is therefore the daily demand during the lead-time plus the safety stock and this is defined mathematically as follows:

$$\mathrm{ROP} = \mathrm{Ld} + \mathrm{ss}$$

Example 10.5 A trading firm has an expected usage of 50,000 units of a product during next year. The cost of processing an order is US$180 and carrying cost per unit is US$2 for a year. Lead time on an order is seven days and the firm will keep a reserve supply equivalent to four days usage.

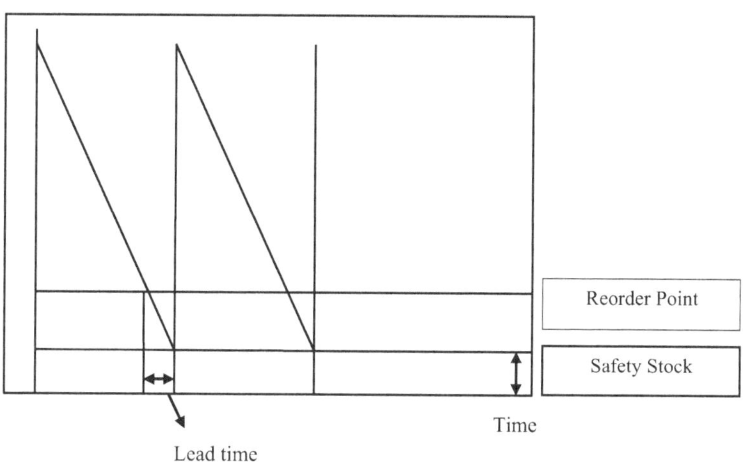

Fig. 10.1 Investment in inventory

Required:

(a) Calculate the EOQ.
(b) Calculate the reorder level assuming the firm is open for 250 days in a year.

Answer 10.5 (a) Economic order quantity (EOQ)

$$EOQ = \sqrt{\frac{2DCo}{HC}} = \sqrt{\frac{(2)(50{,}000)(US\$180)}{US\$2}} = \sqrt{9{,}000{,}000} = 3{,}000 \text{ units}$$

(b) Reorder point (ROP)

$$ROP = Ld + ss$$

$$\text{Daily demand or usage} = \frac{50{,}000}{250} = 200 \text{ units}$$

Safety stock = 200 × 4 days = 800 units.
Therefore, the reorder point will be:

$$ROP = Ld + ss$$

$$ROP = (7)(200) + 800 = 2{,}200 \text{ units}$$

10.4.3 Just-in-Time Inventory System

Another inventory management system is the just-in-time (JIT) model. It was first introduced by Toyota Motor Company in Japan but it has spread rapidly and has been adopted by many other firms. It is particularly useful to those firms that produce a variety of products. The JIT model, also known as stock-less production, aims at obtaining inventory from suppliers at the point when they are needed, and so avoiding the need to carry any materials or components stock. This inventory management system attempts to match physical need with inventory at the point in time the inventory is needed. This means the firm carries little or no inventory, but obviously there is the danger or risk of running out of stock and not being able to meet customers' demands. Therefore, the use of the JIT system requires close coordination between suppliers and the firm. If the firm reduces it levels by introducing the JIT system, it means that it will require a lower level of investment in working capital. A restaurant, for instance, might find it preferable to use the EOQ approach for staple non-perishable food stocks but adopt JIT for perishable and 'exotic' items. In a hospital, a stock-out could have serious repercussion and as such JIT would be quite unsuitable.

10.4.4 The ABC System of Inventory Management

The ABC system is concerned with treating stock items differently, based on the volume of sales they generate or how important they are to the firm's manufacturing process. The essence of the ABC system is that detailed stock control is costly and time consuming, therefore, efforts should be directed where they are most needed and produce the greatest returns. The ABC system ranks inventory according to value, which allows the firm to set control and carrying cost constraints based on inventory investment. The ranks are:

- 'A rank'—the few very expensive items
- 'B rank'—larger number of less expensive items
- 'C rank'—relatively inexpensive items

'A rank' items account for the bulk of total value, usually put at 80 %, although they actually represent 10 % to 20 % of the items. Such items require close day-to-day control. 'B rank' items account for 15 % of total value and represent about 30 % of items. They require regular review while class 'C rank' items account for 10 % of total value, although they represent 50 % of items. These are reviewed infrequently. The ABC system ensures that the firm's resources are put to optimal use. It also saves time and labour since it counts only the inventory required by the cycle for the class of inventory as compared to counting all inventory items every cycle. However, more resources are required to maintain the ABC system compared with the traditional costing systems.

10.5 Accounts Receivable Management

Accounts receivable is money owed to a firm from the sale of its goods and services in the normal course of business. A firm extends credit in order to stimulate sales, however, there are costs involved in granting credit. Accounts receivable management is therefore aimed at achieving optimum investment in debtors through controlled credit allowed to customers. Entrepreneurs and managers of MSMEs need to understand the importance of accounts receivable management so as to better manage their accounts receivable, and not expose themselves to high default risks. Management of accounts receivable requires a credit policy to be established, properly implemented and regularly monitored. The credit policy decision involves a trade-off or the balance between the benefits of increased sales as a result of allowing the credit and the costs of granting credit.

10.5.1 Establishing Credit Policy

Credit policy is an important determinant of the firm's level of sales. It refers to the management guidelines the firm establishes in granting trade credit and the management of accounts receivable. A lenient accounts receivable credit policy is to provide credit to all customers who request it and also allow these customers a long credit period and also a delay in taking steps to ensure collections of overdue accounts. Such lenient policy will attract new customers but it comes with some costs. On the other hand a very strict credit policy could keep the cost at a lower level but it will also mean loss of sale as customers will turn to competing firms. The credit policy of the firm consists of a credit standard set to extend credit, terms of trade and collection procedure. We will discuss these credit variables one after the other.

10.5.1.1 Credit Standards

Credit standards refer to the creditworthiness and financial strength a customer must demonstrate in order to qualify for the credit. The credit worthiness of the customer is an indication of whether the customer is likely to settle the debt or default. In evaluating customers for credit, some of the common considerations are the six Cs of credit—character, capacity, collateral, capital, conditions and control. **Character** refers to the honesty and integrity of the customer. It has to do with ascertaining whether that customer will pay on time based on past experience, and if it is a new customer, whether a favourable credit references can be obtained from other creditors or suppliers. **Capacity** deals with determining whether the customer has sufficient cash flow or income to settle the outstanding debt. **Collateral** shows the ability of the customer to settle the debt by selling assets for cash. It is represented by assets provided by the customer as a pledge for security of the credit extended. **Capital** represents the net worth of the customer. It is an indication of the general financial position of the customer. **Condition** has to do with the impact of recent developments in the customer's area of business or industry and how trends in general economic conditions might affect the customer's ability to meet the debt obligation. **Control** is determining whether changes in law and regulation could adversely affect the customer's ability to honour the indebtedness.

10.5.1.2 Terms of Credit

Terms of credit are the requirements that a firm puts in place for the use of credit by its customers. The credit terms would typically specify the credit period, the discount period, and the discount rate. The credit period is the length of time for which credit is granted, and it shows the period elapsing between the date when the customer receives her/his statement of accounts and the date when payment is due. The discount period is the period, which elapses between the date the customer receives its statement of accounts and the date when the discount is foregone. The discount rate expresses the price reduction the customer will receive for paying within the discount period. For instance, if a firm indicates *n*/40 on the invoice to the customer, it means there is no discount but the credit period is 40 days. If the firm states 3/10 net 30, it means if the customer pays within ten days of the invoice, a 3 % discount is offered. Other than that the entire net is due 20 days later or at the 30th day.

10.5.1.3 Collection Policy

Collection policy refers to the procedures that the firm follows for obtaining payment for goods and services previously sold to customers on credit and which have become due. It involves monitoring accounts receivable to spot trouble and obtaining payment on past-due accounts. The longer a debt is allowed to run, the higher the probability of eventual default. A system of follow-up procedures is required, bearing in mind the risk of offending a valued customer to such an extent that their business is lost. The critical problem here is the need to recognise when the accounts warrant special attention. Some of the techniques that could be used in collecting overdue debts include sending reminder letters, making telephone calls, withholding supplies, engaging a debt collection agency and taking legal action against the customer.

10.5.1.4 Analysing Accounts Receivable

It is also important for the firm to analyse its accounts receivable in order to determine how well it is able to match the credit granted with its collection policy. This exercise is very useful in controlling credit. The firm should be able to evaluate its credit performance and compare it with the credit policy. Assuming a small business has established its credit policy of 60 days. This means the firm's customers are supposed to settle their debt within 60 days after purchasing on credit. We saw in Chap. 8 that accounts receivable turnover is calculated by dividing credit sales by accounts receivable. It is stated as follows:

$$\text{Accounts receivable turnover} = \frac{\text{Credit sales}}{\text{Accounts receivables}}$$

If the small business has sold goods on credit to the tune of US$800,000 and its accounts receivable stood at US$160,000, we can compute the accounts receivable turnover as:

$$\text{Accounts receivable turnover} = \frac{\text{US\$800,000}}{\text{US\$160,000}} = 5 \text{ times}$$

If we divide the number of days in the year by the accounts receivable turnover, we get the collection period.

$$\text{Collection period} = \frac{365}{5} = 73 \text{ days}$$

Remember we mentioned in Chap. 8 that the collection period can also be stated as follows:

$$\text{Accounts receivable collection period} = \frac{\text{Accounts receivables}}{\text{Credit sales}} \times 365$$

So, we calculate the collection days as follows:

$$\text{Accounts receivable collection period} = \frac{\text{US\$160,000}}{\text{US\$800,000}} \times 365 = 73 \text{ days}$$

This means the firm's actual collection period of 73 days exceeds its credit policy of 60 days. Therefore, the firm will have to intensify its collection effort to speed up collections in order to better manage accounts receivable. This will require the firm to reconsider its credit policy. It has to re-evaluate the six Cs of credit and adopt a more stringent credit policy.

On the other hand, if the firm's collection period is less than its credit terms or credit policy, it means the firm has increased its liquidity. It would then be prudent to consider adopting a more lenient credit policy.

10.5.1.5 Aging of Accounts Receivable

In monitoring accounts receivable to track the ones that are due for payment and ensure that payments are obtained on time, the firm may use aging analysis. This involves preparing an aging schedule to determine the amounts of accounts receivable, the various lengths of time for which these accounts have been due, and the proportion of accounts that falls within each time frame.

Let us consider how an aging schedule of accounts receivable schedule is prepared. The aging schedule shows a breakdown of the firm's accounts receivable by age of account. Table 10.1 illustrates the aging report of a small business. It shows that 16 % of the accounts are less than 20 days old, 32 % are between 21 and 60 days, 36.7 % are between 61 and 80 days old, while 15.3 % are over 80 days old. Considering that the firm has a 60-day credit period in its credit policy, it means 52 % of the accounts are overdue, while 48 % are on time.

Table 10.1 Aging of accounts receivable

Customer	Outstanding balance (US$)	Days outstanding
A	24,000	18
B	25,000	65
C	26,000	55
D	30,000	65
E	22,000	30
F	23,000	90
Total	150,000	

Aging schedule

Customer	Days outstanding 0–20	21–60	61–80	80+
A	US$24,000			
B			US$25,000	
C		US$26,000		
D			30,000	
E		22,000		
F				US$23,000
Total	US$24,000	US$48,000	US$55,000	US$23,000
Percentage outstanding	16 %	32 %	36.7 %	15.3 %

With 52 % of accounts receivable being overdue, the firm has a number of options. The first is to communicate to the customers to settle their debt. The second may involve refusing further credit terms to such customers until they pay the outstanding as expected. The third option available to the firm is to hand over such delinquent customers to a debt collection agency. The final option may require the firm to determine how much of the debt is not recoverable in order to write off as a bad debt. In such a case, the customer may have folded up or 'closed shop'.

10.5.2 Financing Accounts Receivable

Most businesses will have to extend credit to their customers to keep in line with industry practice and thus maintain sales. They must then wait until the customer pays to realise the cash. However, there are ways that the business may raise finance on the strength of its outstanding sales invoices through the practices of factoring and invoice discounting.

Factoring involves turning over the responsibility for collecting the firm's debts to a specialist institution (the factor). The factor provides financing by means of advances and uses the firm's accounts receivable balances as security. The factor typically takes over the running of the firm's sales ledgers. This may be by non-recourse or with recourse. With non-recourse financing, the factoring house bears the credit or default risk and does not fall on the firm. In the case of factoring with recourse, the factoring house does not bear the credit risk, meaning when the firm's customers' default on the debt, the factoring house is not affected. The firm still assumes the risks and will have to refund the outstanding to the factoring house if the customers default. Factoring is most suitable for MSMEs, which cannot afford sophisticated credit control and sales accounting systems, and for those firms, which are expanding rapidly.

Invoicing discounting is a source of financing accounts receivable, which involves obtaining finance and using the sales debtors as security. However, unlike factoring, invoice discounting involves only the provision of the finance. The financial institution providing the invoice discounting does not provide a sales ledger service or any protection against bad debts. This type of accounts receivable financing is with recourse to the client firm.

10.6 Cash and Marketable Securities Management

MSMEs and entrepreneurs are mostly confronted with cash flow problem challenges, which tend to adversely affect their operations and impede their growth and development. A good appreciation of cash management would be useful for them to better manage their cash position. The cash management is concerned with managing cash flows and cash balances of the firm. Managing the cash flow has to do with ensuring that collections and disbursement of cash are as efficient as possible. Cash management also involves exercising control over the cash position so as to keep the firm sufficiently liquid and profitable.

The aim of cash management is to obtain the highest return possible on cash. This requires the firm ensuring that it has enough cash to take care of its daily operations or meet its disbursal needs and at the same time minimise its investment in idle cash balances. A firm incurs opportunity cost (interest income forgone) if it holds excess or too much idle cash. If the firm maintains a very small cash balance, it may run out of cash and might have to incur costs selling its marketable securities (trading cost) or to borrow short-term (interest expense). Effective and efficient cash management requires the firm speeding up on its inflows and delaying outflows as much as possible.

Cash mainly consists of petty cash, cash in hand and cash at bank. Sometimes cash is defined to include short-term marketable securities, which are referred to as *cash equivalents* and they include Treasury bills, negotiable certificates of deposit, commercial paper and so on. (We have described the different types of short-term marketable securities in this chapter.) The firm's balance sheet will typically have cash to include short-term marketable securities. Therefore, cash management involves managing all the components of cash as well as the management of short-term marketable securities.

10.6.1 Reasons for Holding Cash

Cash is normally held for transaction, precautionary and speculative motives. Transaction motive is concerned with the need to hold cash to carry out a firm's normal business activities such as payment to suppliers of raw material, payment of salaries, payment of utility bills and so on.

Precautionary motive has to do with the need to hold cash to take care of unexpected needs or emergencies such as strikes, fire outbreaks, floods, competitors' marketing campaigns and so on.

Speculative motive involves the need to hold cash to take advantage of future investment opportunities, such as special offers from suppliers, attractive interest rates and favourable fluctuation in exchange rates and so on.

10.6.2 Managing Collection and Disbursement of Cash

The firm can better manage its cash position by managing its collection and disbursement effectively. This will entail speeding up collections and delaying disbursements or managing the float. The term ***float*** is sometimes used to describe the amount of money tied up between the time when a payment is initiated (e.g. when a customer sends a cheque in payment, probably through the mailing system), and the time when the funds become available for use in the recipient's bank account. Float management involves controlling the collection and disbursement of cash.

There are broadly two types of float, these are the collections float and the disbursement float. The disbursement float is the time that elapses between payment by a firm and the time that the cheque actually clears at the bank and the funds moves out of the firm's bank account. The longer the disbursement float, the longer the firm still has the funds in its bank account which can even earn interest. The collections float, on the other hand, is the amount of time that elapses between when a firm's customer makes a payment by cheque and when the cheque clears for the funds to be available in firm's account. Since funds in the bank account may earn some interest, it is better to speed up the collection time. A lengthy collection float suggests inefficient cash management.

A lengthy float may be due to a transmission delay, a lodgement or processing delay, a clearing delay. Transmission delay is the delay in terms of the length of time it takes for a customer to make payment by mailing the cheque for it to reach the firm. Lodgement or processing delay is the delay in terms of the length of time it takes the firm to deposit the cheque or cash at the bank.

Clearing delay is the delay with respect to the time needed for the bank to clear the cheque.

There are several measures that could be taken by the firm in order to reduce the float and to better manage collections float. These include:

(i) The firm should ensure that the lodgement delay is kept to a minimum. Cheques received should be presented to the bank on the day of receipt.
(ii) The firm might, in some cases, arrange to collect cheques from the payer's premises. This would be possible with only local customers. The payment will have to be large to make the extra effort worthwhile.
(iii) The firm's customer might be asked to deposit the cheque into the firm's account through the customer's bank branch, provided both parties have the same bank.
(iv) Electronic fund transfers can be used. This involves a computerised system for the immediate transfer of funds from one bank account to another.
(v) The firm can also ask the customer to make a standing orders or a direct debit. This is an order or instruction the customers give to their bank to make regular transfer into the firm's bank account. It is advisable to use this system if it involves regular payments.
(vi) The firm can use the Lock Box Collection System. A lockbox is a post office box that the firm rents and authorises its bank to pick up cheques sent by the customers from and immediately deposit them into the firm's bank account. Utility firms normally use a modern form of the lock box system, where they ask their customer to pay their bills at the post office or at the bank directly.

10.6.3 Management of Marketable Securities

Marketable securities management is an important aspect of cash management. Though marketable securities include both long-term and short-term marketable, we are interested in short-term marketable securities because they are near cash (cash equivalents) or can easily be converted to cash. An MSME with surplus cash can invest it in short-term marketable securities. Short-term **marketable securities** are financial instruments that are considered to be near cash because they are easily converted to cash at short notices at lower cost. Recall we mentioned in Chap. 4 that the market for short-term marketable securities is the *money market.* Investment in short-term marketable securities serves as substitutes for cash to avoid holding a large cash balance, and part of the investment can be liquidated any time the firm needs cash. Examples of short-term marketable securities are Treasury bills, negotiable certificates of deposit, commercial papers, bankers' acceptances, repurchase agreements, money market mutual funds and so on.

Short-term marketable securities have shorter maturity, they are safer, have less default risk, are more marketable or liquid and attract less or no tax. These characteristics serve as advantages for investing in short-term marketable securities

10.6.4 Cash Management Models

Cash management models attempt to minimise the total costs associated with cash movements between the bank account and short-term investments by determining when, and how much, cash should be transferred each time. Holding too much idle funds comes with an opportunity cost of lost interest. Investing too much funds in marketable securities will be associated with transaction costs as the firm sells part of the short-term investment. The cash management models attempt to find the optimum cash management strategy that will minimise the total costs. There are two main models and these are the Baumol Model and the Miller–Orr Model.

10.6.4.1 The Baumol Model

The mechanics involved in using this model are very similar to what we saw under the EOQ inventory model. The Baumol model has the following assumptions:

(i) There is steady or constant demand for cash over time.
(ii) Firms would hold stock of marketable securities which can be sold in order to replenish cash balance.
(iii) The main carrying cost of holding cash is the interest foregone or the opportunity cost for not investing the excess cash.
(iv) The cost of placing an order is the administrative cost incurred for each sale of marketable securities.
(v) The model identifies the optimum amount of marketable securities to sell by value each time cash needs replenishing.

The model is stated as follows:

$$OC = \sqrt{\frac{2DT}{r}}$$

Where:
D = total annual cash disbursement
T = transaction cost of each sale of marketable securities
r = interest rate per annum
OC = optimal amount of marketable securities to sell to optimise transaction costs and interest income

Example 10.6 Omega Enterprise is a small-sized retail outlet. Its annual requirement for cash is US$300,000 spread evenly throughout the year. The current yield on government securities is 10 % per annum. Switching cost is US$20 per transaction.

Required:

(a) Calculate the optimum amount of cash to be transferred to enterprise's current account.
(b) Calculate the number of transactions to undertake in a year.
(c) What is the average cash balance in the current account?
(d) Calculate the cost of holding cash in the current account.

Answer 10.6 (a) **Optimal cash**

$$OC = \sqrt{\frac{2DT}{T}} = \sqrt{\frac{(2)(\text{US\$ } 300{,}000)(\text{US\$ } 20)}{0.10}} = \sqrt{120{,}000{,}000} = \text{US\$ } 10{,}954$$

The amount US$10,954 is the of Treasury bills to be sold by the firm anytime it needs cash.

(b) **Number of transactions in a year**

$$= \frac{Annual\ Demand}{Optimal\ Cash}\ or\ \frac{D}{OC} = \frac{\$300{,}000}{\$10{,}954} = 27\ times$$

(c) **Average cash balance for the period:**

$$= \frac{\text{Optimal cash}}{2} = \frac{\text{OC}}{2} = \frac{\text{US\$ }10{,}954}{2} = \text{US\$ }5477$$

(d) **Total cost of holding the account balance in the year:**

$$\text{TC} = \frac{\text{D}}{\text{OC}}(\text{T}) + \frac{\text{OC}}{2}(\text{r})$$

$$\text{TC} = \frac{\text{US\$ }300{,}000}{\text{US\$ }10{,}954}(\text{US\$ }20) + \frac{\text{US\$ }10{,}954}{2}(0.10)$$

$$\text{TC} = \text{US\$ }547.7 + \text{US\$ }547.7 = \text{US\$ }1095$$

10.6.4.2 The Miller–Orr Model

In the late 1950s, Miller and Orr presented a second model on cash management. Miller–Orr assumed that cash flows are entirely unpredictable. The model sets upper and lower cash limits and when the balance reaches an upper limit, the firm will purchase short-term investments to bring the cash balance back to a predetermined level known as the ***return point***. When the cash balance falls to the lower limit, the firm will sell short-term investments to bring the cash balance back to the return point.

The model takes into account uncertainty in both receipts and payments of cash. All cash receipts and payments are met from the cash balance and the firm's cash balance is allowed to vary freely between the two limits. The lower limit needs to be specified by the firm and the upper limit is obtained the model. On any day that the cash balance moves outside these limits, appropriate action needs to be taken. This is illustrated in Fig. 10.2.

At point 1, the cash balance gets to the lower limit and must be replenished by either selling marketable securities or borrowing. The size of this withdrawal is indicated on the diagram (*W*), and it is the distance between the return point (usually set in Miller–Orr as the lower limit plus one-third of the distance up to the upper limit) and the lower limit.

At point 2, the cash balance gets to the upper limit and a certain amount (*D*) must be invested in marketable securities or put in a deposit account. Again, this is computed by the model as the distance between the upper limit and the return point.

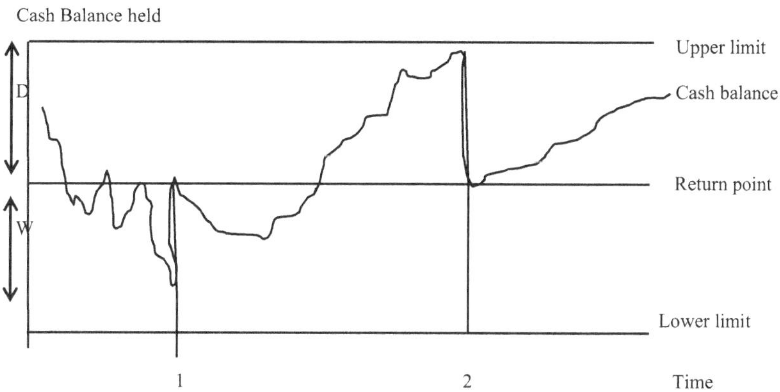

Fig. 10.2 The Miller–Orr cash management model

The minimum cost upper limit is computed by reference to brokerage costs, holding costs and the variance of cash flows. The model assumes normally distributed cash flows. Miller and Orr saw the model to be fairly robust and provide significant potential cost savings for firms.

If cash reaches the lower limit, the firm must sell securities one-third of spread for cash. If it reaches upper limit, it must purchase securities two-thirds of spread. The spread is the difference between the upper limit and lower limit.

The formula for calculating the spread is given as follows:

$$\text{Spread} = 3\left[\frac{\frac{3}{4} \times \text{Transaction cost} \times \text{Variance of cash flow}}{\text{Daily interest rate}}\right]^{\frac{1}{3}}$$

The upper limit is given as:

$$\text{Upper limit} = \text{Lower limit} + \text{Spread}$$

The return point is also computed as:

$$\text{Return point} = \text{Lower limit} + \left(\frac{1}{3} \times \text{Spread}\right)$$

Example 10.7 If a firm sets its minimum cash balance of US$5,000 and estimates transaction cost to be US$15 per sale or purchase of securities and interest rate of 7.3 % per annum (0.02 % per day). Standard deviation of cash flows is US$1,200 per day (so variance is equal to US$1,440,000 per day).

Answer 10.7 The spread is calculated as:

$$\text{Spread} = 3\left[\frac{\frac{3}{4} \times \text{Transaction cost} \times \text{Variance of cash flow}}{\text{Daily interest rate}}\right]^{\frac{1}{3}}$$

$$\text{Spread} = 3\left[\frac{\frac{3}{4} \times \text{US\$15} \times \text{US\$1,440,000}}{0.0002}\right]^{\frac{1}{3}} = \text{US\$ 12,980}$$

If the lower limit (set by the firm) is US$5000, then the upper limit will be:

$$\text{Upper limit} = \text{Lower limit} + \text{Spread} = \text{US\$5,000} + \text{US\$12,980} = \text{US\$17,980}$$

$$\text{Return point} = \text{Lower limit} + \left(\frac{1}{3} \times \text{Spread}\right) = \text{US\$5,000} + \left(\frac{1}{3} \times \text{US\$12,980}\right) = \text{US\$9,327}$$

10.7 Current Liabilities Management

Current liabilities are amounts owed by the firm which are due in one accounting year including, short-term debt, accrued expenses or liabilities, and accounts payable. Therefore, current liabilities management involves ensuring effective and efficient management of short-term debt, accrued liabilities and accounts payable in order to minimise the firm's obligations and payments for these.

10.7.1 Short-Term Debt Management

Short-term debt consists of business obligations that will be paid within the current accounting period. It consists of current payments on long-term debt, bank lines of credit, notes payable, short-term loan for one year or less. The aim of short-term debt management is to ensure that the firm pays the debt as and when it falls due.

Short-term debt is generally cheaper compared to long-term debt because it has lower default risk and is more flexible than long-term debt. However, there might be renewal problems associated with short-term debt. Under difficult economic conditions or difficult financial situation of the firm, it may be tough for the firm to get renewal for the short-term finance facility. Even if no renewal problem is encountered, the cost of negotiation in terms of the entrepreneur's time may be high, and this must be taken into consideration. The firm may also be exposed to fluctuations in short-term interest rates if it has to always renew its financing arrangements.

10.7.2 Accrued Liabilities Management

Accrued liabilities are accrued taxes the firm is expected to pay during the normal course of business. The firm is expected to meet its obligations on accrued liabilities since failing may result in penalties being imposed on the firm. The focus on accrued liabilities management is to ensure the firm pays these obligations in a timely manner in order to avoid being slapped with penalties.

10.7.3 Accounts Payable Management

Accounts payable refers to obligations of the firm resulting from the purchase of goods and services on credit. The aim of accounts payable management is to minimise payments to suppliers or creditors. The entrepreneur must seek to stretch out accounts payable as long as possible without destroying the firm's credit profile. Continuous delayed payment to suppliers may compel them to begin to supply on cash basis, which may adversely affect the firm's cash flow, or they may stop doing business with the firm. Suppliers typically offer credit terms to their customers in order to boast sales and encourage prompt payment. The credit terms of the supplier would also indicate the credit period, the discount period, and the discount rate. There are three different types of discount that suppliers offer including cash discounts, trade discounts and quantity discounts. The firm can take advantage especially of cash discounts offered by suppliers so as to minimise payments to the suppliers.

10.7.3.1 Cash Discounts

Cash discounts are often offered by a supplier if payment is made promptly. The terms of the cash discount is important in ascertaining how the invoice amount will be paid. The cash discount is stated as a/b net c, which means 'deduct *a* % off the invoice price if payment is made within *b* days, otherwise pay full price within *c* days'. If cash discounts are quoted on the invoice in terms such as 3/20 net 60, it means 'deduct 3 % if paid within 20 days, otherwise pay the entire amount within 60 days'. In other words, the supplier will give a discount of 3 % off the invoice price if the invoice is paid within 20 days. But the entire amount is due 40 days later or at the 60th day.

The firm should always consider the cost of the discount and compare with other sources of finance. This is because the firm may probably have to borrow funds at a cost to take advantage of that discount. Therefore, the cost of the discount must be considered in deciding on whether or not to accept the discount. The annual opportunity cost of not taking the discount is given as:

$$\text{Effective interest rate} = \frac{\text{Discount amount}}{\text{Net payment}} \times \frac{365}{\text{Full payment days} - \text{Discount days}}$$

Example 10.8 A firm needs US$4,800 to take a trade discount within five days. After five days, the full invoice amount of US$5,000 is due within 40 days. A bank is ready to lend the firm US$4,800 for 40 days and charge US$190.

Required:

(a) What is the effective interest rate on trade credit?
(b) What advice will you give to the firm?

Answer 10.8 (a) **The effective interest rate or opportunity cost of not taking the discount is:**

$$\text{Effective interest rate} = \frac{\text{Discount amount}}{\text{Net payment}} \times \frac{365}{\text{Full payment days} - \text{Discount days}}$$

$$\text{Effective interest rate} = \frac{\text{US\$200}}{\text{US\$4800}} \times \frac{365}{40-5} = 43.45\%$$

(b) **The cost of the bank loan will be:**

$$\text{Cost of bank loan} = \frac{\text{Charge}}{\text{Loan amount}} \times \frac{365}{n}$$

$$\text{Cost of bank loan} = \frac{\text{US\$190}}{\text{US\$4,800}} \times \frac{365}{40} = 36.1\%$$

The firm should go for the bank loan since that gives it a lower cost of financing.

10.7.3.2 Trade Discounts

Trade discounts represent the amount deducted from the purchase of the goods and services. These are amounts deducted from the invoice prices of goods or services when specific services are performed by the purchasing firm. For instance, a trade discount may be expressed as 12 % off the invoice price and if the invoice price is given as US$50,000, then the discount amount will be US$6,000 (i.e. 0.12 × US$50,000). The customer or firm will pay US$44,000 (i.e. US$50,000 – US$6,000).

10.7.3.3 Quantity Discounts

Quantity discounts are offered by suppliers to customers who purchase in bulk quantities. Suppliers offer quantity discount in order to increase their sales and cash flow. An effect of quantity discount is the reduction in the unit price. For example, assuming a supplier offers an item with the following listing as shown in Table 10.2. If the firm purchases any quantity up to 49 units, it will buy them at a price of US$30 per unit. If the firm buys any quantity

Table 10.2 Quantity discounts

Stock number	Quantity	Unit price
11101	1–49	US$30
	50–99	29
	100–199	28
	200–300	26

within the range of 100 and 199, it will pay a unit price of US$28. This means the larger the quantity, the lower the unit price.

10.8 Summary and Conclusions

Working capital is the capital available for conducting the daily operations of a firm, represented by its current assets. The small business manager has the responsibility of managing the levels of working capital in order to maximise the value of the firm. Ensuring efficient working capital management is necessary for enhancing the overall objective of the firm. The small business owner or manager must be interested in increasing current assets and minimising current liabilities. Current assets include stocks, debtors and cash. Current liabilities are creditors and accruals. The difference between the current assets and current liabilities is the net current assets.

Working capital management is the management of all aspects of both current assets and current liabilities to minimise the risk of insolvency, while maximising the returns on assets. Efficient working capital management ensures that the firm maintains a certain level of stock, debtors and cash and at the same time making sure that too much funds are not tied in the current assets.

Discussion Questions and Problems

1. What would you describe as efficient working capital management?
2. Masnat Enterprise is trying to get a handle on its cash management. Reviewing the books, it was found that over the past year accounts receivable have averaged 75 days. Sales and inventory have averaged 60 days. Masnat Enterprise has paid its creditors 25 days after receiving the bill. Masnat Enterprise produces evenly over the year and is expected to spend a huge amount during the year for materials and suppliers. Compute the cash cycle.
3. Samtel produces 160,000 telephones per annum but uses five units of raw materials to produce each unit. The demand for telephones is stable throughout the year. It costs US$200 each time raw materials are ordered, and carrying cost is US$8 per unit of raw materials per annum. Calculate the EOQ and the total inventory costs.
4. Explain the inventory management system that is useful for MSMEs operating in the manufacturing sector.

5. An MSME is saddled with huge accounts receivable. How can it finance such accounts receivable?
6. Happy Feet Ltd. has a T-bill that can be sold on the secondary market for cash each time it needs cash. The cost of discounting the T-bill is US$30. The interest rate on T-bills is 14 % per annum. If the firm's demand for cash is US$14,000 per month, what is the optimal amount of T-bills that the firm should sell each time it needs to do so in order to optimise transaction costs and interest income.
7. A firm experiences a constant demand for cash totalling US$2,000,000 per annum. It replenishes its bank account (which does not pay interest) by selling constant amounts of securities, which are held as an investment earning 6 % per annum. The cost per sale of securities is a fixed US$12 per sale. Required:

   (a) Calculate the optimum amount of cash to be transferred to the firm's current account.
   (b) Calculate the number of transactions to undertake in a year.
   (c) Find the average cash balance in the current account.
   (d) Calculate the total cost per year of maintaining cash balances.

8. A medium-sized firm has US$6,000 as the firm's lower cash control limit. Interest rate on investments is 15 per annum. The firm's standard deviation of daily cash has been measured as US$7,000. Switching cost or transaction is US$25 per transaction. You are required to calculate the following:

   (i) The spread
   (ii) The upper limit
   (iii) The return point

9. A firm of chartered accountants has rendered taxation and accounting services to Excom Pty Limited on terms of 2/30 net 60, which means Excom Pty may deduct 2 % off the invoice amount if it pays within 30 days, else the full amount of the invoice is due by the 60th day. You are required to compute the annual interest rate of the discount terms to the firm.
10. Samtech requires US$5,500 to take a trade discount within ten days. After ten days, the full invoice amount of US$6,000 is due within 40 days. A bank is ready to lend the firm US$5,500 for 40 days and charge US$200. What is the effective interest rate on trade credit? What advice will you give to the firm?

Part IV

Valuation

11

Time Value of Money

Learning Objectives
By the end of this chapter, you should be able to:

- appreciate the concept of 'time value of money'
- compare simple and compound interest
- calculate future value lump sum and prevent value lump sum
- distinguish between effective rate and stated rate
- explain and calculate perpetuities
- calculate future and present values based on annuities
- distinguish between ordinary annuity and annuity due
- explain and calculate amortisation

11.1 Introduction

The concept of *time value of money* deals with the fact that 'a dollar today is worth more than a dollar tomorrow'. This means it will take more future dollars than current dollars to buy the same quantity of goods and services because of the effect of inflation. If you have the opportunity to receive US$2,000 today or US$2,000 in a year from today, which would you prefer? Naturally, you would take the US$2,000 today because you recognise the *time value of money*. Receiving the US$2,000 today gives you the opportunity to invest the money in order to earn interest. In a year's time you are likely to receive an amount bigger than the US$2,000. Assuming the US$2,000 can be put in fixed deposit with interest rate of 16 % per annum. Then, the value

J.Y. Abor, *Entrepreneurial Finance for MSMEs*,
DOI 10.1007/978-3-319-34021-0_11

of the investment after one year will be worth US$2,000 plus US$320 or US$2,320. We got the interest amount of US$320 by multiplying the interest rate of 16 % by the principal of US$2,000. The dollar of US$2,000 today is obviously worth more than the US$2,000 in future. For you to be convinced to part with your money for some time, you would need to be convinced of a rate of interest. In a world where there is certainty in all cash flows, the *rate of interest* can be used to express the time of money. With the rate of interest, it is possible to adjust the cash flows to any particular point in time.

The concept of time of money is an important concept in finance. Most financial decisions, whether personal or business, are based on time of value of money. Understanding how to move money through time is critical in almost every business decision. In fact, it is difficult to appreciate finance without understanding the time value of money. We learned in Chap. 1 that the focus of entrepreneurial finance is to maximise value for the entrepreneur, and this depends partly on the timing of cash flows. A good appreciation of the time value of money will enable the entrepreneur to use the techniques to evaluate capital budgeting decisions and other business and financial decisions.

There are four different ways of solving problems on time value of money. These include the use of time value of money tables, which have been provided in the appendix of this book, the use of financial calculator, the use of spreadsheet, and the use of formulas. In this book, we shall focus mainly on the use of formulas.

In this chapter, we discuss the concepts of simple interest, compound interest, future value of a lump sum, present value of a future lump sum, effect of compounding, perpetuities, annuities and amortisation.

11.2 Simple Interest

Simple interest is the interest paid (earned) on only the principal amount stated. The **principal amount stated** is original amount that is borrowed (lent). The dollar amount of simple interest is computed based on the original amount or principal, the interest rate and the time span. In simple interest, only the principal amount attracts interest and that interest earned does not attract interest. The interest earned on the principal amount is added to the principal to get the total amount due. Simple interest is calculated as follows:

$$\mathrm{SI} = P_0(r)(n)$$

Where:
SI = simple interest in dollars
P_0 = principal
r = interest rate per period
n = number of time periods

For example, let us assume you put US$1,000 in a savings account that promises 12 % interest. If you keep the money for one year, the simple interest would be computed as follows:

$$\text{SI} = \text{US\$1,000}(0.12)(1) = \text{US\$120}$$

The maturity amount at the end of the one year is US$1,120 (i.e. US$1,000 + US$120).

If the US$1,000 is saved for nine months, then the interest amount would be:

$$\text{SI} = \text{US\$1,000}(0.12)\left(\frac{9}{12}\right) = \text{US\$90}$$

Because the interest amount is US$90, the maturity amount at the end of the nine months would be US$1,090.

Let us consider another example. If you borrow US$8,000 from the bank at 16 % for five years, then the simple interest amount would be:

$$\text{SI} = \text{US\$8,000}(0.16)(5) = \text{US\$6,400}$$

The total amount due the bank at the end of the five years would be US$14,400.

It is important to note that, in time value of money, if you know any three of the four values, you can easily compute the missing value. In the third example, assuming you already know the interest amount to be US$6,400 and the interest rate is 16 % and the time is five years, we easily can find the principal as follows:

$$\text{SI} = P_0(r)(n)$$

$$\text{US\$6,400} = P_0(0.16)(5)$$

$$P_0 = \frac{US\$6,400}{(0.16)(5)} = US\$8,000$$

If we want to determine how long it will take to repay the loan, this can be computed as follows:

$$SI = P_0(r)(n)$$

$$US\$6,400 = US\$8,000(0.16)(n)$$

$$n = \frac{US\$6,400}{(US\$8,000)(0.16)} = 5\,\text{years}$$

It means, it will take five years to repay the bank the total amount due of US$14,400 at 16 % interest rate, based on a principal amount of US$8,000. Remember that the simple interest amount is calculated and added to the principal or original amount to arrive at the amount due.

11.2.1 Simple Interest and Treasury Bill Discount

We can use the simple interest rate to compute Treasury bill discount. Treasury bills are short-term financial instrument issued by governments to raise short-term funds. When government issues Treasury bills, it means it is borrowing short-term from the money market. An entrepreneur with excess cash may therefore invest in such bills in order to preserve the value of the funds (safety) and at the same time be able to sell the bills with ease (liquidity). Treasury bills are issued in different denominations for three months, six months and one year. Treasury bills do not pay interest but rather the investor gets what we call a **discount.** The **discount** is the difference between what the investor pays and what he/she gets when the Treasury bill matures. The investor pays a discount amount and gets the face value at maturity.

Assuming the Ghana government issued a 91-day Treasury bill with a face value of GHS 10,000 and a discount rate of 24 %, the discount amount (*D*) will be computed as follows:

$$D = F \times Y_d \times \left(\frac{t}{364}\right)$$

Where:
D = discount amount
F = face value
Y_d = discount yield
t = number of days to maturity

$$D = \text{GHS}10{,}000 \times 0.24 \times \left(\frac{91}{364}\right) = \text{GHS}600$$

The purchase price (P)of the Treasury bill is equal to the face value (F) minus the discount amount (D). This is computed as follows:

$$P = F - D$$
$$\text{P} = \text{GHS}10{,}000 - \text{GHS}600 = \text{GHS}9{,}400$$

This means the investor pays GHS 9,400 to purchase the Treasury bill and gets the face value of GHS 10,000 at maturity. Thus, the investor's return is the GHS 600.

We calculate the discount yield, which is the percentage discount from the face value of the Treasury bill. This is computed as follows:

$$Y_d = \frac{F - P}{F} \times \frac{364}{t}$$

In this example, assuming we know the price to be GHS 940 but we do not have the discount yield, we can calculate it as follows:

$$Y_d = \frac{\text{GHS}10{,}000 - \text{GHS}9{,}400}{\text{GHS}10{,}000} \times \frac{364}{91} = 0.24 = 24\%$$

Note that we use 364 days in this example because that is the convention in Ghana. Treasury bills in Ghana are issued for maturities of 91 and 182 days. Other countries such as South Africa and the USA use 365 days.

11.2.2 Interest Equivalent Yield

We mentioned that investor pays GHS 9,400 to purchase the Treasury bill and gets the face value of GHS 10,000 at maturity. The GHS 9,400 is what government borrows from the investor or lender for 91 days and then pays GHS 600. We notice that the discount yield on the Treasury bill is understated relative to the true value. This is because the denominator is the face value rather than the purchase price of the bill. In order to covert the discount yield to an interest rate that takes into consideration the purchase price or the original cost of the investment, we compute the *interest equivalent yield* (IEY) or *effective annual interest rate* as follows:

$$\text{IEY} = \frac{F - P}{P} \times \frac{364}{t}$$

In the above example, we can compute the interest equivalent yield as follows:

$$\text{IEY} = \frac{\text{GHS}10{,}000 - \text{GHS}9{,}400}{\text{GHS}9{,}400} \times \frac{364}{91} = 0.2553 = 25.53\%$$

The interest equivalent yield of 25.53 % is the actual interest paid taking into consideration the cost of the money borrowed and the actual amount of money used by the government. The interest equivalent yield is higher than the discount yield.

Note that the denominator of the discount yield is the face value, while the denominator of the interest equivalent yield is the price of the security.

11.3 Compound Interest

Compound interest is the interest paid (earned) on both the principal amount and the accrued interest that has been previously paid (earned). This means the interest paid (earned) on a loan (an investment) is periodically added to the principal. The interest-on-interest is known as *compounding* and this is what makes the compound interest different from the simple interest. The concept of compound interest can be used to solve a number of problems in finance.

Table 11.1 Compound value

Year	Amount saved (US$)	Interest (US$)	Compound value (US$)
1	1,000	1,000 × 0.12 = 120	1,120
2	1,120	1,120 × 0.12 = 134	1,254
3	1,254	1,254 × 0.12 = 151	1,405
4	1,405	1,406 × 0.12 = 169	1,574
5	1,574	1,574 × 0.12 = 189	1,762

If US$1,000 is put in a savings account for five years and is compounded annually at 12 % interest, the savings would accumulate to US$1,762 at the end of the five years. This is computed as follows (Table 11.1):

The accumulated amount is known as the future value (FV) or compound value. Instead of going through the process of computing the compound interest as done in Table 11.1, it can be simplified by using the following compound interest formula to determine the future value:

$$FV = PV(1+r)^n$$

Where:

FV = future value
PV = present value, or principal amount
r = interest rate per period of compounding
n = number of compounding periods over which investment is held

Using our example of saving US$1,000 for five years at 12 % compounded annually, the future value can be computed as follows:

$$FV = US\$1{,}000(1+0.12)^5$$

$$FV = US\$1{,}000(1.7623) = US\$1{,}762$$

To compare compound and simple interest, let us assume we wish to obtain the future value by using simple interest. This can be calculated as follows:

$$FV = US\$1{,}000 + \left[(US\$1{,}000)(0.12)(5)\right]$$

$$FV = US\$1{,}000 + [US\$600] = US\$1{,}600$$

In the case of compound interest, because interest compounds on the interest already earned, the interest earned is more than the interest earned under simple interest. Thus, the future value of US$1762 using compound interest is greater than US$1,600 using simple interest.

11.4 Future Value of a Lump Sum

Future (or compound) value is the value at some future time of a present amount of money, or a series of payments, evaluated at a given interest rate. In other words, future value is the cash value of an investment at some time in the future. Assume that you deposit US$5,000 in an account earning 14 % compounded annually for ten years. What is the future value of the deposit? The formula for getting the future value is given as follows:

$$FV = PV(1+r)^n$$

$$FV = US\$5{,}000(1+0.14)^{10}$$

$$FV = US\$5{,}000(3.7072) = US\$18{,}536$$

Remember we mentioned that time value of money can also be solved using tables, financial calculator, and spreadsheet. We shall focus on the use of time value of money tables and financial calculators. Using the tables to solve the problem, the equation can be rewritten as follows:

$$FV = PV\left(FVIF_{r,n}\right)$$

The $(1 + r)^n$ in the equation $FV = PV(1 + r)^n$ is replaced by a future value interest factor(FVIF) at a specific interest rate (r) and a specified time period (n). We can get the (FVIF)from the table (Appendix B-1 of this book) by going to 14 % interest rate in the column and looking down in the row to periods (n) of 10 and obtaining 3.70. We then put this value in the equation to arrive at:

$$FV = US\$5{,}000(3.7072) = US\$18{,}536$$

Using a financial calculator, we need to appreciate that there are five key registers on the calculator and these are defined as follows:

N = the number of periods
I/Y = the interest rate per period
PV = present value
PMT = the amount of payment per period
FV = future value
CPT = is the register used to request the computation of any of the five values.

In order to solve for the any of the five items, you key in any four items and then request for the computation of the fifth item. The two most popular financial calculators are the Hewlett-Packard HP-12C, and the Texas Instruments BA-II PLUS.

Using the example of US$5,000 deposit at 14 % compounded annually for ten years, we obtain the future value by setting the registers as follows:

PV: 5000
I/Y: 14
N: 10
PRESS CPT, FV
Then we get the answer as US$18,536.

11.5 Present Value of a Future Lump Sum

Present (or discount) value is the current value of a future amount of money, or a series of payments, evaluated at a given interest rate. Present value answers the question: how much should be invested today, in order to obtain a certain amount, or streams of amounts in the future?

Finding the present value (or *discounting*) is simply the reverse of *compounding*. Let us recall:

$$\mathrm{FV} = \mathrm{PV}(1+r)^n$$

Rearranging and solving for present value, give us:

$$\mathrm{PV} = \frac{\mathrm{FV}}{(1+r)^n}$$

$$PV = FV\frac{1}{(1+r)^n}$$

Assume that you need US$3,000 in four years. Let us examine the process to determine how much you need to deposit today at a discount rate of 15 % compounded annually.

$$PV = US\$3,000\frac{1}{(1+0.15)^4}$$

$$PV = US\$3,000(0.5718) = US\$1,715.4$$

Note that the term $\frac{1}{(1+r)^n}$ that is known as ***present value of interest factor*** (*PVIF*) is simply the reciprocal of the ***future value of interest factor*** (*FVIF*). Using the table (Appendix B-2 of this book), we get the (PVIF) of 0.5718 by looking at the intersection of 15 % in the column and four years in the row. This is computed as follows:

$$PV = FV(PVIF_{r,n})$$

$$PV = US\$3,000(0.5718) = US\$1,715.4$$

Using the financial calculator, we go through the following:
FV: 3000
I/*Y*: 15
N: 4
PRESS CPT, PV
Then we get the answer as 1,715.4.

Example 11.1
A medium-sized firm intends to undertake a project that will generate the expected cash flows provided below. What is the present value of the expected cash flows given a discount rate of7 %? What is the present value if the discount rate is 12 %? What is the present value considering a discount rate of 17 %? (Table 11.2).

Table 11.2 Future value

Year	Future value (US$000)
1	850
2	740
3	1,090
4	1,310

Table 11.3 Present value of each of the cash flows and totals

Year	Cash flows (US$'000)	7 %	PV@7 % (US$'000)	12 %	PV@12 % (US$'000)	17 %	PV@17 % (US$'000)
1	850	0.9346	794.41	0.8929	758.97	0.8547	726.50
2	740	0.8734	646.32	0.7972	589.93	0.7305	540.57
3	1,090	0.8163	889.77	0.7118	775.86	0.6244	680.60
4	1,310	0.7629	999.39	0.6355	832.51	0.5337	699.15
Total			3,329.89		2,957.26		2,646.82

Answer 11.1

To solve this problem, we need to determine the present value of each of the cash flows and then add them up. The present value of a lump sum is given as (Table 11.3):

$$\mathrm{PV} = \mathrm{FV}\frac{1}{(1+r)^n}$$

11.5.1 Finding the Interest Rate and the Number of Periods

There are instances in solving time value of money problems where you know the future value, the present value and the time periods involved. What is not known is the compound interest rate (r) implicit in an investment.

Let us assume in 2015 Art Gallery sold a sculpture at an auction for a price of US$25,000. The previous owner purchased it in 2010 at a price of US$11,000. What was his annual rate of return on this sculpture?

To solve this question, either the future value or the present value formula can be used. Both approaches will lead to the same answer, since they are the inverse of each other. Let us use the future value formula, which is given as:

$$\mathrm{FV} = \mathrm{PV}(1+r)^n$$

$$\text{US\$25,000} = \text{US\$11,000}(1+r)^n$$

$$(1+r)^5 = \frac{\text{US\$25,000}}{\text{US\$11,000}} = 2.2727$$

$$1+r = (2.2727)^{1/5}$$

$$r = (2.2727)^{1/5} - 1 = 0.1784 \text{ or } 17.84\%$$

Using financial calculator, we have:

FV: 25,000
PV: −11,000
PMT: 0
N: 5
PRESS CPT, *I*/*Y*
Then we get the answer as 17.84 %.

We may also have to solve for the number of years that it will take to arrive at a certain future amount. We can do this by manipulating the basic present or future value formula (remember, one is a reciprocal of the other). There are only four parts to this equation; the present value (PV), the future value (FV), the discount rate (r) and the life of the investment (n). Given any of these, we can always find the fourth.

Let us assume we deposit US$5,000 today in an account paying 14 %, how long does it take to double this amount?

Again to answer this question, we can use either the future value or the present value formula.

Any of them should give us the same answer since they are the inverse of each other. We will use the future value formula. In this question, to double the US$5000, we get a future value of US$10,000, so we have:

$$\text{FV} = \text{PV}(1+r)^n$$

$$\text{US\$10,000} = \text{US\$5,000}(1.10)^n$$

$$(1.10)^n = \frac{\text{US\$10,000}}{\text{US\$5,000}} = 2$$

$$\ln(1.10) \times n = \ln(2)$$

$$n = \frac{\ln(2)}{\ln(1.10)} = \frac{0.6931}{0.0953} = 7.27 \text{ years}$$

Using financial calculator, we have:

FV: 10,000
PV: −5,000
PMT: 0
I/*Y*: 10
PRESS CPT, *N*
Then we get the answer as 7.27.

11.6 Effect of Compounding

We have looked at the issue of future and present values under the assumption that compounding and discounting occur on a yearly basis. But this is not always the case. There are instances when compounding may occur more frequently than just once a year, which can affect the future or present value. For example, let us say an entrepreneur invested US$7,000 in a fixed deposit account for one year with 20 % interest rate 'compounded semi-annually'. This means the entrepreneur's investment of US$7,000 would be worth US$7,000 × 1.10 = US$700 at the end of the sixth month, and US$7,700 × 1.10 = US$8,470 at the end of the one year.

This can be expressed in the following formula:

$$\text{FV} = \text{PV}\left(1 + \frac{r}{m}\right)^{mn}$$

Where:
FV = future value
PV = present value
r = sated annual interest rate
m = number of times the amount is compounded
n = number of years

Putting the values in the formula, we have:

$$\text{FV} = \text{US\$7,000}\left(1 + \frac{0.2}{2}\right)^{2\times 1} = \text{US\$7,000}(1.10)^2 = \text{US\$8,470}$$

Assuming the compounding was done yearly, the future value would have been worth US$8,400 (i.e. US$7,000 × 1.20). Let us note that the future value at the end of one year is greater with semi-annual compounding than with annual compounding. This because one gets 'interest on interest' with semi-annual compounding.

With quarterly compounding at 20 %, the US$7,000 fixed deposit for one year will yield:

$$FV = US\$7,000\left(1+\frac{0.2}{4}\right)^{4\times 1} = US\$7,000(1.05)^{4} = US\$8,508.54$$

If the fixed deposit is compounded monthly, we would have:

$$FV = US\$7,000\left(1+\frac{0.2}{12}\right)^{12\times 1} = US\$7,000(1.0167)^{12} = US\$8,539.10$$

Assuming the compounding occurred daily, then the future would be:

$$FV = US\$7,000\left(1+\frac{0.2}{365}\right)^{365\times 1} = US\$7,000(1.0005)^{365} = US\$8,549.35$$

We see that the entrepreneur's fixed deposit of US$7,000 generates different future values depending on the frequency of compounding. Clearly, we observe that the more frequent the compounding, the greater the future value.

11.6.1 Stated Annual Interest Rate and Effective Annual Rate of Interest

The frequency of the compounding brings us to the issue of **stated annual interest rate** and **effective annual rate (EAR) of interest**. The stated annual interest rate is mainly quoted on an annual basis and it does not consider the issue compounding. The stated annual interest rate is also known as the **annual percentage rate (APR)**. The EAR of interest considers the interest rate that would apply for a given frequency of compounding. The general formula for calculating the EAR of interest is given as follows:

$$EAR = \left(1+\frac{r}{m}\right)^{m} - 1$$

For example, let us assume a loan has a stated annual interest rate of 15 % and the interest on the loan is compounded monthly. The EAR of interest will be computed as follows:

$$\text{EAR} = \left(1 + \frac{0.15}{12}\right)^{12} - 1 = 0.1608 = 16.08\%$$

If the stated annual interest rate is compounded quarterly, then the EAR loan will be:

$$\text{EAR} = \left(1 + \frac{0.15}{4}\right)^{4} - 1 = 0.1587 = 15.87\%$$

It is obvious that the EAR increases with more frequent compounding. In the example we just looked at, we noticed that compounding monthly generates EAR of 16.08 % higher than EAR of 15.87 % when the compounding occurs quarterly.

11.6.1.1 Continuous Compounding

We just discussed that compounding can actually occur more frequently than once a year. Compounding can occur semi-annually, quarterly, monthly or daily. In practice, interest can be compounded continuously. The general formula for the future value of an investment compounded continuously over many periods can be stated as:

$$\text{FV} = \text{PV}(e)^{rn}$$

Where:
FV = future value
PV = initial investment
r = stated annual interest rate
n = number of years
e = a transcendental number approximately equal to 2.718. e^x is a key on your calculator

Let us assume that a small business invested US$30,000 at a continuous compounded rate of 11 % for two years. What is the value of the firm's wealth at the end of two years? We can get the value of the firm's investment at the end of the two years as follows:

$$FV = PV(e)^{rn}$$

$$FV = US\$30,000(2.718)^{(0.11)(2)} = US\$37,381.45$$

We can also look for the present value when the interest rate is compounded continuously. This formula which is simply a reciprocal of the future value computation is given as follows:

$$PV = \frac{FV}{(e)^{rn}}$$

For example, what is the present value of US$20,000 to be received at the end of five years with a discount rate of 13 %, compounded continuously? This calculation will look as follows:

$$PV = \frac{FV}{(e)^{rn}}$$

$$PV = US\$20,000/(2.718)^{(0.13)(5)} = US\$10,441.68$$

11.7 Perpetuities

A **perpetuity** is a constant stream of cash flows occurring forever. Examples are Consol bonds issued in the UK that do not have any maturity and fixed dividend on a preference share that cannot be redeemed. The present value of an amount *C* to be paid is given as:

$$PV = \frac{C}{r}$$

What is the value of a British consol that promises to pay £20 every year forever, given 8 % interest rate?

$$PV = \frac{£20}{0.08} = £250$$

Let us consider another example. Imagine that a US$10,000 preference share pays 14 % annual dividend rate and the required rate of return is 16 %. The annual dividend, which is in perpetuity is US$1,400 (US$10,000 × 14 %). The present value of the perpetuity can be computed as:

$$PV = \frac{US\$1,400}{0.16} = US\$8,750$$

Example 11.2
Shiram Life Insurance Company (South Africa) is offering an investment policy to you that will pay you and your heirs US$15,000 per annum forever. If the required return rate on this investment product is 8 %, how much will you be expected to pay for the policy? Now, suppose Vanguard Life Assurance told you the policy costs US$350,000. At what interest rate will this be considered a fair deal?

Answer 11.2
This cash flow is a perpetuity and therefore to find the present value the perpetuity, we use the equation:

$$PV = \frac{C}{r}$$

$$PV = \frac{US\$15,000}{0.08} = US\$187,500$$

To find the interest rate at which the investment will be a good deal, we work for the interest rate that equates the perpetuity cash flows with the present value of the cash flows. Using the present value of a perpetuity equation:

$$US\$350,000 = \frac{US\$15,000}{r}$$

We can now solve for the interest rate as follows:

$$r = \frac{\text{US\$15,000}}{\text{US\$350,000}} = 0.0429 \text{ or } 4.29\%$$

11.7.1 Growing Perpetuity

A **growing perpetuity** is a stream of cash flows that grows at a constant rate forever. The present value of an amount C that grows at a constant rate of g % annually is given as follows:

$$\text{PV} = \frac{C}{r-g}$$

For example, suppose the expected dividend next year is US$50, and dividends are expected to grow at 5 % annually forever. If the discount rate is 12 %, what is the value of this promised dividend stream? The present value of this growing perpetuity will therefore be:

$$\text{PV} = \frac{\text{US\$50}}{0.12-0.05} = \text{US\$714.29}$$

11.8 Annuities

An **annuity** is a stream of constant cash flows occurring at regular intervals over a fixed period of time. An annuity represents a series of equal payments (or receipts) over a specified number of equidistant periods. Examples of annuities are interest payments on a bond, insurance premiums, mortgage payments, and retirement savings. There are two types of annuities, an ordinary annuity and an annuity due. An **ordinary annuity** is an annuity where the same fixed payments are made or received at the end of the period. An **annuity due** is where the same fixed payments are made or received at the beginning of the period. Examples of annuity due are rents and leases, which are normally paid in advance at the beginning of the period.

11.8.1 Future Value of Ordinary Annuity

The future value ordinary annuity (FVOA) is a stream of equal cash flows occurring at the end of the period for n periods at interest rate of r. This can be obtained using the following formula:

$$\text{FVOA} = C(\text{FVIFA})$$

$$\text{FVOA} = C\left[\frac{(1+r)^n - 1}{r}\right]$$

Where:

FVOA = the future value of an ordinary annuity
C = cash flow of annuity

FVIFA = future value interest factor of annuity = $\left[\frac{(1+r)^n - 1}{r}\right]$

r = the interest rate per time period
n = number of compounding periods per year times the number of years

For example, what is the future value a three-year ordinary annuity of US$100,000 at 10 %?

We can use the formula for obtaining the future value of an annuity, thus:

$$\text{FVOA} = C\left[\frac{(1+r)^n - 1}{r}\right]$$

$$\text{FVOA} = \text{US\$}100{,}000\left[\frac{(1+0.10)^3 - 1}{0.10}\right] = \text{US\$}100{,}000(3.31) = \text{US\$}331{,}000$$

We could also obtain the FVIFA of 3.31 from the financial table in Appendix B-3 by looking at the intersection of 10 % in the column and three years in a row. We then put this value in the equation to arrive at:

$$\text{FVOA} = \text{US\$}100{,}000(3.31) = \text{US\$}331{,}000$$

Using the financial calculator, we go through the following:

I/Y: 10
N: 4
PV: 0
PMT: 100,000
PRESS CPT, FV
Then we get the answer as 331,000.

Example 11.3
ICEK Enterprise has been presented with two different investment plans. Plan A will require the firm depositing US$2500 every six months and receive interest at a 8 % annual rate, compounded semi-annually. With respect to Plan B, ICEK Enterprise will be required to deposit US$5000 each year and receive interest at a rate of 9 %, compounded annually. The initial deposit with Plan A will be made six months from now and that of Plan B will be made one year hence.

(a) Compute the future value of both Plan A and Plan B at the end of ten years.
(b) Recommend which plan ICEK Enterprise should use, considering that the firm is only concerned with the value of its investment at the end of ten years?
(c) Assuming the rate of interest on Plan B were 8 % how would your answer change?

Answer 11.3
(a) For Plan A:

$$\mathrm{FV} = C\left[\frac{\left(1+\frac{r}{2}\right)^{2n}-1}{\frac{r}{2}}\right]$$

$$\mathrm{FVOA} = \mathrm{US\$}2{,}500\left[\frac{(1.04)^{20}-1}{0.04}\right] = \mathrm{US\$}2{,}500(29.7781) = \mathrm{US\$}74{,}445.25$$

(b) For Plan B:

$$\text{FV} = C\left[\frac{(1+r)^n - 1}{r}\right]$$

$$\text{FVOA} = \text{US\$5,000}\left[\frac{(1.09)^{10} - 1}{0.09}\right] = \text{US\$5,000}(15.1929) = \text{US\$75,964.5}$$

(c) Select Plan B over Plan A because it gives the greater future value.
(d) If interest rates were 8 %.

Plan B:

$$\text{FVOA} = \text{US\$5,000}\left[\frac{(1.08)^{10} - 1}{0.08}\right] = \text{US\$5,000}(14.4866) = \text{US\$72,433}$$

If this were the case, Plan A would be better.

Note: We need to also be mindful of a situation where deposits are made yearly but compounding occurs more frequently, say monthly or quarterly. In that case we have to match the mode of compounding with the mode of the annuity (annual payment) to get the right formula.

Example 11.4
BIVA Enterprise puts US$20,000 in a deposit account at the end of every year for five years, but the funds in the account are compounded monthly at an interest rate of 16 %. What is the value of BIVA's deposits at the end of five years?

Answer 11.4
To solve this question, we need to first of all match the mode of compounding with the mode of the annuity payment by finding the EAR. The EAR can be gotten as follows:

$$EAR = \left(1 + \frac{0.16}{12}\right)^{12} - 1 = 0.1723 = 17.23\%$$

The EAR of 17.23 % is the interest rate that matches the mode of annuity payment (i.e. annual payment). We now put this in our *FVOA* formula considering the deposits of US$20,000 annually at the end of every year for five years

$$\text{FVOA} = \text{US\$}20{,}000\left[\frac{(1+0.1723)^5 - 1}{0.1723}\right] = \text{US\$}20{,}000(7.05) = \text{US\$}141{,}000$$

11.8.2 Future Value of Annuity Due

We mentioned that an annuity due is one in which each annuity payment occurs at the beginning of the period. Since an annuity due merely shifts the payments from the end of the year to the beginning of the year, we have to compound the cash flows for one additional year in order to obtain the future value of an annuity due (FVAD). The formula is therefore given as follows:

$$\text{FVAD} = C\left[\frac{(1+r)^n - 1}{r}\right](1+r)$$

Example: A micro-enterprise invests US$8,500 at the beginning of every year for four years at a 12 % interest rate. How much money will the firm have at the end of the four years? Since the cash flow occurs at the beginning of the period, we shall compute the present value of annuity due as follows:

$$\text{FVAD} = C\left[\frac{(1+r)^n - 1}{r}\right](1+r)$$

$$\text{FVAD} = \text{US\$}8{,}500\left[\frac{(1.12)^4 - 1}{0.12}\right](1.12)$$

$$\text{FVAD} = \text{US\$}8{,}500(4.7793)(1.12)$$

$$\text{FVAD} = \text{US\$}8{,}500(5.3528) = \text{US\$}45{,}498.8$$

Let us take another example. An entrepreneur invests US$6,000 at the beginning of each year for 15 years into a retirement account for an interest rate of 5.5 %. How much money will the entrepreneur have at the end of the 15 years? The answer will be:

$$\text{FVAD} = C\left[\frac{(1+r)^n - 1}{r}\right](1+r)$$

$$\text{FVAD} = \text{US\$6,000}\left[\frac{(1.055)^{15} - 1}{0.055}\right](1.055)$$

$$\text{FVAD} = \text{US\$6,000}(22.41)(1.055) = \text{US\$141,855.3}$$

Again, we need to be mindful of a situation where deposits are made yearly but compounding occurs more frequently, say monthly, quarterly or semi-annually. In such a situation, we need to match the mode of compounding with the mode of the annuity payment to get the right formula.

Using the BIVA Enterprise example we looked at previously, but this time the US$20,000 is deposited at the beginning of every year for five years, but the funds in the account are compounded monthly at an interest rate of 16 %.What is the value of BIVA deposits the end of five years?

To solve this question, we need to first of all match the mode of compounding with the mode of the annuity payment by finding the EAR. The EAR can be gotten as follows:

$$\text{EAR} = \left(1 + \frac{0.16}{12}\right)^{12} - 1 = 0.1723 = 17.23\%$$

The EAR of 17.23 % is the interest rate that matches the mode of annuity payment (i.e. annual payment). We now put this in our FVAD formula considering the deposits of US$20,000 annually at the end of every year for five years.

$$\text{FVAD} = \text{US\$20,000}\left[\frac{(1+0.1723)^5 - 1}{0.1723}\right](1.1723)$$

$$\text{FVAD} = \text{US\$20,000}(7.05)(1.1723)$$

$$\text{FVAD} = \text{US\$20,000}(8.26) = \text{US\$165,200}$$

The future value annuity due gives a higher figure than the future value ordinary annuity. In the BIVA example, the FVOA was US$141,000 but the FVAD of US$165,000 is higher. The intuition in the case of annuity due is that, because the payments are made at the beginning of the period, the first payment receives interest at the end of period. This results in one more period than the ordinary annuity for interest to be received.

11.8.3 Present Value Ordinary Annuity

The present value ordinary annuity (PVOA) is a stream of equal cash flows for n periods at interest rate of r when the cash flows are occurring at the end of the period. This can be obtained using the following formula:

$$\text{PVOA} = C(\text{PVIFA})$$

$$\text{PVOA} = C\left[\frac{1-\frac{1}{(1+r)^n}}{r}\right]$$

PVOA = the present value of an ordinary annuity
C = cash flow of annuity

PVIFA = present value interest factor of annuity = $\left[\frac{1-\frac{1}{(1+r)^n}}{r}\right]$

r = the interest rate per time period
n = number of compounding periods per year times the number of years

Example 11.5
Mr. Yinimi, an entrepreneur, intends investing in a financial instrument that will give him US$40,000 per year at the end of each year for 20 years. If the investment can earn 12 %, compounded annually, what is the present value of Mr. Yinimi's investment?

Answer 11.5

$$\text{PVOA} = C\left[\frac{1-\dfrac{1}{(1+r)^n}}{r}\right]$$

$$\text{PVOA} = \text{US\$40,000}\left[\frac{1-\dfrac{1}{(1+0.12)^{20}}}{0.12}\right] = \text{US\$40,000}(7.4694) = \text{US\$298,776}$$

We could also obtain the PVIFA of 7.4694 from the financial table in Appendix B-5 and then multiply the annuity of US$40,000 by the PVIFA to get an identical answer of US$298,776 as the present value. This is what we mean:

$$\text{PVOA} = \text{US\$40,000}(7.4694) = \text{US\$298,776}$$

Using the financial calculator, we go through the following:
I/Y: 12
N: 20
FV: 0
PMT: 40,000
PRESS CPT, PV
Then we get the answer as −298,776.

Example 11.6
Mr. and Mrs. Naba are saving for the University education of their new baby girl, Axelia. The Nabas anticipate that University expenses will involve US$20,000 per year when Axelia enters the University in 18 years. The annual interest rate over the next few decades will be 15 %. How much should the Nabas deposit in a bank account each year to fully finance their daughter's four years of University education? Assume that she enters the university on her 18th birthday.

Answer 11.6

The present value of the four years at the university can be calculated using the annuity formula.

$$\text{PVOA} = \text{US\$20,000}\left[\frac{1-\frac{1}{(1.15)^4}}{0.15}\right] = \text{US\$20,000}(2.8550) = \text{US\$57,100}$$

We assume that Alexia enters University on her 18th birthday, an amount of US$57,100 represents the present value at date 17. We calculate the present value of the university education at date 0 as follows:

$$\text{PV}_0 = \frac{\text{US\$57,100}}{(1.15)^{17}} = \text{US\$5,306.07}$$

Assuming that the Nabas make deposits into the bank account at the end of each of the 17 years, we can compute the annual deposit that will yield a present value of all deposits of US$5,306.07. This is calculated as:

$$\text{US\$5,306.07} = C\left[\frac{1-\frac{1}{(1.15)^{17}}}{0.15}\right]$$

$$\text{US\$5,306.07} = C(6.0472)$$

$$C = \frac{\text{US\$5,306.07}}{6.0472} = \text{US\$877.44}$$

Thus, deposits of US$877.44 made at the end of each of the first 17 years and invested at the rate of 14 % will generate enough funds to enable them pay the tuition of US$20,000 over the following four years.

11.8.4 Present Value Annuity Due

In the case of present value of an annuity due (PVAD), each cash flow is received one year earlier. The cash is received at the beginning of each year rather than at the end of each year. Therefore, the discounting is done for one less period. In order to determine the *PVAD*, we first find the present value of an ordinary annuity and then after multiply by (1 + *r*) which in effect cancels out one year's discounting. The formula is given as follows:

$$\mathrm{PVAD} = C\left[\frac{1-\dfrac{1}{(1+r)^n}}{r}\right](1+r)$$

Example 11.7

Let us say a small business owner expects to receive US$10,000 at the beginning of every year for the next six years. What is the present value of the equal income stream if the interest rate is 11 %?

Answer 11.7

$$\mathrm{PVAD} = C\left[\frac{1-\dfrac{1}{(1+r)^n}}{r}\right](1+r)$$

$$\mathrm{PVAD} = \mathrm{US\$}10{,}000\left[\frac{1-\dfrac{1}{(1.11)^6}}{0.11}\right](1.11)$$

$$\mathrm{PVAD} = \mathrm{US\$}10{,}000(4.2305)(1.11)$$

$$\mathrm{PVAD} = \mathrm{US\$}10{,}000(4.6959) = \mathrm{US\$}46{,}959$$

11.8.5 Growing Annuity

A **growing annuity** is a stream of cash flows growing over a given period of time. The cash flows may grow over time, due either to real growth or to inflation. The general formula for a growing annuity growing at a growth rate g is given as follows:

$$\mathrm{PV} = \frac{C}{r-g}\left[1-\left(\frac{1+g}{1+r}\right)^{n}\right]$$

Example 11.8
A defined-benefit retirement plan is offering to pay US$30,000 per annum for 25 years and increase the annual payment by 4 % every year. Determine the present value at retirement given a discount rate of 12 %. This present value of the growing annuity can be determined as follows:

Answer 11.8

$$\mathrm{PV} = \frac{C}{r-g}\left[1-\left(\frac{1+g}{1+r}\right)^{n}\right]$$

$$\mathrm{PV} = \frac{\mathrm{US\$30{,}000}}{0.12-0.04}\left[1-\left(\frac{1.04}{1.12}\right)^{25}\right] = \mathrm{US\$375{,}000}(0.8432) = \mathrm{US\$316{,}200}$$

11.9 Amortisation

The formula for the present value of equal cash flows can also be used to solve for the payment that would be required to pay off a loan and all the interest that would accumulate on this loan amount. This is the process used by banks to work the periodic loan repayments. When we make payments such that we are able to pay off a loan and its accompanying interest, we are said to be *amortising* the loan.

Example 11.9
A micro-enterprise secured a bank loan for US$100,000 for six years at a 15 % interest rate compounded monthly. Let us use this information to prepare an amortisation schedule.

Answer 11.9

In this example, the loan amount of US$100,000 is the present value of the stream of payments. So, we have to look for the stream of cash flow payments. This time let us denote the cash flow payments as PMT. We calculate this as present value ordinary annuity (PVOA) and this is given as follows:

$$\mathrm{PV} = \mathrm{PMT}\left[\frac{1-\dfrac{1}{(1+r)^n}}{r}\right]$$

We need to bear in mind that the interest is compounded monthly so we have:

$$\mathrm{US\$100{,}000} = \mathrm{PMT}\left[\frac{1-\dfrac{1}{(1+0.15/12)^{6\times 12}}}{0.15/12}\right]$$

$$\mathrm{US\$100{,}000} = \mathrm{PMT}(47.2925)$$

$$\mathrm{PMT} = \frac{\mathrm{US\$100{,}000}}{47.2925} = \mathrm{US\$2{,}114.5}$$

In this example, we now know the total payment to be US$2,114.5. We will thus calculate the interest paid (i.e. beginning loan balance multiplied by the interest rate) and then subtract it from the total payment to get the principal component that has been paid in each payment period. The ending loan balance is arrived at by subtracting the portion of the principal paid from the beginning loan balance.

In the first month, the interest paid is calculated as US$100,000 × 0.15/12 = US$1,250. Since the total payment is US$2,114.5, the principal component paid in the first month will be:

$$\text{Principal paid} = \mathrm{US\$2{,}114.5} - \mathrm{US\$1{,}250} = \mathrm{US\$864.5}$$

The ending loan balance in the first month is therefore computed as:

$$\text{Ending balance} = \mathrm{US\$100{,}000} - \mathrm{US\$864.5} = \mathrm{US\$99{,}135.5}$$

Table 11.4 Loan amortisation schedule

Month	Beginning balance (US$)	Total payment (US$)	Interest paid (US$)	Principal paid (US$)	Ending balance (US$)
1	100,000.00	2,114.50	1,250.00	864.50	99,135.50
2	99,135.50	2,114.50	1,239.19	875.31	98,260.19
3	98,260.19	2,114.50	1,228.25	886.25	97,373.95
4	97,373.95	2,114.50	1,217.17	897.33	96,476.62
5	96,476.62	2,114.50	1,205.96	908.54	95,568.08
…					
…					
…					
30	70,005.85	2,114.50	875.07	1,239.43	68,766.42
31	68,766.42	2,114.50	859.58	1,254.92	67,511.50
32	67,511.50	2,114.50	843.89	1,270.61	66,240.89
…					
…					
…					
…					
65	16,002.94	2,114.50	200.04	1,914.46	14,088.48
66	14,088.48	2,114.50	176.11	1,938.39	12,150.08
67	12,150.08	2,114.50	151.88	1,962.62	10,187.46
68	10,187.46	2,114.50	127.34	1,987.16	8,200.30
69	8,200.30	2,114.50	102.50	2,012.00	6,188.30
70	6,188.30	2,114.50	77.35	2,037.15	4,151.16
71	4,151.16	2,114.50	51.89	2,062.61	2,088.55
72	2,088.55	2,114.50	26.11	2,088.39	0.15

In the second month, the interest paid is US$99,135.5 × 0.15/12 = US$1,239.19 and then the loan balance reduces by US$99,135.5 − US$875.31 = US$98,260.19. We can complete the process by preparing a loan amortisation schedule as shown in Table 11.4. The ending loan balance at the end of the last year or maturity of the loan should be zero or close to zero. The amortisation schedule can best be prepared using a spreadsheet.

11.10 Summary and Conclusions

This chapter has covered the concept of time value of money, which is a useful tool for finance managers, MSME managers and entrepreneurs to deal with the problems in financial decisions. It deals with the fact that 'a dollar today is worth more than a dollar tomorrow'.

Most financial decisions, whether personal or business, are based on time of value of money. In a world where there is certainty in all cash flows, the rate of interest can be used to express the time of money.

Interest rates may be based on simple interest rate or compound interest rate. Simple interest is the interest paid (earned) on only the principal amount stated, while compound interest is the interest paid (earned) on both the principal amount and the accrued interest that has been previously paid (earned).

Future (or compound) value is the value at some future time of a present amount of money, or a series of payments, evaluated at a given interest rate. Present (or discount) value is the current value of a future amount of money, or a series of payments, evaluated at a given interest rate.

To compare alternative investments or loan facilities having different compounding periods, we calculate their EAR of interest. The EAR of interest considers the interest rate that would apply for a given frequency of compounding. The stated annual interest rate or APR is mainly quoted on an annual basis and it does not consider the issue of compounding.

A perpetuity is a constant stream of cash flows occurring forever, and a growing perpetuity is a stream of cash flows that grows at a constant rate forever. An annuity is a stream of constant cash flows occurring at regular intervals over a fixed period of time.

Future value ordinary annuity is a stream of equal cash flows occurring at the end of each period at a given interest rate, and the future value is calculated as of the last cash flow. Future value annuity due is a stream of equal cash flows occurring at the beginning of each period at a given interest rate, and the future value is calculated as one period after the last cash flow.

Present value ordinary annuity is a stream of equal cash flows occurring at the end of each period, and the present value is calculated as of one period before the first cash flow. Present value annuity due is a stream of equal cash flows occurring at the beginning of each period, and the present value is calculated as of the first cash flow.

When amortising a loan, we are interested in making periodic payments such that we are able to pay off the principal and its accompanying interest. The interest payment is calculated on the unpaid principal balance.

Discussion Questions and Problems

1. Look for the unknown variables in each of the following (Table A.11.1):

Table A.11.1 Looking for unknown variables

Present value (US$)	Years	Interest rate	Future value (US$)
6,000	?	8 %	13,500
9,000	?	7 %	15,600
20,500	16	?	300,000
28,500	8.2	?	180,400

2. In seeking financing for expansion to meet a growing demand, the financial manager of a fruit processing company based in Beijing, Bright Blue Limited gets the following quotes from three different banks. The banks and their respective quoted rates are illustrated below:

Industrial Bank	13 % compounded quarterly
Harbin Bank	9 % compounded semi-annually
Bank of Dalian	8 % compounded monthly

Which option should the firm go for?

3. Sambot Ltd., a micro-enterprise, will receive US$50,000 five years from now. If the interest rate is 24 %, what is the present value of the amount to be received? Assuming compounding takes place quarterly, how would your answer change with monthly interest compounding?
4. Assuming an entrepreneur invests an amount of US$85,000 in this instrument, how long will it take for this amount of investment to double.
5. An SME has been offered a five-year annuity of US$35,000 per year. The first payment comes at the end of the first year. How much will the firm have in its special account created for this investment at the end of the five years assuming market interest rate is 16 % per annum?
6. X-Fund pays US$20,000 per year for ten years and P-Fund pays US$35,000 per year for six years. If the discount rate for X-Fund is 12 % per annum, and that of P-Fund is 14 % per annum, indicate which of the two investments has a higher present value.
7. During 2011, The Durban Art Gallery sold a unique painting at an auction for a price of US$25,000. The value of the painting in 2007 was US$21,500. What was the annual rate of return on this painting?

8. An investment offers US$5,800 per annum for 12 years, with the first payment occurring one year from now. If the required return is 8 %, what is the value of the investment? What is the value assuming the payments occurred for 30 years?
9. What is the present value of a financial instrument that promises to pay US$6,500 annually for 25 years? The yield on other instruments with similar risk is 12 %.
10. A small business has two offers for a mortgage loan. The first offer is US$300,000 at an interest rate of 15 % for 20 years and the second offer is US$300,000 at an interest rate of 13.5 % for 15 years.

    (a) Calculate the monthly payment for both mortgage loans.
    (b) Calculate the amount of interest paid over the life of the loans.
    (c) Which offer is a better deal?

12

Evaluating Capital Investment Decisions: Capital Budgeting

Learning Objectives
By the end of this chapter, you should be able to:

- explain the rationale for capital budgeting
- discuss the factors that affect capital budgeting decisions
- list and explain the steps involved in the capital budgeting process
- explain the techniques or methods used in evaluating capital budgeting projects
- show how capital budgeting decisions are arrived at based on independent and mutually exclusive projects
- determine how capital budgeting decisions are influenced by capital rationing
- appreciate the importance of following, monitoring and taking corrective measures after the capital budgeting decision has been made

12.1 Introduction

In Chap. 11, we learned about the concept of time value of money. This concept will be useful for understanding the capital investment, which we shall cover in this chapter. The process of making capital investment decisions is also known as **capital budgeting**.

MSMEs just like other businesses are also confronted with decision of investing in long-term assets or projects. These investments are expected to

J.Y. Abor, *Entrepreneurial Finance for MSMEs*,
DOI 10.1007/978-3-319-34021-0_12

generate returns in the future. The MSME will have to make decisions regarding whether to buy new equipment and or expand its operations by acquiring additional premises. The method the entrepreneur or small business manager will have to go through in arriving at such a decision is referred to as capital budgeting. It is the capital investment decisions of firms and it involves the process by which these firms allocate funds between their long-term projects (capital expenditures).

This chapter deals with capital budgeting, and the steps involved in the capital budgeting process. It also discusses the techniques of capital budgeting such as the payback, discounted payback, Net Present Value (NPV), Internal Rate of Return (IRR), modified IRR, the profitability index (PI) and the accounting rate of return (ARR). These techniques help enterprises in assessing long-term projects and provide a guide in the selection of the good projects into its capital budget. We shall also discuss the other steps involved in capital budgeting, including making the decision, following up, and taking corrective action.

12.2 Capital Budgeting: An Overview

Capital budgeting is the process of analysing capital investment opportunities and deciding which ones to accept. It refers to the whole process of analysing long-term projects (involving fixed assets) and deciding which ones to include in the firm's planned investments. In taking capital budgeting decisions, the enterprise has to ensure that the projects it has included in its planned investment provide the owners or shareholders with reasonable returns over and above the required investment. Firms' investments in long-term or capital projects involve cash outlay with the expectation of some benefits in the future. The benefits derived from capital investments typically go beyond one year in the future. Examples include investment in fixed assets, introducing a new product on the market, undertaking research and development, embarking on a marketing communication campaign, embarking on an expansion project and acquiring a new business.

Let us assume that Print-Solutions Limited, a renowned printing company wants to expand its business into photocopying, with specific concentration on colour photocopying, since the market for colour photocopying is untapped. Before embarking on this expansion, Print-Solutions Limited has to determine the costs and benefits of the photocopying business. It will then determine whether this expansion project will yield the owners with greater benefits than what they would earn on other investments on the market. If the returns are high, then Print-Solutions Limited can go ahead to invest in the project. If the returns are low, then it would be better if it distributed the cash on the project to the owners.

Capital budgeting decisions are crucial to the future success of businesses. In order to simplify our discussion on the subject, we make the following assumptions:

- Investments in long-term assets will generate increased cash flow by improving the level of effectiveness and efficiency.
- Rates of return on investments and the current rate of inflation will continue to be the same.

12.3 Factors Affecting Capital Budgeting

Capital budgeting decisions are affected by a number of factors, including changes in government regulations, research and development, and changes in business strategy.

12.3.1 Changes in Government Regulations

Changes in government regulations on certain businesses could lead to increased cost to an enterprise in complying with such regulations. Capital budgeting is useful for determining whether to comply with a particular regulation and stay in the area of business or quit that business. The firm would have to ascertain the present value of the expected benefits of complying with the new regulation and compare with the cost of compliance. If the firm expects the present value of the future benefits to exceed the cost of compliance, then the firm will go ahead and comply with the necessary regulations. This means by complying with the new regulation the firm may experience improved efficiency, which will translate into increased future revenues. However, if the firm expects that the present value of the expected benefits of complying with the new regulation is less than the cost of compliance, then the firm will discontinue that business and therefore not comply.

For example, assuming there is a new government regulation for all small-scale mining firms to investment in a particular type of technology or machinery. The mining firm would have to evaluate the viability of such an investment in order to ascertain whether it makes economic sense to comply with the new regulation and or to exit the business altogether. Another example could be a situation where there is a ban on all equipment with carbon emissions. This will require firms with such equipment to abandon what they have and invest in new equipment. Would it be economically viable to comply with such a directive? The firm would need to evaluate the economic viability of the investment by going through capital budgeting process to ascertain that.

12.3.2 Research and Development

Research and development is essential in a firm's new-product development programme. Firms seek to introduce new products on the market in order to stay competitive. Capital budgeting can also be used to determine whether such research and development is necessary and will yield the expected benefits in excess of the costs involved in the research and development. In order to justify the research and development costs associated with the new products, the expected benefits from the introduction of the new products must be greater than the costs to be incurred. Otherwise, it does not make economic sense to go ahead with such research and development. Coming out with a new product can be risky, especially when such a programme is inconsistent with the firm's strategy. A critical evaluation of the present value of the expected benefits and costs of the new-product development is necessary to justify whether or not the firm should undertake the research and development.

12.3.3 Changes in Business Strategy

Firms' must be mindful of changing their business strategy when there are changes in economic factors. Such changes in strategy are needful in order to avoid business failure and remain relevant to clients. An enterprise wishing to change its business strategy will have to ascertain through capital budgeting decision-making whether such strategic moves are economically viable. If a firm wishes to expand into new areas or markets, it needs to weigh the expected benefits from such expansion against the costs of the strategic change. If the expected benefits exceed the costs, then the firm is more likely to adopt the new strategy. For example, if a firm wishes to enter the export market, it would have to determine the present value of the benefits to be derived from exporting and compare them with the costs involved in such export trade to arrive at a decision. Another example of a change in business strategy is when a firm decides to acquire another business. Again the present value of the benefits from the acquisition needs to be weighed against the cost of the acquisition in order to determine whether it is economically viable to pursue the acquisition strategy.

12.4 Steps in Capital Budgeting

In order to ensure that the MSME takes the right decision, it must carefully follow the necessary steps in making capital budgeting or capital investment decisions. There are five key steps involved in capital budgeting and these are:

- Formulating a proposal: This involves identifying the costs and expected benefits to be derived in the form of cash flows.
- Evaluating the data: This involves determining whether the cost and benefits generated make the investment viable.
- Making a decision: This entails choosing the course of action that provides the best outcome.
- Following up: This consists of monitoring and controlling the cash flows to ensure the actual benefits received exceed the additional cost incurred.
- Taking corrective action: This involves taking the necessary actions to bring the actual benefits received in line with expectations.

These five key steps are discussed in more details.

12.5 Formulating an Investment Proposal

In order to formulate a proposal, the firm must first identify all the costs and benefits associated with the project.

12.5.1 Costs in Capital Budgeting

The entrepreneur or MSME manager needs to take into consideration the costs that are relevant in capital budgeting decision. Such relevant costs include start-up costs, working capital commitment costs and tax factor costs.

Start-up costs are the total costs incurred to start the project. These costs include acquisition costs, costs of equipment, training costs, maintenance costs, costs of service agreements, hiring new employees, inventory, storage and so on. The firm's new project does not generate cash flows and revenue at the stage prior to the start-up or initial costs being incurred. Initial financing is therefore required by the firm to cover the start-up costs. Cash flows are normally generated after the initial investment or costs of the project have been incurred.

Working capital commitment costs entail maintaining specific levels of working capital necessary to meet the requirements of lending institutions. Banks and other lenders usually require firms that have borrowed from them to finance capital projects to maintain a certain level of working capital. This is to enable the borrowing firm to honour the periodic repayments of the loan and interest. Because the working capital is locked up and cannot be invested to earned returns, it constitutes an opportunity cost to the firm and as such should be included as part of the costs in the proposal formulation.

Tax factor costs arise from additional taxes that have to be paid by the firm as a result of acquisition of a new asset or an appreciation in the value of the firm's property. For instance, if a medium-sized manufacturing firm buys a new machine or expands its factory building, this will attract additional property tax because of the improvement in the value of the asset. These additional taxes add to the total costs of the investment and must also be considered in formulating the proposal.

It is important to note that *sunk costs* must be ignored in determining the costs of the capital project. Sunk costs are unrecoverable costs which have already been incurred and are not related to a particular project, therefore, they are not considered in the capital budgeting decision process.

12.5.2 Benefits and Importance of Capital Budgeting

Investments in capital projects by businesses are mainly in anticipation of the benefits of enhanced cash flow and the increased level of efficiency in the firms' operations. Another benefit could be in the form of tax-savings or reduction in tax liability. This is because of being allowed to write off portions of the investment (depreciation or capital allowance) which reduces taxable profit. It is however important to caution that the benefit in terms of tax-savings may not be reliable because it depends on the country's tax laws which are subject to frequent changes. The main benefits are the increased cash flows and improvement in the efficiency level associated with the capital investment.

Capital budgeting is a very important finance function for a number of reasons. The results of capital budgeting decisions continue for several years, and therefore investments in fixed assets will result in the firm losing some level of flexibility. For instance, once Print-Solutions Limited decides to invest in the photocopying business and goes ahead to purchase photocopying machines and other assets it needs, it cannot easily rescind that decision.

Capital budgeting shapes a firm's strategic direction. This is necessary in the sense that expansion into new products or markets must be preceded by capital expenditure.

Capital budgeting requires long-term sales forecast, over the whole life of the project. For instance, if the photocopying business has a ten-year life span, the firm has to make a ten-year sales forecast.

Appropriate forecast of asset requirements is important to prevent unnecessary costs and lost sales. If the firm invests too much in assets, depreciation costs, maintenance costs and so on will increase, quite unnecessarily. On the other hand, if it underestimates its asset requirements and invests too little in assets, the firm will not be able to meet the total demand for its products and will lose some of its sales.

Timing is also very important. First of all, capital budgets must be ready, as and when they are needed, to avoid losses in a competitive business environment. Furthermore, the firm has to be accurate in the timing of its forecasts (sales, assets requirements, etc.). This way it will be able to produce sufficiently to meet its demand over the life of the project, without incurring unnecessary costs.

Effective capital budgeting improves the timing and quality of asset acquisitions. It assists the firm to forecast its needs for capital assets and enable it acquire the assets before they are needed. This will reduce costs and improve sales and profits.

Capital budgeting ensures proper planning, and considering the huge expenditures, the firm must be sure it has the required amount of funds. However, large amounts of money are not available automatically. Therefore, the firm considering a major expenditure programme should plan its financing in advance to ensure that funds are available when they are needed.

12.6 Techniques of Capital Budgeting

After considering the costs and benefits associated with capital budgeting decisions, we will now discuss the techniques of evaluating the data obtained in the capital budgeting proposal. These techniques help us to assess long-term projects and guide us in selecting the good projects. The capital budgeting techniques include the payback, discounted payback, NPV, PI, IRR, modified IRR (MIRR) and accounting rate of return (ARR). We shall discuss these techniques one after the other.

Table 12.1 Cummulative net cash flows

Period	Net cash flows (NCF) US$	Cumulative NCF US$
0	−10,000	−10,000
1	5,000	−5,000
2	4,000	−1,000
3	3,000	2,000
4	1,000	3,000

12.6.1 Payback Period

The payback period is the expected number of years required to recover the money invested in a project. It is based on the notion that a project that pays its initial investment quickly is a good project. To apply the payback period rule, you first calculate the amount of time it takes to pay back the initial investment (the payback period). The firm sets a maximum acceptable payback period, which is used to compare with the actual payback period calculated for the project. If the payback period is less than a pre-specified payback period, the project is accepted, otherwise, it is rejected.

Example 12.1
The photocopying project of Print-Solutions Limited is expected to yield the following cash flows (both inflows and outflows) over the next four years. At the start of the project, an amount of US$10,000 will be spent in setting up the photocopying office and purchasing the photocopying machines needed. The project will start yielding cash flows from year 1 and the finance manager of the company has forecasted that there will be a cash inflow of US$5,000 in year 1, US$4,000 in year 2, US$3,000 in year 3 and US$1,000 in year 4. The pre-specified payback period for the firm is three years.

Calculate the payback period of the project.

Based on the payback rule, should the project be accepted or rejected (Table 12.1)?

Answer 12.1
As can be seen, by the end of year 3, the cumulative inflows have more than recovered the initial outflow. Thus, the payback occurred during the third year. We therefore calculate the payback period as follows;

$$\text{Payback Period} = \text{Year before full recovery} + \frac{\text{Unrecovered cost } at \text{ start of year}}{\text{cash flow during year}}$$

In our example, the year before full recovery is year 2. The unrecovered amount at the start of the year of recovery (year 3) is US$1,000 and the cash flow during year 3 is US$3,000.

Therefore,

$$\text{Payback period} = 2 + \frac{1,000}{3,000}$$

$$\text{Payback period} = 2 + 0.33$$

$$\text{Payback period} = 2.33\text{years}$$

Acceptance Criterion If the payback period calculated is less than the maximum acceptable payback period, the project's proposal should be accepted, otherwise the proposal should be rejected. In Example 12.1, based on the payback rule, the firm should accept the project because the payback period for this project of 2.33 years is less than the pre-specified payback period of three years.

Advantages

The advantages of using the payback period method include:

- The payback period method is mostly used for very short-term and small projects.
- It is simple to calculate and easy to understand.
- It provides an indication of the project's risk and liquidity since it is interested in how quickly the costs of the project can be recovered.

Disadvantages

There are advantages with using the payback period method, including:

- It is not reliable because it ignores the time value of money and as such, decisions made with the payback rule do not depend on the cost of capital.

- It also ignores all cash flows after the cut-off or payback period.
- If a project has higher cash flows in later years, the payback rule may reject this project, even though it may be viable.
- The maximum acceptable payback period set by the firm can be subjective.

12.6.2 Discounted Payback Period

In trying to address some of the problems with using the payback, some use the discount payback period method, which is a variant form of the payback. The discounted payback period is similar to the payback period, except that the expected cash flows of the project are discounted at the project's cost of capital. It is the number of years required to recover the investment from the *discounted* NCF.

Example 12.2
Using our Photocopying project, at a 10 % discount rate, we calculate the discounted payback period as follows (Table 12.2).

Answer 12.2

$$\text{Discounted payback period} = 2 + \frac{2{,}149}{2{,}254}$$

$$\text{Discounted payback period} = 2.95\text{years}$$

Acceptance Criterion If the discounted payback period calculated is less than the maximum acceptable, accept the project, otherwise it should be rejected.

Table 12.2 Discounted net cash flows

Period	Net cash flows (NCF) US$	Discounted NCF US$
0	−10,000	10,000
1	5,000	4,545
2	4,000	3,306
3	3,000	2,254
4	1,000	683

Assuming the pre-specified discounted payback period of the company is three years, this project will still be accepted under this rule.

Advantages

The discounted payback period has the advantages of the payback period. In addition, it is better than the payback rule in the sense that it uses the discounted cash flow of the project.

Disadvantages

The disadvantages of the discounted payback period are that:

- The decision rule also ignores cash flows after the cut-off period, a problem, which could lead to the rejection of profitable investments.
- It also requires an arbitrary cut-off period.

12.6.3 Net Present Value

The NPV method is an improvement on the payback and the discounted payback methods, because it relies on the time value of money or discounted cash flow technique and it also makes use of all the cash flows that accrue to the project. The NPV is implemented by the following procedure:

- Discount each of the cash flows of the project (both inflows and outflows) at the project's cost of capital to obtain their present values.
- Sum these discounted cash flows (both the inflows and outflows, the inflows will assume positive signs, whiles the outflows assume negative signs) to obtain the project's NPV.

In mathematical notations, NPV is calculated as follows:

$$\text{NPV} = \text{CF}_0 + \frac{\text{CF}_1}{(1+\text{k})^1} + \frac{\text{CF}_2}{(1+\text{k})^2} + \cdots + \frac{\text{CF}_n}{(1+\text{k})^n}$$

$$\text{NPV} = \sum_{t=0}^{n} \frac{\text{CF}_t}{(1+k)^t}$$

Where CF_t is the expected NCF at period t, k is the project's cost of capital and n is the life span of the project. (Note that expenditures such as the cost of buying equipment or building factories are treated as negative cash flows.)

Acceptance Criterion If the NPV is positive, the project should be accepted. If the NPV is negative, the project should be rejected. If two projects are mutually exclusive (the occurrence of one precludes the occurrence of the other), the one with the higher NPV must be chosen. There are instances where the firm may still go ahead with a project with zero NPV, especially when the project has some social benefits such as increased employment or improvements in the standard of living of people.

Example 12.3

Assuming the following cash flows are expected on the photocopying project of Print-Solutions Limited. If the opportunity cost of capital is 10 %, what is the NPV of the project (Table 12.3)?

Answer 12.3

$$\text{NPV} = -\text{US\$}10{,}000 + \frac{\text{US\$}5{,}000}{(1.10)^1} + \frac{\text{US\$}4{,}000}{(1.10)^2} + \frac{\text{US\$}3{,}000}{(1.10)^3} + \frac{\text{US\$}1{,}000}{(1.10)^4}$$

$$\text{NPV} = -\text{US\$}10{,}000 + \text{US\$}4{,}545 + \text{US\$}3{,}306 + \text{US\$}2{,}254 + \text{US\$}683 = \text{US\$}788$$

This project should be accepted given that the NPV is positive.

The cost of capital used in discounting the cash flows is the interest rate the firm must pay on an annual basis to obtain the necessary financing for the project. Where the firm plans on using both debt and equity to finance the

Table 12.3 Cash flows

Period	Cash flows US$
0	−10,000
1	5,000
2	4,000
3	3,000
4	1,000

project, then the cost of capital is based on the WACC. The cost of capital will be made up of (1) the interest on borrowed funds and (2) the interest that the firm could earn by putting its own funds in a different investment (opportunity cost).

The WACC is obtained by multiplying the cost of debt (interest rate on borrowed funds) by the proportion of borrowed funds, and multiplying the cost of equity (opportunity cost to the owner) by its proportion of owner's equity.

Example 12.4 A firm is buying a new fixed asset for US$120,000. It will use US$40,000 from its own resources and finance the balance of US$80,000 with a bank loan. Assuming the firm's opportunity cost is 9 % and the interest rate on the loan is 15 %, what is the WACC?

$$\text{WACC} = \left(\text{Cost of debt} \times \frac{\text{Proportion of debt}}{\text{Total finance}}\right) + \left(\text{Cost of equity} \times \frac{\text{Proportion of equity}}{\text{Total finance}}\right)$$

$$\text{WACC} = \left(0.15 \times \frac{\text{US\$80,000}}{\text{US\$120,000}}\right) + \left(0.09 \times \frac{\text{US\$40,000}}{\text{US\$120,000}}\right)$$

$$\text{WACC} = (0.10) + (0.03) = 0.13 = 13\%$$

The WACC is the interest rate used in discounting the cash flows in order to obtain the NPV in capital budgeting decisions of firms.

Following from Example 12.4, what is the NPV of investing in this new asset, assuming the future cash flows on the project are as follows?

Year 1	US$25,000
Year 2	US$34,000
Year 3	US$40,000
Year 4	US$50,000
Year 5	US$55,000

Answer 12.4

Considering the cost of the asset is US$120,000 and our calculated cost of capital is 13 %, we shall calculate the NPV as follows:

$$\text{NPV} = -\text{US\$120,000} + \frac{\text{US\$25,000}}{(1.13)^1} + \frac{\text{US\$34,000}}{(1.13)^2} + \frac{\text{US\$40,000}}{(1.13)^3} + \frac{\text{US\$50,000}}{(1.13)^4} + \frac{\text{US\$55,000}}{(1.13)^5}$$

$$NPV = -US\$120,000 + US\$22,123.89 + US\$26,626.99 + US\$27,722.01 + US\$30,665.94 + US\$29,851.80$$

$$NPV = US\$16,990.63$$

Advantages

The advantages of using the NPV method are that:

- It is often used in practice and it is useful in the sense that future cash flows that will be paid and received can be discounted back to the present so that a decision on the investment can be made now.
- Interest rates are determined by and based on the WACC that takes risk into consideration.

Disadvantages

The disadvantages of the NPV method are that:

- It is difficult to compute.
- It is difficult to interpret because NPV does not provide a measure of a project's actual rate of return.

12.6.4 Internal Rate of Return

The IRR is the actual rate of return of an investment project and it also considers the time value of money in its calculation. The IRR is the interest or discount rate, which equates the present value of a project's expected inflows to the present value of the project's costs.

$$PV(\text{Inflows}) = PV(\text{Investment costs})$$

If the IRR is the interest rate that equates the present value to the cost, then it means the NPV will be equal to zero. Therefore, the IRR is also defined as the interest rate that makes the NPV of the project to be zero.

$$NPV = CF_0 + \frac{CF_1}{(1+IRR)^1} + \frac{CF_2}{(1+IRR)^2} + \cdots + \frac{CF_n}{(1+IRR)^n} = 0$$

$$\text{NPV} = \sum_{t=0}^{n} \frac{\text{CF}_t}{(1+\text{IRR})^t} = 0$$

Interpolation Finding the IRR sometimes requires the trial-and-error approach. It is however easier to use financial calculator and spreadsheet to get the IRR. There are instances where one is compelled to still use the trial-and-error method or we can interpolate. Interpolation is the process of using mathematics to find an unknown value between two known values. Let us try and illustrate that in Example 12.5.

Example 12.5

Using the cash flows from our Photocopy project, determine the IRR. If the opportunity cost of capital of the project is 10 %, should the project be accepted or rejected?

First, let us discount the cash flows from the project at the project's cost of capital of 10 % to determine if that equates the NPV of the project to zero (Table 12.4).

We still do not have the discount rate that equates the NPV of the project to zero. However, because we have two NPVs and the two discount rates, we can through interpolation find the IRR of the project. Since we know that the NPV of 788 corresponds to 10 % and the NPV of −83 corresponds to 15 %, therefore we interpolate and find the unknown interest rate, which lies between 10 % and 15 %. The IRR can be computed using the following formula:

Table 12.4 Discounted cash flows

Project period	0	1	2	3	4
Cash flows	−10,000	5,000	4,000	3,000	1,000
Discount factor (10 %)	1.000	0.9091	0.8264	0.7513	0.683
Present values	−10,000	4,545	3,306	2,254	683
Net present value	788				
Since the NPV of the project is positive, it means the IRR is higher than 10 %. Let us use a higher discount rate, say 15 %					
Cash flows	−10,000	5,000	4,000	3,000	1,000
Discount factor (15 %)	1.000	0.8696	0.7561	0.6575	0.5718
Present values	−10,000	4,348	3,024	1,973	572
Net present value	−83				

$$\mathrm{IRR} = a + (b - a)\frac{\mathrm{NPV}_a}{\mathrm{NPV}_a - \mathrm{NPV}_b}$$

$$\mathrm{IRR} = 0.1 + (0.15 - 0.1)\frac{788}{788 - (-83)}$$

$$\mathrm{IRR} = 0.1 + (0.15 - 0.1)\frac{788}{788 + 83} = 0.14.52 = 14.52\%$$

Where a is the lower discount rate and b is the higher discount rate.

Acceptance Criterion The IRR of the project is compared to the project's cost of capital (or the required rate of return). If the IRR is greater than the project's cost of capital, then the project is accepted, otherwise, the project is rejected.

12.6.4.1 Problems of Using the Internal Rate of Return

The NPV rule and the IRR rule, in most conditions, yield the same results, since both of them use the discounted cash flow technique and also use all the cash flows accruing to the project. However, the NPV rule is preferred to the IRR rule. This is because the IRR cannot take care of certain complications associated with capital budgeting. These shortfalls are discussed below.

Delayed Investments This refers to projects that record positive cash flows before negative cash flows. For instance, if you borrow money, you will have a positive cash flow at the beginning of the period and negative cash flows subsequently, when you start paying off your interests and principal. Further, you could be involved in a project, where you are paid up front, but under which you spend money in subsequent years to execute the contract. Because the cash flows of such a project do not follow the conventional cash outflow followed by cash inflows pattern, the IRR decision rule is turned upside down. Under this condition, the NPV is preferred to the IRR.

Non-existent IRR Sometimes the nature of some projects may be such that at all discount rates, and the NPV is either positive or negative (that is, the NPV is never zero, no matter what discount rate you are using). Since the IRR is defined as the discount rate that equates the NPV of the project to zero, the IRR in such a situation provides no recommendation and so it cannot be used. Under this condition, the NPV is preferred.

Multiple IRR Sometimes the nature of the cash flows from a project may be such that it has more than one IRR. Since you would not know which IRR is the correct one to be compared to the cost of capital, it is better to use the NPV under this condition.

When you have to choose from two projects such that the selection of one project precludes the selection of the other, the IRR could lead to an erroneous rule. You can only use the IRR under this condition if you look at the incremental expenditure (if the projects are of different scales). Thus, under such conditions, it is better to use the NPV.

12.6.5 Modified Internal Rate of Return

The MIRR is a modification of the IRR. Unlike the IRR, which assumes cash flows are reinvested at the project's own IRR, the MIRR assumes cash flows are reinvested at the project's cost of capital (a more realistic assumption).

In using the MIRR, all cash outflows (COF) are discounted to year 0, while all cash inflows (CIF) are compounded to their terminal values, using the project's cost of capital. The MIRR is the rate that equates the terminal values (TV) or future values of all the inflows to the present values of all the outflows. The MIRR can be gotten using the following expression:

$$\mathrm{PV}(\mathrm{Cost}) = \frac{\mathrm{TV}}{(1+\mathrm{MIRR})^n}$$

$$\sum_{t=0}^{n} \frac{\mathrm{COF}_t}{(1+\mathrm{k})^t} = \left\{ \sum_{t=0}^{n} \mathrm{CIF}_t (1+k)^{n-t} \right\} / (1+\mathrm{MIRR})^n$$

Example 12.6

Using the cash flows of the photocopying project, and the opportunity cost of capital of 10 %, calculate the MIRR. Based on the MIRR rule, should the project be accepted or rejected (Table 12.5)?

Table 12.5 Terminal value

Year	Cash flows (CIF)	Future values $[CIF_t(1 + k)^{n-t}]$
1	US$5,000	US$6,655
2	4,000	4,840
3	3,000	3,300
4	1,000	1,000
	Terminal value	US$15,795

Answer 12.6

Remember the cost of the project is US$10,000.

So, the MIRR is the rate the will equate US$15,795 to US$10,000 when discounted. We therefore get MIRR as follows:

$$\frac{\text{US\$15,795}}{(1+\text{MIRR})^n} = \text{US\$10,000}$$

$$(1+\text{MIRR})^4 = \frac{\text{US\$15,795}}{\text{US\$10,000}}$$

$$(1+\text{MIRR}) = (1.5795)^{1/4}$$

$$\text{MIRR} = 1.1211 - 1$$

$$\text{MIRR} = 0.1211 \text{ or } 12.11\%$$

Since 12.11 % is the rate that equates the terminal value of the cash inflows to the present value of the cash outflows, then we conclude that the MIRR of the project is 12.11 %. Since the 12.11 % is above the cost of capital of the project, 10 %, this project should be accepted.

12.6.6 Profitability Index

So far, it seems the NPV is the best capital budgeting rule. However, when different opportunities demand different amounts of a particular resource, which is fixed in supply (resource constraints), you may be restricted to selecting only some projects and leaving others. For instance, if you have US$10,000, to invest in different projects with a total cost of US$10,500, you will be forced to select only some of the projects and leave others. Especially if all the projects have positive NPVs, selecting the projects with the highest NPVs might not lead to the best decision. For instance, the project with the highest NPV might take up the whole amount and prevent you from taking a combination of other projects, which might result in a higher NPV (when put together). Thus, under conditions of resource constraints, we use the PI, which compares the projects NPV (value added) to the resource required for the project. The PI is the NPV per unit of resource used.

The PI is the benefit–cost ratio and is defined as the ratio of the present value of the cash flows to the cost of the project. It is computed as:

$$PI = \frac{\text{Total present value of future cash fows}}{\text{Initital investment}}$$

Acceptance Criterion Accept the project if the PI is greater than one, otherwise reject. Where there are competing projects, rank the projects beginning from the one with the highest PI and select till your resource is totally consumed.

Example 12.7
Assuming a project has a total present value of US$250,000 with a cost of US$160,000, what is the PI?

The PI for this project is:

$$PI = \frac{\text{US\$250,000}}{\text{US\$160,000}} = 1.56$$

Since the PI is greater than one, we accept the project. The project is profitable, because for every dollar invested, the project will return US$1.56 in benefit. Note that when the NPV is positive, the PI will be greater than one, and when the NPV is negative, the PI will be less than one. In this example, our NPV is US$90,000; therefore, the PI is greater than one. Assuming a project produced a PI of say 0.76, it would mean that for every dollar invested, the project returned 76 cent (less than one dollar) in benefit.

Table 12.6 Sharp Engineering example Pt.1

Projects we can include		
Project	Present value	Engineer head count
Router	67.7	50
Project A	69.7	47
Project B	52.1	44
Project C	54	40
Project D	72.5	61
Project E	78.6	58
Project F	44.9	32

Example 12.8

Sharp Engineering is a small engineering firm with 190 engineers. It has the following projects, with their NPVs and resource requirements (Table 12.6). Which of the projects should Sharp Engineering invest in?

Answer 12.8

Because this project involves the issue of resource constraint (190 engineers), the best technique to use is the PI. Further, the total number of engineers required for all the projects are 332, which means we have to select some of the projects and leave out others (Table 12.7).

The ranks of the projects, beginning from the one with the highest PI, are indicated in the last column. We therefore rank them accordingly and calculate the amount of resources consumed to determine which of the projects we can include in our capital budget as follows (Table 12.8).

Because there are only 190 engineers, we cannot take any other project (since there is no project which requires only three engineers). Therefore, we select Projects A, F, E and the Router into our capital budget.

Advantages

The advantages of using a PI are:

- It is easy to calculate and interpret.
- It may be useful when available investment funds are limited.
- It provides an indication of cost–benefit analysis, and also, correct decision is made when evaluating independent projects.

Table 12.7 Sharp Engineering example Pt.2

Project	Present value	Engineer head count	Profitability index	Rank
Router	67.7	50	1.354	4
Project A	69.7	47	1.483	1
Project B	52.1	44	1.184	7
Project C	54	40	1.35	5
Project D	72.5	61	1.189	6
Project E	78.6	58	1.355	3
Project F	44.9	32	1.403	2

Table 12.8 Sharp Engineering example Pt. 3

Decision:			
Project	Profitability index	Resource required	Resource consumed
Project A	1.483	47	47
Project F	1.403	32	79
Project E	1.355	58	137
Router	1.354	50	187
Project C	1.350	40	
Project D	1.189	61	
Project B	1.184	44	

Disadvantages

The disadvantages of the PI include:

- It may give a wrong indication of the project's viability, if interest rate estimates are too low or cash flow projections are too high.
- There are also problems using the PI involving mutually exclusive projects.

12.6.7 Accounting Rate of Return

The ARR is a measure of the project's profitability from a conventional accounting standpoint. It is the average return from income generated over the life of an investment. It is determined as the average annual income from the project, divided by the average cost of the project. This method is easy to calculate but it does not consider the time value of money or the present value of the cash flows. The ARR is calculated as follows:

$$\text{ARR} = \frac{\text{Average annual income}}{\text{Average cost Investment}}$$

Acceptance Criterion Accept the project if the ARR is equal or greater than the target set by the firm, otherwise we reject the project. In ranking projects that have the same target ARR, the project with the highest ARR should be chosen because it is the most profitable.

Example 12.9
A medium-sized firm is considering a project with an initial cost of US$78,500. The project has a five-year life and generates annual income of US$10,800, US$12,500, US$12,800, US$13,300 and US$13,700 over the five years, respectively.

What is the ARR on this project?
Should this project be accepted if the ARR is 15 %?

Answer 12.9

$$\text{ARR} = \frac{\dfrac{\text{US\$10,800} + \text{US\$12,500} + \text{US\$12,800} + \text{US\$13,300} + \text{US\$13,700}}{5}}{\text{US\$78,500}}$$

$$\text{ARR} = \frac{12{,}620}{78{,}500} = 0.1608 = 16.08\%$$

This project should be accepted since the ARR of 16.08 % is greater than the required ARR of 15 %.

Advantages
The advantages include:

- The ARR is the return from income generated over the life an investment and it is easy to calculate.
- The accounting information is usually available to compute the ARR.

Disadvantages
The disadvantages are that:

- It ignores the time value of money.
- It uses an arbitrary benchmark cut-off rate.
- It is based on book values, not on cash flows and market values.

12.7 Making the Decision

In practice most businesses, especially MSMEs, have limited access to financial resources. Therefore, it will require that they make capital rationing decisions. **Capital rationing** is a constraint placed on the amount of financial resources that can be invested in a given period of time. This constraint is mainly a result of limited finances. In that case, the firm will have to choose among projects, especially if they are **mutually exclusive**. Projects are said to be mutually exclusive projects if they serve a similar purpose. Firms are compelled to choose some alternatives and ignore others when the projects are mutually exclusive. Such situations require ranking the projects and choosing the one with the highest NPV. For instance, a firm is considering whether to acquire a boat to transport its workers across a river to and from its factory or to construct a bridge to facilitate the movement of the workers. The firm will choose the project, which gives the higher NPV and ignore the other. It will not choose both projects, even though they both give positive NPV, because the two projects are mutually exclusive or they serve the same purpose.

However, in the absence of capital rationing, the firm can choose all independent projects as long as they add value to the firm. Independent projects are not mutually exclusive, which means choosing one project does not preclude you from choosing the other. This suggests that, where the projects are not mutually exclusive, they are all chosen provided they all have positive NPVs. On the other hand, all the projects are rejected provided they all have negative NPVs. It is important to mention that, if the firm has abundant resources, it can choose all independent projects as long as the projects have positive NPVs.

12.8 Following Up

This stage of the capital budgeting process requires monitoring and controlling the firm's cash flows. Monitoring involves establishing standards and procedures that ascertain how well the decision taken compares with the proposal. It also involves setting up budgets to monitor all cash inflows and cash outflows and to determine whether the proposed cost and expected benefits are realised. Controlling entails establishing standards for measuring a project, measuring actual performance of the project against the standards that have been set up, and taking corrective measures to remedy the situation. Establishing standards involves setting up annual budgets based on the firm's capital decisions. The annual budget gives an idea of the expected costs and benefits for the year, though the annual budget is in practice broken into monthly budgets. Measuring actual performance focuses on comparing actual costs and benefits with the budgeted costs and benefits. Taking corrective measures is necessary in capital budgeting decisions in case the actual costs and benefits deviate from the budgeted figures significantly.

12.9 Taking Corrective Action

When the difference between the actual cash flows deviate from the budgeted cash flows, then we have a variance. The variance could be positive or negative. Positive variance is when the actual benefits exceed the budgeted benefits or when the actual costs fall short of the budgeted costs. On the other hand, negative variance occurs when the actual benefits are less than the budgeted benefits or when the actual costs exceed the budgeted costs. Taking corrective action entails reducing cost or increasing cash inflows in the case of negative variance. It also involves investing excess cash in the case of positive variance.

12.10 Summary and Conclusions

Capital budgeting is the process of analysing investment opportunities and deciding which ones to accept. It refers to the whole process of analysing long-term projects and deciding which ones to include in the firm's planned investments. Capital budgeting decisions are affected by a number of factors including, changes in government regulations, research and development and changes in business strategy.

In order to ensure that firms take the right decision, they must carefully follow the necessary steps in making capital budgeting or capital investment decision and these steps include: (1) formulating a proposal, (2) evaluating the data, (3) making a decision, (4) following up and (5) taking corrective action.

A number of techniques are used in evaluating the data obtained in the capital budgeting proposal and these techniques assist in assessing long-term projects and providing a guide in selecting good projects. These techniques include the payback, discounted payback, NPV, PI, IRR, modified MIRR and ARR. In practice, most firms use the NPV and IRR methods.

Discussion Questions and Problems

1. Ms. Darko is the Finance Officer of Grace Ltd. She has proposed two investment plans to management/Plan A requires a deposit of US$6,000 every six months, with an interest receivable at a 5 % annual rate, compounded semi-annually. Plan B requires a deposit of US$8,000 yearly, with an interest rate of 7.5 % compounded annually. The initial deposit in Plan A would be made six months from now, and that of Plan B in a year's time.

   (a) What is the future value of Plan A at the end of five years?
   (b) What is the future value of Plan B at the end of five years?
   (c) Which plan should management approve, assuming management's only concern is the value of the investment at the end of five years?
   (d) Would management's choice of plan change if the rate of interest in Plan B were 6.5 %?

2. Winlett Enterprise, a small business maintains a capital structure of 2:3. The firm is considering expanding its area of operation with an initial cost estimation of US$100,000. The interest rate on loans is 12 %, while the opportunity cost on the firm's own funds is 8 %. The expected annual free cash flows from the project are as follows:

Year	Cash flows (US$)
1	72,000
2	75,000
3	85,000
4	95,000
5	98,000

Using NPV and MIRR project evaluation methods, on the assumption that the cash flows are reinvested at the cost of capital rate, is the project a viable one?

3. Consider the following projects:

Year	Project A	Project B	Project C
0	(10,000)	(20,000)	(30,000)
1	10,000	10,000	10,000
2	0	10,000	10,000
3	0	10,000	0
4	0	10,000	10,000
5	0	10,000	10,000

(a) Given an opportunity cost of capital of 8 %, which projects result in a positive NPV?
(b) Calculate the payback period for each project, if the cut-off period is three years. Which project should be accepted?
(c) Briefly discuss the advantages and disadvantages of using the payback and NPV methods of investment appraisal.

4. Glax Limited is considering embarking on a bottling water project with the following cash flows. The opportunity cost of capital of the project is 10 %.

Year	Cash flows
0	−300,000
1	150,000
2	120,000
3	90,000
4	30,000

(a) Assuming the payback period of Glax Limited is three years. Should the project be accepted based on the payback rule?
(b) If the discounted payback period of Glax Limited is 3.5 years, should the project be accepted based on the discounted payback period rule?
(c) Based on the NPV rule, should the project be accepted?
(d) Based on the IRR rule, should the project be accepted?
(e) Based on the Modified IRR rule, should the project be accepted?

5. Patosh Ltd, a medium-sized business is considering two independent projects, Project X and Project Y. The initial cost of project X is US$350,000 and that of Project Y is US$600,000. Considering cost of capital for both projects is 10 % and the expected cash flows from each project are:

Year	Project X	Project Y
	$	$
0	−350,000	−600,000
1	150,000	180,000
2	170,000	180,000
3	160,000	200,000
4	140,000	210,000
5	150,000	250,000
6	150,000	160,000

(a) Compute the payback period and discounted payback period for each project.
(b) Calculate the NPV and PI for each project.
(c) Indicate if the projects should be accepted based on the NPV and PI methods.
(d) Why would you prefer the NPV method to other methods of project evaluation?
(e) Outline the steps involved in capital budgeting decisions.

6. IYA Ltd is considering a project with an initial cash outlay of US$75,000 and a required rate of return of 11 %. The expected annual free cash flows from the project given as:

Year	Cash flows
	US$
1	17,000
2	19,800
3	25,300
4	29,800
5	38,500
6	45,000

(a) Indicate whether this project is viable or not using the NPV and PI methods.
(b) Compute the MIRR for this project assuming the cash flows are reinvested.

7. Best World Limited, a small business is considering expanding its area of operation with an initial cost estimation of US$65,000. The entrepreneur intends investing US$26,000 from retained earnings and financing the remainder with a bank loan. The interest rate on loans is 12 % while the

opportunity cost on the firm's own funds is 10 %. The expected annual free cash flows from the project are as follows:

Year	Cash flows
	US$
1	20,000
2	22,600
3	27,200
4	30,000
5	35,000
6	38,000
7	40,000

Show whether this project is viable or not, using the NPV and MIRR methods assuming the cash flows are reinvested at the cost of capital rate.

8. Naxtell Limited is seeking to purchase a major piece of equipment which cost US$20 million.

The machine is expected to be sold at scrap by the end of the fifth year for US$5 million. The machine will generate US$4.5 million at the end of every year throughout the life of the machine. The company requires 15 % on the return on its investment. Using the NPV, method should the machine be bought?

13

Valuation of New Ventures and Small Businesses

Learning Objectives
By the end of this chapter, you should be able to:

- explain how new ventures and small businesses are valued
- use the various valuation methods
- appreciate the strengths and weaknesses of the valuation methods
- understand the criteria for selecting a venture valuation model

13.1 Introduction

An entrepreneur is interested in turning opportunities into a viable business, grow the business and eventually harvest the resulting value on such a business venture investment. Investors, including venture capitalists and other private equity investors, are also interested in how new ventures or entrepreneurial firms are valued. Determining the value of the venture is critical for establishing the percentage of ownership the business's external investors may be interested in. The perceived value of the venture, as well as the capabilities of the entrepreneur to enhance the value of the firm, is critical to the external investor. The entrepreneur may also be interested in whether the external investor can contribute to the overall value and whether the external investor has the financial resources and organisational capacity to invest in the firm.

In this chapter, we look at how entrepreneurial firms are valued. We specifically discuss valuation of business ventures. We also examine the various

J.Y. Abor, *Entrepreneurial Finance for MSMEs*,
DOI 10.1007/978-3-319-34021-0_13

methods of valuation and the criteria for selecting a new venture valuation model. The knowledge acquired in time value of money and capital budgeting is important in appreciating the issues discussed under valuation of new ventures and small businesses.

13.2 Valuation of Business Ventures

Valuation is a difficult yet an important aspect of the business investment process and this exercise is required to be carried out on regular basis. What value should an entrepreneur place on the firm when they initially seek equity from external investors? What should the external investor pay to invest in the firm? What is the appropriate valuation when additional financing is required? What is the appropriate valuation at the time of existing or harvesting the investment?

Valuation is concerned with the process of determining the amount an investor needs to pay to invest in a firm. When investors invest in a firm, they assume ownership interest and therefore, in exchange for their investment, they receive the firm's shares. If an investor is interested in holding say 20 % of the firm, it will be necessary to first determine what the entire firm is worth. The investor will then ascertain exactly how much to offer for the 20 % stake in the firm. On the other hand, the entrepreneur will decide whether he/she is prepared to give up 20 % ownership in the firm for the price offered by the investor. The value of the firm may be expressed in total (say US$20 million) or on a per share basis (say US$3.25 per share).

In the case of publicly listed companies, the value of the firm is determined on per second basis by investors (buyers and sellers of the shares) on the stock exchange. The problem however, is with respect to valuing new ventures, private companies and small businesses that are not listed on the public exchange. That is, there is no efficient mechanism involving multiple buyers and sellers for setting the share price (SP) for private companies. The problem is further compounded by the fact that these firms have little or no track record of performance making it difficult to provide any forecast for future years.

Essentially, valuing new venture and small businesses is difficult because of the problem of estimating future cash flows and the appropriate discount rate for determining the present value of the future cash flows. In spite of these difficulties, earnings or cash flows forecasts are captured in most business plans and investors who are looking for deals make forecasts for cash flows and earnings. In Chap. 9, we examined how to forecast performance and how to forecast financial information to determine financing needs. We can use those approaches to estimate the future cash flow and also follow required procedure to determine appropriate discount rates.

13.3 Valuation Methods

Various methods exist for valuing new ventures and small businesses. These different methods can result in varying outcomes, and therefore it is necessary to consider valuation from different perspectives to arrive at an appropriate valuation range. The various valuation methods discussed in this chapter include:

- Discounted cash flow method
- Risk-adjusted net present value
- Certainty equivalent method
- Venture capital method
- Free cash flow to equity
- Free cash flow to firm
- Valuation using comparable firms

13.3.1 Discounted Cash Flow Method

Under the discounted cash flow (DCF) method, the value of the business is estimated based on its expected future cash flows, discounted at a rate that reflects the riskiness of the cash flows. In the DCF method, the value of an asset is computed as the present value of the asset's expected cash flows. The intrinsic value of an asset is estimated based upon its characteristics in terms of expected cash flows, growth potential and risk. The expected future cash flows are discounted to present values using a discount rate that reflects the riskiness of the asset. The present value of the series of cash flows is determined as:

$$PV_j = \frac{FCF_1}{(1+r)^1} + \frac{FCF_2}{(1+r)^2} + \frac{FCF_3}{(1+r)^3} + \frac{FCF_4}{(1+r)^4} + \cdots + \frac{FCF_n}{(1+r)^n} \tag{13.1}$$

This can be simplified in Eq. (13.2):

$$PV_j = \sum_{t=1}^{N} \frac{CF_t}{(1+r)^t} \tag{13.2}$$

Table 13.1 Print Direct Limited example

Year	1	2	3	4	5
Cash flows	US$300,000	US$400,000	US$620,000	US$850,000	US$980,000

where:
N = life of the asset
FCF_n = free cash flows emanating from the project
CF_t = future cash flows at period t
r = discount rate reflecting the riskiness of the estimated cash flows

Example 13.1
Print Direct Limited operating in designing and printing of wedding cards and posters in Kampala, has a five-year investment plan that will generate the following cash flows (Table 13.1):

The firm can earn 12 % on similar investments. How much is this investment worth today?

Answer 13.1

$$\text{Value of asset} = \frac{\text{US\$300,000}}{(1.12)^1} + \frac{\text{US\$400,000}}{(1.12)^2} + \frac{\text{US\$620,000}}{(1.12)^3} + \frac{\text{US\$850,000}}{(1.12)^4} + \frac{\text{US\$980,000}}{(1.12)^5} = \text{US\$2,124,307.13}$$

Advantages

The advantages of the DCF method are that:

- It provides an objective framework for assessing a firm's risk and cash flows to estimate value.
- It requires users to think about key drivers of value.
- It may be useful when no comparable companies are available.

Disadvantages

The disadvantages of the DCF method are as follows:

- It is extremely sensitive to cash flow projections, which may be inherently difficult to predict, particularly as the projection horizon lengthens.

- The terminal value may be distorted by incorrect estimations of either cash flow or terminal multiples.
- The validity of the discount rate depends on assumptions for β and the market risk premium.

13.3.2 Risk-Adjusted Net Present Value

This method is used to value risky future cash flows. It uses a discount rate that reflects the time value of money and riskiness of the future cash flows to discount those risky future cash flows to present value. To be able to value the risk-adjusted NPV of any asset, we consider two main approaches: the use of higher discount rates to discount expected cash flows when valuing riskier assets, and the use lower discount rates when valuing safer assets. Academics and financial analysts employ risk and return models to determine the discount rates for the valuation of risk-adjusted discount rates (RADRs) models.

13.3.2.1 Risk and Return Models

In the discounted cash flow model above, we determine the value of the asset using free cash flows, the life of the asset and discount rates all provided in the information of a given firm. In this scenario, however, the riskiness and the return of the asset will be determined using econometric and financial models such as the capital asset pricing model (CAPM) and the multifactor models of today. The output of these models is what we call the ***expected rate of return*** for any investment given its risk or the ***risk-adjusted rate*** of any given asset.

The CAPM measures the relationships between risk and return of any asset. In the CAPM, the expected return on an asset is a function of its β, relative to the market portfolio. It can be written as:

$$\text{Expected return} = \text{Risk free rate} + \text{Market } \beta \times \text{Equity risk premium} \quad (13.3)$$

Algebraically, the relationship between risk and return can be expressed as follows:

$$E(r_j) = r_f + \beta_j (r_m - r_f) \quad (13.4)$$

In Eq. (13.3), the market risk premium is defined as $r_m - r_f$. β_j is the β risk of the asset. The value of β_j, the β risk of the asset jth asset, depends on its non-diversifiable risk. Specifically, β_j is measured as follows:

$$\beta_j = \frac{\text{cov}\left(r_j, r_m\right)}{\sigma_m^2} \tag{13.5}$$

where cov(r_j, r_m) is defined as the covariance between the returns on the assets and the returns of the market and σ_m^2 is the variance of the market returns.

In Eq. (13.3), which measures the risk and return relationship, two key inputs are common. Thus, the risk-free rate and the equity risk premium. The ***risk-free rate*** guarantees the investors his or her return with certainty. It is measured as the current market interest rate on default free assets (usually government securities). Note that the risk-free rate varies across currencies since the expected inflation rate differs with currencies.

In the case of the ***equity risk premium***, it is estimated in two different ways. The first is the historical risk premium obtained from returns earned on shares, relative to the risk-free investment. The second is to calculate the implied premium based on the prices of shares, relative to the expected cash flows generated from such investment.

Example 13.2

In January 2016, the Indian government issued a 182-day Treasury bill with a discount rate of 8.125 %. The regression β for BBuy was 1.95; the standard error was 0.45; and the bottom-up β for BBuy was 2.45, considering other e-commerce firms. Assuming the latter is accepted as the best estimate of the β, using the implied risk premium of 5.39 %, what would be the expected return on BBuy shares?

Answer 13.2

$$\text{Expected return } on \text{ BBuy} = r_f + \beta_j\left(r_m - r_f\right) = 8.125 + 2.45(5.39) = 21.3305\%$$

If we were to evaluate BBuy equity cash flows, we would have used 21.3305 % as the RADR to discount the risky future cash flows.

Example 13.3
A project costs US$100,000 today and offers US$50,000, US$60,000, US$80,000 cash inflows for the next three years, respectively. Its β is 1.5 and the market return is 19 %. Given a risk-free rate of 9 %, compute the NPV of the project?

Answer 13.3

$$\text{Expected return} = r_f + \beta_j\left(r_m - r_f\right) = 9 + 1.5(19 - 9) = 24\%$$

$$\text{Project value} = -\text{US\$}100{,}000 + \frac{\text{US\$}50{,}000}{(1.24)^1} + \frac{\text{US\$}60{,}000}{(1.24)^2} + \frac{\text{US\$}80{,}000}{(1.24)^3}$$

$$= \text{US\$}21{,}303.41$$

The risk-adjusted NPV can therefore be stated as:

$$PV_j = \sum_{t=1}^{N} \frac{CF_{jt}}{\left(1 + r_f + \beta_{jt}\left(r_m - r_f\right)\right)^t} \tag{13.6}$$

Advantages
The advantages of the risk-adjusted NPV method are that:

- It values assets based on expected future cash flows.
- The discount rate is considered the opportunity cost of capital.
- It can use market β to estimate cost of capital.
- It is not necessary to estimate the total risk.

Disadvantages
The main disadvantages of the risk-adjusted NPV method are:

- It is unlikely to get true comparable firms for new ventures.
- It may be difficult to value complicated financial claims on the assets, if information on total risk is not available.
- It is difficult to use because the appropriate discount rate for valuing a single cash flow cannot normally be determined based on data from comparable firms.

13.3.3 Certainty Equivalent Method

Sometimes it is difficult to use the RADR form of the CAPM to value real investment opportunities with risky cash flows. This is because risk-averse investors will always prefer more to less and will not want to lose their investments. You may either adjust the discount rate for risk in DCF valuation or adjust the expected cash flows for risk. In adjusting the cash flow, you are simply replacing the uncertainty of expected cash flows with the certainty equivalent cash flows, using a risk adjustment procedure similar to what is used in adjusting discount rates.

Let us go back to the problem we evaluated using the BBuy in our previous Example 13.2. Let us assume that BBuy's investment yield a cash flow of US$250,000 per annum. This cash flow is uncertain with the same risk as the market. Given the information in Example 13.2, we can discount at the risk-adjusted rate of 21.33 % rather than the 8.125 % risk-free rate of interest. This gives us a present value of US$ 250 , 000/1.2133 = US$ 206 , 049.62.

Supposing that BBuy has decided not to consider the market interest rate and that of the sensitivity in the market with respect to the bond and has decided to rely solely on the government to pay back all the money with surety. It means that BBuy is certain that the money will be paid at the end of the year. This guarantee will remove all the uncertainty about the payoff on the investment. This means that BBuy will accept a figure less than the original US$250,000 it could have received. But how much less will BBuy receive considering the risk-free rate of 8.125 % and the present value of US$206,049.62?

$$PV = \frac{\text{Certain cash flow}}{1.08125} = \text{US\$206,049.62}$$

Certain cash flow = US$222,791.15

This certain cash flow of US$222,791.15 has the same value as the earlier risky cash flow of US$250,000. The difference between the cash flow of US$250,000 and the present value of US$ 206 , 049.62 is US$ 43 , 950.38, which shows the time value of the money component of the entire investment. However, the other aspect compensates for the risk attached to the forecasted cash flows.

Thus, US$250,000 – US$222,791.15 = US$27,208.85. This figure is known as the **markdown** or the **haircut** used to compensate for the risk.

This scenario we presented illustrates two ways of valuing risky cash flows:

Method 1: We first discounted the cash flow at the RADR, r is greater than the risk-free rate, r_f. This accounts for both the time value of money and for risk.

Method 2: In the second scenario, find the certainty cash flow and discount at the risk-free interest rate, r_f. Here, you opt to find out the smallest *certain payoff* for which you will exchange the risky cash flows for. This is what is called the *certainty equivalent* (CEQ). Since the CEQ is the certainty equivalent of the cash flow, we discount it using the risk-free interest rate, r_f. The certainty equivalent makes separate adjustments for risk and time.

The mathematical expression for the PV of a cash flow at period t is:

$$PV = \frac{C_t}{(1+r)^t} = \frac{CEQ_t}{(1+r_f)^t} \tag{13.7}$$

Advantages

The advantages of the CEQ method are that:

- It is an alternative method of incorporating risk into project evaluation.
- It allows the decision maker to deduce that aspect of the investment amount that contains the risk because of risk deduction.

Disadvantages

The disadvantages of the CEQ method include:

- The decision maker should be willing to accept the smallest cash flow as a result of the certainty equivalent.
- Certainty equivalent cash flows depend on the RADRs to arrive at its present value.

13.3.4 Venture Capital Method

Investors look out for businesses that have potential to provide large payouts for investors. The investors intend to supply funds to such businesses with the anticipation that they will yield profit in the long run. Venture capital (VC) firms also provide equity to start-ups and other firms that have a limited track record and do not have access to the capital market. The VC firm normally looks out for new and small businesses with potential for growth that will lead to high future returns or payouts. When investors and other VC firms invest in a firm, they take ownership or an equity stake in that firm. They actually receive shares in exchange for the investment they make in that firm.

The venture capital method is traditionally used for valuing VC investment, which combines elements of the multiples-based valuation and discounted cash flow valuation methods. It is generally used by venture capitalists, private equity investors and business angels, and is useful in providing a rough estimate of the current value of such future-oriented, uncertain investments.

The venture capital method follows a very simple procedure:

1. A terminal value (V_t) of the firm is estimated for the time of disinvestment (exit). In order to do this, multiples (comparable companies) are often used and the kind of comparable to be used at any point in time depends on factors such as the expected financial situation of the company and the industry it operates in. Following this method, the estimation is based on a 'success scenario', which is a situation in which the firm meets its performance objectives and the investor's expectations.
2. This terminal value is then converted into a present value (V_0^{Post}) using a comparably high discount rate (r) specified by the investor. This is known as a *post money* valuation, meaning the investment by the investor (I) has already been included.[1] The conversion may be done either by using the NPV framework, or by applying the concept of internal rates of return (IRRs). Whichever way, the results should be identical.
3. The fraction of ownership (F) the investors require in exchange for contributed capital is determined by the ratio of the amount of their investment (I) and the present value of the firm.
4. The number of shares is determined based on the fraction set in relation to the number of total shares, which comprises the number of existing shares (K) and the number of new shares (Y) to be issued to the investor. The SP is also obtained by dividing the amount of new investment by the number of new shares to be issued.

The general forms of the equations for the valuations based on the NPV framework can be summarised in Table 13.2 following the steps outlined above.

[1] Post-money is pre-money plus the new investment ($V_0^{Post} = V_0^{Pre} + I$)
Pre-money is the value of the firm before money goes in ($V_0^{Pre} = V_0^{Post} - I$).

Table 13.2 Venture capital method—NPV framework

Step 1	Estimating terminal value	V_t = Earnings × *P*/*E* Ratio
Step 2	Determining present value	$V_O^{Post} = \frac{V_t}{(1+r)^t}$
Step 3	Calculating the fraction of ownership investors require	$F = \frac{I}{V_O^{Post}}$
Step 4	Obtaining number and price of new shares	$Y = K\frac{F}{1-F}; SP = \frac{I}{Y}$

Example 13.4

A newly established company, Japxy Solutions Limited, plans to provide software solutions in the area of accounting and billing to ensure efficient collection of electricity tariffs of the power supplier, Electricity Company Limited (ECL). Currently, the existing capital is divided equally among the five founding entrepreneurs who hold 180,000 of Japxy's shares each. The entrepreneurs try to raise external capital from the early-stage venture capitalist, sound capital fund (SCF). They indicate that at the end of SCF's four-year investment horizon in Japxy, revenues are expected to be at the level of US$20 million per annum. In order to achieve their goals and get the company started, they require US$800,000 additional capital. Existing companies with a similar business model as Japxy's, is normally valued with a sales multiple around 1.85. The IT experts of SCF are of the view that the market and the business model are very attractive, but it is a risky business considering the team's lack of experience and other factors. Therefore, a discount rate of 65 % per year may be considered appropriate in their opinion.

In order to put Japxy in shape to manage the accounting and the electricity tariffs for ECL, how many shares will SCF obtain and at which price?

Answer 13.4

We follow the procedure outlined earlier:

Step 1: Estimating terminal value

The terminal value is estimated using the sales multiple because Japxy is not expected to generate any profit by the end of the investment horizon. Therefore, Japxy's value four years from now is anticipated as:

$$V_t = \text{Earnings} \times P / E\text{Ratio} = \text{US\$ } 20{,}000{,}000 \times 1.85 = \text{US\$ } 37{,}000{,}000$$

Step 2: Determining present value

We used the discount rate (r) provided in the case as 65 % to determine the present value of Japxy.

$$V_O^{Post} = \frac{V_t}{(1+r)^t} = \frac{\text{US\$ }37{,}000{,}000}{(1.65)^4} = \text{US\$ }4{,}991{,}900.81$$

Step 3: Calculating fraction of ownership investors require
The ownership fraction of F is determined using:

$$F = \frac{I}{V_O^{Post}} = \frac{\text{US\$ }800{,}000}{\text{US\$ }4{,}991{,}900.81} = 0.16025959 = 16.025959\%$$

Step 4: Obtaining number and price of new shares
We first of all determine the number of existing shares (K) by the five founding entrepreneurs. Thus, $K = 5 \times 180{,}000$ shares $= 900{,}000$ existing shares available to the entrepreneurs.
Therefore, the number of new shares (Y) to be issued to SCF will be

$$Y = 900{,}000 \times \frac{0.16025959}{1 - 0.16025959} = 171{,}759 \text{ shares}$$

with an SP of

$$\text{SP} = \frac{\text{US\$ }800{,}000}{171{,}759} = \text{US\$ }4.6577$$

An alternative method of valuing the firm aside from the NPV is the use of the internal rate of return (IRR). Here, we are not discounting the cash flow to its present value but we are interested in looking at a way of determining the fraction of ownership (and eventually the number of shares) to be bought by the investor. In the final analysis, we will arrive at the same figures using both approaches.

The mathematical expressions based on the IRR framework are shown in Table 13.3.

Using Example 13.4 and based on the IRR framework, determine the value of the firm as follows:

Step 1: Estimating terminal value
We estimate the terminal value using the same way as the NPV case.

$$V_t = \text{US\$ }20{,}000{,}000 \times 1.85 = \text{US\$ }37{,}000{,}000$$

Table 13.3 Venture capital method—IRR framework

Step 1	Estimating terminal value	V_t = Earnings × P/E Ratio
Step 2	Determining desired future wealth by investor	$W = I \times (1 + i)^t$
Step 3	Calculating the needed fraction of ownership	$F = \frac{W}{V_t}$
Step 4	Obtaining number and price of new shares	$Y = K\frac{F}{1-F}; SP = \frac{I}{Y}$
Step 5	Determining current valuation	$V_0^{Post} = \frac{I}{F}$ or $V_0^{Post} = SP \times (K + Y)$
		$V_0^{Pre} = V_0^{Post} - I$ or $V_0^{Pre} = SP \times K$

Step 2: Determining desired future wealth by investor

We will determine the desired future wealth of the investor using the discount rate applied above.

$$W = \text{US\$ } 800{,}000 \times (1.65)^4 = \text{US\$ } 5{,}929{,}605$$

Step 3: Calculating the needed fraction of ownership

To achieve this wealth by the given valuation at the terminal date, the investor has to hold

$$F = \frac{\text{US\$ } 5{,}929{,}605}{\text{US\$ } 37{,}000{,}000} = 0.16025959 = 16.025959\%$$

Step 4: Obtaining number and price of new shares

Considering 900,000 existing shares, the number of new shares to be issued to investor is

$$Y = 900{,}000 \times \frac{0.16025959}{1 - 0.16025959} = 171{,}760 \text{ shares}$$

with an SP of

$$SP = \frac{\text{US\$ } 800{,}000}{171{,}760} = \text{US\$ } 4.6577$$

Step 5: Determining current valuation

The valuation can then be estimated as follows: If US$800,000 acquires 16.025959 % of the company, then 100 % or the entire company is valued at

$$V_O^{Post} = \frac{100\%}{16.0259595\%} \times US\$\,800,000 = US\$\,4,991,900.8$$

We can obtain the same results by multiplying the SP by the total number of shares:

$$V_O^{Post} = US\$\,4.6577 \times (900,000 + 171,760)$$

We can determine the pre-money valuation (i.e. the value of the company before the additional investment of US$800,000). We show that by subtracting the additional investment of US$800,000 from the post investment calculated above.

$$V_O^{Pre} = V_O^{Post} - I = US\$\,4,991,900.8 - US\$\,800,000 = US\$\,4,191.900.8$$

We can also calculate it by multiplying the SP by the number of existing shares:

$$V_O^{Pre} = SP \times K = US\$\,4.6577 \times 900,000$$

13.3.4.1 Valuation Assuming Future Dilution

In our preceding example (Example 13.4), Japxy Solutions Limited was valued with the assumption that it would only receive a single round of financing (US$800,000) from the SCF in the four-year period. In practice, VC financing does not involve a single round of financing but rather it is staged over a number of financing rounds depending on the achievement of certain milestones. In the subsequent financing rounds, lower discount rates are used (lower returns), since it does not involve raising one large sum of money in these rounds unlike the first round.

As Japxy will be involved in the issuance of new shares to investors in the new rounds of financing, the stake of the existing shareholders stands the risk of being diluted. What this means is that initial investors might lose part of their controlling interest or ownership in Japxy because of the issuance of the new shares.

Bearing in mind that the early-stage investors risk the chance of losing part of their ownership in the company to new investors, they will demand a higher fraction of ownership in order to achieve their desired ownership position. It is however important to note that, if more shares are issued to the earlier investor, future investors will also have to receive a higher stake in order to attain a desired fraction of ownership. Therefore, to determine the existing ownership position, the previous investor needs to consider the number of shares to be issued in the future, which will partially depend on the number of shares originally issued in the first round. How then do we solve this paradox?

The mathematical procedure to address the valuation of share dilution of a venture capitalist is outlined in Table 13.4.

Example 13.5 We refer to Example 13.4 on Japxy Solutions Limited. Assuming after the first two years, Japxy plans on raising additional capital of US$5 million, which was provided by another venture capital company, Business Growth Fund (BGF). At this stage, Japxy Solutions Limited is expected to expand further with a lower overall risk and therefore have a lower discount rate of 35 %.

Table 13.4 Venture capital method—considering multiple rounds of financing

Step 1	Estimating terminal value	V_t = Earnings × P/E Ratio
Step 2	Determining present value	$V_0^{Post} = \frac{V_t}{(1+r)^t}$
Step 3	Calculating required fraction of ownership	$F = \frac{I}{V_0^{Post}}$
Step 4	Considering dilution	
	(a) Calculating fractions of ownership for dilutive (future) investments	$V_{td}^{Post} = \frac{V_t}{(1+r)^{t-td}}$ $F = \frac{I}{V_{td}^{Post}}$ with td as the time of dilutive investment
	(b) Determining retention rate	$RET = 1 - \sum_{m=1}^{n} F_m$
	(c) Calculating increased required fraction of ownership (dilution adjusted).	$F_0^{Post} = \frac{F_t}{RET}$
Step 5	Obtaining number and price of new shares	$Y^* = X\frac{F_0^{Post}}{1-F_0^{Post}}$ $SP^* = \frac{I}{Y^*}$

Note: Depending on the number of times of future investments, Step (4a) might have to be applied as many times as there are future investments, because of the dilution of existing ownership positions

Answer 13.5

Step 1: Estimating terminal value

The terminal value is estimated as follows.

$$V_t = \text{Earnings} \times P\,/\,E\text{Ratio} = \text{US\$}\,20{,}000{,}000 \times 1.85 = \text{US\$}\,37{,}000{,}000$$

Step 2: Determining present value

We used the discount rate (r) provided in the case as 65 % to determine the present value of Japxy.

$$V_0^{Post} = \frac{V_t}{(1+r)^t} = \frac{\text{US\$}\,37{,}000{,}000}{(1.65)^4} = \text{US\$}\,4{,}991{,}900.81$$

Step 3: Calculating fraction of ownership investors require

The ownership fraction of F is determined using:

$$F = \frac{I}{V_0^{Post}} = \frac{\text{US\$}\,800{,}000}{\text{US\$}\,4{,}991{,}900.81} = 0.16025959 = 16.025959\%$$

Step 4(a): Calculating fraction of ownership for dilutive (future) investments

Then in Step 4(a) exactly the same calculations are done from Business Growth Fund's point of view. Beginning with the valuation at the end of year 4: V_4 = US$37,000,000, BGF would value Japxy in year 2 (the time of BGF's investment) at

$$V_{td}^{\text{Post}} = \frac{V_t}{(1+r)^{t-td}} = V_2^{\text{Post}} = \frac{\text{US\$}\,37{,}000{,}000}{(1+0.35)^{4-2}} = \text{US\$}\,20{,}301{,}783.26$$

Considering the amount of the investment as I_{BGF} = US$5,000,000 this investor would require a fraction of ownership of Japxy Solutions Limited as

$$F_{BGF} = \frac{\text{US\$}\,5{,}000{,}000}{\text{US\$}\,20{,}301{,}783.26} = 0.2463 = 24.63\%$$

Step 4(b): Determining retention rate

The investor's retention rate is RET = 1 – 0.2463 = 0.7537.

$$RET = 1 - \sum_{m=1}^{n} F_m = 1 - 0.2463 = 0.7537$$

Therefore, the existing owners of the firm (the five founding entrepreneurs and SCF) would retain only 75.37 % of the company's shares altogether.

Step 4(c): Calculating increased demand fraction of ownership

In order to compensate for this dilution, the increased ownership demand of SCF at the current point of time is calculated as

$$F_0^{Post} = \frac{F_t}{RET} = \frac{0.1603}{0.7537} = 0.2127$$

It is important to note that at the end of the year 4, SCF will not hold 21.27 % of the company but rather it will hold 21.27 % of the remaining 75.37 % of the company, which is equal to 16.03 % of the firm. It means by increasing the demanded ownership fraction, SCF would be able to fully compensate for the anticipated dilution caused by the financing round in year 2.

Step 5: Obtaining corresponding number and price of new shares

Considering 900,000 existing shares, SCF's demanded ownership fraction equals

$$Y^* = 900{,}000 \times \frac{0.2127}{1 - 0.2127} = 243{,}147 \text{ shares}$$

with an SP of

$$SP^* = \frac{\text{US\$ } 800{,}000}{243{,}147} = \text{US\$ } 3.2902$$

Determining the number of shares to be issued to BGF we arrive at this as follows:

The total of the founders' shares and all other shares, which have been issued to earlier investors is 900,000 + 243,147 = 1,143,147.

The number of shares being issued to BGF is:

$$Y^* = 1{,}143{,}147 \times \frac{0.2463}{1 - 0.2463} = 373{,}567 \text{ shares}$$

with an SP of

$$SP^{*} = \frac{\text{US\$ } 5{,}000{,}000}{373{,}567} = \text{US\$ } 13.3845$$

13.3.5 Free Cash Flow to Equity

The free cash flow to equity (FCFE) method of valuation involves estimating the future cash flows to providers of capital and capitalising these to determine the value of the company.

13.3.5.1 Estimates of Cash Flows

A number of approaches have been used in estimating cash flows, adding to the confusion about how a company should be valued in the literature. For instance the traditional accounting valuation of a company is the use of the **earnings before depreciation and amortisation (EBDA)**. This calculation is simple and uses information only from the cash flow statements. It is shown below:

$$\text{EBDA} = \text{Net income} + \text{Depreciation} + \text{Amortisation} \tag{13.8}$$

In the EBDA, we are adding the primary non-cash expenses that have been deducted to arrive at the net income.

In valuing a company, we consider that the cash flows should be the one available to the suppliers of capital (owners and creditors). In this case, interests are deducted to arrive at the net income of the company. So, to properly estimate the company's cash flow, we have to now apply the **earnings before interest, depreciation and amortisation** (**EBIDA**). EBIDA is also known as operating income before depreciation and amortisation (**OIBDA**). The EBIDA provides a new cash flow that could be paid to both creditors and owners of the company. This is shown in Eq. (13.9):

$$\text{EBIDA} = \textit{Net}\text{ income} + \text{Interest} + \text{Depreciation} + \text{Amortization} \tag{13.9}$$

Free cash flow from operation (CFO) is another measure. Companies are required to prepare statement of cash flow and this provides useful information in financial analysis and valuation. This statement shows cash flows by operation, financing and investment activities. The cash flow is computed by adjusting net income for non-cash expenses and income, and also for changes in working capital accounts.

The computation uses a company's statement of comprehensive income (income statement), and statement of financial position (balance sheet). This is shown in Eqs. (13.10) and (13.11):

$$\text{CFO} = \text{Net income} + \text{Depreciation} + \text{Amortization} + \text{Other non cash charges} - \text{Increase in net working capatal} \quad (13.10)$$

Where:

$$\text{Net working capital} = \text{Current assets} - \text{Current liabilities} \quad (13.11)$$

From Eq. (13.11), we can deduce that if net working capital increases, it is a reduction in cash flow from operations and if net working capital decreases it is an increase in cash flow from operations. It is important to note that cash flow from operations is an indication of the financial health of the firm and the survival of a firm is more dependent on its financial potency. So, a firm's ability to generate cash flow from operations will help to ensure its survival and growth.

Free cash flow (FCF) is measured by deducting capital expenditure from the cash flow from operations. It has always been argued that cash flow, no matter how it is computed does not necessarily reflect the cash available for providers of capital (owners and creditors). This is because in order to ensure the continuous existence of companies, they must carry out capital expenditure to guarantee their existence and growth. It is the FCF that considers these expenditures. This is expressed in the Eq. (13.12):

$$\text{FCF} = \text{CFO} - \text{Capital expenditure required to maintain curent growth} \quad (13.12)$$

However, it is not possible to ascertain the amount a firm spends on capital expenditure required to maintain current growth from the financial statements. Therefore, a common approach is to calculate FCF, using the entire capital expenditure for the period.

$$\text{FCF} = \text{CFO} - \text{Capital expenditure} \quad (13.13)$$

13.3.5.2 Valuation Using Free Cash Flow to Equity

In the valuing a firm's equity, it is important to recognise that the owners (who are the residual claimants) are affected by the firm's use of debt financing. Thus, the FCFE is the FCF adjusted for the debt cash flow. The debt cash flow adjustment or net borrowing is given as:

$$\text{Net borrowing} = \text{New debt financing} - \text{Debt repayment} \tag{13.14}$$

Therefore, the FCFE is computed starting with the FCF operations:

$$\begin{aligned}\text{FCFE} = {} & \text{Cash flow from operation} - \text{Capital expenditure} - \\ & \text{Increase in working capital} + \text{Net borrowing}\end{aligned} \tag{13.15}$$

Alternatively, we can start the calculation with the net income and add non-cash charges (or subtract non-cash income) such as depreciation and amortisation, charges from write-down assets and deferred taxes:

$$\begin{aligned}\text{FCFE} = {} & \text{Net income} + \text{Non cash charges} - \text{Capital expenditure} + \\ & \text{Net borrowing}\end{aligned} \tag{13.16}$$

13.3.6 Free Cash Flow to Firm

The FCF to the firm is made up of the cash flows to all claim holders in the firm, including ordinary shareholders, preference shareholders and debt holders. Free cash flow to the firm (FCFF) can be measured by adding up the cash flows to the claim holders, including cash flows to equity, cash flows to preference shares and cash flows to lenders. We show these in the following equations:

We can calculate the FCFF by starting with the FCF operations:

$$\begin{aligned}\text{FCFF} = {} & \text{Cash flow from operation} + \text{Interest}\left(1 - \text{Tax rate}\right) - \\ & \text{Capital expenditure}\end{aligned} \tag{13.17}$$

An alternative approach is to begin with earnings before interest and taxes:

$$\begin{aligned}\text{FCFF} = {} & \text{EBIT}\left(1 - \text{Tax rate}\right) + \text{Non cash charges} - \\ & \text{Capital expenditure} - \text{Increase in working capital}\end{aligned} \tag{13.18}$$

Recognising that:

$$\text{EBIT}(1-\text{Tax rate}) = \text{Net income} + \text{Interest}(1-\text{Tax rate}) \tag{13.19}$$

Eq. (13.18) can be rewritten in terms of net income:

$$\begin{aligned}\text{FCFF} = \text{Net income} + \text{Interest}(1-\text{Tax rate}) + \text{Non}-\text{cash charges} - \\ \text{Capital expenditure} - \text{Increase in working capital}\end{aligned} \tag{13.20}$$

The FCFF is often known as the unlevered FCF since it is the cash flow before considering interest on debt.

You must note that the FCF to the firm can be reconciled with the FCFE by recognising that the differences between the two are: interest paid on debt, and net new debt financing.

The FCFF can be stated as:

$$\text{FCFF} = \text{FCFE} + \text{Interest expenses}(1-\text{Tax rate}) - \text{Net borrowing} \tag{13.21}$$

13.3.6.1 Free Cash Flow Valuation

To value a firm, you have to discount the future (forecasted) cash flows to the present. The model used in determining the value of the FCF today depends on the assumptions regarding the growth of the FCF. The appropriate cost of capital and FCF depends on what is being valued. For instance:

(i) In the valuation of equity, the cost of equity is the cost of capital and the value of the FCF is the FCFE.
(ii) In the valuation of firm, the cost of capital is the weighted average cost of capital (WACC) and the FCF is the FCFF.

Table 13.5 shows the appropriate growth models used for valuation of free cash flows:

13.3.6.2 Valuing a Firm's Equity

If you are valuing equity of a company, and the free cash flows grow at a constant rate indefinitely, then we have to use the Gordon growth model. This is shown below:

Table 13.5 Appropriate growth models used for valuation of free cash flows

Growth assumption	Model	General formula
No growth	Perpetuity	$\text{Value} = \frac{\text{FCF}}{r}$
Constant growth	Gordon growth model	$\text{Value} = \frac{\text{FCF}_1}{r-g}$
Non-constant growth	Discount cash flow	$\text{Value} = \sum_{t=1}^{\infty}\frac{\text{FCF}_1}{r}$

$$\text{Value of equity} = \frac{\text{FCF}_1}{r_e - g} \tag{13.22}$$

where r_e is the cost of equity.

Example 13.6

Assuming that the FCFE for Berband Limited is US$30,000,000 to its shareholders. This cash grows at a constant rate of 4 % forever. Assuming that the equity cost of capital is 10 %. What is the value of the equity of the company?

Answer 13.6

$$\text{Value of equity} = \frac{\text{FCF}_1}{r_e - g} = \frac{\text{US\$ }30{,}000{,}000}{0.1-0.04} = \text{US\$ }500{,}000{,}000$$

13.3.6.3 Valuing the Entire Firm

You may decide to value the entire firm. Let us assume that the cash flow will grow from g_1 for t_1 periods and then g_2 thereafter. The appropriate formula to apply is:

$$\text{Value of the firm} = \sum_{t=1}^{t_1}\frac{\text{FCFF}_0(1+g)^t}{(1+r_c)^t} + \left(\frac{\text{FCFF}_0(1+g_1)^{t_1}(1+g_2)/(r_c-g_2)}{(1+r_c)^{t_1}}\right) \tag{13.23}$$

where r_c is the WACC.

Table 13.6 Lapell Limited's annual financial report example

Item	Amount US$'000	Income statement US$'000	Balance sheet US$'000	Statement of cash flow US$'000
Cash flow from operations	4,800			4,800
Net income	3,440	3,400		
EBIT	5,482.31			
Depreciation and amortisation	1,340			1,340
Other non-cash adjustment	160		160	160
Change in working capital	140			140
Capital expenditure	4,100			4,100
Net debt financing	470			470
Interest expense	190	190		
Tax rate	35 %	35 %		

Table 13.7 Lapell Limited's free cash flow example

Free cash flow	Equation	Calculations
Free cash flow to equity (FCFE)	(13.15)	4800 – 4100 + 470 = 1170
	(13.16)	3440 + 1340 + 160 – 4100 – 140 + 470 = 1170
Free cash flow to firm (FCFF)	(13.17)	4800 + 190(1 – 0.35) – 4100 = 823.5
	(13.18)	5482.31(1 – 0.35) + 1340 + 160 – 4100 – 140 = 823.5
	(13.20)	3440 + 190(1 – 0.35) + 1340 + 160 – 4100 – 140 = 823.5
	(13.21)	1170 + 190(1 – 0.35) – 470 = 823.5

Example 13.7

Let us consider Lapell Limited's annual financial report for the year 2015 (Table 13.6).

Let us assume that all capital expenditure is necessary in order to maintain the current growth. The FCF in US$'000 in 2015 for Lapell Limited is shown below:

In Table 13.7, we showed the different calculations of FCFE and firm. The earlier illustrations of the formulae are used for the calculations.

Suppose Lapell Limited cash flow are expected to grow at a rate of 21 % each year for the next five years and then 4.5 % thereafter. If the cost of equity is 8.5 % and weighted average cost capital is 7.5 %. What is the valuation of Lapell Limited and its equity?

Table 13.8 shows the FCFE and that of the firm for Lapell Limited for the five-year period.

Table 13.8 Lapell Limited's free cash flow to equity example

US$' 000	FCF_1	FCF_2	FCF_3	FCF_4	FCF_5
Value of firm	996.44	1,205.69	1,458.89	1,765.25	2,135.96
Value of equity	1,415.70	1,713.00	2,072.73	2,508.00	3,034.68

$$\text{FCFF} = \text{FCFF}_0\left(1+g\right)^t = 823.5\left(1.21\right)^1 = \text{US\$996.44}$$

$$\text{FCFE} = \text{FCFE}_0\left(1+g\right)^t = 1{,}170(1.21)^1 = \text{US\$1,415.7}$$

$$\text{Value of the firm} = \frac{\text{US\$ 996.44}}{(1.075)^1} + \frac{\text{US\$ 1,205.69}}{(1.075)^2} + \frac{\text{US\$ 1,458.89}}{(1.075)^3} + \frac{\text{US\$ 1,765.25}}{(1.075)^4} + \frac{\text{US\$ 2,135.96}}{(1.075)^5} + \left(\frac{\text{US\$ } 823.5(1.21)^1(1.045)/(0.075-0.045)}{(1.075)^1}\right) = \text{US\$38,232.82}$$

$$\text{Value of equity} = \frac{\text{FCFE}_1}{r_e - g} = \frac{\text{US\$4 1,415.7}}{0.085-0.045} = \text{US\$35,392.5}$$

13.3.7 Valuation Using Comparable Firms

We have shown the value of the firm, by considering its expected cash flow through the calculations of the free cash flows to the owner. According to the concept of the law of one price, the present value of a firm's cash flow is its future value. This is because we have to invest the present value somewhere else with the same risk to be able to obtain its future value. We can equally apply the law of one price in the method of comparables. Under this method, we estimate the value of the firm based on other firms' value that we expect to give the same cash flows in the future. For instance, let us consider a new firm that is identical to a publicly listed firm. If these two firms are set to generate similar cash flows, then the law of one price suggests that the value of the existing (publicly listed) firm can be used to estimate the value of the new firm.

However, because identical firms do not exist in the real world, even if they belong to the same industry, the law of one price cannot be applied to value the new company. This is because even if firms belongs to the same industry or are perfectly competitive, they cannot be valued the same way because of the differences in size or scale of operations.

In this discussion, we want to find ways of adjusting for this scale or size differences through the use of comparables to value firms with similar business acumen.

13.3.7.1 Valuation Multiples

We therefore adjust for the differences in the firm scale or size by using multiples. A valuation multiple is the ratio of the value to some measure of the firm scale.

Let as consider this hypothetical scenario of valuing an office building located in a business district in Nairobi. To value this office building, we can consider the same type of office space with similar identical properties in the same area. In this case, price per square foot of buildings in the same area would be an appropriate measure to consider. Therefore, multiplying the size of the building concerned by the average price per square foot will give a fair estimate of the value of the building. This same idea can be applied to valuing shares.

Price earnings (P/E) ratio is the most popular valuation multiple and is mostly used for public companies. P/E is defined as the SP divided by its earnings per share (EPS). The financial intuition is that any investor who buys the share of a firm is automatically buying the future earnings of the firm. This is because differences will likely to exist in the size of firms' earnings. This means that an investor should be willing to pay proportionally more for a share with higher current earnings. Therefore, the value of a firm's share can be estimated by multiplying its current EPS by the average *P*/*E* ratio of comparable firms. This is shown in the model below:

$$P_0 = \frac{Div_1}{r_E - g} \tag{13.24}$$

If we divide both sides of this equation by EPS_1, we have the following formula:

Forward:

$$\frac{P}{E} = \frac{P_0}{EPS_1} = \frac{Div_1 / EPS}{r_E - g} = \frac{\text{Dividend payout rate}}{r_E - g} \tag{13.25}$$

From Eq. (13.25), the formula provides for the firm's forward *P*/*E*, which is the computed *P*/*E* multiple based on its forward earnings (expected earnings over the next 12 months).

Eq. (13.25) suggests that if the shares of two firms have the identical dividend payout, EPS growth rates, risk and cost of capital, then it stands to reason that they would have the same *P*/*E*. It also means that firms and industries that exhibit high growth rates, generate excess cash and maintain high payout rates, should have high *P*/*E* multiples.

We can also compute the firms' trailing ratio using trailing earnings (earnings over the period of 12 months). The firms trailing earnings is defined as:

$$\text{Trailing } P/E = \frac{P_0}{EPS_0} = \frac{(1+g_0)P_0}{EPS_1} = (1+g_0)\left(\text{Forward}\frac{P}{E}\right) \tag{13.26}$$

Eq. (13.26) shows that trailing multiples tend to be higher for growing firms. Thus, when comparing the multiple, you must be sure to be consistent in the use of either trailing or forward multiples firms. Therefore, for valuation purposes, the forward *P*/*E* ratio is preferred because we are more interested in future earnings. Since we are mostly concerned about the persistent components of the firm's earnings, it is imperative to follow the common practice that suggests that we exclude extra ordinary items that are not repeated, when computing a *P*/*E* ratio for purpose of valuation.

Example 13.8

Suppose a local clothing manufacturer, HMS Kickers Limited's EPS is US$5.24. If the average *P*/*E* of comparable clothing firm is 28.4, estimate a value for HMS Kickers Limited using the *P*/*E* as a valuation multiple.

Answer 13.8

We estimate an SP for HMS Kickers Limited by multiplying its EPS by the *P*/*E* of comparable firms. Thus,

$$P_0 = \text{US\$ } 5.24 \times 28.4 = \text{US\$ } 148.82$$

This estimate assumes that HMS Kickers Limited has similar risk, payout rates, and growth rates to comparable firms in the industry.

Total enterprise value (TEV) multiple is also a common valuation multiple. TEV represents the entire value of the firm, not just the equity. It represents the total value of the firm before debt payment, to constitute an appropriate multiple. To do this, the enterprise value is divided by a measure of earnings or cash flows before payment of interest. We can consider TEV to EBIT, EBITDA and FCF as common multiples. Most practitioners rely on TEV/EBITDA multiples. TEV is useful as it takes into consideration different capital structures. Using only market capitalisation (i.e. equity value) does not recognise the fact that the firm may be using its equity more efficiently (or in a riskier manner) because it is leveraging the equity with debt.

From Eq. (13.22) under the FCFE valuation, if the expected FCF is constant, then Eq. (13.22) could be adjusted to form Eq. (13.27)

$$\frac{V_0}{\text{EBITDA}_1} = \frac{\text{FCF}_1 / \text{EBITDA}_1}{r_{WACC} - g_{FCF}} \qquad (13.27)$$

The *P*/*E* multiple is generally higher for firms with high growth rates and low capital requirement. This makes free cash flows to be greater in proportion to EBITDA.

Example 13.9

Suppose HMS Kickers Limited has EPS of US$8.74 and EBITDA of US$58.5 million. HMS Kickers Limited has 9.5 million shares outstanding and debt of US$250 million (net cash). Jackers Wear Limited is considered comparable to HMS Kickers Limited, but Jackers Wear Limited does not have debt. If Jackers Wear Limited has a price earnings ratio of 15.3 and an enterprise value to EBITDA multiple of 8.3, estimate value of HMS Kickers Limited's shares using both multiples. Which estimate is likely to be more accurate?

Answer 13.9

We can use Jackers Wear Limited's *P*/*E* to estimate an SP for HMS Kickers Limited.

Thus,

$$P_0 = \text{US\$}\,8.74 \times 15.3 = \text{US\$}\,133.722$$

Using the enterprise value to EBITDA multiple, we will estimate HMS Kickers Limited's enterprise value to be:

$$V_0 = \text{US\$ } 58{,}500{,}000 \times 8.3 = \text{US\$ } 485{,}550{,}000$$

We therefore subtract debt, and divide by the number of shares to estimate HMS Kickers Limited's SP: This is shown below:

$$P_0 = \left(\text{US\$ } 485{,}550{,}000 - \text{US\$ } 250{,}000{,}000\right) / 9{,}500{,}000 = \text{US\$ } 24.79$$

This value shows that because of the large difference in leverage between the two firms, we would expect the second estimate, which is based on enterprise value, to be more reliable.

13.3.7.2 Other Multiples

Other valuation multiples, such as ratio of total enterprise value to revenue (TEV/revenue), ratio of total enterprise value to forecast revenue (TEV/forecast revenue), and ratio of total enterprise value to gross profit (TEV/gross profit) can be used. TEV/revenue multiple may be suitable if the firms will be assumed to maintain similar margins in the future. In the case of firms with considerable tangible assets, the ratio of price to book value of equity per share is often appropriate. Some multiples are considered as industry specific. For instance, in the Telecom industry, it is possible to consider enterprise value per subscriber.

13.3.7.3 How to Identify Comparable Companies

In using the comparables method, it is important to address the question: What are comparable companies? In order to arrive at a reasonable answer, a number of issues need to be addressed, including the following:

- Are the comparison companies in the same industry as the target company? It is important to note that comparables, in terms of industry, are not necessarily competitors.
- Do the comparison companies have the same size in terms of the revenue as the target company?

- Are the cost structures of the comparison companies similar to the company of interest? For instance, are the companies spending the same proportion on marketing communication or research and development expenses?
- Do the comparison companies have similar growth rates as the company of interest? Investors prepare to pay more for companies that are fast growing than competitors that are not growing. This is because companies that grow fast have the potential to give higher return in the future.
- Do the companies use similar distribution strategies? For instance, is the target company using a direct sales force, while all the competitors are using distributors?
- Do the comparison companies have similar prospects for profitability to those of the target company? The goal of every business is wealth or profit maximisation. So, it is important to understand the profit muzzle of the businesses, a company is to be compared with.
- Are there other metrics that are relevant for predicting future financial success?

Apart from determining comparability, it is also important to identify comparable valuations.

13.3.7.4 Identifying Comparable Valuations

There are different ways to find comparable indices for valuing a company and these include using publicly traded companies, using prices paid for related private companies when they are acquired by another company, and considering similar venture investments. Each of these methods has their strength and weaknesses.

Using Publicly Traded Companies

This involves looking at the value placed on publicly traded companies. Publicly traded companies have attractive information to use because the data is readily available. The entrepreneurs or external investors do not only see the information on the prices of their shares but there are other important elements of information available to them that can be used. Some of this information includes the research reports of their comparable investment banks, which will include the financial forecasts, and the research analyst's view of where the SPs are heading. Using publicly traded companies as comparables has some challenges:

- Publicly traded companies are almost always much larger than the private company of interest. This means that the greater size leads to stability and hence less risk.
- Publicly traded companies are almost always profitable and/or cash flow positive, while private companies are always the opposite. Thus, profitability equates to lower risk.
- Companies do not always get to be public unless they have shown consistent financial performance. Private companies have not been around that much to have such history, or their growing pains have led to inconsistent results. In addition, when looking at public companies, you are likely comparing against the best performance rather than sampling from the entire universe.
- Publicly traded companies have greater liquidity, meaning it is easier for the initial investors to offload their shares on the stock exchange.

In spite of these, publicly traded comparables can still be used as long as the necessary adjustments have been made.

Using Mergers and Acquisition Transactions

How private companies are valued for a venture investment may also involve considering the prices paid for comparable private companies acquired by another company in M&A) transactions. The approach is useful to the extent that it avoids the problems of size and lack of liquidity, associated with the use of publicly traded companies' transactions. Care needs to be taken when identifying similar companies for comparison.

Information on such M&A transactions may be obtained from the media and investment banks' research reports over time. However, such information involving private companies is often difficult to acquire. For instance, an acquirer may provide information on the purchase price but not other financial information, making it impossible to calculate ratios such as TEV/revenue or TEV/EBITDA for the purpose of venture valuation.

Using Other Venture Investment

Venture investment made in a comparable company can also be used as a suitable comparable. For instance, if an investor or venture capitalist paid four times the revenue for competitor A, another investor or venture capitalist should also pay four times the revenue to invest in Competitor B. This allows the venture capitalist to be able to track a lot of transactions and will over time build up their own database of information. This explains why venture capitalists tend to specialise. Again, these venture capitalists will have the opportunity to negotiate prices better than entrepreneurs. Entrepreneurs need to be mindful of this kind of information to figure out what is going on with their competitors so as to ascertain what their own company is worth. However, entrepreneurs find it difficult to do this and it is imperative that they find financial advisors with access to private companies' comparables as a way of levelling the playing field. Both parties must have a sense that there is a fair deal at the end of the day.

Information of venture transactions on private companies may not be subject to any form of regulation and may be inaccurate. In the case of M&A, useful detailed information, apart from the price, may not be available to determine whether it is a comparable situation or to assist in computing the relevant ratios.

13.4 Selecting a Valuation Model

Valuation is very important not only for estimating the value of the business venture but also critical when negotiating for financial contracts between entrepreneurs and investors. Methods of valuation include the use of comparables involving the application of multiples to income statement information or balance sheet information, or the use of discounted cash flow. The multiples may be obtained from market information on publicly traded companies, M&A's transactions, and other venture investment. The DCF method is often based on market information regarding the appropriate discount rate.

In valuing new ventures or early-stage ventures with significant potential for growth, the primary approach is the use of the DCF methods. Different discounting approaches are often used, and the differences among these approaches are in respect of the cash flows, the discount rates used and how uncertainty is taken into consideration. These various approaches have their own strengths and limitations, thus it is necessary to consider the following questions in ascertaining the strengths of each valuation approach (see Smith et al. 2011):

- Is the valuation based on expected future cash flows?
- Is cost of capital used as the discount rate?
- How does the model deal with cash flows that vary in risk?

- Can the model be used to value embedded options and complex financial claims?
- How difficult is it to estimate the information required for the valuation?

In establishing the value of the business venture, it is important to note that eventually the value arrived at will be based on negotiation. This is to suggest there is no right answer. However, the external investor and the entrepreneur need to do their own background analysis to ascertain an appropriate value and what each of them is prepared to accept as a fair value.

13.5 Summary and Conclusions

Investors, including venture capitalists and other private equity investors are also interested in how new ventures or entrepreneurial firms are valued. Determining the value of the venture is critical for establishing the percentage of ownership the business external investors may be interested in. The perceived value of the venture as well as the capabilities of the entrepreneur to enhance the value of the firm is critical to the external investor. The entrepreneur may also be interested in whether the external investor can contribute to the overall value and whether the external investor has the financial resources and organisational capacity to invest in the firm.

Valuation is concerned with the process of determining the amount an investor needs to pay to invest in a firm. When investors invest in a firm, they assume ownership interest and therefore, in exchange for their investment, they receive the firm's shares. Valuing new ventures and small businesses can be difficult considering the problem of estimating future cash flows and appropriate discount rate for determining the present value of the future cash flows. In spite of these difficulties, earnings or cash flows forecasts are captured in most business plans, and investors who are looking for deals make forecasts for cash flows and earnings.

There are various methods of valuing new ventures and small businesses and these include, DCF method, risk-adjusted NPV, CEQ method, venture capital method, FCFE, free cash flow to firm and valuation using comparable firms (multiples). These approaches have their own strengths and limitations, and therefore it is important to consider a number of issues in gauging the strengths of each valuation approach. It is however important to note that the value arrived at will eventually be based on negotiation, after the external investor and the entrepreneur have carried out their own background analysis to ascertain an appropriate value.

Discussion Questions and Problems

1. What is valuation? Explain how early-stage businesses are valued.
2. What criteria should be used in selecting a valuation model for new businesses?
3. A project produces cash flows of US$435 in year 1, US$185 in year 2, US$732 in year 3 and US$846 in year 4. If the cost of capital is 16 %, what is the projects PV?
4. A project cost US$285,000. It generates a cash flow of US$35,400 in year 1, US$18,300 in year 2 and US$25,300 in year 3. If the project pays US$12,500 in perpetuity at an interest rate of 9 %, what will be the NPV of the project? Supposing that you want to adjust for risk. In this situation, you consider the market return to be 18 % and the risk-free rate to be 8 %. If the β is 1.80. What is the NPV of the project?
5. A small business located in New Delhi, India will cost US$750,000. It is expected to produce an operating cost of US$155,000 a year for the next eight years. If the cost of capital is 15 %, what is the NPV of the business? What will be the worth of the business after four years?
6. A factory located in Nairobi, Kenya, costs US$500,000. It will produce an inflow after operating cost of US$120,000 in year 1, US$230,000 in year 2, US$300,000 in year 3, US$350,000 in year 4. The opportunity cost of capital for the project is 13 %, calculate the NPV of the project?
7. A project has a forecasted cash flow of US$2100 in year 1, US$3200 in year 2, US$4100 in year 3. Assume the interest rate is 5 % and the risk premium is 11 %. If the project β is 1.15, calculate the PV of the project.
8. A small business located in Lagos, Nigeria forecasts the following free cash flows over a five-year period (Table A.13.1):

Assuming the free cash flows are expected to grow by 4 % per annum after the fifth year. Given a WACC of 14 %:

(a) What is the value of the business?
(b) If the business has debt of US$300,000 and 40,000 shares outstanding, estimate its SP.

Table A.13.1 Small business cash flow example

Year	1	2	3	4	5
Free cash flows	US$53,500	US$68,000	US$78,500	US$75,000	US$82,500

Table A.13.2 TransValley Properties Limited cash flows example

Year	1	2	3	4
Free cash flows	–US$185,000	–US$12,000	US$99,000	US$240,000

9. TransValley Properties Limited intends to start a new real estate firm in Kampala, Uganda. The expected free cash flows of the firm for the next four years are given below (Table A.13.2):

Consider the cash flows after the fourth year growing by 5 % per annum forever. Assume the firm's cost of capital is 15 %, estimate the continuation value at the end of the fourth year and the value of TransValley Properties Limited today.

10. BSky Products Limited had sales of US$385 million in 2015. As a financial analyst you expect it to grow by 8 % in 2016, but that this growth will slow by 2 % per annum to a long-run growth rate for the food industry of 3.5 % by 2021. On the basis of BSky's past profitability and investment needs, EBIT is expected to be 8 % of sales, increases in net working capital requirements to be 9 % of any increase in sales, and capital expenditure to be equivalent to depreciation expenses. If BSky has US$50 million in cash, US$1.5 million in debt, and 11 million shares outstanding, a tax rate of 31 %, and WACC of 10 %.

    (a) Compute the value of BSky's share in early 2016.
    (b) If BSky's EBIT was given as 8 % of sales and its operating expenses can be reduced and EBIT increased to 9 % of sales, what would be the share's value change?

11. As a financial analyst you notice that Samsung has a stock price of US$87.62 and EPS of US$7.80. Its competitor Apple, has an EPS of US$3.85. Estimate the value of Apple stock using only this information.
12. MGL Limited has EPS of US$7.35 and EBITDA of US$75.23 million. MGL Limited has 11.5 million shares outstanding and debt of US$350 million (net cash). As a financial analyst, you believe VNL Limited is comparable to MGL Limited in terms of underlying business, but VNL Limited has no debt. If VNL Limited has a price earnings ratio of 21.35 and an enterprise value to EBITDA multiple of 9.23.

    (a) Estimate the value of MGL Limited's shares using both multiples?
    (b) Indicate which estimate is likely to be more accurate.

13. The existing capital of a newly found medium-sized firm in South Africa, SFS Enterprise, is divided evenly among its eight founding investors who own at least 250,000 shares each in SFS Enterprise. The investors aim to raise foreign capital and bring together their ideas to the early-stage venture capitalist, Iporo Capital Fund (ICF). They stated that at the end of each investor's six-year investment horizon, they expect revenue of US$32 million per annum. To get their company in full swing they needed a start-up capital of US$1,200,000. The existing company in the industry that is almost equivalent to SFS Enterprise has a multiple around 2.35. The financial advisers of the investors concluded that because the business is a start-up, there seems to be uncertainty regarding the future performance of the company. So, they consider a risk premium of 25 %, a β of 2.5 and a Treasury bill rate of 8.5 %, which is appropriate for the business. Based on this scenario, how many shares will the investors demand to put SFS Enterprise in shape to do business in South Africa? What will be the SP of SFS Enterprise?

    (a) Using the NPV method.
    (b) Using the IRR method.
    (c) Assuming SFS later decides to raise an additional US$ 7 million from another VC firm, Opportunity Capital Fund (OCF). The business is expected to expand further with a lower risk premium of 13 % while the risk-free rate and the β remain the same.

        (i) How many shares will be issued to Business Opportunity Fund?
        (ii) What will the SP be?

Part V

Financing Choice and Harvesting

14

Financing Choice

Learning Objectives
By the end of this chapter, you should be able to:

- identify the various financing options available to MSMEs
- explain how to determine financing requirement
- discuss factors that affect the financing choice of MSMEs

14.1 Introduction

Businesses require various forms of finance in order to acquire permanent or fixed assets such as land, buildings, vehicle(s) and equipment (fixed capital). These forms of finance can be used to support normal short-term operations such as purchase inventory, pay bills and to pay wages and salaries (working capital) and also for expansion or to change the direction of the business (growth capital). Though there appear to be various sources of finance available for businesses, MSMEs have been identified to encounter difficulties in accessing most of these sources of financing. MSMEs are said to have a 'constrained' financing choice and therefore are often compelled to make do with whatever come to them. Entrepreneurs or MSMEs tend to cast a wide net to capture the financing they need from various sources to start a new venture or expand an existing business. We mentioned in Chap. 2 that MSMEs adopt *layering*, which involves piecing together capital from multiple sources.

The financing source a firm may access depends on several factors. This chapter builds on the knowledge obtained in previous chapters. In Chap. 2, we

J.Y. Abor, *Entrepreneurial Finance for MSMEs*,
DOI 10.1007/978-3-319-34021-0_14

discussed the various sources of financing new ventures and small businesses. In this chapter, we identify these financing options available to MSMEs and then explain how they determine their financing needs or requirement. The chapter also examines more closely the factors that affect the choice of financing among the various sources.

14.2 Financing Options

MSMEs finance their operations with a combination of debt and equity finance. Sources of debt finance include bank loans, trade credit, factoring, asset based lenders, public debt offer, commercial papers, leasing, microfinance loans, finance from DFIs and public sector support schemes. Sources of equity finance include personal savings, family and friends, business angels, venture capital, corporate venturers, private placements of equity and public offering of equity. We have provided a list of financing sources for MSMEs in Table 14.1. The various financing sources do not have a similar focus. The providers of these various financing sources have different objectives, conditions, capabilities and constraints. Also, the firms, which use these financing sources, have different financing needs or requirements. Some firms may require long-term financing, while others may need short-term working capital. Some may also require a substantial amount of capital and others may ask for small amounts.

Even though the financing menu seems to be vast, in practice, the financing alternatives available to MSMEs are highly limited. Debt finance is usually unsuitable for firms with unpredictable cash flows, high business and financial risk and high operational gearing. Generally, debt finance is usually not available to start-up enterprises since they do not yet have a track record or operational and financial history. Therefore, new businesses are more likely to

Table 14.1 Various financing sources for MSMEs and new ventures

Equity sources	Debt sources
Personal savings	Bank lending
Family and friends	Trade credit
Business angels	Factoring
Venture capital	Asset-based lending
Corporate venturers	Public offering of debt
Private placement of equity	Leasing
Public offering of equity	Microfinance loans
	Finance from DFIs
	Public sector support schemes

rely on equity finance such as the entrepreneur's personal savings, to finance their operations. Debt financing, though expensive, does not result in the dilution of the entrepreneur's stake in the venture. Also, if the project offers return greater than that required for the project, then debt finance is beneficial though it introduces increased financial risk. A downside for small businesses is that the bank may request a personal guarantee by the entrepreneur, regardless of any business collateral that has been offered.

The choice between debt and equity also depends to a large extent on the industry in which the enterprise is operating. Some businesses cannot support much debt and therefore have an observed capital structure that is heavily tilted towards equity. High technology firms, for example, tend to use a lot of equity compared to debt. With debt, the enterprise has to make periodic payments of interest and principal. Payments of dividends to shareholders are not mandatory and depend primarily on the dividend policy of the enterprise. Most firms maintain a mix of debt and equity in their capital structure. Entrepreneurs should also bear in mind that, usually equity financing provided by family and friends are likely to be converted into a loan or debt if the business fails.

14.3 Determining Financing Requirement

The financing requirement can be determined by forecasting financial statements. These financial statements include the statement of comprehensive income (income statement), statement of financial position (balance sheet) and statement of cash flows. Usually, businesses also prepare a cash budget, which aids in planning for funding requirements. The most popular technique of forecasting the finance needed is the percentage of sales method. This method assumes that most items in the financial statement change in proportion to changes in sales.

The firm should be able to ascertain whether it requires short-term or long-term financing. After the financing needs have been determined, the business will have to determine the appropriate source to obtain the finance. If the firm needs short-term finance, it will have to avoid financing sources that require a more elaborate evaluation and approval process such as bank loans, venture capital and the issue of shares, either through private placement or through public offering. Short-term financing needs are best financed with the use of short-term sources such as accounts payable, bank overdrafts, delayed payment of bills and so on. Raising finance from short-term sources usually involves small amounts and as such does not require a detailed and rigorous credit evaluation process. Therefore, the transaction costs involved in short-term financing are lower than long-term sources of financing. Short-term sources are mostly used to finance current assets or assets that can easily be converted into cash, such as inventory and accounts receivable.

Long-term financing needs are also best financed using long-term sources such as long-term bank loans, venture capital, the issue of shares and so on. It is difficult to raise long-term finance from short-term sources since such sources may not be able to provide the financing required. Long-term financing usually involves larger amounts with higher transaction costs.

Firms would want to apply the asset maturity matching principle, which involves matching the duration of their assets and liabilities. Empirical studies have shown that MSMEs try to finance their fixed assets with long-term finance and their current assets with short-term finance. This strategy is important in avoiding any cash flow mismatch. For example, a business which finances a long-term asset with short-term debt finance may find that it will be constrained in its ability to meet the required payments. This is because the asset will not have generated enough cash flows to meet the repayments associated with the short-term debt. Another case of mismatching is when the business finances a current asset with long-term debt finance. After a short while, the current assets may have generated enough cash flows to pay off the debt for themselves. The business will then be left with a loan that it no longer requires. It will, however, have to continue making interest payments on such a loan, and if it wants to pay off the entire loan, it may find that it will have to make a prepayment penalty to the provider of the loan.

The enterprise, in raising finance must also endeavour to maintain financial flexibility. An enterprise generally would not want to utilise all its borrowing capacity. Maintaining financial flexibility is essential because the business can get into hard times, and the economy generally could go down. If the business has not maintained financial slack, then it will find that it has no capacity to borrow during such times. The ability to borrow during periods like this too may be constrained by the state of the business as well as the state of the economy. Therefore, it is prudent for the enterprise not to utilise all its borrowing capacity, by maintaining some financial slack. Maintaining financial slack gives the enterprise options for future funding requirements.

14.4 Factors Affecting Financing Choice

The menu of financing choices is varied because of demand and supply conditions. There are various suppliers of funds with varied specialities and capabilities. Also, businesses that demand funds differ in terms of size, age and industry and therefore have different financing needs. Ideally, providers of finance want to tailor their capabilities and specialities to a particular segment(s) of clients whose peculiar needs make such financing desirable. Specifically, several factors influence the particular choice of finance that an entrepreneur will employ to finance an enterprise. In making any decision, the aim of the entrepreneur will be to maximise the enterprise's NPV and therefore increase its value. The choice of finance is a crucial decision, as it can make or unmake the enterprise. Some of the factors which can affect the choice of finance include: the stage of the enterprise, the conditions attached to financing, taxes, profits and cash flow levels, the value of assets, the cost of obtaining the finance, the relationship with the provider of finance and its ability to provide value increasing services, the time frame in which the finance can be arranged, and how soon the business requires the money.

14.4.1 Stage of the Firm

One of the important factors to consider in financing an enterprise is the stage or age of the business. Early stage enterprises are likely to find it difficult to raise debt finance. From the life-cycle perspective, as a firm gets older, it establishes itself as a continuing business and also gains a reputation among debt providers, like banks. Therefore, it is able to gain access to debt finance. Since MSMEs do not have access to the public equity market, long years of business may imply a long business relationship with external debt providers and this increases MSMEs chances of obtaining external debt finance.

Early stage or younger firms usually have to rely on self-financing and financing from friends and family. Also, business angels and venture capitalists are usually willing to provide equity capital to young enterprises in the start-up and early growth phase. Business angels are more likely to invest at an earlier stage in a business, compared to venture capitalists. The amount provided by business angels, however, is likely to be less than the amount that a typical venture capitalist will want to invest in the enterprise. Other finance providers, such as debt capital providers, will usually not invest in a start-up enterprise. Also, if the entrepreneur is able to delay raising finance, then the entrepreneur is likely to get a higher valuation for the enterprise since much more uncertainty regarding the prospects associated with the enterprise will have been resolved over time. Therefore, the stage of an enterprise is an important factor to consider in the choice of the financing that the entrepreneur wishes to use.

14.4.2 Conditions Attached to the Finance

The entrepreneur must also consider the conditions attached to the finance. This is because these conditions restrict and limit the flexibility of the enterprise as well as the options that are open to it. Providers of finance may limit the strategic options available to the enterprise, and they may request to be consulted and involved in key decisions. Providers of debt capital can write several restrictive covenants into the contract with the enterprise. These include restricting the enterprise's ability to raise future debt, restricting the levels of managerial compensation and restricting the payment of dividends to shareholders.

Also, venture capital financiers may want an option of first refusal in case the enterprise needs to raise subsequent financing. Company law may also require that a company undertakes a rights issue if it wants to raise subsequent equity finance. The type of financing being sought is also related to the restrictions that are likely to be in place. Short-term financing is likely to be associated with fewer restrictions compared to longer-term financing sources. This is because much more can go wrong in the long-term, and therefore the provider of finance will want to protect himself from opportunistic behaviour by the entrepreneur.

14.4.3 Tax Implications

The choice of finance might have tax implications. We know at this stage that interest on debt is tax deductible and therefore can generate a tax shield for the business. The present value of the tax shield adds to the value of the enterprise. Dividends to shareholders are not tax deductible for the firm. This is because they are regarded as an appropriation of profit rather than a charge against profit. Interests are regarded as valid costs of carrying out businesses and therefore the tax authorities allow them as valid deductions against profits. When it comes to equity, investors or shareholders can choose when to sell their shares to realise any capital gains made. There is a tax gain for the investor in delaying the payment of capital gains tax. This is because the present value of the tax obligation is lower as time goes by. It means that, since interest on debt reduces firms' tax burden, it may encourage firms to go in for more debt rather than equity.

14.4.4 Profitability and Cash Flows

Some financing methods will require regular payments or outflows. The enterprise must therefore be sufficiently profitable and be able to generate enough and regular cash flows to meet the payments. Therefore, the entrepreneur must have in mind the cash flow consequences of using a particular financing method. This is because some cash flows require frequent payments, others require less frequent payments, while some may not require cash outflows. Businesses may also find that it is possible to structure a financing arrangement to reduce the strain on their cash flows. An entrepreneur may negotiate a suspended interest payment on a loan for the first year. This means that in the first year the business does not have to make interest payments. This gives the business time to settle so that it is in a better position to meet interest payments once they begin. Also, the entrepreneur can negotiate a loan with only interest payments. In this case, the entrepreneur makes only interest payments. The remaining balance or principal is paid on maturity of the loan. Such loans, therefore, are known as balloon loans as the payments that have to be made balloon from the relatively small interest payment to the bulk ballooned amount that has to be settled. To go for such an option, the entrepreneur must have confidence, that the business can generate substantial retained earnings to pay the bulk balance upon maturity.

It is also important to mention that profitable firms are believed to rely on less debt because they can retain the profits and plough these back into the business. The firm will only go for debt when the retained profits are not adequate to finance the business operations. Generally, firms go beyond debt to raise external equity if the debt is also not enough. This process is known as the pecking order theory (POT). In the case of MSMEs, they are said to face an extreme form of the POT known as the constraint POT or modified POT. This is because they have less access to external equity, thus they rely on internal funds or profits first and then go on to debt finance.

14.4.5 Value of Assets

The value of the enterprise's assets can also matter in determining the choice of finance. Generally, a higher asset value suggests a bigger firm size. MSMEs with a relatively large asset base can afford to borrow money from various financiers. This is because the large asset base can serve as good collateral for the provider of the finance. Therefore, MSMEs with a relatively larger tangible asset base find it easier to raise debt finance compared to their counterparts with a lower tangible asset base. Large firms or firms with high asset value are also generally considered to be more diversified and as such have less risk, thus, increasing their ability to absorb more debt.

Firms with a large intangible asset base, however, may find it more difficult to borrow or raise debt finance. This is because the value of the intangible asset may be subjectively determined. Examples of firms that may have high intangible assets are firms engaged in active research and development such as pharmaceutical firms, video games developers and software developers.

14.4.6 Cost of Finance

The entrepreneur must also consider the costs of raising the required finance. These include explicit costs, such as the cost of hiring consultants (like lawyers, accountants, auditors and investment banks), and application and processing fees. They also include implicit costs such as the time spent in negotiating and arranging the deal. If the firm decides to raise public equity it will have to go through an initial public offering. The cost of the initial public offering sometimes can be high and can range between 15 % and 20 % of the funds raised. Another cost associated with an IPO is the cost of the under-pricing of the issue. Therefore, considering the costs involved in doing an IPO, more mature firms are more likely to go public through an IPO compared to younger enterprises and start-up firms.

Also, for trade credit, the entrepreneur would want to consider the cost of the trade credit against alternative financing that can be utilised. If alternative financing can be arranged at a low cost, then there is no point taking the trade credit. The key point is that the higher the cost of raising the finance, the lower the net proceeds that will accrue to the firm. However, the firm may have to incur such cost to be able to raise finance in the amounts that it requires. After the finance has been raised, the enterprise may still have to incur costs to keep investors informed of what is going on in the enterprise. The cost of keeping investors informed differs based on the type of finance obtained. Raising public equity will mean that the firm will have to periodically send annual reports to its diverse shareholder base. The cost of printing such material and meeting ongoing requirements associated with a listed public company can be very expensive indeed. Also, depending on the shareholder structure, the cost of keeping investors informed could differ. A diverse shareholder base may involve more cost because of a higher level of agency costs. A shareholder base made up of more institutional and large investors is likely to involve less cost for the firm in keeping shareholders informed because of lower agency costs. Therefore, apart from the initial cost of raising finance, the entrepreneur must take into consideration the ongoing costs of keeping investors informed.

14.4.7 Relationship with Finance Providers

Another important factor is the relationship between the entrepreneur and the provider of finance. This relationship can determine whether a business will be able to raise the required funding. A good relationship with the potential provider of finance increases the likelihood that the business will be able to obtain the required funding. Banks are relationship-based organisations as their main business is to get to know their clients better and to collect the needed information about their businesses so that they are in a better position to make a good lending decision. Venture capitalists, for example, look for a good chemistry between themselves and the firms that they invest in. The continued healthy relationship between the entrepreneur and the finance providers is important. Also, the entrepreneur may be able to raise funds based on the relationship with friends and family and not through the merit of the proposed investment per se.

The relationship between the entrepreneur and providers of finance is likely to break down when the business is experiencing financial distress, making it difficult to raise additional financing that may be needed. Firms in financial distress have most likely squandered their reputational capital and goodwill with finance providers. Financial distress constrains the menu of financing options that may be available to the small enterprise. Therefore, raising finance under financial distress conditions may be even more difficult than raising start-up finance.

The entrepreneur must also consider the extent to which the finance provider is likely to be involved in the affairs of the enterprise. Some providers of finance, such as venture capitalists and business angels, take a hands-on approach and are usually quite involved in the enterprises in which they invest. Venture capitalists and business angels usually desire to be involved because they usually have the capacity to add value to the enterprise. Others may not wish to be involved, and since their involvement in the enterprise can be destabilising and therefore detract from value, making the entrepreneur lose focus. Providers of debt finance, such as banks, are usually not interested in being involved in the activities of the enterprise so far as they receive their interest payments and the business is not in financial distress.

14.4.8 Time Frame Within Which Financing Is Required

Finally, the entrepreneur must consider how soon the finance can be arranged and the urgency of the finance for the enterprise. Generally, given an enterprise has to raise finance quickly, it may find that the alternatives available are few, and that some plausible financing sources may take time to materialise. The enterprise may therefore be forced to borrower at a comparatively high cost, because of the urgency with which the funds are needed. When the finance is needed immediately and cannot be raised from profit or the personal resources of the entrepreneur, drawing on past relations with family and friends and suppliers (who may grant further trade credit) is likely to prove beneficial. Another option to generate funds, is a sale and lease back of property. The enterprise can also factor its receivables to a factoring company or accelerate the collection of receivables while delaying the settlement of its accounts payable. These strategies may be used to obtain some funds in the short-term for the business.

However, most methods to acquire funds usually take some time. Obtaining funds from government sponsored programmes, for example, can take time since it usually involves a lot of bureaucracy and a long queue of applicants waiting to be served. Investors such as venture capitalists also take some time to evaluate the proposed investment before they decide to commit their time and resources. A bank will also take time to conduct due diligence before it approves a loan facility. Therefore, the entrepreneur needs to plan for its future financing requirements ahead. Planning for the financing need should take into consideration the amount of financing that will be required as well as when the finance will be required (i.e. timing). The financing need can either be immediate or short-term, medium-term or long-term in nature. Planning financial requirements ensures that the enterprise can borrow at an appropriate cost and that it can match the need for financing with the nature of the investment being made.

14.5 Summary and Conclusions

In this chapter, we have discussed the financing choice of MSMEs. We saw that MSMEs mostly have difficulty accessing finance, and therefore they cast a wide net to capture the financing they need from various sources to start a new venture or to expand an existing business. MSMEs finance their operations with a combination of debt and equity finance. Sources of debt finance include bank loans, trade credit, factoring, asset based lenders, public debt offer, commercial papers, leasing, microfinance loans, finance from DFIs and public sector support schemes. Sources of equity finance include personal savings, family and friends, business angels, venture capital, corporate venturers, private placements of equity and public offering of equity.

The menu of financing choices is varied, because of demand and supply conditions. There are various suppliers of funds with varied specialities and capabilities. Also, businesses that demand funds differ in terms of size, age and industry and therefore have different financing needs. MSMEs need to maintain financial flexibility and not to utilise all of its borrowing capacity. Maintaining financial flexibility by maintaining some financial slack will help enhance the enterprises options for future funding requirements.

The choice of finance is a crucial decision and some of the factors which can affect the choice of finance include the stage of the enterprise, the conditions attached to financing, taxes, profits and cash flow levels, the value of assets, the cost of obtaining the finance, the relationship with the provider of finance and its ability to provide value increasing services, the time frame within which the financing is required or how soon the business needs the finance.

Discussion Questions and Problems

1. Identify the various types of capital.
2. Explain why MSMEs are said to have a 'constrained' financing choice.
3. What are the various financing options available for MSMEs?
4. Is debt a good source of financing MSMEs?
5. Discuss the advantages and disadvantages of using equity finance.
6. How different are business angels from venture capital?
7. Discuss what is involved in determining the financing requirement of MSMEs.
8. Examine the factors that influence MSMEs' choice of financing.
9. Explain the life-cycle theory and how age affects the financing choice of firms.
10. Explain the POT within the context of MSMEs.

15

Harvesting the Business Venture Investment

Learning Objectives
By the end of this chapter, you should be able to:

- identify the various techniques involved in harvesting
- describe the process involved in going public and how investors can use going public to harvest their investment
- explain how investors can harvest their investing through acquisitions
- show how management buyout can be used as a form of harvesting
- describe how employee stock ownership can be used for harvesting
- discuss the factors that influence the investors' harvesting decisions

15.1 Introduction

The Book of Genesis rightly states 'While the earth remains, **seedtime and harvest**, cold and heat, and summer and winter, day and night shall not cease'. This suggests that farmers who sow or plant will have to wait to harvest their yield after several months or years. It stands to reason that you can only harvest or reap what you sowed. In a similar fashion, initial investors or entrepreneurs who invest capital and operate a business for several years, may wish to exit the business or sell their stake or reduce their percentage holding in the enterprise. The process of doing this is known as *harvesting*. Harvesting is the final stage of investment, where the entrepreneurs or initial investors liquidate their investments.

J.Y. Abor, *Entrepreneurial Finance for MSMEs*,
DOI 10.1007/978-3-319-34021-0_15

This stage in the investment process is very important. It is a critical element in informing investors' initial investment decisions. Investors enter into a venture with the mind of realising a return at the end of the investment. What would be realised may be influenced by how and when the investment will be harvested. The entrepreneur may have different inclinations in terms of harvesting. Some entrepreneurs may wish to harvest all their investment and therefore shift their attention to some other project or venture. Other entrepreneurs may consider the venture as an investment in perpetuity. The harvesting inclination of the investor or entrepreneur may have implications for the type of harvesting technique to adopt. Whatever the inclination may be, the harvesting should be able to generate appropriate returns for the investors, considering the investments they have made, the risks they have absorbed and the amount of work they have put into the venture. Harvesting may take various forms, including going public Mergers and Acquisitions (M&A's), Management Buyouts (MBOs) and Employee Stock Ownership Plans (ESOPs). In this chapter, we examine these various harvesting techniques, one after the other. The chapter also discusses the factors that must be considered before harvesting decisions are taken.

15.2 Going Public

An enterprise going public involves doing an IPO. An IPO takes place when a private firm first offers its shares to the investing public. IPOs take place in the primary market where the shares are sold for the first time. During the IPO, the funds raised go to the firm as well as initial investors who are selling their stake or interest in the enterprise. The IPO is important because it is a liquidity event, which enables early stage investors to harvest or exit the investment. For venture capitalists investing private equity, an IPO may be a precondition for investing in the enterprise. The entrepreneur may also want to sell their investment in order to pursue another venture or to diversify his/her personal investment.

A firm that has already issued shares to the public can issue additional shares to raise more capital through a 'seasoned new issue' or a 'secondary offering'. Seasoned new issue may appear similar to 'secondary offering' and the two terms are sometimes used interchangeable, but they are not the same. Seasoned new issue, which is also known as seasoned offering, involves the firm issuing additional shares out of its authorised shares to shareholders. In this case, the funds raised go to the firm issuing the shares. In the case of a secondary offering, the shares being sold were previously issued by the firm and are being resold through a public offering process. The already issued shares are held by existing shareholders, such as the founder or the entrepreneur, private equity investors and institutional investors. These shareholders can offload their shares during the secondary offering. The total issued shares of the firm concerned therefore will not change and the funds raised will go to the sellers.

After the shares have been sold in the primary market, they are subsequently listed and traded on the secondary market. The stock exchange is the secondary market for public stock offerings.

The firm requires the services of an investment bank or an underwriter to take it through the IPO process.

15.2.1 The Role of Investment Banks

The investment bank performs several functions and the enterprise's choice of an investment bank depends on its satisfaction with the services that the investment banker is proposing to offer. The functions performed by the investment bank or underwriter include valuation of the equity issue, issuing and selling, distribution of issue, providing analysis and coverage of the stock after the IPO.

The investment bank assists the issuing firm in preparing the necessary registration documents, timing the issue and establishing the right price for the issue. Investment banks help in pricing and designing securities to make them attractive to investors. Considering the active engagement of investment banks in the primary market, they are often in the position to advise the customer on the right pricing of new securities. Proper pricing ensures that the issue obtains the highest price possible, which allows the issue to be sold out in the shortest time possible. Private companies are mostly associated with high information asymmetries. The investment bank therefore acts as an intermediary between the public capital market investors and the company. The enterprise will want to raise funds at the highest price possible and this will mean issuing less of its shares. Public capital market investors want to pay the lowest price possible. For this reason, and based on the information asymmetry that exists between capital market investors and the enterprise, the investment bank uses its reputation to certify the value of the shares that are being offered. Venture capitalists also help with the certification of value of the companies that they are involved with. Therefore, it is no surprise that venture capital-backed companies tend to experience less under-pricing compared to non-venture capital-backed companies. The reputation of the investment bank may be severely tarnished if it gets the valuation wrong. Not only will it have a reduced ability to charge higher future premiums, but it also faces the risk of being sued by investors. Therefore, the investment banker sets the offer price based on information gathered about the enterprise, as well as its estimate about demand for the issue.

In issuing the shares, the investment bank may offer a ***bought deal*** or a ***best efforts*** arrangement. The bought deal is also known as 'firm commitment' which involves the investment banker buying the entire issue from the issuer and reselling this to its clients made up of institutional and individual investors. The investment banker guarantees the price that the issuer receives. The investment banker therefore bears the risk that the market price will decline and that it will not be able to sell the entire issue. With a best efforts arrangement, the investment banker simply promises to try and sell the entire issue for the issuer. The investment bank promises to use its in-house facilities, expertise and goodwill to sell the shares at the best price. It does not guarantee the price that will be obtained or the quantities that can be sold. The investment banker earns fees or a commission from underwriting the issue, known as the gross spread or the underwriter discount. This is the difference between the price paid to the issuing firm and the price at which the investment bank sells the securities to the investing public.

Apart from pricing and selling the shares, investment banks help in distributing the issue to the general public. The distribution may be done alone or with other investment banks. If the distribution is done with other investment banks, it is known as 'syndication'. The main investment bank is known as the lead underwriter. The lead underwriter is responsible for coordinating the activities of the other members of the syndicate. Syndications enable the lead investment bank to spread the risk associated with the issue to the members of the syndication team. The lead syndicator or investment bank, however, has to share the underwriting fees with the other members of the syndication team.

The investment banker can also offer to provide an investment analysis on the shares of the issuer after the IPO. This is important for the issuing firm, because having analysts cover its stock can lead to interest in the shares and therefore more trading on the company's equity. This is good for the issuer, because it establishes a good liquid market for its shares and this can lead to a more accurate reflection of the value of the company. This is one of the main reasons why firms go public, that is, to establish a suitably determined price for their shares. This is very important for the company for several reasons. The company may want to use its shares subsequently in takeovers or acquisitions. The company may also want to issue more shares in the future to finance its activities. An appropriate market valuation ensures that the firm gets appropriate value for its shares. Usually, public companies issue additional shares close to or at a discount to the price on the stock exchange in the recent past. Therefore, inappropriately priced shares could lead to expropriation of value from the company or existing shareholders.

15.2.2 Advantages of Going Public

There are several benefits of choosing to go public. It enables entrepreneurs to easily diversify their investment portfolio. The entrepreneurs will have invested a lot of time and effort in the enterprise and therefore may have significant wealth locked up in the enterprise. Going public enables the entrepreneurs to unlock this value and to diversify their portfolio. This is because the entrepreneurs can sell some of their holdings in the enterprise and invest in other businesses. The public market also provides the opportunity for private equity investors and venture capitalists to easily harvest their investment.

Similarly, a public equity market provides liquidity which makes it easier for an investor to sell their shares and realise capital gains. Liquidity is important because it facilitates investments in the economy since investors can easily sell their shares when necessary and therefore their investment horizon do not need to coincide with that of the firm that needs the funds. A stock exchange listing is beneficial for investors since they can easily get out of their investment if they want to. This promotes investment because investors know that they can have access to their capital when they need to.

One key benefit of going public is the ability of the firm to raise large amounts of capital. This is because the shares are offered to the general public, which is made up of a large pool of potential investors. This is one advantage public offering has over private placement. After going through the IPO, the firm will have the necessary funding to invest in fixed asset, for expansion, research and development projects, boost sustaining and growth capital and sometimes repay debt.

Going public could lead to an improved corporate governance of the company. Listed companies are required to comply with corporate governance requirements and various disclosure requirements, such as quarterly disclosure of their results and the provision of price sensitive information to the market. Investors' interests are therefore better protected in a listed company. Listed firms are also subjected to various kinds of scrutiny by market analysts and monitors, who ensure that the mangers of the firms are taking decisions and behaving in ways that seek to protect the interest of the shareholders. Corporate governance assists the firm to adopt better management practices, to institute an effective internal auditing system and to ensure greater opportunities for growth and a new strategic outlook.

Another advantage of going public is the improved corporate image of the firm. The stock exchange listing increases the reputation and visibility of the listed firm. The firm tends to receive a lot of media attention during the IPO process, and this gives it so much visibility. The reputation and visibility of the firm to stakeholders, such as customers, employees, suppliers and providers of funds is improved and this can create new business for the firm. Becoming a listed company improves the firm's prestige, brand image and competitive edge in the industry it operates. The improved brand image of the firm enables the firm to increase its revenue and market share. The enhanced reputation enables the firm to attract and retain key employees. Going public enables a company to provide long-term incentive schemes such as stock options to its employees. This can increase employee morale and loyalty because they become more committed to the company. It also enables the firm to negotiate for better terms with its suppliers and gain easier access to future funding from other finance providers and from the market.

A stock exchange listing facilitates the process of price discovery. Due to the fact that a company is listed on a stock exchange and its shares are publicly traded, its share price should gravitate towards its natural equilibrium. An appropriate value is therefore placed on the stock of the company.

15.2.3 Disadvantages of Going Public

Going public also comes with some disadvantages. One key disadvantage is the costs associated with going public and continuing to be a public company. Public offering is an expensive option of raising long-term capital. The costs include filing fees, cost of hiring an investment bank, auditor, lawyer and so on. For a small business, the costs of raising the capital may be high in relation to the capital being raised. Being listed on the stock exchange requires the firm to regularly send annual reports to shareholders, provide and communicate all price sensitive information, and maintain correspondence with investors and market regulators. All these come with additional huge costs.

Another disadvantage of going public is the dilution of the founder's ownership. Going public may involve the firm issuing additional shares, and or the founder or entrepreneur off-loading part of his/her investment. This will lead to the dilution of the founder's stake in the business.

The entrepreneur or founder may run the risk of losing control. By going public, the founder loses the extent of control he/she has in the firm. If a high percentage of the shares are bought by investors who do not like the founder, they could vote the existing management team, including the founder, out.

Firms that decide to go public certainly lose the privacy they enjoyed in the past before going public. Information on listed companies is available in the public domain and this can be used by competitors, regulators and other market analysts. In such a situation, competitors, which are not listed, may have undue advantage over the listed firm by gaining access to their public information to out-perform them. Since the unlisted competing firm is still a private firm, its information will not be available on the public market, thus, it will continue to enjoy some level of privacy which the listed firm will not.

Going public can also bring about pressure on the firm to perform in the short-term. Private firms are normally not under pressure to produce results immediately. The entrepreneur and other owners may decide to grow at their own pace, even if it will take years to generate the expected results. However, in the case of public companies, investors or shareholders are often impatient and want immediate results. They may engage in all kinds of shareholder activism to put pressure on the firm to perform so as to pay dividends. Also, because listed firms are subject to all kinds of scrutiny by market analysts, they may be compelled to post profits in the short-term to impress shareholders and market analysts. In the process, they may adopt creative accounting techniques to present interesting financial results.

The time involved and the timing of the public offering can also be a disadvantage. Going public takes time for the process to be completed and it requires so much time. If the firm needs finance immediately or urgently, IPO will be a wrong option because of the detailed and time-consuming process involved. The process could take a substantial amount of the time of the entrepreneur and other managers of the firm. Managers shifting attention from the core business to the demands of the IPO could adversely affect the business. The timing of the issue is very important, and it is usually advisable to issue the shares when the stock market is at its peak. When the shares are issued at the wrong time, this may lead to under-subscription and the public offer will be unsuccessful.

Firms that become successful candidates for public offerings are those that consistently exhibit high growth rates, have a strong record of earnings, have a solid position in a rapidly growing industry, have a sound management team with experience and have a strong board of directors in place. Successful candidates for public offering also tend to be in existence for a longer period with many years of audited financial records and also meet Securities and Exchange Commission's standards or requirements.

15.3 Acquisition

Harvesting the investment in a firm can be done by a merger or an acquisition. Technically, a merger occurs when one firm becomes one with another, and an acquisition is a situation when one firm acquires or takes over another. Usually, the bigger firm acquires or takes over the smaller one. M&A's are an essential component of the market for corporate control. The market for corporate control in principle should ensure that managers are always on their feet, since inefficient managers can be booted out through the takeover process. However, in practice it can lead to small efficient firms being taken over by large inefficient firms to ensure the survival of the large firm.

We mentioned that bigger firms usually acquire smaller ones. However, it is possible to have a small firm taking over a bigger firm through what is known as a ***reverse acquisition***. In this case, the reverse acquisition allows the private firm to obtain a stock market listing or go public. The publicly listed firm is usually a failed company, which just exists as a shell but still has a public listing. The public listing can attract the private enterprise to acquire this shell company. The publicly listed company notionally acquires the private firm by a share exchange through an accounting transaction. The publicly listed company needs not have the resources to undertake the acquisition. In substance however, what is happening is that the private firm has acquired the publicly listed company. After the acquisition, the private firm can change the name of the publicly listed company to its name. The private firm can use this route to go public but avoid the high costs of the IPO. However, its shares may remain under-valued for some time, since no investment bank may be involved to provide a certification of value. Due to the low valuation in the short-term, harvesting in the short-term may generate lower proceeds compared to an IPO process.

15.3.1 Forms of Mergers and Acquisitions

The acquirer or predator may purchase a target firm for either cash or by using its shares. There are several considerations regarding whether cash or equity should be used to seal the merger. We now discuss the various forms of M&A's.

15.3.1.1 Purchase of Shares of the Venture for Cash

One form of M&A's is when the acquirer purchases the target firm's outstanding shares for cash. Selling investors may prefer to receive cash to enable them harvest or exit their investment. However, receiving cash may generate taxable gains that must be paid to the tax authorities. However, venture capitalists may not mind receiving cash because the limited partners are not taxable on the gain. This is because the limited partners may be pension funds and other investors who do not have to pay tax on their gains. If this is the case, then tax considerations become unimportant. For the entrepreneur, a cash purchase of the entire business means that they have been bought out and therefore can no longer partake in the business. Using a cash offer can be risky for the acquirer since mistakes about valuation can easily be made. The acquirers who prefer a cash offer must be very confident of their valuation since they are exchanging a relatively safe asset (cash) for a risky asset (the shares of the seller or target firm). To use a cash offer the acquirers must do due diligence so that they are confident that they are not over-paying to acquire the target firm. It may also require the seller to give warranties as to the value of the shares that they are purchasing. If the seller cannot open its books up for a detailed due diligence because it wants to protect commercially sensitive information, it may want to give the acquirer more warranties to be reassured. Therefore, warranties and due diligence may serve as substitutes. If the acquirer is not able to conduct sufficient due diligence and is not satisfied with the warranties that it has received, then it would want to discount the price that it pays for the seller or target firm.

15.3.1.2 Purchase of Assets of the Venture for Cash

Another form of M&A's is by purchasing the assets of the target firm for cash. The acquirer purchases the assets that are needed and are essential for the operation of the business of the seller. In this case, the acquirer does not assume the liabilities of the seller. The seller is still responsible for paying off all the liabilities of the venture. Considering that the acquirer does not assume the liabilities of the enterprise, the seller receives larger proceeds from the transaction. This is because the acquirer does not need to deduct the value of the liabilities of the enterprise from the transaction value. The higher proceeds received by the seller can be used to defray the liabilities of the enterprise. The venture whose shares have been bought may end up becoming a shell and may have to liquidate or enter a new business. Purchase of asset is common in the automobile industry, where an acquirer of a dealership is likely to purchase just the assets of the seller. The seller will have to settle any liabilities that may be associated with the inventory of cars sold.

15.3.1.3 Purchase of Equity of the Venture for Equity of the Acquirer

Purchasing equity of the target firm for equity of the acquiring firm can also be used. This involves the seller giving up its equity to acquire equity in the acquirer or buyer. Equity in the acquiring or new firm can allow the sellers to continue to partake in the activities of the new firm. An acquirer will want to use equity if it is not that confident in its valuation. This is because a share offer mitigates the possibility of overvaluation or undervaluation of both entities. Due to the fact that acquirers are likely to use shares rather than cash to undertake a takeover when they perceive that their share price is overvalued, their share price is likely to drop if it announces a merger deal financed by shares. When the acquirer is uncertain about the value, it can use earn-out provisions, which ensures that the price finally received by the seller depends on the post-merger performance of the entity. Earn-out provisions may not be too fair on the seller since post-merger performance may not entirely be within their control. Using a share for share exchange can be beneficial for the acquirer because it conserves liquidity and improves borrowing capacity that can be used to finance future deals. Again, using a share for share exchange enables the acquirer to expand faster through more M&As compared to if it utilises cash offers. Therefore, an acquirer, which wants to expand quickly through M&A's, is most likely to utilise its share to finance the acquisitions. If the acquirer is not listed, then valuing its share may be difficult. In this case, shares of both firms are associated with risk and therefore the parties have to conduct due diligence and valuation exercises to ensure that they receive appropriate value. Due to the riskiness associated with shares of both entities, they may have to provide guarantees or warranties as to the value of their equity.

If a share for share exchange is used, the objective of harvesting becomes extremely difficult if the acquirer is also not listed. This means that there is no clear path to harvesting. However, if the acquirer has better prospects of going public, then the transaction may be beneficial in the long-term. On the other hand, if the acquirer is listed, then there is a clear path to harvesting. Also, if the acquirer is listed, value can be created by the transfer of shares from under-diversified investors to diversified capital market investors. The sellers benefit because they can achieve diversification in this case because the shares that they receive is freely tradable. They can therefore achieve diversification because they can easily sell the shares they receive and invest in other firms.

15.3.2 Types of Mergers and Acquisitions

There are different types of M&A's and these are vertical, horizontal and conglomerate. Vertical mergers involve firms in related lines of business but at different levels of the production or different stages along the value chain. Vertical mergers involve a firm integrating backwards towards its raw material source or forwards towards its ultimate consumer. For example, a manufacturer of detergents could merge with its distributor if the distributor is a separate business. This is an example of integrating forwards towards the ultimate consumer. If the detergents manufacturer merged with a producer of palm oil then we have a backwards integration. These two firms are at different stages of production and therefore the merger is a vertical merger.

If two firms in the same line of business come together, this kind of merger is known as a horizontal merger. An example is the merger of two detergent manufacturers.

Conglomerate mergers involve two or more firms with unrelated business lines. Conglomerates are large businesses which have a portfolio made up of different business lines. An example of a conglomerate merger could be a manufacturer of detergents merging with a producer of chocolates, or a real estate firm. These businesses are very varied and unrelated. A conglomerate M&A may take place if the acquirer wants to diversify its business line. The main synergies that are likely to be obtained from a conglomerate may be expected to come from economies of scale, utilising higher quality management and a stronger brand.

15.3.3 Reasons for Mergers and Acquisitions

The finance literature indicates M&A's come in waves, known as the merger waves. When merger waves are on, a lot of M&A's tend to take place. The main purpose of M&A's is for the firms involved to experience synergistic benefits. These leads to the whole (the new firm) being greater than the sum of the parts (the individual firms as standalone firms). This means, we can add one to one and obtain something greater than two due to synergies. Synergies are the value drivers that spike M&A activity. Synergies are generated or may be anticipated due to a variety of reasons. Synergies could come from operating on scale economies, eliminating inefficiencies and duplicated services, and complementarities in using factors of production.

Synergies lead to increased revenues and lower costs due to larger economies and one of the ways to create synergy is to eliminate duplicated services. For example, instead of having two IT departments, the new firm can utilise just one IT department. Also, an acquirer may benefit financially from a merger because it can utilise tax shields or accumulated losses of the target that would not have been available without the merger. Economies of scale operate in several ways to create value. One way is that the bigger firm can obtain supplies at a cheaper cost because it orders in larger quantities. Economies of scale can also occur because fixed operating and production costs can be spread over larger volumes of production. In terms of complementarities, the two firms can complement each other in several ways by combining their strengths to make them even stronger because they are together. For example, one of the firms may be good at production while the other may be good at marketing. Combining these two firms will lead to a firm that is a greater producer and marketer at the same time. M&A can also occur in industries with too many players and spare capacity. In this case M&A activity leads to a consolidation of the industry. Also, a firm with excess cash may decide to use the excess cash to acquire another firm, instead of paying out this free cash flow as dividends to its shareholders or repurchase its shares. M&A's therefore occur because a firm with free cash flow is using its excess cash to acquire a firm with a high market share and growth rate.

The gain from a merger is expressed as follows:

$$\text{Gain} = PV_{AB} - \left(PV_{\text{A}} + PV_{\text{B}}\right)$$

The expression shows that for there to be a gain from the merger, the value of the whole must be greater than the sum of the individual parts. The gain represents the synergistic benefits we have been talking about. *For our purposes the main reason of the merger apart from creating synergies is to provide an exit route for investors such as venture capitalists and the entrepreneur or founder. Therefore, venture capitalists as well as other investors can sell their stakes through an M&A.* M&A's, however, may raise conflict of interests between the entrepreneur who also happens to be the manager and other equity investors who have no managerial interests at stake. This is because the entrepreneur is likely to lose his/her role or have a diminished position in any new firm that is created.

Some of the reasons for mergers can be outright 'silly'. One of these silly reasons is to provide diversification for capital market investors. The problem with trying to achieve diversification is that it only serves the managers' interests but not investors. This is because investors can achieve diversification more easily, quicker and at a far cheaper cost than the firm can.

Another reason that may not be sensible is to merge just to reduce borrowing costs. This is because even though the merged firm can obtain lower borrowing costs they reduce their valuable option to default on their debt. This is because the two firms now guarantee each other's debt. Therefore, the gain from lower borrowing costs can be exactly offset by the mutual guarantee that is provided to debt holders leading to no net gain from the merger.

The anticipated gains from mergers do not always occur. There are several reasons why these anticipated benefits seem to fizzle out and are not realised. Integrating systems, corporate cultures and processes, in practice can turn out to be very difficult in deed. These factors mean that the anticipated synergies may not be realised. Another reason is that the acquirer tends to pay too much, for the seller it is probably because it gets involved in a bidding contest. This leads to the acquirer paying a very high premium for the seller. Also, the cost of the acquisition may be very high, because the seller's stock anticipates the merger and therefore rises above its fundamental value. Also, managers tend to be too optimistic in estimating the supposed synergies that are likely to be achieved from the merger. Therefore, behavioural finance concepts may help explain this over optimism that leads to some of the merger 'catastrophes' that we observe in the real world. Also, the merged firm may experience diseconomies of scale and therefore lead to the destruction of value. M&A's can be multibillion dollar deals but the evidence suggests that the ex-ante expectations of synergies tend not to be realised. These are some of the reasons why the firms may be better off apart than together.

Another reason why a merger may not achieve its intended benefits may be due to the fact that priced employees of the seller may leave after the merger because they probably were opposed the merger. In some businesses such as service and R&D industries, the value of the business is very much attributable to the quality of its staff. Therefore, the acquirer may sign agreements and give incentives to employees to let them stay. Related to the point above, employees who leave may set up a similar firm, which ends up competing with the new firm that is created. If the acquirer is worried about this happening, it can sign non-competition agreements, which restrict the ability of previous employees to set up rival firms.

15.4 Management Buyouts

MBOs constitute another means by which investors in an enterprise may exit or liquidate their investment. The MBO is a special form of a leveraged buyout in which management uses debt finance to finance the purchase of the shares of selling investors. In an MBO, investors or shareholders are interested in selling their shares to the management of the enterprise. MBOs usually take place in low interest rate environments and when the stock market is booming. For a closely held enterprise, management may be the majority shareholder. Investors such as venture capitalists may want to exit their investment by sending the enterprise public. The management may want to keep the firm private and therefore will want to buy -out the investors. It may also be that the seller (a venture capitalist) may have already located a buyer for their stake. Management may not want the party to be involved in the activities of the enterprise and therefore may offer a counter proposal to the seller (the venture capitalist). The bid for the seller's interest in the enterprise may lead to a beauty contest which may lead to management paying too much for the seller's stake. An MBO can also take place in a company that is already public. In this case, the MBO is likely to lead to the company to become a private enterprise. The private enterprise may however go public again after the MBO. This may be due to the higher debt burden that may have been imposed on the enterprise, especially if the MBO was financed with debt.

Management would want to undertake an MBO because they are confident and optimistic about the prospects of the enterprise. One key reason for this is that managers are insiders in the enterprise and therefore are likely to have more information about the prospects of the enterprise, compared to other investors. The purchase of equity by management is likely to lead to management being more under-diversified because they have concentrated their investments in the enterprise. Despite being under-diversified, managers are likely to undertake an MBO to protect their jobs and careers. An MBO is also likely to entail lower costs compared to an IPO. This is because the level of information asymmetry is low because management has personal knowledge about the value of the enterprise and also a financier providing debt financing only needs to be concerned about the debt servicing ability of the enterprise and not the valuation of the entire enterprise (which is more costly).

Managers usually do not have the money to finance the purchase of the seller's equity. They tend to raise funds to buy- out investors. One method by which the management can raise funds to finance the buyout is by borrowing from their bankers. The loans acquired from the banks are used to pay off investors who want to sell their stake. Banks are very concerned about the debt servicing capacity of the enterprise. This is because the capital structure of the enterprise will be more geared towards survival, as the debt component soars. Therefore, apart from the prospects of the enterprise, it needs to have good cash generating abilities. Where the MBO is mainly finance with debt, it is known as leveraged buyouts (LBOs). Providers of finance, including debt financiers, would usually want management to personally contribute part of the financing required for the MBO.

15.5 Employee Stock Ownership Plans

Another way of providing liquidity or harvesting opportunities for investors is through ESOPs. ESOPs are set up to enable employees acquire ownership interests in an enterprise. ESOP's act as retirement programmes for employees, just that the bulk of the employee's retirement funds are invested in the shares of the employer. Setting up and administering an ESOP can be costly. These costs include set-up costs, administrative costs and the cost of getting frequent valuations from an external party to assess the value of the enterprise's equity amongst others. ESOP's are usually utilised by private and closely held companies, such as family owned businesses. The ESOP may have rights to appoint members to the board of the enterprise. There may be qualifying conditions such as a stipulated minimum number of working years with the enterprise before an employee becomes qualified to purchase enterprise's shares. Apart from qualifying conditions, there may be vesting conditions, which may require the employee to work with the enterprise for a given number of years.

ESOPs differ a bit from employee stock options. They all, however, have the same effect in that employees end up holding shares of their employer. Stock options give the employee the right, but not the obligation, to purchase the enterprise's shares. They therefore give the employee a call option on the enterprise's shares. The options are given to employees at an agreed strike price. It is hoped that the price of the enterprise's shares will rise in future. If this occurs, then employees can exercise the option at the lower strike price and sell the acquired shares at higher future market prices. However, the enterprise must perform well before its share price can rise for the options to be of value to them. Therefore, employees are motivated to work hard because they have a direct financial interest in the good performance of the enterprise. The recent trend of new ventures to grant company-wide stock options plans is an alignment of the interests of management, shareholders and non-managerial employees (Kraizberg and Gargalas 2002). Just like employee stock options, actual shares can lead theoretically to the alignment of the interests of employees to the interest of the enterprise. It is believed that ownership interests in the enterprise can increase the motivation of employees, align their interests to that of the company, as well as give employees a feeling of being part of the enterprise.

There are two main types of ESOPs. These are leveraged and unleveraged ESOPs. First of all, the company sets up the ESOP. The ESOP is usually administered and managed by a trust. The entrepreneur or other investors then sell shares to the ESOP. However, before the shares are sold they have to be valued by an independent third party. The independent third party establishes a value for the shares. The shares are usually sold at a discount to the ESOP. There are several reasons for this. One is that the value that is determined is subjective, especially because the value determined is not based on a market-determined value (such as the price prevailing on a stock exchange). Also, the shares are being sold to an under-diversified group of employees. This is due to the fact that the bulk of the retirement funds of employees are going to be invested in the shares of the enterprise. Ordinarily, asset pricing models such as the Capital Asset Pricing Model (CAPM) assume that the investors' portfolio are diversified and therefore investors need only be compensated for market or unsystematic risk. This results in a lower discount rate that will be used in the valuation model and therefore a higher price. For employees, investing in the company's shares, such an assumption cannot be made. Employees investing in ESOPs need to be compensated for the unsystematic risk associated with the enterprise, which will result in a higher discount rate and therefore a lower valuation or price that has to be paid by the employees.

After a price has been determined for the shares of the enterprise, the ESOP purchases a large amount of shares from the entrepreneur. This provides a significant liquidity event for the entrepreneur. To finance this purchase, the ESOP will usually borrow from a bank. This is why it is known as a leveraged ESOP. The loan will be collateralised or secured by the shares of the enterprise. Also the enterprise may be required by the lending institution to provide guarantees for the repayment of the loan. The ESOP, after acquiring the shares distributes these to employees. The amount allocated to employees is usually based on a formula, which takes into account the employee's salary level. Contributions from the employer towards employees' retirement are then channelled into the ESOP. The enterprise's contribution to the ESOP, depending on the jurisdiction, is likely to be a tax-deductible expense for the enterprise. Also, employees benefit because the amounts contributed on their behalf are not taxable until they transfer out of the plan. ESOP will use these payments to settle or retire the loan balance owed to the lending institution.

For our purposes, ESOPs provide liquidating opportunities for the various parties involved in the activities of the enterprise. ESOPs provide liquidity for the entrepreneur, investors in the enterprise's shares, such as venture capitalists and business angels, family members who want to opt out of the firm as well as employees who are retiring, or have resigned. Venture capitalists, business angels and other investors who may have invested equity in the enterprise can harvest their investment by selling their equity stake based on a fair valuation to the ESOP. Also, because ESOPs are utilised by closely held enterprises such as family owned businesses, family members who want to opt out can do so by selling their shares to the ESOP. They can be used as a succession management instrument. Family feuds have been known to run down and destroy family empires especially after the death of the founder. For employees who are retiring or those who are resigning from the enterprise, they can transfer out of the plan by selling their shares to the ESOP. The main difference between a leveraged and an unleveraged ESOP is that an unleveraged ESOP is not financed with debt. The ESOP uses contributions made into it to purchase the enterprise's equity overtime. Therefore, the initial amount received by the entrepreneur will be higher under the leveraged ESOP. Even though ESOP's provide liquidity, the enterprise remains private, as shares are sold within an internal market.

15.6 Harvesting Decisions

Various factors, which affect harvesting alternative, will be attractive to management and investors. The harvesting decision is a complex one because various forces may be at play at the same time. The various stakeholders involved in the enterprise therefore consider some of the factors that are detailed in the discussion below.

15.6.1 Current Market Conditions and Valuation Considerations

One of the very important factors to consider in the harvesting decision is the current market conditions. Current market conditions affect the value that an enterprise is likely to receive from a public offer. The enterprise is likely to achieve the highest value for its shares through a public offering. This is because capital market investors are believed to be well diversified and need only to be compensated for systematic risk. However, the value that can be obtained in a public offer very much depends on the prevailing conditions in the capital market. In a bull run, when share prices are buoyant and rising, the price that can be obtained from an IPO is likely to be higher compared to when markets are exhibiting bearish conditions and sentiments. A private deal may suit the enterprise better during market downturns. It is no wonder that companies usually withdraw their public offerings when market conditions change adversely. Recent evidence shows that IPO activity reduced drastically during the 2007 global financial crisis when markets were down, beaten and shy.

15.6.2 Size of the Enterprise

In choosing how an investment should be harvested, the size of the enterprise concerned should be taken into account. This is because the size of the enterprise has implications for the cost of harvesting the investment. As mentioned earlier, IPOs involve higher fixed costs and these costs are huge for smaller firms. Therefore, larger firms find IPOs to be a more viable option compared to smaller firms, because they incur lower costs relatively. An option to reduce cost for smaller firms to achieve a publicly listed status may be to merge with a company that is already public. The costs in this case are likely to be lower for the smaller enterprise because fewer parties are involved in the process and the private nature of the contracting process. Apart from the initial costs, public companies incur high ongoing costs that are likely to be incurred in an effort to comply with stock exchange and other regulatory requirements, which aim at keeping capital market investors protected and informed of relevant information pertaining to public companies.

15.6.3 Stage of the Enterprise's Development

An entrepreneur must also consider the stage of the enterprise before deciding on a harvesting option. Not all companies can access public capital markets. Early stage and start-up enterprises are usually not good candidates for a public market offering. Enterprises that can make it to the public market are likely to be more mature companies with a sound business model, a good track record, stable and predictable earnings and cash flows, as well as a potential for future growth that will reward later stage capital market investors. It is no surprise that early stage companies have to be nursed by private equity and venture capital investors before they become ripe for a public market harvesting. Therefore, early stage companies, which have investors who want to harvest, may have to look for other private equity and venture capital investors to invest in the enterprise. This implies that an IPO will not be an option for some enterprises, and a private deal will be more probable in these circumstances.

15.6.4 Synergies

In some instances, the possibility of achieving synergistic benefits from an equity sale may be a consideration for the entrepreneur. This could be a key consideration, if growth cannot be achieved quickly by the enterprise expanding organically. M&A's may then be an option since M&A's can provide the anticipated and needed synergies that are being sought. IPOs, ESOPs and MBOs as harvesting alternatives cannot provide such synergistic benefits.

15.6.5 Control of Firm

The level of control retained by the entrepreneur can also affect the harvesting alternative chosen. In an IPO, for example, it is likely to lead to a reduction in the equity stake of the enterprise. However, even with a significantly reduced shareholding, the entrepreneur is likely to have some control over the activities of the enterprise as well as maintain management of the enterprise. The entrepreneur can maintain even more control depending on the jurisdiction in which the enterprise is operating. In some countries, companies can sell various classes of shares. Some shares have voting rights while others do not have voting rights. The voting share may be reserved for the founders of the enterprise. Such voting share retains significant control over the enterprise in the hands of the entrepreneur. In such jurisdictions, entrepreneurs are likely to sell non-voting share to the public, reducing outside investors control over the activities of the enterprise. However, by going public the entrepreneur will have to cede some control to outside investors since such investors become part owners of the enterprise. If an MBO is chosen, the management of the enterprise, who may also be the owners, will retain control over the enterprise after the MBO transaction. In an M&A, the entrepreneur or the management team is very likely to lose control over the enterprise after the M&A.

15.6.6 Tax Considerations

The choice of harvesting can be based on tax considerations. The various harvesting options can have very different tax implications. ESOPs contributions by the organisation, as mentioned earlier, are likely to be tax deductible for the enterprise. Also, employees obtain a tax benefit because investments in the ESOP are not taxable until they are realised. By taking the option to go public, investors in the enterprise can decide when to sell their stake and therefore generate taxable gains. Investors therefore can choose and time when they want to incur a tax liability such that it is beneficial for them. Also, by delaying selling and the payment of capital gains, the present value of the capital gains tax is reduced. Listed companies usually receive favourable tax treatments compared to non-listed companies in frontier and emerging markets. This preferential treatment can be in the area of corporate taxation, where listed companies pay a lower corporate tax rate compared to non-listed companies. Also, investors in listed companies may be granted concessions on the payment of capital gains tax and tax on dividend income. There may also be tax consequences for harvesting by M&A's. The seller may have to pay tax on the gains from the transaction.

15.7 Summary and Conclusions

This chapter examined harvesting of MSMEs. We discussed the various forms of harvesting and the factors that influence firms' harvesting choice. Harvesting is a critical aspect of micro-enterprise finance. It provides opportunities for the initial investors to sell off their stake in the business. It is the final stage of investment where the entrepreneur or initial investors liquidate their investments. Harvesting may take various forms including, Going Public, M&A, MBOs and ESOPs.

There are a number of factors that must be taken into consideration in adopting a particular harvesting technique. These include current market conditions and valuation, cost and size of the enterprise, stage of the enterprise's development, synergies, control of firm and taxes.

Discussion Questions and Problems

1. Identify the forms of harvesting available to an entrepreneur or an initial investor.
2. What are the functions of investment banks in the IPO process?
3. Discuss the advantages and disadvantages of a small business that decides to go public.
4. How do entrepreneurs harvest their investment using acquisitions?
5. Explain the various forms of M&A's.
6. Explain the three main types of M&A's.
7. Do M&A's always create the necessary synergies?
8. What is the difference between MBO and LBO and how is MBO used as a form of harvesting?
9. How effective is ESOP as a harvesting option?
10. What factors should be taken into consideration in harvesting decisions?

Appendix A: Formula Sheet

The following is useful formulae

1. **Simple Interest Formula**

$$SI = P_0 \times r \times n$$

2. **Compound Interest (Single deposit)/ Future Value**

   a. Single compounding

$$FV_n = PV_0 \left(1 + r\right)^n$$

   b. Compounding more than once

$$FV_n = PV_0 \left(1 + \frac{r}{m}\right)^{mn}$$

3. **Future Value of an Annuity**

   a. Ordinary annuity

$$FVOA = C\left[\frac{\left(1 + r\right)^n - 1}{r}\right]$$

J.Y. Abor, *Entrepreneurial Finance for MSMEs*,
DOI 10.1007/978-3-319-34021-0

b. Annuity due

$$\text{FVAD} = C\left[\frac{(1+r)^n - 1}{r}\right](1+r)$$

4. **Future Value of Perpetuity**

Since a perpetuity is designed to live infinitely, it is not possible to work its future value.

5. **Present Value of a Single Deposit**

$$\text{PV}_0 = \frac{\text{FV}_n}{(1+r)^n}$$

6. **Present Value of an Annuity**

a. Ordinary annuity

$$\text{PVOA} = C\left[\frac{1 - \frac{1}{(1+r)^n}}{r}\right]$$

b. Annuity due

$$\text{PVAD} = C\left[\frac{1 - \frac{1}{(1+r)^n}}{r}\right](1+r)$$

7. **Growing annuity**

$$\text{PV} = \frac{C}{r-g}\left[1 - \left(\frac{1+g}{1+r}\right)^n\right]$$

8. **Present Value of a Perpetuity**

$$\mathrm{PV} = \frac{C}{r}$$

9. **Rate Implicit on an Investment**

$$r = \left(\frac{\mathrm{FV}}{\mathrm{PV}}\right)^{\frac{1}{t}} - 1$$

10. **Number of Years**

$$n = \frac{\ln\left(\frac{\mathrm{FV}}{\mathrm{PV}}\right)}{\ln(1+i)}$$

11. **Effective Annual Rate of Interest**

$$\mathrm{EAR} = \left(1 + \frac{r}{m}\right)^{m} - 1$$

12. **External Funds Needed**

$$\mathrm{EFN} = \frac{A}{S}(\Delta S) - \frac{L}{S}(\Delta S) - (\mathrm{PM})(\mathrm{PS})(1-d)$$

13. **Break-Even Quantity**

$$Q_B = \frac{F}{P - V}$$

14. **Economic Order Quantity**

$$\mathrm{EOQ} = \sqrt{\frac{\mathrm{2DCo}}{\mathrm{HC}}}$$

15. **Total Inventory Cost**

$$\mathrm{TC} = \frac{D}{Q}(\mathrm{Co}) + \frac{Q}{2}(\mathrm{HC})$$

16. **Subsidy Dependence Index**

$$\mathrm{SDI} = \frac{\text{Net Subsidy}}{\text{Loan Portfolio} \times \text{Interest rate on loan}}$$

17. **Operational Sustainability**

$$\mathrm{OSS} = \frac{\text{Total Operational Income}}{\text{Interest Expense} + \text{Loan Loss Provision} + \text{Administrative Expenses}}$$

18. **Financial Sustainability**

$$\mathrm{PAR} = \frac{\text{Total Loan Principal on Overdue or Delinquent Loans Outstanding}}{\text{Total Loan Principal Outstanding}}$$

Appendix B: Financial Tables

Table B.1 Future value of US$1 at '*n*' period
Formula: $FVLS = PV(1+r)^n$

Periods (*n*)	1 %	2 %	3 %	4 %	5 %	6 %	7 %	8 %	9 %	10 %	11 %	12 %	13 %	14 %	15 %	16 %	17 %	18 %	19 %	20 %
1	1.0100	1.0203	1.0308	1.0415	1.0524	1.0632	1.0746	1.0862	1.0981	1.1103	1.1112	1.1341	1.1314	1.1602	1.1602	1.1879	1.2050	1.2207	1.2366	1.2529
2	1.0201	1.0404	1.0609	1.0816	1.1025	1.1236	1.1449	1.1664	1.1881	1.2100	1.2321	1.2544	1.2769	1.2996	1.3225	1.3456	1.3689	1.3924	1.4161	1.4400
3	1.0303	1.0612	1.0927	1.1249	1.1576	1.1910	1.2250	1.2597	1.2950	1.3310	1.3676	1.4049	1.4429	1.4815	1.5209	1.5609	1.6016	1.6430	1.6852	1.7280
4	1.0406	1.0824	1.1255	1.1699	1.2155	1.2625	1.3108	1.3605	1.4116	1.4641	1.5181	1.5735	1.6305	1.6890	1.7490	1.8106	1.8739	1.9388	2.0053	2.0736
5	1.0510	1.1041	1.1593	1.2167	1.2763	1.3382	1.4026	1.4693	1.5386	1.6105	1.6851	1.7623	1.8424	1.9254	2.0114	2.1003	2.1924	2.2878	2.3864	2.4883
6	1.0615	1.1262	1.1941	1.2653	1.3401	1.4185	1.5007	1.5869	1.6771	1.7716	1.8704	1.9738	2.0820	2.1950	2.3131	2.4364	2.5652	2.6996	2.8398	2.9860
7	1.0721	1.1487	1.2299	1.3159	1.4071	1.5036	1.6058	1.7138	1.8280	1.9487	2.0762	2.2107	2.3526	2.5023	2.6600	2.8262	3.0012	3.1855	3.3793	3.5832
8	1.0829	1.1717	1.2668	1.3686	1.4775	1.5938	1.7182	1.8509	1.9926	2.1436	2.3045	2.4760	2.6584	2.8526	3.0590	3.2784	3.5115	3.7589	4.0214	4.2998
9	1.0937	1.1951	1.3048	1.4233	1.5513	1.6895	1.8385	1.9990	2.1719	2.3579	2.5580	2.7731	3.0040	3.2519	3.5179	3.8030	4.1084	4.4355	4.7854	5.1598
10	1.1046	1.2190	1.3439	1.4802	1.6289	1.7908	1.9672	2.1589	2.3674	2.5937	2.8394	3.1058	3.3946	3.7072	4.0456	4.4114	4.8068	5.2338	5.6947	6.1917
11	1.1157	1.2434	1.3842	1.5395	1.7103	1.8983	2.1049	2.3316	2.5804	2.8531	3.1518	3.4785	3.8359	4.2262	4.6524	5.1173	5.6240	6.1759	6.7767	7.4301
12	1.1268	1.2682	1.4258	1.6010	1.7959	2.0122	2.2522	2.5182	2.8127	3.1384	3.4985	3.8960	4.3345	4.8179	5.3503	5.9360	6.5801	7.2876	8.0642	8.9161
13	1.1381	1.2936	1.4685	1.6651	1.8856	2.1329	2.4098	2.7196	3.0658	3.4523	3.8833	4.3635	4.8980	5.4924	6.1528	6.8858	7.6987	8.5994	9.5964	10.6993
14	1.1495	1.3195	1.5126	1.7317	1.9799	2.2609	2.5785	2.9372	3.3417	3.7975	4.3104	4.8871	5.5348	6.2613	7.0757	7.9875	9.0075	10.1472	11.4198	12.8392
15	1.1610	1.3459	1.5580	1.8009	2.0789	2.3966	2.7590	3.1722	3.6425	4.1772	4.7846	5.4736	6.2543	7.1379	8.1371	9.2655	10.5387	11.9737	13.5895	15.4070
16	1.1726	1.3728	1.6047	1.8730	2.1829	2.5404	2.9522	3.4259	3.9703	4.5950	5.3109	6.1304	7.0673	8.1372	9.3576	10.7480	12.3303	14.1290	16.1715	18.4884
17	1.1843	1.4002	1.6528	1.9479	2.2920	2.6928	3.1588	3.7000	4.3276	5.0545	5.8951	6.8660	7.9861	9.2765	10.7613	12.4677	14.4265	16.6722	19.2441	22.1861
18	1.1961	1.4282	1.7024	2.0258	2.4066	2.8543	3.3799	3.9960	4.7171	5.5599	6.5436	7.6900	9.0243	10.5752	12.3755	14.4625	16.8790	19.6733	22.9005	26.6233
19	1.2081	1.4568	1.7535	2.1068	2.5270	3.0256	3.6165	4.3157	5.1417	6.1159	7.2633	8.6128	10.1974	12.0557	14.2318	16.7765	19.7484	23.2144	27.2516	31.9480
20	1.2202	1.4859	1.8061	2.1911	2.6533	3.2071	3.8697	4.6610	5.6044	6.7275	8.0623	9.6463	11.5231	13.7435	16.3665	19.4608	23.1056	27.3930	32.4294	38.3376
21	1.2324	1.5157	1.8603	2.2788	2.7860	3.3996	4.1406	5.0338	6.1088	7.4002	8.9492	10.8038	13.0211	15.6676	18.8215	22.5745	27.0336	32.3238	38.5910	46.0051
22	1.2447	1.5460	1.9161	2.3699	2.9253	3.6035	4.4304	5.4365	6.6586	8.1403	9.9336	12.1003	14.7138	17.8610	21.6447	26.1864	31.6293	38.1421	45.9233	55.2061
23	1.2572	1.5769	1.9736	2.4647	3.0715	3.8197	4.7405	5.8715	7.2579	8.9543	11.0263	13.5523	16.6266	20.3616	24.8915	30.3762	37.0062	45.0076	54.6487	66.2474
24	1.2697	1.6084	2.0328	2.5633	3.2251	4.0489	5.0724	6.3412	7.9111	9.8497	12.2392	15.1786	18.7881	23.2122	28.6252	35.2364	43.2973	53.1090	65.0320	79.4968
25	1.2824	1.6406	2.0938	2.6658	3.3864	4.2919	5.4274	6.8485	8.6231	10.8347	13.5855	17.0001	21.2305	26.4619	32.9190	40.8742	50.6578	62.6686	77.3881	95.3962
26	1.2953	1.6734	2.1566	2.7725	3.5557	4.5494	5.8074	7.3964	9.3992	11.9182	15.0799	19.0401	23.9905	30.1666	37.8568	47.4141	59.2697	73.9490	92.0918	114.4755
27	1.3082	1.7069	2.2213	2.8834	3.7335	4.8223	6.2139	7.9881	10.2451	13.1100	16.7386	21.3249	27.1093	34.3899	43.5353	55.0004	69.3455	87.2598	109.5893	137.3706
28	1.3213	1.7410	2.2879	2.9987	3.9201	5.1117	6.6488	8.6271	11.1671	14.4210	18.5799	23.8839	30.6335	39.2045	50.0656	63.8004	81.1342	102.9666	130.4112	164.8447
29	1.3345	1.7758	2.3566	3.1187	4.1161	5.4184	7.1143	9.3173	12.1722	15.8631	20.6237	26.7499	34.6158	44.6931	57.5755	74.0085	94.9271	121.5005	155.1893	197.8136

(continued)

Table B.1 (continued)

Periods (n)	1 %	2 %	3 %	4 %	5 %	6 %	7 %	8 %	9 %	10 %	11 %	12 %	13 %	14 %	15 %	16 %	17 %	18 %	19 %	20 %
30	1.3478	1.8114	2.4273	3.2434	4.3219	5.7435	7.6123	10.0627	13.2677	17.4494	22.8923	29.9599	39.1159	50.9502	66.2118	85.8499	111.0647	143.3706	184.6753	237.3763
31	1.3613	1.8476	2.5001	3.3731	4.5380	6.0881	8.1451	10.8677	14.4618	19.1943	25.4104	33.5551	44.2010	58.0832	76.1435	99.5859	129.9456	169.1774	219.7636	284.8516
32	1.3749	1.8845	2.5751	3.5081	4.7649	6.4534	8.7153	11.7371	15.7633	21.1138	28.2056	37.5817	49.9471	66.2148	87.5651	115.5196	152.0364	199.6293	261.5187	341.8219
33	1.3887	1.9222	2.6523	3.6484	5.0032	6.8406	9.3253	12.6760	17.1820	23.2252	31.3082	42.0915	56.4402	75.4849	100.6998	134.0027	177.8826	235.5625	311.2073	410.1863
34	1.4026	1.9607	2.7319	3.7943	5.2533	7.2510	9.9781	13.6901	18.7284	25.5477	34.7521	47.1425	63.7774	86.0528	115.8048	155.4432	208.1226	277.9638	370.3366	492.2235
35	1.4166	1.9999	2.8139	3.9461	5.5160	7.6861	10.6766	14.7853	20.4140	28.1024	38.5749	52.7996	72.0685	98.1002	133.1755	180.3141	243.5035	327.9973	440.7006	590.6682
36	1.4308	2.0399	2.8983	4.1039	5.7918	8.1473	11.4239	15.9682	22.2512	30.9127	42.8181	59.1356	81.4374	111.8342	153.1519	209.1643	284.8991	387.0368	524.4337	708.8019
37	1.4451	2.0807	2.9852	4.2681	6.0814	8.6361	12.2236	17.2456	24.2538	34.0039	47.5281	66.2318	92.0243	127.4910	176.1246	242.6306	333.3319	456.7034	624.0761	850.5622
38	1.4595	2.1223	3.0748	4.4388	6.3855	9.1543	13.0793	18.6253	26.4367	37.4043	52.7562	74.1797	103.9874	145.3397	202.5433	281.4515	389.9983	538.9100	742.6506	1020.6747
39	1.4741	2.1647	3.1670	4.6164	6.7048	9.7035	13.9948	20.1153	28.8160	41.1448	58.5593	83.0812	117.5058	165.6873	232.9248	326.4838	456.2980	635.9139	883.7542	1224.8096
40	1.4889	2.2080	3.2620	4.8010	7.0400	10.2857	14.9745	21.7245	31.4094	45.2593	65.0009	93.0510	132.7816	188.8835	267.8635	378.7212	533.8687	750.3783	1051.6675	1469.7716

Table B.2 Present value of US$1 at 'n' period

$$PV = \frac{FV}{(1+r)^n}$$

Periods (*n*)	1 %	2 %	3 %	4 %	5 %	6 %	7 %	8 %	9 %	10 %	11 %	12 %	13 %	14 %	15 %	16 %	17 %	18 %	19 %	20 %
1	0.9901	0.9804	0.9709	0.9615	0.9524	0.9434	0.9346	0.9259	0.9174	0.9091	0.9009	0.8929	0.8850	0.8772	0.8696	0.8621	0.8547	0.8475	0.8403	0.8333
2	0.9803	0.9612	0.9426	0.9246	0.9070	0.8900	0.8734	0.8573	0.8417	0.8264	0.8116	0.7972	0.7831	0.7695	0.7561	0.7432	0.7305	0.7182	0.7062	0.6944
3	0.9706	0.9423	0.9151	0.8890	0.8638	0.8396	0.8163	0.7938	0.7722	0.7513	0.7312	0.7118	0.6931	0.6750	0.6575	0.6407	0.6244	0.6086	0.5934	0.5787
4	0.9610	0.9238	0.8885	0.8548	0.8227	0.7921	0.7629	0.7350	0.7084	0.6830	0.6587	0.6355	0.6133	0.5921	0.5718	0.5523	0.5337	0.5158	0.4987	0.4823
5	0.9515	0.9057	0.8626	0.8219	0.7835	0.7473	0.7130	0.6806	0.6499	0.6209	0.5935	0.5674	0.5428	0.5194	0.4972	0.4761	0.4561	0.4371	0.4190	0.4019
6	0.9420	0.8880	0.8375	0.7903	0.7462	0.7050	0.6663	0.6302	0.5963	0.5645	0.5346	0.5066	0.4803	0.4556	0.4323	0.4104	0.3898	0.3704	0.3521	0.3349
7	0.9327	0.8706	0.8131	0.7599	0.7107	0.6651	0.6227	0.5835	0.5470	0.5132	0.4817	0.4523	0.4251	0.3996	0.3759	0.3538	0.3332	0.3139	0.2959	0.2791
8	0.9235	0.8535	0.7894	0.7307	0.6768	0.6274	0.5820	0.5403	0.5019	0.4665	0.4339	0.4039	0.3762	0.3506	0.3269	0.3050	0.2848	0.2660	0.2487	0.2326
9	0.9143	0.8368	0.7664	0.7026	0.6446	0.5919	0.5439	0.5002	0.4604	0.4241	0.3909	0.3606	0.3329	0.3075	0.2843	0.2630	0.2434	0.2255	0.2090	0.1938
10	0.9053	0.8203	0.7441	0.6756	0.6139	0.5584	0.5083	0.4632	0.4224	0.3855	0.3522	0.3220	0.2946	0.2697	0.2472	0.2267	0.2080	0.1911	0.1756	0.1615
11	0.8963	0.8043	0.7224	0.6496	0.5847	0.5268	0.4751	0.4289	0.3875	0.3505	0.3173	0.2875	0.2607	0.2366	0.2149	0.1954	0.1778	0.1619	0.1476	0.1346
12	0.8874	0.7885	0.7014	0.6246	0.5568	0.4970	0.4440	0.3971	0.3555	0.3186	0.2858	0.2567	0.2307	0.2076	0.1869	0.1685	0.1520	0.1372	0.1240	0.1122
13	0.8787	0.7730	0.6810	0.6006	0.5303	0.4688	0.4150	0.3677	0.3262	0.2897	0.2575	0.2292	0.2042	0.1821	0.1625	0.1452	0.1299	0.1163	0.1042	0.0935
14	0.8700	0.7579	0.6611	0.5775	0.5051	0.4423	0.3878	0.3405	0.2992	0.2633	0.2320	0.2046	0.1807	0.1597	0.1413	0.1252	0.1110	0.0985	0.0876	0.0779
15	0.8613	0.7430	0.6419	0.5553	0.4810	0.4173	0.3624	0.3152	0.2745	0.2394	0.2090	0.1827	0.1599	0.1401	0.1229	0.1079	0.0949	0.0835	0.0736	0.0649
16	0.8528	0.7284	0.6232	0.5339	0.4581	0.3936	0.3387	0.2919	0.2519	0.2176	0.1883	0.1631	0.1415	0.1229	0.1069	0.0930	0.0811	0.0708	0.0618	0.0541
17	0.8444	0.7142	0.6050	0.5134	0.4363	0.3714	0.3166	0.2703	0.2311	0.1978	0.1696	0.1456	0.1252	0.1078	0.0929	0.0802	0.0693	0.0600	0.0520	0.0451
18	0.8360	0.7002	0.5874	0.4936	0.4155	0.3503	0.2959	0.2502	0.2120	0.1799	0.1528	0.1300	0.1108	0.0946	0.0808	0.0691	0.0592	0.0508	0.0437	0.0376
19	0.8277	0.6864	0.5703	0.4746	0.3957	0.3305	0.2765	0.2317	0.1945	0.1635	0.1377	0.1161	0.0981	0.0829	0.0703	0.0596	0.0506	0.0431	0.0367	0.0313
20	0.8195	0.6730	0.5537	0.4564	0.3769	0.3118	0.2584	0.2145	0.1784	0.1486	0.1240	0.1037	0.0868	0.0728	0.0611	0.0514	0.0433	0.0365	0.0308	0.0261
21	0.8114	0.6598	0.5375	0.4388	0.3589	0.2942	0.2415	0.1987	0.1637	0.1351	0.1117	0.0926	0.0768	0.0638	0.0531	0.0443	0.0370	0.0309	0.0259	0.0217
22	0.8034	0.6468	0.5219	0.4220	0.3418	0.2775	0.2257	0.1839	0.1502	0.1228	0.1007	0.0826	0.0680	0.0560	0.0462	0.0382	0.0316	0.0262	0.0218	0.0181
23	0.7954	0.6342	0.5067	0.4057	0.3256	0.2618	0.2109	0.1703	0.1378	0.1117	0.0907	0.0738	0.0601	0.0491	0.0402	0.0329	0.0270	0.0222	0.0183	0.0151
24	0.7876	0.6217	0.4919	0.3901	0.3101	0.2470	0.1971	0.1577	0.1264	0.1015	0.0817	0.0659	0.0532	0.0431	0.0349	0.0284	0.0231	0.0188	0.0154	0.0126
25	0.7798	0.6095	0.4776	0.3751	0.2953	0.2330	0.1842	0.1460	0.1160	0.0923	0.0736	0.0588	0.0471	0.0378	0.0304	0.0245	0.0197	0.0160	0.0129	0.0105
26	0.7720	0.5976	0.4637	0.3607	0.2812	0.2198	0.1722	0.1352	0.1064	0.0839	0.0663	0.0525	0.0417	0.0331	0.0264	0.0211	0.0169	0.0135	0.0109	0.0087
27	0.7644	0.5859	0.4502	0.3468	0.2678	0.2074	0.1609	0.1252	0.0976	0.0763	0.0597	0.0469	0.0369	0.0291	0.0230	0.0182	0.0144	0.0115	0.0091	0.0073

(*continued*)

Table B.2 (continued)

Periods (*n*)	1 %	2 %	3 %	4 %	5 %	6 %	7 %	8 %	9 %	10 %	11 %	12 %	13 %	14 %	15 %	16 %	17 %	18 %	19 %	20 %
28	0.7568	0.5744	0.4371	0.3335	0.2551	0.1956	0.1504	0.1159	0.0895	0.0693	0.0538	0.0419	0.0326	0.0255	0.0200	0.0157	0.0123	0.0097	0.0077	0.0061
29	0.7493	0.5631	0.4243	0.3207	0.2429	0.1846	0.1406	0.1073	0.0822	0.0630	0.0485	0.0374	0.0289	0.0224	0.0174	0.0135	0.0105	0.0082	0.0064	0.0051
30	0.7419	0.5521	0.4120	0.3083	0.2314	0.1741	0.1314	0.0994	0.0754	0.0573	0.0437	0.0334	0.0256	0.0196	0.0151	0.0116	0.0090	0.0070	0.0054	0.0042
31	0.7346	0.5412	0.4000	0.2965	0.2204	0.1643	0.1228	0.0920	0.0691	0.0521	0.0394	0.0298	0.0226	0.0172	0.0131	0.0100	0.0077	0.0059	0.0046	0.0035
32	0.7273	0.5306	0.3883	0.2851	0.2099	0.1550	0.1147	0.0852	0.0634	0.0474	0.0355	0.0266	0.0200	0.0151	0.0114	0.0087	0.0066	0.0050	0.0038	0.0029
33	0.7201	0.5202	0.3770	0.2741	0.1999	0.1462	0.1072	0.0789	0.0582	0.0431	0.0319	0.0238	0.0177	0.0132	0.0099	0.0075	0.0056	0.0042	0.0032	0.0024
34	0.7130	0.5100	0.3660	0.2636	0.1904	0.1379	0.1002	0.0730	0.0534	0.0391	0.0288	0.0212	0.0157	0.0116	0.0086	0.0064	0.0048	0.0036	0.0027	0.0020
35	0.7059	0.5000	0.3554	0.2534	0.1813	0.1301	0.0937	0.0676	0.0490	0.0356	0.0259	0.0189	0.0139	0.0102	0.0075	0.0055	0.0041	0.0030	0.0023	0.0017
36	0.6989	0.4902	0.3450	0.2437	0.1727	0.1227	0.0875	0.0626	0.0449	0.0323	0.0234	0.0169	0.0123	0.0089	0.0065	0.0048	0.0035	0.0026	0.0019	0.0014
37	0.6920	0.4806	0.3350	0.2343	0.1644	0.1158	0.0818	0.0580	0.0412	0.0294	0.0210	0.0151	0.0109	0.0078	0.0057	0.0041	0.0030	0.0022	0.0016	0.0012
38	0.6852	0.4712	0.3252	0.2253	0.1566	0.1092	0.0765	0.0537	0.0378	0.0267	0.0190	0.0135	0.0096	0.0069	0.0049	0.0036	0.0026	0.0019	0.0013	0.0010
39	0.6784	0.4619	0.3158	0.2166	0.1491	0.1031	0.0715	0.0497	0.0347	0.0243	0.0171	0.0120	0.0085	0.0060	0.0043	0.0031	0.0022	0.0016	0.0011	0.0008
40	0.6717	0.4529	0.3066	0.2083	0.1420	0.0972	0.0668	0.0460	0.0318	0.0221	0.0154	0.0107	0.0075	0.0053	0.0037	0.0026	0.0019	0.0013	0.0010	0.0007

Table B.3 Future value of an ordinary annuity of US$1 at '*n*' period

$$FV_{\text{ordinary annuity}} = C\left[\frac{(1+r)^n - 1}{r}\right]$$

Periods (*n*)	1.0 %	2.0 %	3.0 %	4.0 %	5.0 %	6.0 %	7.0 %	8.0 %	9.0 %	10.0 %	11.0 %	12.0 %	13.0 %	14.0 %	15.0 %	16.0 %	17.0 %	18.0 %	19.0 %	20.0 %
1	1.0000	1.0000	1.0000	1.0000	1.0000	1.0000	1.0000	1.0000	1.0000	1.0000	1.0000	1.0000	1.0000	1.0000	1.0000	1.0000	1.0000	1.0000	1.0000	1.0000
2	2.0100	2.0200	2.0300	2.0400	2.0500	2.0600	2.0700	2.0800	2.0900	2.1000	2.1200	2.1200	2.1400	2.1400	2.1500	2.1600	2.1700	2.1800	2.1900	2.2000
3	3.0301	3.0604	3.0909	3.1216	3.1525	3.1836	3.2149	3.2464	3.2781	3.3100	3.3744	3.3744	3.4396	3.4396	3.4725	3.5056	3.5389	3.5724	3.6061	3.6400
4	4.0604	4.1216	4.1836	4.2465	4.3101	4.3746	4.4399	4.5061	4.5731	4.6410	4.7793	4.7793	4.9211	4.9211	4.9934	5.0665	5.1405	5.2154	5.2913	5.3680
5	5.1010	5.2040	5.3091	5.4163	5.5256	5.6371	5.7507	5.8666	5.9847	6.1051	6.3528	6.3528	6.6101	6.6101	6.7424	6.8771	7.0144	7.1542	7.2966	7.4416
6	6.1520	6.3081	6.4684	6.6330	6.8019	6.9753	7.1533	7.3359	7.5233	7.7156	8.1152	8.1152	8.5355	8.5355	8.7537	8.9775	9.2068	9.4420	9.6830	9.9299
7	7.2135	7.4343	7.6625	7.8983	8.1420	8.3938	8.6540	8.9228	9.2004	9.4872	10.0890	10.0890	10.7305	10.7305	11.0668	11.4139	11.7720	12.1415	12.5227	12.9159
8	8.2857	8.5830	8.8923	9.2142	9.5491	9.8975	10.2598	10.6366	11.0285	11.4359	12.2997	12.2997	13.2328	13.2328	13.7268	14.2401	14.7733	15.3270	15.9020	16.4991
9	9.3685	9.7546	10.1591	10.5828	11.0266	11.4913	11.9780	12.4876	13.0210	13.5795	14.7757	14.7757	16.0853	16.0853	16.7858	17.5185	18.2847	19.0859	19.9234	20.7989
10	10.4622	10.9497	11.4639	12.0061	12.5779	13.1808	13.8164	14.4866	15.1929	15.9374	17.5487	17.5487	19.3373	19.3373	20.3037	21.3215	22.3931	23.5213	24.7089	25.9587
11	11.5668	12.1687	12.8078	13.4864	14.2068	14.9716	15.7836	16.6455	17.5603	18.5312	20.6546	20.6546	23.0445	23.0445	24.3493	25.7329	27.1999	28.7551	30.4035	32.1504
12	12.6825	13.4121	14.1920	15.0258	15.9171	16.8699	17.8885	18.9771	20.1407	21.3843	24.1331	24.1331	27.2707	27.2707	29.0017	30.8502	32.8239	34.9311	37.1802	39.5805
13	13.8093	14.6803	15.6178	16.6268	17.7130	18.8821	20.1406	21.4953	22.9534	24.5227	28.0291	28.0291	32.0887	32.0887	34.3519	36.7862	39.4040	42.2187	45.2445	48.4966
14	14.9474	15.9739	17.0863	18.2919	19.5986	21.0151	22.5505	24.2149	26.0192	27.9750	32.3926	32.3926	37.5811	37.5811	40.5047	43.6720	47.1027	50.8180	54.8409	59.1959
15	16.0969	17.2934	18.5989	20.0236	21.5786	23.2760	25.1290	27.1521	29.3609	31.7725	37.2797	37.2797	43.8424	43.8424	47.5804	51.6595	56.1101	60.9653	66.2607	72.0351
16	17.2579	18.6393	20.1569	21.8245	23.6575	25.6725	27.8881	30.3243	33.0034	35.9497	42.7533	42.7533	50.9804	50.9804	55.7175	60.9250	66.6488	72.9390	79.8502	87.4421
17	18.4304	20.0121	21.7616	23.6975	25.8404	28.2129	30.8402	33.7502	36.9737	40.5447	48.8837	48.8837	59.1176	59.1176	65.0751	71.6730	78.9792	87.0680	96.0218	105.9306
18	19.6147	21.4123	23.4144	25.6454	28.1324	30.9057	33.9990	37.4502	41.3013	45.5992	55.7497	55.7497	68.3941	68.3941	75.8364	84.1407	93.4056	103.7403	115.2659	128.1167
19	20.8109	22.8406	25.1169	27.6712	30.5390	33.7600	37.3790	41.4463	46.0185	51.1591	63.4397	63.4397	78.9692	78.9692	88.2118	98.6032	110.2846	123.4135	138.1664	154.7400
20	22.0190	24.2974	26.8704	29.7781	33.0660	36.7856	40.9955	45.7620	51.1601	57.2750	72.0524	72.0524	91.0249	91.0249	102.4436	115.3797	130.0329	146.6280	165.4180	186.6880
21	23.2392	25.7833	28.6765	31.9692	35.7193	39.9927	44.8652	50.4229	56.7645	64.0025	81.6987	81.6987	104.7684	104.7684	118.8101	134.8405	153.1385	174.0210	197.8474	225.0256
22	24.4716	27.2990	30.5368	34.2480	38.5052	43.3923	49.0057	55.4568	62.8733	71.4027	92.5026	92.5026	120.4360	120.4360	137.6316	157.4150	180.1721	206.3448	236.4385	271.0307
23	25.7163	28.8450	32.4529	36.6179	41.4305	46.9958	53.4361	60.8933	69.5319	79.5430	104.6029	104.6029	138.2970	138.2970	159.2764	183.6014	211.8013	244.4868	282.3618	326.2369
24	26.9735	30.4219	34.4265	39.0826	44.5020	50.8156	58.1767	66.7648	76.7898	88.4973	118.1552	118.1552	158.6586	158.6586	184.1678	213.9776	248.8076	289.4945	337.0105	392.4842
25	28.2432	32.0303	36.4593	41.6459	47.7271	54.8645	63.2490	73.1059	84.7009	98.3471	133.3339	133.3339	181.8708	181.8708	212.7930	249.2140	292.1049	342.6035	402.0425	471.9811
26	29.5256	33.6709	38.5530	44.3117	51.1135	59.1564	68.6765	79.9544	93.3240	109.1818	150.3339	150.3339	208.3327	208.3327	245.7120	290.0883	342.7627	405.2721	479.4306	567.3773
27	30.8209	35.3443	40.7096	47.0842	54.6691	63.7058	74.4838	87.3508	102.7231	121.0999	169.3740	169.3740	238.4993	238.4993	283.5688	337.5024	402.0323	479.2211	571.5224	681.8528
28	32.1291	37.0512	42.9309	49.9676	58.4026	68.5281	80.6977	95.3388	112.9682	134.2099	190.6989	190.6989	272.8892	272.8892	327.1041	392.5028	471.3778	566.4809	681.1116	819.2233
29	33.4504	38.7922	45.2189	52.9663	62.3227	73.6398	87.3465	103.9659	124.1354	148.6309	214.5828	214.5828	312.0937	312.0937	377.1697	456.3032	552.5121	669.4475	811.5228	984.0680
30	34.7849	40.5681	47.5754	56.0849	66.4388	79.0582	94.4608	113.2832	136.3075	164.4940	241.3327	241.3327	356.7868	356.7868	434.7451	530.3117	647.4391	790.9480	966.7122	1181.8816
31	36.1327	42.3794	50.0027	59.3283	70.7608	84.8017	102.0730	123.3459	149.5752	181.9434	271.2926	271.2926	407.7370	407.7370	500.9569	616.1616	758.5038	934.3186	1151.3875	1419.2579
32	37.4941	44.2270	52.5028	62.7015	75.2988	90.8898	110.2182	134.2135	164.0370	201.1378	304.8477	304.8477	465.8202	465.8202	577.1005	715.7475	888.4494	1103.4960	1371.1511	1704.1095
33	38.8690	46.1116	55.0778	66.2095	80.0638	97.3432	118.9334	145.9506	179.8003	222.2515	342.4294	342.4294	532.0350	532.0350	664.6655	831.2671	1040.4858	1303.1253	1632.6698	2045.9314

(continued)

Table B.3 (continued)

Periods (n)	1.0 %	2.0 %	3.0 %	4.0 %	5.0 %	6.0 %	7.0 %	8.0 %	9.0 %	10.0 %	11.0 %	12.0 %	13.0 %	14.0 %	15.0 %	16.0 %	17.0 %	18.0 %	19.0 %	20.0 %
34	40.2577	48.0338	57.7302	69.8579	85.0670	104.1838	128.2588	158.6267	196.9823	245.4767	384.5210	384.5210	607.5199	607.5199	765.3654	965.2698	1218.3684	1538.6878	1943.8771	2456.1176
35	41.6603	49.9945	60.4621	73.6522	90.3203	111.4348	138.2369	172.3168	215.7108	271.0244	431.6635	431.6635	693.5727	693.5727	881.1702	1120.7130	1426.4910	1816.6516	2314.2137	2948.3411
36	43.0769	51.9944	63.2759	77.5983	95.8363	119.1209	148.9135	187.1021	236.1247	299.1268	484.4631	484.4631	791.6729	791.6729	1014.3457	1301.0270	1669.9945	2144.6489	2754.9143	3539.0094
37	44.5076	54.0343	66.1742	81.7022	101.6281	127.2681	160.3374	203.0703	258.3759	330.0395	543.5987	543.5987	903.5071	903.5071	1167.4975	1510.1914	1954.8936	2531.6857	3279.3481	4247.8112
38	45.9527	56.1149	69.1594	85.9703	107.7095	135.9042	172.5610	220.3159	282.6298	364.0434	609.8305	609.8305	1030.9981	1030.9981	1343.6222	1752.8220	2288.2255	2988.3891	3903.4242	5098.3735
39	47.4123	58.2372	72.2342	90.4091	114.0950	145.0585	185.6403	238.9412	309.0665	401.4478	684.0102	684.0102	1176.3378	1176.3378	1546.1655	2034.2735	2678.2238	3527.2992	4646.0748	6119.0482
40	48.8864	60.4020	75.4013	95.0255	120.7998	154.7620	199.6351	259.0565	337.8824	442.5926	767.0914	767.0914	1342.0251	1342.0251	1779.0903	2360.7572	3134.5218	4163.2130	5529.8290	7343.8578

Table B.4 Future value of an annuity due of US$1 at '*n*' period

$$FV_{\text{annuity due}} = C\left[\frac{(1+r)^n - 1}{r}\right](1+r)$$

Periods (*n*)	1%	2%	3%	4%	5%	6%	7%	8%	9%	10%	11%	12%	13%	14%	15%	16%	17%	18%	19%	20%
1	1.0100	1.0200	1.0300	1.0400	1.0500	1.0600	1.0700	1.0800	1.0900	1.1000	1.1100	1.1200	1.1300	1.1400	1.1500	1.1600	1.1700	1.1800	1.1900	1.2000
2	2.0301	2.0604	2.0909	2.1216	2.1525	2.1836	2.2149	2.2464	2.2781	2.3100	2.3421	2.3744	2.4069	2.4396	2.4725	2.5056	2.5389	2.5724	2.6061	2.6400
3	3.0604	3.1216	3.1836	3.2465	3.3101	3.3746	3.4399	3.5061	3.5731	3.6410	3.7097	3.7793	3.8498	3.9211	3.9934	4.0665	4.1405	4.2154	4.2913	4.3680
4	4.1010	4.2040	4.3091	4.4163	4.5256	4.6371	4.7507	4.8666	4.9847	5.1051	5.2278	5.3528	5.4803	5.6101	5.7424	5.8771	6.0144	6.1542	6.2966	6.4416
5	5.1520	5.3081	5.4684	5.6330	5.8019	5.9753	6.1533	6.3359	6.5233	6.7156	6.9129	7.1152	7.3227	7.5355	7.7537	7.9775	8.2068	8.4420	8.6830	8.9299
6	6.2135	6.4343	6.6625	6.8983	7.1420	7.3938	7.6540	7.9228	8.2004	8.4872	8.7833	9.0890	9.4047	9.7305	10.0668	10.4139	10.7720	11.1415	11.5227	11.9159
7	7.2857	7.5830	7.8923	8.2142	8.5491	8.8975	9.2598	9.6366	10.0285	10.4359	10.8594	11.2997	11.7573	12.2328	12.7268	13.2401	13.7733	14.3270	14.9020	15.4991
8	8.3685	8.7546	9.1591	9.5828	10.0266	10.4913	10.9780	11.4876	12.0210	12.5795	13.1640	13.7757	14.4157	15.0853	15.7858	16.5185	17.2847	18.0859	18.9234	19.7989
9	9.4622	9.9497	10.4639	11.0061	11.5779	12.1808	12.8164	13.4866	14.1929	14.9374	15.7220	16.5487	17.4197	18.3373	19.3037	20.3215	21.3931	22.5213	23.7089	24.9587
10	10.5668	11.1687	11.8078	12.4864	13.2068	13.9716	14.7836	15.6455	16.5603	17.5312	18.5614	19.6546	20.8143	22.0445	23.3493	24.7329	26.1999	27.7551	29.4035	31.1504
11	11.6825	12.4121	13.1920	14.0258	14.9171	15.8699	16.8885	17.9771	19.1407	20.3843	21.7132	23.1331	24.6502	26.2707	28.0017	29.8502	31.8239	33.9311	36.1802	38.5805
12	12.8093	13.6803	14.6178	15.6268	16.7130	17.8821	19.1406	20.4953	21.9534	23.5227	25.2116	27.0291	28.9847	31.0887	33.3519	35.7862	38.4040	41.2187	44.2445	47.4966
13	13.9474	14.9739	16.0863	17.2919	18.5986	20.0151	21.5505	23.2149	25.0192	26.9750	29.0949	31.3926	33.8827	36.5811	39.5047	42.6720	46.1027	49.8180	53.8409	58.1959
14	15.0969	16.2934	17.5989	19.0236	20.5786	22.2760	24.1290	26.1521	28.3609	30.7725	33.4054	36.2797	39.4175	42.8424	46.5804	50.6595	55.1101	59.9653	65.2607	71.0351
15	16.2579	17.6393	19.1569	20.8245	22.6575	24.6725	26.8881	29.3243	32.0034	34.9497	38.1899	41.7533	45.6717	49.9804	54.7175	59.9250	65.6488	71.9390	78.8502	86.4421
16	17.4304	19.0121	20.7616	22.6975	24.8404	27.2129	29.8402	32.7502	35.9737	39.5447	43.5008	47.8837	52.7391	58.1176	64.0751	70.6730	77.9792	86.0680	95.0218	104.9306
17	18.6147	20.4123	22.4144	24.6454	27.1324	29.9057	32.9990	36.4502	40.3013	44.5992	49.3959	54.7497	60.7251	67.3941	74.8364	83.1407	92.4056	102.7403	114.2659	127.1167
18	19.8109	21.8406	24.1169	26.6712	29.5390	32.7600	36.3790	40.4463	45.0185	50.1591	55.9395	62.4397	69.7494	77.9692	87.2118	97.6032	109.2846	122.4135	137.1664	153.7400
19	21.0190	23.2974	25.8704	28.7781	32.0660	35.7856	39.9955	44.7620	50.1601	56.2750	63.2028	71.0524	79.9468	90.0249	101.4436	114.3797	129.0329	145.6280	164.4180	185.6880
20	22.2392	24.7833	27.6765	30.9692	34.7193	38.9927	43.8652	49.4229	55.7645	63.0025	71.2651	80.6987	91.4699	103.7684	117.8101	133.8405	152.1385	173.0210	196.8474	224.0256
21	23.4716	26.2990	29.5368	33.2480	37.5052	42.3923	48.0057	54.4568	61.8733	70.4027	80.2143	91.5026	104.4910	119.4360	136.6316	156.4150	179.1721	205.3448	235.4385	270.0307
22	24.7163	27.8450	31.4529	35.6179	40.4305	45.9958	52.4361	59.8933	68.5319	78.5430	90.1479	103.6029	119.2048	137.2970	158.2764	182.6014	210.8013	243.4868	281.3618	325.2369
23	25.9735	29.4219	33.4265	38.0826	43.5020	49.8156	57.1767	65.7648	75.7898	87.4973	101.1742	117.1552	135.8315	157.6586	183.1678	212.9776	247.8076	288.4945	336.0105	391.4842
24	27.2432	31.0303	35.4593	40.6459	46.7271	53.8645	62.2490	72.1059	83.7009	97.3471	113.4133	132.3339	154.6196	180.8708	211.7930	248.2140	291.1049	341.6035	401.0425	470.9811
25	28.5256	32.6709	37.5530	43.3117	50.1135	58.1564	67.6765	78.9544	92.3240	108.1818	126.9988	149.3339	175.8501	207.3327	244.7120	289.0883	341.7627	404.2721	478.4306	566.3773
26	29.8209	34.3443	39.7096	46.0842	53.6691	62.7058	73.4838	86.3508	101.7231	120.0999	142.0786	168.3740	199.8406	237.4993	282.5688	336.5024	401.0323	478.2211	570.5224	680.8528
27	31.1291	36.0512	41.9309	48.9676	57.4026	67.5281	79.6977	94.3388	111.9682	133.2099	158.8173	189.6989	226.9499	271.8892	326.1041	391.5028	470.3778	565.4809	680.1116	818.2233
28	32.4504	37.7922	44.2189	51.9663	61.3227	72.6398	86.3465	102.9659	123.1354	147.6309	177.3972	213.5828	257.5834	311.0937	376.1697	455.3032	551.5121	668.4475	810.5228	983.0680
29	33.7849	39.5681	46.5754	55.0849	65.4388	78.0582	93.4608	112.2832	135.3075	163.4940	198.0209	240.3327	292.1992	355.7868	433.7451	529.3117	646.4391	789.9480	965.7122	1180.8816
30	35.1327	41.3794	49.0027	58.3283	69.7608	83.8017	101.0730	122.3459	148.5752	180.9434	220.9132	270.2926	331.3151	406.7370	499.9569	615.1616	757.5038	933.3186	1150.3875	1418.2579
31	36.4941	43.2270	51.5028	61.7015	74.2988	89.8898	109.2182	133.2135	163.0370	200.1378	246.3236	303.8477	375.5161	464.8202	576.1005	714.7475	887.4494	1102.4960	1370.1511	1703.1095
32	37.8690	45.1116	54.0778	65.2095	79.0638	96.3432	117.9334	144.9506	178.8003	221.2515	274.5292	341.4294	425.4632	531.0350	663.6655	830.2671	1039.4858	1302.1253	1631.6698	2044.9314
33	39.2577	47.0338	56.7302	68.8579	84.0670	103.1838	127.2588	157.6267	195.9823	244.4767	305.8374	383.5210	481.9034	606.5199	764.3654	964.2698	1217.3684	1537.6878	1942.8771	2455.1176
34	40.6603	48.9945	59.4621	72.6522	89.3203	110.4348	137.2369	171.3168	214.7108	270.0244	340.5896	430.6635	545.6808	692.5727	880.1702	1119.7130	1425.4910	1815.6516	2313.2137	2947.3411

(*continued*)

Table B.4 (continued)

Periods (n)	1 %	2 %	3 %	4 %	5 %	6 %	7 %	8 %	9 %	10 %	11 %	12 %	13 %	14 %	15 %	16 %	17 %	18 %	19 %	20 %
35	42.0769	50.9944	62.2759	76.5983	94.8363	118.1209	147.9135	186.1021	235.1247	298.1268	379.1644	483.4631	617.7493	790.6729	1013.3457	1300.0270	1668.9945	2143.6489	2753.9143	3538.0094
36	43.5076	53.0343	65.1742	80.7022	100.6281	126.2681	159.3374	202.0703	257.3759	329.0395	421.9825	542.5987	699.1867	902.5071	1166.4975	1509.1914	1953.8936	2530.6857	3278.3481	4246.8112
37	44.9527	55.1149	68.1594	84.9703	106.7095	134.9042	171.5610	219.3159	281.6298	363.0434	469.5106	608.8305	791.2110	1029.9981	1342.6222	1751.8220	2287.2255	2987.3891	3902.4242	5097.3735
38	46.4123	57.2372	71.2342	89.4091	113.0950	144.0585	184.6403	237.9412	308.0665	400.4478	522.2667	683.0102	895.1984	1175.3378	1545.1655	2033.2735	2677.2238	3526.2992	4645.0748	6118.0482
39	47.8864	59.4020	74.4013	94.0255	119.7998	153.7620	198.6351	258.0565	336.8824	441.5926	580.8261	766.0914	1012.7042	1341.0251	1778.0903	2359.7572	3133.5218	4162.2130	5528.8290	7342.8578
40	49.3752	61.6100	77.6633	98.8265	126.8398	164.0477	213.6096	279.7810	368.2919	486.8518	645.8269	859.1424	1145.4858	1529.9086	2045.9539	2738.4784	3667.3906	4912.5914	6580.4965	8812.6294

Table B.5 Present value of an ordinary annuity of US$1 at '*n*' period

$$PV_{\text{ordinary annuity}} = C\left[\frac{1-\frac{1}{(1+r)^n}}{r}\right]$$

Periods (*n*)	1 %	2 %	3 %	4 %	5 %	6 %	7 %	8 %	9 %	10 %	11 %	12 %	13 %	14 %	15 %	16 %	17 %	18 %	19 %	20 %
1	0.9901	0.9804	0.9709	0.9615	0.9524	0.9434	0.9346	0.9259	0.9174	0.9091	0.9009	0.8929	0.8850	0.8772	0.8696	0.8621	0.8547	0.8475	0.8403	0.8333
2	1.9704	1.9416	1.9135	1.8861	1.8594	1.8334	1.8080	1.7833	1.7591	1.7355	1.7125	1.6901	1.6681	1.6467	1.6257	1.6052	1.5852	1.5656	1.5465	1.5278
3	2.9410	2.8839	2.8286	2.7751	2.7232	2.6730	2.6243	2.5771	2.5313	2.4869	2.4437	2.4018	2.3612	2.3216	2.2832	2.2459	2.2096	2.1743	2.1399	2.1065
4	3.9020	3.8077	3.7171	3.6299	3.5460	3.4651	3.3872	3.3121	3.2397	3.1699	3.1024	3.0373	2.9745	2.9137	2.8550	2.7982	2.7432	2.6901	2.6386	2.5887
5	4.8534	4.7135	4.5797	4.4518	4.3295	4.2124	4.1002	3.9927	3.8897	3.7908	3.6959	3.6048	3.5172	3.4331	3.3522	3.2743	3.1993	3.1272	3.0576	2.9906
6	5.7955	5.6014	5.4172	5.2421	5.0757	4.9173	4.7665	4.6229	4.4859	4.3553	4.2305	4.1114	3.9975	3.8887	3.7845	3.6847	3.5892	3.4976	3.4098	3.3255
7	6.7282	6.4720	6.2303	6.0021	5.7864	5.5824	5.3893	5.2064	5.0330	4.8684	4.7122	4.5638	4.4226	4.2883	4.1604	4.0386	3.9224	3.8115	3.7057	3.6046
8	7.6517	7.3255	7.0197	6.7327	6.4632	6.2098	5.9713	5.7466	5.5348	5.3349	5.1461	4.9676	4.7988	4.6389	4.4873	4.3436	4.2072	4.0776	3.9544	3.8372
9	8.5660	8.1622	7.7861	7.4353	7.1078	6.8017	6.5152	6.2469	5.9952	5.7590	5.5370	5.3282	5.1317	4.9464	4.7716	4.6065	4.4506	4.3030	4.1633	4.0310
10	9.4713	8.9826	8.5302	8.1109	7.7217	7.3601	7.0236	6.7101	6.4177	6.1446	5.8892	5.6502	5.4262	5.2161	5.0188	4.8332	4.6586	4.4941	4.3389	4.1925
11	10.3676	9.7868	9.2526	8.7605	8.3064	7.8869	7.4987	7.1390	6.8052	6.4951	6.2065	5.9377	5.6869	5.4527	5.2337	5.0286	4.8364	4.6560	4.4865	4.3271
12	11.2551	10.5753	9.9540	9.3851	8.8633	8.3838	7.9427	7.5361	7.1607	6.8137	6.4924	6.1944	5.9176	5.6603	5.4206	5.1971	4.9884	4.7932	4.6105	4.4392
13	12.1337	11.3484	10.6350	9.9856	9.3936	8.8527	8.3577	7.9038	7.4869	7.1034	6.7499	6.4235	6.1218	5.8424	5.5831	5.3423	5.1183	4.9095	4.7147	4.5327
14	13.0037	12.1062	11.2961	10.5631	9.8986	9.2950	8.7455	8.2442	7.7862	7.3667	6.9819	6.6282	6.3025	6.0021	5.7245	5.4675	5.2293	5.0081	4.8023	4.6106
15	13.8651	12.8493	11.9379	11.1184	10.3797	9.7122	9.1079	8.5595	8.0607	7.6061	7.1909	6.8109	6.4624	6.1422	5.8474	5.5755	5.3242	5.0916	4.8759	4.6755
16	14.7179	13.5777	12.5611	11.6523	10.8378	10.1059	9.4466	8.8514	8.3126	7.8237	7.3792	6.9740	6.6039	6.2651	5.9542	5.6685	5.4053	5.1624	4.9377	4.7296
17	15.5623	14.2919	13.1661	12.1657	11.2741	10.4773	9.7632	9.1216	8.5436	8.0216	7.5488	7.1196	6.7291	6.3729	6.0472	5.7487	5.4746	5.2223	4.9897	4.7746
18	16.3983	14.9920	13.7535	12.6593	11.6896	10.8276	10.0591	9.3719	8.7556	8.2014	7.7016	7.2497	6.8399	6.4674	6.1280	5.8178	5.5339	5.2732	5.0333	4.8122
19	17.2260	15.6785	14.3238	13.1339	12.0853	11.1581	10.3356	9.6036	8.9501	8.3649	7.8393	7.3658	6.9380	6.5504	6.1982	5.8775	5.5845	5.3162	5.0700	4.8435
20	18.0456	16.3514	14.8775	13.5903	12.4622	11.4699	10.5940	9.8181	9.1285	8.5136	7.9633	7.4694	7.0248	6.6231	6.2593	5.9288	5.6278	5.3527	5.1009	4.8696
21	18.8570	17.0112	15.4150	14.0292	12.8212	11.7641	10.8355	10.0168	9.2922	8.6487	8.0751	7.5620	7.1016	6.6870	6.3125	5.9731	5.6648	5.3837	5.1268	4.8913
22	19.6604	17.6580	15.9369	14.4511	13.1630	12.0416	11.0612	10.2007	9.4424	8.7715	8.1757	7.6446	7.1695	6.7429	6.3587	6.0113	5.6964	5.4099	5.1486	4.9094
23	20.4558	18.2922	16.4436	14.8568	13.4886	12.3034	11.2722	10.3711	9.5802	8.8832	8.2664	7.7184	7.2297	6.7921	6.3988	6.0442	5.7234	5.4321	5.1668	4.9245
24	21.2434	18.9139	16.9355	15.2470	13.7986	12.5504	11.4693	10.5288	9.7066	8.9847	8.3481	7.7843	7.2829	6.8351	6.4338	6.0726	5.7465	5.4509	5.1822	4.9371
25	22.0232	19.5235	17.4131	15.6221	14.0939	12.7834	11.6536	10.6748	9.8226	9.0770	8.4217	7.8431	7.3300	6.8729	6.4641	6.0971	5.7662	5.4669	5.1951	4.9476
26	22.7952	20.1210	17.8768	15.9828	14.3752	13.0032	11.8258	10.8100	9.9290	9.1609	8.4881	7.8957	7.3717	6.9061	6.4906	6.1182	5.7831	5.4804	5.2060	4.9563
27	23.5596	20.7069	18.3270	16.3296	14.6430	13.2105	11.9867	10.9352	10.0266	9.2372	8.5478	7.9426	7.4086	6.9352	6.5135	6.1364	5.7975	5.4919	5.2151	4.9636
28	24.3164	21.2813	18.7641	16.6631	14.8981	13.4062	12.1371	11.0511	10.1161	9.3066	8.6016	7.9844	7.4412	6.9607	6.5335	6.1520	5.8099	5.5016	5.2228	4.9697

(*continued*)

Table B.5 (continued)

Periods (n)	1 %	2 %	3 %	4 %	5 %	6 %	7 %	8 %	9 %	10 %	11 %	12 %	13 %	14 %	15 %	16 %	17 %	18 %	19 %	20 %
29	25.0658	21.8444	19.1885	16.9837	15.1411	13.5907	12.2777	11.1584	10.1983	9.3696	8.6501	8.0218	7.4701	6.9830	6.5509	6.1656	5.8204	5.5098	5.2292	4.9747
30	25.8077	22.3965	19.6004	17.2920	15.3725	13.7648	12.4090	11.2578	10.2737	9.4269	8.6938	8.0552	7.4957	7.0027	6.5660	6.1772	5.8294	5.5168	5.2347	4.9789
31	26.5423	22.9377	20.0004	17.5885	15.5928	13.9291	12.5318	11.3498	10.3428	9.4790	8.7331	8.0850	7.5183	7.0199	6.5791	6.1872	5.8371	5.5227	5.2392	4.9824
32	27.2696	23.4683	20.3888	17.8736	15.8027	14.0840	12.6466	11.4350	10.4062	9.5264	8.7686	8.1116	7.5383	7.0350	6.5905	6.1959	5.8437	5.5277	5.2430	4.9854
33	27.9897	23.9886	20.7658	18.1476	16.0025	14.2302	12.7538	11.5139	10.4644	9.5694	8.8005	8.1354	7.5560	7.0482	6.6005	6.2034	5.8493	5.5320	5.2462	4.9878
34	28.7027	24.4986	21.1318	18.4112	16.1929	14.3681	12.8540	11.5869	10.5178	9.6086	8.8293	8.1566	7.5717	7.0599	6.6091	6.2098	5.8541	5.5356	5.2489	4.9898
35	29.4086	24.9986	21.4872	18.6646	16.3742	14.4982	12.9477	11.6546	10.5668	9.6442	8.8552	8.1755	7.5856	7.0700	6.6166	6.2153	5.8582	5.5386	5.2512	4.9915
36	30.1075	25.4888	21.8323	18.9083	16.5469	14.6210	13.0352	11.7172	10.6118	9.6765	8.8786	8.1924	7.5979	7.0790	6.6231	6.2201	5.8617	5.5412	5.2531	4.9929
37	30.7995	25.9695	22.1672	19.1426	16.7113	14.7368	13.1170	11.7752	10.6530	9.7059	8.8996	8.2075	7.6087	7.0868	6.6288	6.2242	5.8647	5.5434	5.2547	4.9941
38	31.4847	26.4406	22.4925	19.3679	16.8679	14.8460	13.1935	11.8289	10.6908	9.7327	8.9186	8.2210	7.6183	7.0937	6.6338	6.2278	5.8673	5.5452	5.2561	4.9951
39	32.1630	26.9026	22.8082	19.5845	17.0170	14.9491	13.2649	11.8786	10.7255	9.7570	8.9357	8.2330	7.6268	7.0997	6.6380	6.2309	5.8695	5.5468	5.2572	4.9959
40	32.8347	27.3555	23.1148	19.7928	17.1591	15.0463	13.3317	11.9246	10.7574	9.7791	8.9511	8.2438	7.6344	7.1050	6.6418	6.2335	5.8713	5.5482	5.2582	4.9966

Table B.6 Present value of annuity due of US$1 at '*n*' period

$$PV_{\text{annuity due}} = C\left[\frac{1-\frac{1}{(1+r)^n}}{r}\right](1+r)$$

Periods (*n*)	1 %	2 %	3 %	4 %	5 %	6 %	7 %	8 %	9 %	10 %	11 %	12 %	13 %	14 %	15 %	16 %	17 %	18 %	19 %	20 %
1	1.0000	1.0000	1.0000	1.0000	1.0000	1.0000	1.0000	1.0000	1.0000	1.0000	1.0000	1.0000	1.0000	1.0000	1.0000	1.0000	1.0000	1.0000	1.0000	1.0000
2	1.9901	1.9804	1.9709	1.9615	1.9524	1.9434	1.9346	1.9259	1.9174	1.9091	1.9009	1.8929	1.8850	1.8772	1.8696	1.8621	1.8547	1.8475	1.8403	1.8333
3	2.9704	2.9416	2.9135	2.8861	2.8594	2.8334	2.8080	2.7833	2.7591	2.7355	2.7125	2.6901	2.6681	2.6467	2.6257	2.6052	2.5852	2.5656	2.5465	2.5278
4	3.9410	3.8839	3.8286	3.7751	3.7232	3.6730	3.6243	3.5771	3.5313	3.4869	3.4437	3.4018	3.3612	3.3216	3.2832	3.2459	3.2096	3.1743	3.1399	3.1065
5	4.9020	4.8077	4.7171	4.6299	4.5460	4.4651	4.3872	4.3121	4.2397	4.1699	4.1024	4.0373	3.9745	3.9137	3.8550	3.7982	3.7432	3.6901	3.6386	3.5887
6	5.8534	5.7135	5.5797	5.4518	5.3295	5.2124	5.1002	4.9927	4.8897	4.7908	4.6959	4.6048	4.5172	4.4331	4.3522	4.2743	4.1993	4.1272	4.0576	3.9906
7	6.7955	6.6014	6.4172	6.2421	6.0757	5.9173	5.7665	5.6229	5.4859	5.3553	5.2305	5.1114	4.9975	4.8887	4.7845	4.6847	4.5892	4.4976	4.4098	4.3255
8	7.7282	7.4720	7.2303	7.0021	6.7864	6.5824	6.3893	6.2064	6.0330	5.8684	5.7122	5.5638	5.4226	5.2883	5.1604	5.0386	4.9224	4.8115	4.7057	4.6046
9	8.6517	8.3255	8.0197	7.7327	7.4632	7.2098	6.9713	6.7466	6.5348	6.3349	6.1461	5.9676	5.7988	5.6389	5.4873	5.3436	5.2072	5.0776	4.9544	4.8372
10	9.5660	9.1622	8.7861	8.4353	8.1078	7.8017	7.5152	7.2469	6.9952	6.7590	6.5370	6.3282	6.1317	5.9464	5.7716	5.6065	5.4506	5.3030	5.1633	5.0310
11	10.4713	9.9826	9.5302	9.1109	8.7217	8.3601	8.0236	7.7101	7.4177	7.1446	6.8892	6.6502	6.4262	6.2161	6.0188	5.8332	5.6586	5.4941	5.3389	5.1925
12	11.3676	10.7868	10.2526	9.7605	9.3064	8.8869	8.4987	8.1390	7.8052	7.4951	7.2065	6.9377	6.6869	6.4527	6.2337	6.0286	5.8364	5.6560	5.4865	5.3271
13	12.2551	11.5753	10.9540	10.3851	9.8633	9.3838	8.9427	8.5361	8.1607	7.8137	7.4924	7.1944	6.9176	6.6603	6.4206	6.1971	5.9884	5.7932	5.6105	5.4392
14	13.1337	12.3484	11.6350	10.9856	10.3936	9.8527	9.3577	8.9038	8.4869	8.1034	7.7499	7.4235	7.1218	6.8424	6.5831	6.3423	6.1183	5.9095	5.7147	5.5327
15	14.0037	13.1062	12.2961	11.5631	10.8986	10.2950	9.7455	9.2442	8.7862	8.3667	7.9819	7.6282	7.3025	7.0021	6.7245	6.4675	6.2293	6.0081	5.8023	5.6106
16	14.8651	13.8493	12.9379	12.1184	11.3797	10.7122	10.1079	9.5595	9.0607	8.6061	8.1909	7.8109	7.4624	7.1422	6.8474	6.5755	6.3242	6.0916	5.8759	5.6755
17	15.7179	14.5777	13.5611	12.6523	11.8378	11.1059	10.4466	9.8514	9.3126	8.8237	8.3792	7.9740	7.6039	7.2651	6.9542	6.6685	6.4053	6.1624	5.9377	5.7296
18	16.5623	15.2919	14.1661	13.1657	12.2741	11.4773	10.7632	10.1216	9.5436	9.0216	8.5488	8.1196	7.7291	7.3729	7.0472	6.7487	6.4746	6.2223	5.9897	5.7746
19	17.3983	15.9920	14.7535	13.6593	12.6896	11.8276	11.0591	10.3719	9.7556	9.2014	8.7016	8.2497	7.8399	7.4674	7.1280	6.8178	6.5339	6.2732	6.0333	5.8122
20	18.2260	16.6785	15.3238	14.1339	13.0853	12.1581	11.3356	10.6036	9.9501	9.3649	8.8393	8.3658	7.9380	7.5504	7.1982	6.8775	6.5845	6.3162	6.0700	5.8435
21	19.0456	17.3514	15.8775	14.5903	13.4622	12.4699	11.5940	10.8181	10.1285	9.5136	8.9633	8.4694	8.0248	7.6231	7.2593	6.9288	6.6278	6.3527	6.1009	5.8696
22	19.8570	18.0112	16.4150	15.0292	13.8212	12.7641	11.8355	11.0168	10.2922	9.6487	9.0751	8.5620	8.1016	7.6870	7.3125	6.9731	6.6648	6.3837	6.1268	5.8913
23	20.6604	18.6580	16.9369	15.4511	14.1630	13.0416	12.0612	11.2007	10.4424	9.7715	9.1757	8.6446	8.1695	7.7429	7.3587	7.0113	6.6964	6.4099	6.1486	5.9094
24	21.4558	19.2922	17.4436	15.8568	14.4886	13.3034	12.2722	11.3711	10.5802	9.8832	9.2664	8.7184	8.2297	7.7921	7.3988	7.0442	6.7234	6.4321	6.1668	5.9245
25	22.2434	19.9139	17.9355	16.2470	14.7986	13.5504	12.4693	11.5288	10.7066	9.9847	9.3481	8.7843	8.2829	7.8351	7.4338	7.0726	6.7465	6.4509	6.1822	5.9371
26	23.0232	20.5235	18.4131	16.6221	15.0939	13.7834	12.6536	11.6748	10.8226	10.0770	9.4217	8.8431	8.3300	7.8729	7.4641	7.0971	6.7662	6.4669	6.1951	5.9476
27	23.7952	21.1210	18.8768	16.9828	15.3752	14.0032	12.8258	11.8100	10.9290	10.1609	9.4881	8.8957	8.3717	7.9061	7.4906	7.1182	6.7831	6.4804	6.2060	5.9563
28	24.5596	21.7069	19.3270	17.3296	15.6430	14.2105	12.9867	11.9352	11.0266	10.2372	9.5478	8.9426	8.4086	7.9352	7.5135	7.1364	6.7975	6.4919	6.2151	5.9636

(*continued*)

Table B.6 (continued)

Periods (*n*)	1 %	2 %	3 %	4 %	5 %	6 %	7 %	8 %	9 %	10 %	11 %	12 %	13 %	14 %	15 %	16 %	17 %	18 %	19 %	20 %
29	25.3164	22.2813	19.7641	17.6631	15.8981	14.4062	13.1371	12.0511	11.1161	10.3066	9.6016	8.9844	8.4412	7.9607	7.5335	7.1520	6.8099	6.5016	6.2228	5.9697
30	26.0658	22.8444	20.1885	17.9837	16.1411	14.5907	13.2777	12.1584	11.1983	10.3696	9.6501	9.0218	8.4701	7.9830	7.5509	7.1656	6.8204	6.5098	6.2292	5.9747
31	26.8077	23.3965	20.6004	18.2920	16.3725	14.7648	13.4090	12.2578	11.2737	10.4269	9.6938	9.0552	8.4957	8.0027	7.5660	7.1772	6.8294	6.5168	6.2347	5.9789
32	27.5423	23.9377	21.0004	18.5885	16.5928	14.9291	13.5318	12.3498	11.3428	10.4790	9.7331	9.0850	8.5183	8.0199	7.5791	7.1872	6.8371	6.5227	6.2392	5.9824
33	28.2696	24.4683	21.3888	18.8736	16.8027	15.0840	13.6466	12.4350	11.4062	10.5264	9.7686	9.1116	8.5383	8.0350	7.5905	7.1959	6.8437	6.5277	6.2430	5.9854
34	28.9897	24.9886	21.7658	19.1476	17.0025	15.2302	13.7538	12.5139	11.4644	10.5694	9.8005	9.1354	8.5560	8.0482	7.6005	7.2034	6.8493	6.5320	6.2462	5.9878
35	29.7027	25.4986	22.1318	19.4112	17.1929	15.3681	13.8540	12.5869	11.5178	10.6086	9.8293	9.1566	8.5717	8.0599	7.6091	7.2098	6.8541	6.5356	6.2489	5.9898
36	30.4086	25.9986	22.4872	19.6646	17.3742	15.4982	13.9477	12.6546	11.5668	10.6442	9.8552	9.1755	8.5856	8.0700	7.6166	7.2153	6.8582	6.5386	6.2512	5.9915
37	31.1075	26.4888	22.8323	19.9083	17.5469	15.6210	14.0352	12.7172	11.6118	10.6765	9.8786	9.1924	8.5979	8.0790	7.6231	7.2201	6.8617	6.5412	6.2531	5.9929
38	31.7995	26.9695	23.1672	20.1426	17.7113	15.7368	14.1170	12.7752	11.6530	10.7059	9.8996	9.2075	8.6087	8.0868	7.6288	7.2242	6.8647	6.5434	6.2547	5.9941
39	32.4847	27.4406	23.4925	20.3679	17.8679	15.8460	14.1935	12.8289	11.6908	10.7327	9.9186	9.2210	8.6183	8.0937	7.6338	7.2278	6.8673	6.5452	6.2561	5.9951
40	33.1630	27.9026	23.8082	20.5845	18.0170	15.9491	14.2649	12.8786	11.7255	10.7570	9.9357	9.2330	8.6268	8.0997	7.6380	7.2309	6.8695	6.5468	6.2572	5.9959

Glossary

Aa

Accounting rate of return (ARR) It is the average return from income generated over the life of an investment. It is used in investment appraisal and is determined as the average annual income from the project divided by the average cost of the project.

Accounts payable It is the obligations of the firm resulting from the purchase of goods and services on credit.

Accounts payable management Set of policies, procedures and practices employed to manage credit purchases and other payables by the firm.

Accounts receivable It is money owed to a firm from the sale of its goods and services in the normal course of business.

Accounts (Average) receivable collection period A ratio that indicates the average length of time that the firm must wait after making sale before receiving cash. It is calculated as the number of days in a year divided by accounts receivable turnover.

Accounts receivable management This entails establishing policies to ensure optimum investment in debtors, through controlled credit allowed to customers.

Accounts receivable turnover A ratio that determines how fast a firm is turning its credit sales into cash. It indicates the number of times in a year a firm collects its average accounts receivable and is calculated as credit sales divided by accounts receivable.

Accrued liabilities These are expenses that have already been incurred by a firm but not yet paid for. Could be short or long-term liabilities on the firm's statement of financial position.

Acid test ratio A ratio that measures the ability of the firm to use its near cash conversion assets to pay off current liabilities as and when they fall due.

J.Y. Abor, *Entrepreneurial Finance for MSMEs*,
DOI 10.1007/978-3-319-34021-0

Activity (efficiency) ratios These are ratios that examine the efficiency with which a firm's management uses its assets and capital.

Acquisition This is a situation when one firm takes over another.

Adverse selection Where the finance provider selects wrongly because the applicant has information about the success or otherwise of a project that is not available to the finance provider.

Aging of accounts receivable This involves preparing an aging schedule to determine the amounts of accounts receivable, the various lengths of time for which these accounts have been due, and the proportion of accounts that fall within each time frame.

Amortisation It is the gradual writing off of a liability, such as a bank loan or the cost of a non-current asset, in regular payments over a particular period of time.

Angel investors Investors who provide equity capital to entrepreneurs or start-ups.

Annuity It is a stream of constant cash flows occurring at regular intervals over a fixed period of time.

Annuity due An annuity where same fixed payments made or received at the beginning of the period.

Assets These are the resources controlled by the entity as a result of past events, and from which future economic benefits are expected to flow to the entity.

Asset-based lending This is a type of financing where the lender gives the loan based on the borrower's assets that are used as collateral. These assets may be inventory, accounts receivable and equipment.

Bb

Balance sheet A financial position statement showing assets, capital and liabilities of a firm at a particular period of time.

Banker's acceptances Short-term debt instrument guaranteed by a bank, which is issued by a firm as part of a commercial transaction.

Bankruptcy A state of insolvency where the liabilities of an entity are greater than its assets and the entity is not able to pay its debts as and when the debts fall due.

Best effort Where the investment banker simply promises to try and sell the entire issue for the issuer. The investment bank promises to use its in-house facilities, expertise and goodwill to sell the shares at the best price.

Board of directors A body of appointed or elected members who are responsible jointly to oversee the affairs of a company or an organisation.

Bond(s) A long-term debt instrument issued by an entity (company or government) purposely to raise capital by borrowing.

Book value The value of a fixed asset on a firm's books after deducting depreciation. It is also the value of a share of ordinary shares based on the amount of ordinary shares divided by the number of outstanding ordinary shares.

Bootstrapping Starting of a self-sustaining process that is supposed to proceed with the external input.

Break-even analysis A process of determining the number of units of a product that must be sold or the amount of revenue that must be made before the firm begins to make profit. It helps determine what to sell in a specific period of time to cover cost of business activities.

Break-even dollars (BE$) The dollar amount of revenue that equals the total costs. It is calculated as the fixed costs divided by one minus variable costs expressed as a percentage of net sales.

Break-even quantity (BEQ) The number of units of a product that must be produced in order to cover the total costs of production. It is calculated as fixed costs divided by sales prices minus variable costs.

Bridge financing A source of financing or credit granted by an investment bank or a venture capital until a long-term financing is arranged or an obligation is removed. Interest rates are relatively high if bridge financing is a loan.

Budget It is a projection of future financial plans expressed in numerical form, usually for a limited period.

Budgeting process The procedure by which a financial plan is created and managed by an entity.

Business angel *See* Angel investors.

Business plan A formal statement of the goals and objectives of the firm and how to meet those goals and objectives.

Buyout It is acquiring or purchasing of a controlling interest or share in a firm, especially by its own managers.

Cc

Callable preference shares These are preference shares that give the issuer the right to call or redeem the shares at a specified price after a specific date or time.

Capacity The maximum amount of loan that a client can obtain from a bank.

Capital Any economic resources measured in monetary terms used by entrepreneurs and firms to undertake production and distribution of goods and services.

Capital asset An asset owned and controlled by an entity in which benefit is derived from its use. They include long-term investments such as land and equipment.

Capital asset pricing model (CAPM) A model that describes the relationship between expected return and the risk on an investment and that is used to determine the appropriate price of the investment.

Capital budgeting It is the process of analysing capital investment opportunities and deciding which ones to accept.

Capital gains The amount by which an investment or asset selling price exceeds its initial cost or purchase price.

Capital intensive When a firm invests heavily in machinery and equipment and has low labour cost.

Capital market A financial market where long-term securities such as shares and bonds are traded.

Capital rationing The process of allocating capital among different investment projects as a strategy to maximise shareholders wealth as a result of capital constraints.

Cash Money in the form of current notes and coins.

Cash management It involves exercising control over cash position so as to keep the firm sufficiently liquid and profitable.

Cash budget This is a financial projection of a firm's cash receipts and disbursements for a specified future time period.

Cash discount A deduction allowed by a goods seller or by services provider in order to induce customers to pay within a particular period of time. For example 3/20 net 60

Cash equivalent An asset that is easily converted into cash. Examples are Treasury bill and certificates of deposit (CDs).

Cash flow Movement of money in or out of a business, product or project within a particular period of time.

Cash flow from financing activities Section of the cash flow statement that shows the cash inflow and outflow pertaining to transactions with finance providers of a firm. Includes cash received from the issuance of shares, proceeds from short and long-term borrowings, repayment of loans and redeeming shares.

Cash flow from investing activities Section of the cash flow statement that shows the long-term investments of the firm. It includes cash paid for acquisition and cash received from sale of investments.

Cash flow from operating activities Section of the cash flow statement that provides information on the cash flows inflows and outflows from the firm's usual business activities such as the production of goods and the rendering of services.

Cash flow statement A financial statement that indicates how changes in the balance sheet accounts and income affect cash and cash equivalents, and shows the operating, investing and financing activities.

Cash management This is concerned with managing cash flows and cash balances of the firm.

Certificates of deposit (CDs) Promissory notes or certificates issued by a bank to a client who deposits money for a specified length of time at an agreed rate of interest.

Character One of the key factors considered in evaluating a customer's or loan applicant's credit history and reputation.

Credit unions They are financial institutions or intermediaries owned by members with a common bond.

Collateral A specified asset pledged as a subordinate security by a borrower or a guarantor. It could be a landed property or business cash flow.

Collection float The amount of time that elapses between an entity depositing a debtor's cheque and the cheque clearing at the bank.

Collection policy This refers to the procedures that the firm follows for obtaining payment for goods and services previously sold to customers on credit and which have become due.

Commercial paper A short-term promissory note issued by corporate institutions or reputable companies to raise working capital. It could be unsecured or secured by assets.

Compound interest An interest added to the principal of a loan so that the additional interest also earns interest. Interest earned on both the principal amount and the previously accrued interest of an investment

Contractual savings institutions These are financial institutions that acquire funds periodically on a contractual basis and promise their clients future compensation.

Contribution margin The excess of sales per unit over variable cost per unit.

Controlling Involves establishing standards for measuring a project, measuring actual performance of the project against the standards that have been set up, and taking corrective measures to remedy the situation.

Convertible preference shares Preference shares that give the owner the option to convert the shares to ordinary shares at particular period of time.

Corporate bond A bond issued by a company with the intention of borrowing money to finance projects.

Company (Corporation) A legal entity that is given rights similar to that of the individual and with separate affairs different from that of its owners. A company can sue and be sued.

Commercial banks They are financial intermediaries that take deposits from the public and give out short-, medium- and long-term loans to individual and businesses.

Cost of goods sold (COGS) Accumulated cost of all inputs used to create a product or service, which has been sold.

Coupon rate Periodic percentage amount of interest paid on the face value of a bond.

Creditor An entity could be an individual supplier or a bank that has provided credit to a firm. Amount owed to creditors are reported as part of liabilities on the balance sheet of statement of financial position.

Credit evaluation A method of determining the credit worthiness of a borrower based on established standards.

Credit terms These are the requirements that a firm puts in place for the use of credit by its customers. The credit terms would typically specify the credit period, the discount period and the discount rate.

Cumulative discounts Discount offered to a customer by a vendor based on the aggregate quantity of goods purchased by the customer in the fiscal year of the vendor.

Cumulative preference shares Preferred shares, which entitle the holder or owner to receive dividend for previous years where a company did not pay dividend.

Current assets These are assets that have a useful life of less than one year. Examples, inventory, accounts receivables and cash.

Current liabilities These are all obligations that a firm is expected to pay within the accounting year. Examples include; notes payable, taxes payable, account payable.

Current ratio A liquidity ratio of total current assets to total current liabilities. It is calculated as current assets divided by current liabilities.

Dd

Debenture A corporate bond that is not backed by the company's collateral.

Debt-to-equity ratio A ratio that indicates the proportion of the owner's equity that is debt. It is calculated by dividing total liabilities by owner's equity.

Debt ratio A ratio of total debt to total assets expressed in terms of percentages and can be interpreted as a proportion of the total assets of a firm financed with debt.

Debt-to-total-assets ratio A ratio that indicates the total assets financed with total debt. It is the ratio of total liabilities to total assets.

Depository institutions They are financial intermediaries that accept deposits from individuals and institutions and also give out loans.

Depreciation It is the wear and tear of the tangible fixed assets during the useful life of the asset.

Development capital Capital used to further launch the business and grow market share so as to increase profitability.

Development finance institution (DFIs) These are alternative financial institutions including, microfinance institutions, state development banks and community development institutions which provide long-term loans, equity finance and risk guarantee instruments to private investments in developing countries.

Disbursement float It is the time that elapses between payment by an entity and the time that the cheque actually clears at the bank and the funds moves out of entity's bank account.

Discount rate It is the minimum interest rate set by the central bank for lending to other banks.

Dividend The proportion of net profit after tax paid to the shareholders of a firm as their gain. It is usually declared by the board of directors.

Due diligence This involves the process of obtaining and verifying information associated with an investment decision.

Ee

Earnings before taxes The income of a firm before taxes are paid to the government.

Earnings per share This ratio represents the amount of a firm's income earned during the period per unit of ordinary shares.

Economic order quantity (EOQ) The quantity of goods or inventory that minimises holding cost and ordering cost. It is the most efficient quantity that minimises the overall inventory costs

Effective annual rate of interest (EAR) The annual rate of interest actually earned when compounding is considered.

Effectiveness The degree to achieve desired results of goals.

Efficiency The ability to achieve possible higher results with the minimum use of resources.

Electronic funds transfer The process used to transmit funds from one bank account to another through computer application.

Employee stock ownership plans (ESOP) A scheme set up by a firm that enables employees acquire ownership interests in an enterprise. It acts as retirement programmes for employees just that the bulk of the employee's retirement funds are invested in the shares of the employer.

Entrepreneur An individual who bears the risk of starting a business. An entrepreneur combines labour, land and capital to produce goods and services to create value in the society.

Executive summary It is the part of the business plan that summarises it in a way that helps readers know the purpose and the content of a material before reading further.

Ff

Face value *See* Par value.

Factoring It is the process of selling accounts receivable to another firm at a discount of the initial selling price.

Finance A field that deals with resource allocation as well as resource management, acquisition and investment. It involves assets and liabilities allocation over time under conditions of different degrees of uncertainty and risk. It also involves raising money through the issuance of debt and /or equity instruments.

Finance companies They are non-depository financial institutions that acquire funds by issuing financial instruments such as commercial paper, shares and bonds.

Financial assets Assets used to increase revenue and acquire capital assets. Examples include shares, bonds and money market securities.

Financial instrument

Financial leverage Financing the operations and projects of a firm with debt. The higher the debt financing in the capital structure of the firm, the higher its financial leverage.

Financial planning The act of establishing goals in monetary terms and developing strategies to realise them.

Finished goods These are goods or inventory that have gone through all the production processes and are ready to be sold or distributed to retailers and consumers.

Firm commitment (Bought deal) This involves the investment banker buying the entire issue from the issuer and reselling this to its clients.

Fixed assets These are assets that have a useful life of more than one accounting year. They are also known as tangible assets.

Fixed asset turnover A ratio that measures the ability of the business to use fixed assets to generate revenue. It is calculated by dividing net sales by total fixed assets.

Fixed costs These are costs that do not vary with output.

Fixed expenses These are expenses that a firm has limited or no control over such as rent, mortgage payments, insurance, property taxes and income taxes.

Float Used sometimes to describe the amount of money tied up between the time when a payment is initiated (e.g. when a customer sends a cheque in payment, probably through the mailing system) and the time when the funds become available for use in the recipient's bank account.

Forecast A quantitative future estimate.

Forecasting The process of making a forecast.

Financial institutions These are financial intermediaries that ensure the transfer of funds between the savers and the borrowers.

Financial regulators These are government institutions that regulate the financial market to maintain financial market stability and to promote financial market efficiency.

Financial markets They are markets where financial instruments are traded.

Franchise A business practice in which a firm (franchisee) acquires the right to sell the goods and services of another (franchiser) for a specific period of time.

Gg

General partner The partner in charge of the day-to-day operations of the partnership firm.

Generally accepted accounting principles (GAAP) These are rules, guidelines, standards and procedures that govern accounting practices.

Goals These are measurable objectives that can be realised within a specific time frame.

Gross income The accumulated amount of money received from all sources of income of an entity during the year.

Gross profit The amount left after cost of sales has been deducted from net sales.

Gross profit margin A ratio used to determine the amount of gross profit generated by each dollar of net sales.

Gross working capital This is the aggregate of current assets of a business, which include inventory, receivables, cash and marketable securities and prepayments.

Group-based lending This is a lending model used by microfinance institutions in which loans are given to members in a group and the entire group is liable if a single member of the group defaults or does not pay the loan that has been taken.

Growth capital Capital for financing the expansion of the business in areas such as launching into foreign markets, creating new product/ technology lines, accelerating production and/or acquiring competitors.

Hh

Harvesting This is the final stage of investment, where the entrepreneurs or initial investors liquidate their investments.

Horizontal analysis The process of determining the percentage change in an account on the face of the financial statement by using a base time period to subsequent time periods.

Human resource (labour) The set of individuals that form the workforce of a firm, an organisation or an entity.

Ii

Income statement A financial statement that measures the performance or the operations of a business over a particular accounting period. It matches the revenue, income and expenditure within the accounting period.

Individual banking is when the MFI lends to individuals and the individual is responsible for repaying the loan. In this case, the liability rests on the applicant and cannot be passed on to other people.

Inflation It is an increase in the general prices of goods and services. It is mostly measured by the Consumer Price Index (CPI).

Information asymmetry A situation in which a party in a transaction has superior information relative to the other.

Informal finance This involves financial activities and services that take place beyond the scope of a country's formal financial institutions and lie outside financial sector regulations.

Initial public offering (IPO) This is the first offer or sale of shares by a private firm to the public.

Insurance It is the promise of compensation for particular future losses in exchange of a premium (periodic payment).

Insurance companies Financial institutions that receive premiums by selling insurance policies and also invest the funds to earn sufficient funds to meet insurance compensation.

Interest The amount of money paid to a lender for a credit used by a borrower.

Interest expense This is interest accrued during the accounting period on amount borrowed by an entity. It is usually shown on the income statement.

Internal rate of return (IRR) The discount rate that gives a zero net present value of an investment. It is the discount rate that equates the present value to the cost of the investment.

Interpolation The use of mathematics to find an unknown figure that lies within two known figures.

Inventory The items a firm has in stock not yet sold.

Inventory management It is concerned with ensuring that sufficient levels of inventory or stock are maintained in order to meet the demand of customers while minimising the associated holding, administrative and stock out costs

Inventory turnover A ratio that indicates how efficient a firm uses its inventory to generate revenue.

Investment banks These are financial institutions that raise funds through the issue of debt and equity securities in the money and capital markets for firms and government.

Investment companies These are financial intermediaries that issue their own shares to the investing public and use the funds they raise to invest in a diversified portfolio of securities.

Invoicing discounting It involves obtaining finance and using the sales debtors as security.

Jj

Joint venture The coming together of separate entities to undertake a business activity with the goal of making profit.

Just-in-time model An inventory system that aims at obtaining inventory from suppliers at the point when they are needed, and so avoiding the need to carry any materials or components stock. This inventory management system attempts to match physical need with inventory at the point in time the inventory is needed.

Ll

Labour intensive Where a firm has relatively low investment in machinery and has relatively high labour costs as a proportion of it production costs.

Land It is naturally occurred resources whose supply is fixed.

Leasing This is an agreement in which one party (lessee) agrees to rent property from another party (lessor).

Leverage (debt) ratios A ratio that indicates what proportion of the assets of the firm belongs to the owners and creditors.

Leverage, financial The percentage change in earnings per share as a result of the percentage change in operating income.

Leverage, operating The percentage change in operating income as a result of the percentage change in sales.

Liabilities The future obligations of the firm as a result of past transactions or events with economic benefit.

LIBOR London Interbank offered rate

Life insurance A contract between the insured and the insurer, where the insurer promises to pay the insured an amount of money upon the death or incapacitation of the insured in exchange for a premium.

Life insurance companies They are insurance companies that insure people against financial hazards following death or incapacitation. They raise funds from the premiums paid by policyholders and the funds they acquire are then invested in securities.

Limited liability company A company in which the liability of the owners is limited to the amount of capital they have invested in the company.

Limited partner A partner who is not involved in the daily operations of the partnership and whose liability is limited to the amount of capital he/she has invested.

Limited partnership A partnership agreement where partners have the liabilities of partners limited to their capital contribution.

Line of credit A credit limit extended to a firm that may be drawn upon by the firm when required.

Liquidity The degree by which an asset can be converted to cash.

Liquidity ratios These are ratios that determine how a firm's current assets can cover its current liabilities.

Lockbox Financial services offered by banks to firms and other organisation in order to simplify the collection and processing of receivables by keeping the customers of the firms and organisations informed about sending their cheque to a location easily accessible by the bank.

Long-term debt A debt owed by a firm, which is not expected to be paid within the current accounting year.

Mm

Management The process of working through or with people to realise a specific goal by effective and efficient use of resources.

Management buyout *See* Buyout.

Marginal The additional unit of output added by employing another unit of input.

Marginal cost The additional cost of hiring an additional labour or the cost of producing one more unit of output.

Market An organised effort or arrangement where buyers and sellers meet to exchange goods and services.

Market ratios These are used by investors to determine whether to invest their funds in a firm in exchange of ownership.

Market research An organised effort to gather information about customers or a target market through surveys, tests and observation.

Market value The selling price of something in a particular market. It is the value of a share of ordinary shares that an investor is willing to pay in the marketplace.

Marketable securities These include Treasury bills, bonds and shares which are easily traded on the financial market.

Marketing plan A business plan, which describes or specifies how a firm intends to move products or services from production to customers or consumers.

Maturity value *See* Par value.

Mergers The combination of two different firms to become one.

Mezzanine finance A type of finance with features of both debt and equity. It is debt finance that can be converted into an equity interest.

Microcredit This is the provision of small loans to low-income or poor individuals, households and other economic entities with little or no collateral.

Microfinance This is the provision of financial services to low-income clients and micro-enterprises that often do not have access to formal financial services.

Microfinance institution (MFIs) These are institutions that are dedicated to providing financial services to small businesses and those who have no access to conventional banking services.

Micro-saving This is a microfinance service that allows the poor and low-income earners to safeguard money and other valuable items and even earn an interest.

Mission statement A statement that explains the purpose and the principles of a firm.

Monetary policy The process of controlling the supply of money in a country with the aim of managing inflation rate in order to stabilise price and also build confidence in the local currency.

Money market A financial market where short-term securities such as shares and bonds are traded.

Moral hazards An instance where the borrower applies the funds for a different purpose other than the purpose for which the funds were sourced.

Mutual Funds These are investment companies that raise funds by issuing their own shares and invest the funds in diversified portfolios of shares, bonds and other securities.

Money Market Mutual Funds These are a form of mutual funds that focus on money market instruments such as Treasury bills and commercial paper.

Mutually exclusive A situation where the occurrence of an event prevents the occurrence of the other. It is impossible for mutually exclusive events to happen at the same time.

Nn

Negotiable Certificates of Deposits (NCDs) These are short-term marketable securities issued by banks and savings and loans institutions to raise additional deposits. Investments in NCDs are for a specified period of time at a specified fixed or variable interest rate. They are negotiable because investors can negotiate on the terms of the issue.

Net income The earnings after taxes, interest and deductions of other expenses.

Net present value (NPV) It is the sum of present values of cash inflows and out flows over a period of time.

Net profit margin A ratio that measures how much a firm earned on each dollar of net sales after payment of interest and taxes. It is calculated as net profit divided by net sales.

Net return on assets (ROA) A ratio that shows how much a firm earns on each dollar in assets after payment of interest and taxes. It is calculated as net profit divided by total assets. It is also, known as return on investment (ROI).

Net sales Gross sales or revenue less returns and allowance.

Net working capital This is the difference between total current assets and total current liabilities of an entity. It is a measure of the entity's liquidity.

Net worth The assets of an entity less its liabilities.

Non-life insurance companies They are insurance that insure their policyholders against general casualty apart from life, such as loss from theft, fire, and accidents.

Notes payable A promise to pay a creditor an amount owed with interest for a specified period of time, normally within a year.

Oo

Open market operation (OMO) A tool of monetary policy that involves the purchase and sale of securities by the central bank.

Operational self sufficiency (OSS) A ratio that measures the ability of the microfinance institution to cover its operating expenses given its operational income.

Operating expenses These are costs associated with a firm's operating activities and reported on the income statement.

Operating income The excess of gross profit over operating expenses and reported on an income statement.

Operating profit margin *See* Gross profit margin

Operating return on assets This measures how much a firm earns on each unit of an asset prior to the payment of interest and taxes. It is calculated as operating income divided by total assets.

Opportunity costs The value of next highest alternative forgone in order to make a decision.

Ordinary annuity An annuity where same fixed payments are made or received at the end of a particular period.

Ordinary shares (Common stock) These are shares issued by companies (either public or private) to raise long-term capital (equity). Ordinary shares represent ownership right in the company and shareholders have voting rights.

Organised markets These are markets with comprehensive regulatory framework with traders linked to one platform.

Organising An orderly process of defining, structuring, integrating the activities and resources of an enterprise in order to realise specific objectives.

Over-the-counter market (OTC) This is a largely unregulated market, whereby geographically dispersed traders, who are linked to one another via telecommunication systems and computers, trade in securities.

Owners' equity The net worth of the firm or an entity. It is calculated by deducting total liabilities from total asset.

Pp

Par value The value by which a bond or a share is issued or can be redeemed.

Partnership An arrangement where parties carry out a business as owners with the aim of making profit.

Payback A method used in capital budgeting to determine the period within which the initial cost of investment of a project can be recouped.

Percentage of sales method for calculating a pro forma balance sheet A method of calculating a pro forma balance sheet based on the fact the assets and liabilities vary with sales.

Percentages sales method for determining new financing A method of determining the amount of new source of finance for a firm in the future based on the fact that asset and liabilities vary with sales.

Petty cash A fund used to pay for small amount of daily expenses such as postages, transportation and stationery.

Preference shares (Preferred stock) These are shares that have the features of a bond and an ordinary share. Preference shareholders are guaranteed a percentage return on their investment as dividends but they do not have voting rights.

Pension funds They are depository institutions that provide pension benefits to retired employees by receiving regular pension contributions from the employees and their employers.

Portfolio at risk (PAR) A ratio that measures the percentage of the loan portfolio of the microfinance institution that is overdue or is likely to be exposed to significant risks in the future.

Price The cost of a product or service charged by an entity.

Price–earnings (P/E) ratio This indicates the earning per share investors are willing to pay for a share.

Primary market A market for initial issue of shares by a firm to the public.

Prime rate The lowest interest rate at which money could be borrowed from a bank.

Principal value *See* Par value.

Private company It is a company that does not sell it shares to the public and therefore has a limited number of investors or shareholders.

Private limited company *See* Private company.

Private placement This is the issue of securities to specific investors (usually large institutional investors). Under private placement, the issuing firm arranges and places the securities with few institutional investors as opposed to issuing to the general public.

Pro forma balance sheet A statement of financial position for a future period.

Pro forma cash budget A projection of the cash inflows and outflows for the future period of a firm. It usually has three sections, namely, operating, investing, and financing activities.

Pro forma income statement A financial statement that measures the performance or the operations of a business for a future period.

Proceeds The amount received after all deductions have been made out of the value of a loan. It is money received or earn out of an activity or event.

Profit An amount that is earned on an investment or from carrying out a business activity.

Profitability The return on investment. It is calculated by dividing net profit by assets.

Profitability index The ratio of payoff to the cost of investment of a proposed project. It is computed as the present value of the benefits divided by the present value of the costs. It is used to rank alternative projects in capital budgeting.

Profitability ratios These are ratios that measure the firm's ability to generate profit out of its operations to pay a return to equity and debt holders. They also measure the entity's potential to earn income in excess of its operating costs.

Public company This is a company whose ownership is opened to the general public. It can therefore offer its shares to the public and subsequently list these shares on the organised stock exchange.

Public limited company *See* Public company.

Qq

Quantity discount Type of discount offered by suppliers to customers who purchase in bulk quantities.

Quick ratio This measures the liquidity of a firm without liquidating its inventory. It is calculated by deducting inventory and prepayments from current assets and dividing by current liabilities.

Quoted rate *See* Stated rate.

Rr

Ratio The relationship between two variables expressed as a fraction.

Ratio analysis The process involved in establishing the mathematical relationship between variables and it involves comparing one figure against another to produce a ratio and assessing whether the ratio indicates a weakness or strength in an entity's affairs. It is useful for determining the health of a business.

Raw materials The type of inventory used by firm in producing final goods.

Repurchase agreements It is the sale of securities by one party to another with the agreement of repurchasing the securities at a specified price on a predetermined future date. It is also known as repo.

Reserve requirement A proportion of deposit used by banks in their daily operations without giving it out as loans. It is usually established by the central bank. Reserve requirement is either kept with the central bank or in the bank's vault.

Retained earnings The amount of a firm's profit that is not distributed as dividend to shareholders but kept for future investment.

Return on assets (ROA) *See* Return on Investment (ROI).

Return on equity (ROE) A ratio that indicates the net income as a percentage of shareholders equity. This is a profitability indicator of the firm.

Return on investment (ROI) A measure of performance used to examine the efficiency of an investment. It is used to the measure the earnings or returns of an investment relative to the cost of investment.

Revenues The amount amount of money received for undertaking a business activity over a specific period.

Risk The degree of uncertainty surrounding the returns of an investment.

Rural and Community Banks (RCBs) They are unit banks owned by members of a rural community through purchase of shares.

Ss

Salvage (residual) value The estimated resale value of an asset at the end of its estimated useful life. It is the value of an asset after depreciation over its useful life. Used as one of the variables in calculating for depreciation.

Savings and loans institutions They operate just like commercial banks but they are either mutually owned or have corporate share ownership. They also accept deposits and give out loans.

Secondary market A type of financial market where already issued financial securities are traded.

Secured debt A debt that is backed by a specific asset or resources of the firm.

Securities *See* Financial instrument.

Securities and Exchange Commission (SEC) A government institution established to protect the interest of investors and maintain the integrity of the securities market of the country.

Seed capital Capital for financing the preliminary operations such as market research and product development. Seed capital is invested in research and development before the business can start investing.

Shareholders These are individuals or institutions that legally own shares of a firm.

Short-term debt This is an obligation that is due to be paid in the current accounting year, usually one year or less.

Simple interest The amount paid (earned) on only the principal amount stated.

Sole proprietorship A form of business owned wholly by an individual who operates it for the purpose of making profit

Staffing The process of employing competent personnel in a firm to implement business plans.

Start-up capital Capital used in setting up a business venture. It is used to finance activities such as the hiring of staff, renting of office space, equipping the production system among other things.

Start-up costs The costs incurred in setting up a business such as registration charges, legal fees and employee training cost.

Stated (quoted) rate The interest rate that is listed, normally on annual basis and does not consider the effect of compounding. It is also known as listed rate.

Statement of cash flows *See* Cash flow statement

Statement of financial position *See* Balance sheet

Statement of comprehensive income *See* Income statement

Stockholders *See* Shareholders.

Stocks *See* Inventory

Strategic planning The process of developing the long-term plan of the business.

Strategic plans The long-term plans of the entire firm.

Subsidy dependence index (SDI) A ratio that measures how much average yields have to increase in order for the microfinance institution to exit subsidy dependence given its portfolio size.

Tt

Tax factor benefits The opportunity granted by the tax law for a firm to deduct or write off once a new investment is made.

Tax factor costs These are costs resulting in additional taxes that have to be paid by a firm.

Taxes These are payments made to the government in return for the goods and services it provides.

Taxes payable The accrued taxes not yet paid by the firm.

T-bill *See* Treasure bill.

Terms of credit *See* Credit terms.

Times-interest-earned This is a ratio that shows the relationship between operating income and the amount of interest to be paid on debt to creditors on yearly basis.

Time value of money The loss of value of money as a result of inflation

Total assets The aggregate of current and non-current (fixed) assets of a firm.

Trade credit This is the provision of credit by suppliers to their customers. Trade credit provides financing because the firm does not have to pay upfront.

Trade discount This is the amount deducted from the selling price of a good or service purchased by a customer.

Treasury bills Short-term debt instruments or securities issued by the central bank on behalf of government to meet the short-term needs of the government.

Trust A legal entity that has a legal persona of its own. Properties or assets placed in the trust are separate form that of its owners.

Uu

Underwriter An investment bank or a person that buys securities issued by an entity and resells them to investors.

Underwriting The process by which an investment banker purchases, packages and resells a security on behalf of a client. It is also defined as the process of determining the creditworthiness of a potential borrower by a lender or financial service provider.

Unit trusts They are investment companies, which buy a fixed, often unmanaged portfolio of securities and thereafter issue units (shares) in the trust to investors.

Unsecured debt A debt that is not supported by collateral security.

Unsystematic risk Risk that is specific to a business. It does not affect the entire market or economy.

Use assets *See* Fixed assets.

Vv

Variable costs The costs of production that varies with output level.

Variable expenses The type of expenses that an entity has control over.

Variance A deviation from the expected or the estimated.

Venture capital This is money provided by investors to start-up firms and small businesses with perceived long-term growth potential.

Venture capitalists Investors who provide funds towards the expansion and the latter stages of a business development.

Venture capital companies *See* Venture capitalists.

Vertical analysis A method of financial statement analysis where assets, liabilities and equities on the statement of financial position is expressed as a proportion of total assets. Also, the items in the statement of comprehensive income are expressed as a proportion of revenue.

Village banking This is a model used by microfinance institutions where neighbours come together in financial support groups called 'village banks'. The village bank then invites people who want loans to come and write their names. Once a certain number has been reached, the people on the list are used to form a group.

Ww

Warranty The guarantee that a product or service purchased will work under certain terms and conditions. In the event of failure of the product not being able to work under those terms and conditions, the purchaser is entitled to a specified remedy.

Weakness The areas where an entity falls short and as such needs improvement.

Weighted average cost of capital (WACC) The computation of a firm's cost of capital where each category (namely, ordinary shares, preference shares and bonds) of capital is weighted proportionately.

Will A document that directs how the estate of a deceased is to be distributed among beneficiaries

Work-in-progress The stock of goods that are yet to pass out of production as finished goods.

Working capital The aggregate of current assets and current liabilities.

Working capital commitment cost The cost of maintaining specific levels of working capital necessary to meet requirements of lending institutions.

Working capital management The policies and strategies to effectively and efficiently control the user of current assets and current liabilities to provide the firm with a maximum return at a minimum cost.

Bibliography

Abor, J. (2007). Industry classification and the capital structure of Ghanaian SMEs. *Studies in Economics and Finance, 24*(3), 207–219.

Abor, J. (2013). *Finance and small and medium enterprises development in Ghana.* Accra: Sedco Publishing.

Abor, J., & Biekpe, N. (2006a). An empirical test of the agency problems and capital structure of South African quoted SMEs. *SA Journal of Accounting Research, 20*(1), 51–65.

Abor, J., & Biekpe, N. (2006b). SMEs' access to debt finance: A comparison of male-owned and female-owned businesses in Ghana. *International Journal of Entrepreneurship and Innovation, 7*(2), 105–112.

Abor, J., & Biekpe, N. (2007). Small business reliance on bank financing in Ghana. *Emerging Markets Finance and Trade, 43*(4), 93–102.

Abor, J. Y., Agbloyor, E. K., & Kuipo, R. (2014). Bank finance and export activities of small and medium enterprises. *Review of Development Finance, 4*(2), 97–103.

Adams, D. W., & von Pischke, J. D. (1992). Microenterprise credit programs: de¨ja vu. *World Development, 20*, 1463–1470.

Adelman, P. J., & Marks, A. M. (2009). *Entrepreneurial finance* (5th ed.). New Jersey: Pearson Prentice Hall.

Adjasi, C. K. D., & Kyereboah-Coleman, A. (2006). Sustainability and success of microfinance: The case of Ghana. Final report submitted to the African Economic Research Consortium, Nairobi.

Adjei, J. K. (2010). *Microfinance and poverty reduction: The case of Ghana.* Accra: Bold Communications Ltd.

Al-Bagdadi, H. (2002). Microfinance associations: The case of the Ghana Microfinance Institutions Network (GHAMFIN), Deutsche Gesellschaft für Technische Zusammenarbeit (GTZ) Division 41 Economic Development and Employment Promotion.

J.Y. Abor, *Entrepreneurial Finance for MSMEs*,
DOI 10.1007/978-3-319-34021-0

Altman, E. I. (1968). Financial ratios, discriminate analysis and the prediction of corporate bankruptcy. *Journal of Finance, 23*(4), 589–609.

Antrill, P. (2009). Being an angel, ACCA Technical Article. Retrieved from http://www.accaglobal.com/content/dam/acca/global/pdf/sa_march09_attrill.pdf

Armendariz, B., & Morduch, J. (2010). *The economics of microfinance*. Cambridge, MA: Massachusetts Institute of Technology (MIT).

Aryeetey, E. (1993). *Sectoral credit allocation policy and credit flows to small enterprises in Ghana*. Accra: The British Council.

Aryeetey, E. (1998). *Informal finance for private sector development in Africa* (Economic research papers 41). Abidjan: The African Development Bank.

Aryeetey, E., & Udry, C. (1997). The characteristics of informal financial markets in Sub-Saharan Africa. *Journal of African Economies, 6*, 161–203.

Asiamah, J. P., & Osei, V. (2007). Microfinance in Ghana: An overview. Bank of Ghana. Retrieved from https://www.economicswebinstitute.org

Asiedu-Mante, E. (2011). *Rural banking in Ghana*. Accra: Combert.

Baker, H. K. (1987). *Financial management*. New York: Harcourt College Publishers, Harcourt Brace.

Baker, H. K., & Powell, G. (2009). *Understanding financial management, a practical guide*. New Jersey: Wiley.

Ballowe, T. (2010). What is the difference between a business plan and a strategic plan? Retrieved from http://onstrategyhq.com/resources/what-is-the-difference-between-a-business-plan-and-a-strategic-plan

Bangs, D. H. (1998). *The business planning guide: Creating a plan for success in your own business* (8th ed.). Chicago: Upstart Publishing.

Bear Stearns. (2005). Discounted cash flow methodology. Retrieved from http://www.grahamanddoddsville.net/wordpress/Files/SecurityAnalysis/Valuation/7239393-Discounted-Cash-Flow.pdf

Berk, J., & DeMarzo, P. (2014). *Corporate finance* (3rd ed.). Boston: Pearson Education.

Berry, A. (1997, January). SME competitiveness: The power of networking and sub-contracting. Inter-American Development Bank, Washington DC, No. IFM-105.

Berry, A., von Blottnitz, M., Cassim, R., Kesper, A., Rajaratnam, B., & van Seventer, D. E. (2002). The economics of SMMEs in South Africa, Trade and Industrial Policy Strategies. Retrieved from http://www.tips.org.za/files/506.pdf

Biekpe, N. (2004). Financing small business in Sub-Saharan Africa: Review of some key credit lending models and impact of venture capital. *Journal of African Business, 5*(1), 29–44.

Binks, M. R., Ennew, C. T., & Reed, G. V. (1992). Information asymmetries and the provision of finance to small firms. *International Small Business Journal, 11*(1), 35–46.

Blanton, W. R., & Dorman, T. L. (1994). Small business spotlight: SBA loans for community banks. *Journal of Commercial Lending, 76*(6), 32–36.

Brealey, R. A., Myers, S. C., & Allen, F. (2008). *Principles of corporate finance* (9th ed.). Boston: McGraw-Hill International.

Brealey R. A., Myers, S. C., Marcus, A. J., Maynes, E. M., & Mitra, D. (2009). *Fundamentals of corporate finance* (Fourth Canadian Edition). Toronto: McGraw Hill Ryerson.

Brookefield, D. (2001). Business finance and the SME sector, ACCA Technical Article. Retrieved from http://wenku.baidu.com/view/5a59941aa76e58fafab003a0.html

Brusco, S., & Righi, E. (1989). Local government, industrial policy and social consensus: The case of modern Italy. *Economy and Society, 18*(4), 405–423.

Cantillon, R. (1755). *Essai Sur la Nature du Commerce en Genera*. London: Frank Cass and Co.

Clara, M., Russo, F., & Gulati, M. (2000). *Cluster development and BDS promotion in India: UNIDO's Experience in India*. A Paper presented at the International Conference on Business Services for Small Enterprises in Asia, Hanoi, 3–6 April.

Cook, P. (2000). *Support mechanisms for interfirm linkages among SMEs: Impact and assessment, finance and development research programme*. Manchester: IDPM, University of Manchester.

Deloitte & Touche. (2004). Writing an effective business plan. Retrieved from http://www.deloitte.com/dtt/article

Diamond, D. W. (1989). Reputation acquisition in debt markets. *Journal of Political Economy, 97*, 828–862.

Dickinson, T. (2008). Development finance institutions: Profitability promoting development. Retrieved from www.oecd.org

Drake, P. P. What is free cash flow and how do I calculate it? Florida Atlantic University. Retrieved from http://educ.jmu.edu/~drakepp/general/FCF.pdf

Drucker, P. (1985). *Innovation and entrepreneurship*. Oxford: Butterworth-Heineman Elsevier.

Engel, R. (2002). Teaching note: An introduction to the venture capital method. Stanford University. Retrieved from http://www.cefs.de/files/VCMethod.pdf

Fabozzi, F., & Peterson, P. P. (2003). *Financial management and analysis* (2nd ed.). Hoboken: Wiley.

Fan, Q. (2003). *Creating a conducive legal and regulatory framework for small and medium enterprise development in Russia*. A World Bank Policy Dialogue Workshop on the Importance of SMEs and the Role of Public Support in Promoting SME Development, St. Petersburg, 14–16 September 2003. Retrieved from http://www.academia.edu/8864109/

Fisher, T., & Sriram, M. S. (2002). *Beyond microcredit: Putting development back into microfinance*. New Delhi/Oxford: Vistaar Publications [an imprint of Sage].

Frontier Market Network. (2012). Venture capital in South Africa. Retrieved from http://www.frontiermarketnetwork.com/article/258-venture-capital-in-south-africa

Gallagher, J. T., & Andrew, D. J. (1996). *Financial management: Principles and practice*. London: Prentice-Hall International (UK) Limited.

Gulli, H. (1998). *Microfinance and poverty: Questioning the conventional wisdom*. Washington, DC: The Inter-American Development Bank.

Hallberg, K. (2000). *A market-oriented strategy for small and medium-scale enterprises* (International Finance Corporation discussion paper, No. 40). Washington, DC: The World Bank.

Humphrey, J., & Schmitz, H. (1995). Principles for promoting clusters and networks of SMEs. Paper commissioned by the Small and Medium Industries Branch, United Nations Industrial Development Organization, October.

Jensen, M. C. (1986). Agency costs of free cash flow, corporate finance, and takeovers. *American Economic Review, 76*(2), 323–329.

Kanayula, D., & Quartey, P. (2000). *The policy environment for promoting small and medium sized enterprises in Ghana and Malawi* (Finance and development research programme working paper series, paper No. 15). Manchester: IDPM, University of Manchester.

Keown, J. A., Martin, D. J., Petty, J. W., & Scott, F. D., Jr. (2005). *Financial management, principles and applications* (10th ed.). New Jersey: Pearson Prentice Hall.

Knight, F. (1921). *Risk, uncertainty and profit.* New York: Houghton Mifflin.

KPMG & SAVCA. (2010). Venture capital and private equity industry performance survey of South Africa.

Kraizberg, E., & Gargalas, V. N. (2002). Why new firms grant employee-stock-options. *The Journal of Entrepreneurial Finance, 7*(2), 83–103.

Krugman, P. (1991). *Geography and trade.* Cambridge, MA: MIT Press.

Leach, J. C., & Melicher, R. W. (2012). *Entrepreneurial finance* (5th ed.). Mason: South-Western Cengage Learning.

Lucey, T. (2002). *Quantitative techniques* (6th ed.). London: Book Power.

Lundstrom, A., & Stevenson, L. (2005). *Entrepreneurship policy: Theory and practice.* New York: Springer Science+Business Media.

McClelland, D. (1961). *The achieving society.* New York: Free Press.

Mensah, S. (2004). *A review of SME financing schemes in Ghana.* Paper presented at the UNIDO Regional Workshop of Financing Small and Medium Scale Enterprises, Accra, 15–16 March 2004.

Meyanathan, S. D. (Ed.). (1994). *Industrial structures and the development of small and medium enterprise linkages: Examples from East Asia* (EDI series). Washington, DC: World Bank.

Millinuex, A. W. (1997). *The funding of non-financial corporations (NFCs) in the EU (1971–1993): Evidence of convergence.* Mimeo: Department of Economics, University of Birmingham.

Mishkin, F. S. (2012). *Economics of money, banking and financial markets* (10th ed.). Toronto: Pearson Addison Wesley.

My Capital. Venture Capital 101. Retrieved from https://www.mycapital.com/VenetureCapital101_MyCapital.pdf

NYU Stern School of Business. Risk adjusted value. Retrieved from http://people.stern.nyu.edu/adamodar/pdfiles/valrisk/ch5.pdf

ODA. (1992). *British aid and the private sector: Investments and policies, aid economics and social development.* London: ODA.

OECD. (1995). *Reducing the regulatory burden on business in the Netherlands: How can this be achieved?* (Best practice policies for small and medium-sized enterprises). Paris: OECD.

OECD. (1996a). *SMEs: Employment, innovation and growth: The Washington workshop*. Paris: OECD.

OECD. (1996b). *Technology, productivity and job creation*. Paris: OECD.

OECD. (1997a). *Diffusing technology to industry: Government policies and programmes*. Paris: OECD.

OECD. (1997b). Interim report on technology, productivity and job creation – Towards best policy practice, submitted to the May 1997 Council at Ministerial Level.

Ojeka, S. A. (2011). Tax policy and the growth of SMEs: Implications for the Nigerian economy. *Research Journal of Finance and Accounting, 2*(2), 1–12.

Parker, R., Riopelle, R. & Steel, W. (1995). *Small enterprises adjusting to liberalisation in five African countries* (World Bank discussion paper, No. 271, African Technical Department series). Washington DC: The World Bank.

Peachey, S., & Roe, A. (2006). Perspectives access to finance—What does it mean and how do savings bank foster access. Oxford Policy Management. Retrieved from www.savings-banks.com

Petty, B. (1993). A note on forecasting financial requirements. Retrieved from www.baylor.edu/content/services/document.php/57688.doc

Pinson, L. (1993). *Anatomy of a business plan* (2nd ed.). Chicago: Enterprise Dearborn.

Qimiao, F. (2003). *World Bank, creating a conducive legal and regulatory framework for small and medium enterprise development in Russia*. A Policy Dialogue Workshop, St. Petersburg, 14–16 September 2003.

Riding, A. L., & Short, D. M. (1987). Some investor and entrepreneur perspectives on the informal market for risk capital. *Journal of Small Business and Entrepreneurship, 4*, 19–30.

Robinson, M. (2001). *The microfinance revolution, volume 1: Sustainable finance for the poor*. Washington, DC: The World Bank.

Rogarly, B., Fisher, T., & Mayo, E. (1999). *Poverty, social exclusion and microfinance in Britain*. London: Oxfam.

Rosenberg, T. (2009). *A note on valuation for venture capital*. London: Richard Ivey School, The University of Western Ontario.

Ross, S. A., Westerfield, R. W., & Jaffe J. (2008). *Modern financial management* (International Edition). New York: McGraw-Hill.

Sandee, H. (1994). The impact of technical change on inter-firm linkages: A case study of clustered small-scale roof tile enterprises in Central Java. In P. Pederson, A. Suerrisson, & M. P. van Dijk (Eds.), *Flexible specialisation: The dynamics of small-scale industries in the South*. London: Intermediate Technology.

Say, J.-B. (1803). *A treatise on political economy*. New Brunswick: Transaction Publishers.

Schmitz, H. (1995a). Small shoemakers and fordist giants: Tale of the supercluster. *World Development, 23*(19), 9–28.

Schmitz, H. (1995b). Collective efficiency: Growth path for small-scale industry. *Journal of Development Studies, 31*(4), 529–566.

Schulz, M. (1995). The informal sector and structural adjustment: Strengthening collective coping mechanisms in Tanzania. *Small Enterprise Development, 6*(1), 4–14.

Schumpeter, J. (1934). *The theory of economic development*. Cambridge, MA: Harvard University Press.

Shapira, P., Roessner, D., & Barke, R. (1995). New public infrastructures for small firms: Industrial modernisation in the USA. *Entrepreneurship and Regional Development, 7*, 63–84.

Smith, P., & Shreeveport A. H. (2001, January). SMEs and public sector procurement research Report Prepared for Business Service, Management Consultancy.

Smith, J. K., Smith, R. L., & Bliss, R. T. (2011). *Entrepreneurial finance: Strategy, valuation, and deal structure*. Stanford: Stanford University Press.

Spratt, S. (2008). *Development finance: Debates, dogma and new direction*. London/New York: Routledge/Taylor and Francis.

Steel, W. F., & Andah, D. O. (2003). *Rural and micro finance regulation in Ghana: Implications for development and performance of the industry* (Africa Region working paper series No. 49). Washington, DC: World Bank.

Steve, J. (2003). Selecting sources of financing. ACCA Technical Article. Retrieved from http://www.accaglobal.com/content/dam/acca/global/PDF-students/2012s/sept09_jayv2.pdf

Storey, D. J. (2000). Six steps to heaven: Evaluating the impact of public policies to support small businesses in developed economies. In D. L. Sexton & H. Landstrom (Eds.), *Handbook of entrepreneurship* (pp. 176–194). Oxford: Blackwells.

Storey, D. J. (2003). Entrepreneurship, small and medium sized enterprises and public policies. In Z. J. Acs & D. B. Audretsch (Eds.), *Handbook of entrepreneurship research* (pp. 473–511). Dordrecht: Kluwer.

Storey, D. J. (2008). *Entrepreneurship and SME policy*. Lyon: World Entrepreneurship Forum.

Tagoe, N., Nyarko, E., & Anuma-Amarh, E. (2005). Financial challenges facing urban SMEs under financial sector liberalisation in Ghana. *Journal of Small Business Management, 43*(3), 331–343.

Titman, S., Keown, A. J., & Martin, J. D. (2014). *Financial management: Principles and applications* (12th ed.). New Jersey: Pearson Prentice Hall.

Uribe-Echevarria, F. (1992). *Small-scale industrial development policy and strategic issues* (Working paper series, No. 117). The Hague: Institute of Social Studies.

Valenzuela, L., Graham, D. H., & Baydas, M. M. (1997). *Commercial banks in microfinance: New actors in the microfinance world*. Bethesda: USAID Microenterprise Development Office.

Venture Capital Trust Fund Annual Reports, 2006–9.

Young, R. (2004). *Banks in microfinance: Guidelines for successful partnership*. Bethesda: USAID.

Zimmerer, T., & Scarborough, N. M. (2008). *Essentials of entrepreneurship and small business management* (5th ed.). New Jersey: Pearson Prentice Hall.

Zipkin, P. H. (1999). *Foundations of inventory management*. Boston: McGraw Hill.

Index

J.Y. Abor, *Entrepreneurial Finance for MSMEs*,
DOI 10.1007/978-3-319-34021-0

F

G

FSC
www.fsc.org
MIX
Papier | Fördert gute Waldnutzung
FSC® C083411

Kolibri 360 GmbH
Ferdinand-Jühlke-Straße 7
99095 Erfurt, Deutschland
produktsicherheit@kolibri360.de